The Wounded Self

In the German-speaking world there has been a new wave—intensifying since 2007—of autobiographically inspired writing on illness and disability, death and dying. Nina Schmidt's book takes this writing seriously as literature, examining how the authors of such personal narratives come to write of their experiences between the poles of cliché and exceptionality. Identifying shortcomings in the approaches taken thus far to such texts, she makes suggestions as to how to better read their narratives from the stance of literary scholarship, then demonstrates the value of a literary disability studies approach to such writing with close readings of Charlotte Roche's *Schoßgebete* (2011), Kathrin Schmidt's *Du stirbst nicht* (2009), Verena Stefan's *Fremdschläfer* (2007), and—in the final, comparative chapter—Christoph Schlingensief's *So schön wie hier kanns im Himmel gar nicht sein! Tagebuch einer Krebserkrankung* (2009) and Wolfgang Herrndorf's blog-cum-book *Arbeit und Struktur* (2010–13). Schmidt shows that authors dealing with illness and disability do so with an awareness of their precarious subject position in the public eye, a position they negotiate creatively. Writing the liminal experience of serious illness along the borders of genre, moving between fictional and autobiographical modes, they carve out spaces from which they speak up and share their personal stories in the realm of literature, to political ends.

NINA SCHMIDT holds a doctorate in literary and cultural studies from the University of Sheffield. Her most recent academic position was as a postdoctoral researcher at the Freie Universität Berlin.

Studies in German Literature, Linguistics, and Culture

The Wounded Self

Writing Illness in Twenty-First-Century German Literature

Nina Schmidt

Rochester, New York

Copyright © 2022 Nina Schmidt

All Rights Reserved. Except as permitted under current legislation, no part of this work may be photocopied, stored in a retrieval system, published, performed in public, adapted, broadcast, transmitted, recorded, or reproduced in any form or by any means, without the prior permission of the copyright owner.

First published 2018 by Camden House
Reprinted in paperback 2022

Camden House is an imprint of Boydell & Brewer Inc.
668 Mt. Hope Avenue, Rochester, NY 14620, USA
www.camden-house.com
and of Boydell & Brewer Limited
PO Box 9, Woodbridge, Suffolk IP12 3DF, UK
www.boydellandbrewer.com

Paperback ISBN-13: 978-1-64014-134-6
Hardcover ISBN-13: 978-1-64014-016-5

Cover image: detail from Joseph Beuys's installation "zeige deine Wunde" (show your wound, 1974–75), Kunstforum (Maximiliansforum), Munich, 1976. © VG Bild-Kunst, Bonn 2018. Photo by Ute Klophaus. © bpk / Ernst von Siemens Kunststiftung / Joseph Beuys Archiv / Ute Klophaus Nachlass.

Library of Congress Cataloging-in-Publication Data

Names: Schmidt, Nina, 1986– author.
Title: The wounded self : writing illness in twenty-first-century German literature / Nina Schmidt.
Description: Rochester, New York : Camden House, 2018. | Series: Studies in German literature, linguistics, and culture | Includes bibliographical references and index.
Identifiers: LCCN 2018008448| ISBN 9781640140165 (hardcover) | ISBN 1640140166 (hardcover)
Subjects: LCSH: Diseases in literature. | People with disabilities in literature. | German fiction—21st century—History and criticism. | Autobiographical fiction, German—History and criticism. | German prose literature—21st century—History and criticism.
Classification: LCC PT415.D57 S36 2018 | DDC 830.9/3561—dc23 LC record available at https://lccn.loc.gov/2018008448

For James

Contents

Acknowledgments	ix
Introduction: Contemporary German-Language Illness Writing as Literature; Analyzing Narrative Strategies, Aesthetic Forms, and Experimentations with Genre through the Lens of Disability Theory	1
1: Autofiction, Disgust, and Trauma: Negotiating Vulnerable Subject Positions in Charlotte Roche's *Schoßgebete* (2011)	41
2: Looking Beyond the Self—Reflecting the Other: Staring as a Narrative Device in Kathrin Schmidt's *Du stirbst nicht* (2009)	67
3: Intertextuality and the Transnational in Verena Stefan's *Fremdschläfer* (2007): Writing Breast Cancer from beyond the Border	92
4: Confronting Cancer Publicly: Diary Writing in Extremis by Christoph Schlingensief and Wolfgang Herrndorf	114
Conclusion: "Und was dann"; Recent Developments and Research Desiderata	159
Notes	167
Bibliography	209
Index	229

Acknowledgments

THE INITIAL IDEAS for this book formed in 2011. Over the years since, many people and several institutions have helped shape my work, and I am grateful to them all. Although I would like to, unfortunately I am unable to name them all here. However, there are a few special acknowledgments I feel I have to make.

First and foremost, I must thank Caroline Bland and Sue Vice for their mentorship and the School of Languages and Cultures at the University of Sheffield for providing me with such a supportive and inspiring environment during my PhD years. The Association for German Studies and Women in German Studies have been intellectual homes. I owe the AGS thanks, in a concrete way, for a publication subsidy for this monograph and for helping it become a reality.

I completed work on this manuscript as a postdoctoral researcher affiliated with the Schlegel Graduate School of Literary Studies at the Freie Universität Berlin. My thanks to the Einstein Stiftung Berlin and to Irmela Krüger-Fürhoff, without whom this position would not exist. For further crucial financial help, I am happy to acknowledge support from Irmela Krüger-Fürhoff and the FU fund Leistungsorientierte Mittelvergabe Frauenförderung und Gleichstellung.

Thanks to everyone at Camden House, especially to Jim Walker, for making initial contact with me and for accompanying me through the process ever since. Thank you to both my anonymous reviewers for their time and wonderful feedback—I appreciate it. Lastly, I owe Carrie Watterson thanks for outstanding copyediting.

Earlier versions of parts of chapters 1, 2, and 4 have been published previously as "Autofiction and Trauma: Negotiating Vulnerable Subject Positions in Charlotte Roche's *Schoßgebete*," in *Auto/Fiction* 1, no. 1 (2013): 61–86; "'[E]ndlich normal geworden'? Reassembling an Image of the Self in Kathrin Schmidt's *Du stirbst nicht* (2009)," in *Norms, Normality and Normalization*, edited by Matthias Uecker, Dirk Göttsche, Helen Budd, and Gesine Haberlah (Nottingham: Nottingham eprints, 2014), 65–78; and "Confronting Cancer Publicly: Christoph Schlingensief's *So schön wie hier kanns im Himmel gar nicht sein! Tagebuch einer Krebserkrankung*," in *Oxford German Studies* 44, no. 1 (2015): 100–112. I wish to thank the publishers for permission to reuse this material.

I write these acknowledgments in the light of Verena Stefan's death, of which I learned earlier today. She was generous and curious. May this book play its small part in remembering her and her work the way they deserve.

Berlin, December 1, 2017

Introduction: Contemporary German-Language Illness Writing as Literature; Analyzing Narrative Strategies, Aesthetic Forms, and Experimentations with Genre through the Lens of Disability Theory

IT IS AN IMPRESSIVE, paragraph-long sentence with which Virginia Woolf sets out to explore the relation of illness to literature, and creativity more generally, in 1925:

> Consider how common illness is, how tremendous the spiritual change that it brings, how astonishing, when the lights of health go down, the undiscovered countries that are then disclosed, what wastes and deserts of the soul a slight attack of influenza brings to view, what precipices and lawns sprinkled with bright flowers a little rise of temperature reveals, what ancient and obdurate oaks are uprooted in us by the act of sickness, how we go down in the pit of death and feel the waters of annihilation close above our heads and wake thinking to find ourselves in the presence of the angels and the harpers when we have a tooth out and come to the surface in the dentist's arm-chair and confuse his "Rinse the mouth—rinse the mouth" with the greeting of the Deity stooping from the floor of Heaven to welcome us—when we think of this, as we are so frequently forced to think of it, it becomes strange indeed that illness has not taken its place with love and battle and jealousy among the prime themes of literature.[1]

Motivation for her then to write *On Being Ill* was to lament the lack of attention paid to illness. The literary world, she claims, has not explored illness adequately. In her elegant ways, and loaded with poetic imagery—maybe to prove exactly that it is possible to write illness "literarily," although the role models may be lacking—Woolf emphasizes the extraordinary point of view the experience of illness and pain can give writers (and other artists), grounding them in, rather than enabling them to transcend, the body. Dropping out of "the army of the upright,"[2] thrown back onto their own physicality, ill writers not only recognize nature's indifference but can also appreciate illness, for the intensity of feeling it brings and as a liberating force in the social realm. In this sense, Woolf does "romanticize" the illness experience, with a view to valorizing it. As much as she suffered with illness personally (though this remains strictly between the lines in *On Being Ill*), she ultimately celebrates it in this essay, for broadening a writer's horizon.

In an article for the *New York Times*, Judith Shulevitz has pointed out an element of hyperbole in Woolf's central claim that illness has not been given its deserved place in literature, citing as counterexamples Thomas Mann's *Der Zauberberg* (*The Magic Mountain*, 1924) and Woolf's own *Mrs Dalloway* (which came out in 1925).[3] Virginia Woolf's opening question is nonetheless a valid one, both in and beyond her time. And, indeed, she does not pretend there is no literature dealing with the topic of illness but asks why there is not more of it and why it has not come to occupy a more central place in literary history. This certainly is not "a silly question," as Shulevitz provocatively dismisses it.[4] Lastly, Woolf's point of criticism may be better understood when considering the essay's title. Not called "On Illness" but *On Being Ill*, it stresses illness as lived experience—the stance from which Woolf too was writing her piece. Was it less illness as a general literary theme and more specifically personal explorations of illness as lived experience that Woolf had failed to find in literature?

More than eighty years later, we find the artist and cancer diarist Christoph Schlingensief intervening in the German feuilleton debate that unfolded in 2009 on the (non)place of illness narratives in literature.[5] This was undertaken in reaction to an article in the *Frankfurter Allgemeine* that had presumptuously set out to explain "warum wir keine Krebsliteratur mehr lesen wollen" (why we don't want to read any more cancer literature). Schlingensief responded thus:

> Ich lasse mir ... von niemandem sagen, dass ich ihn mit meinen äußerungen, tagebuchaufzeichnungen zu diesem brutalen einschnitt verschonen soll. ... ich habe in der härtesten zeit meines lebens nach literatur ausschau gehalten, die mir erklärt wie andere in diesen momenten gefühlt haben . und obwohl ich susan sonntag [*sic*] kennenlernen durfte, waren mir ihre bücher leider gar keine hilfe, sondern fast zwanghaft analysierte texte zu tuberkulose, krebs und aids. Distanzierte texte, die ihre eigene ohnmacht neutralisieren sollte [*sic*].[6]

> [I won't have anyone tell me to spare them my remarks, my diary recordings concerning this brutal caesura. ... During the toughest time of my life I was on the lookout for literature that would explain to me how others have felt in these moments. And despite having had the honor of meeting Susan Sontag, unfortunately her books

were of no help to me at all, but they were merely obsessively analytical texts about tuberculosis, cancer, and AIDS. Distanced texts designed to neutralize her own powerlessness.][7]

Under attack by the journalist Richard Kämmerlings, Schlingensief justifies his cancer diary publication and general media presence—on the topic and as an ill person—by pointing out what he saw as a distinct lack of illness narratives in late 2007 / early 2008; a time just ahead of the new wave of German-language literature on illness that motivated this study and into which Schlingensief's own diary publication falls. Those who doubt the veracity of Woolf's finding for her time would certainly find Schlingensief's words here difficult to believe and suspect him of exaggerating, in his typical manner. The additional comment he makes on Susan Sontag's writing on illness (which is just as canonical as Woolf's), however, clarifies what type of literature Schlingensief was searching for: the kind that, being informed by personal experience, invites identification or at least emotional engagement. Beyond that, it appears that he was after contemporary texts, although this remains implicit. Schlingensief could not track down such writing at the time he was first diagnosed with lung cancer. This gap, it seems, was perceived by other people as well. In subsequent years, the German-speaking world saw the publication of a series of German-language texts grounded in the personal experience of illness and disability, including Schlingensief's own, by authors rediscovering the autobiographical and meeting a need in our contemporary times.

These texts have been met with unusual public and critical attention, for two possible reasons: because they constitute the first significant resurgence of a larger number of personal illness writings since the literature of the Neue Subjektivität (New Subjectivity) of the 1970s and because they attend to a remarkable variety of illnesses/disabilities, thus broadening the focus of the cancer and HIV/AIDS literature of the 1980s and 1990s. They are widely published and read, as indicated by their regular appearance on the *Spiegel*-Bestsellerliste. Many of these texts receive increased attention from the review sections of German newspapers as well as from jurors of literary prizes. Among the new illness narratives are titles such as Helmut Dubiel's *Tief im Hirn* (2006), Verena Stefan's *Fremdschläfer* (2007), Ulla Berkéwicz's *Überlebnis* (2008), Kathrin Schmidt's prize-winning novel *Du stirbst nicht* (2009), Miriam Pielhau's *Fremdkörper* (2009), and Jürgen Leinemann's *Das Leben ist der Ernstfall* (2009). Furthermore, one can point to Sandra Schadek's *Ich bin eine Insel*, Christoph Schlingensief's *Tagebuch einer Krebserkrankung*, Georg Diez's *Der Tod meiner Mutter*, and Tilman Jens's *Demenz: Abschied von meinem Vater*—all published in 2009—as well as to Jens's sequel to *Demenz*, a rebuttal of the ferocious public backlash against it, titled *Vatermord: Wider einen Generalverdacht* (2012). The resurgence also includes poetry such as Christian Sighişorean's volumes *Rose und Gebrochen Deutsch* (2009) and *VerLetztes* (2011).

Other yet more recent texts are Miriam Meckel's *Brief an mein Leben: Erfahrungen mit einem Burnout* (2010), Charlotte Roche's *Schoßgebete* (2011), Arno Geiger's *Der alte König in seinem Exil* (2011), Wolfgang Herrndorf's *Arbeit und Struktur* (2010–13), and Alexander Görsdorf's *Taube Nuss: Nichtgehörtes aus dem Leben eines Schwerhörigen* (2013). The comedian Gaby Köster wrote *Ein Schnupfen hätte auch gereicht: Meine zweite Chance* (2011) together with colleague and friend Till Hoheneder—and has since published a second book, *Die Chefin* (2015), which is a novel featuring a stroke survivor and wheelchair user as protagonist. David Wagner's *Leben*—the expansion of the short story *Für neue Leben* (2008)—was published in 2013 and won that year's Leipzig Book Fair Prize. Even more recently, Richard Wagner's *Herr Parkinson* (2015) came out, and in November 2015 former foreign minister Guido Westerwelle's *Zwischen zwei Leben* was published, the result of his collaboration with journalist Dominik Wichmann about his leukemia. The list could go on. It includes what traditionalists would class as popular literature as well as what has been praised as high art, and it spans a whole range of writing styles from the prosaic to the poetic and from nonfictional writing (documentary, essay, journalism, diary, memoir) to more fictional or novelistic forms (autofiction, experimental autobiographical novels). These texts have been published by a variety of publishing houses, including many respected imprints. Although work by first-time writers does get published, it is conspicuous that professional writers (academics, journalists, literary authors) and celebrities dominate the picture, the latter with a tendency to produce collaborative narrative.

Nonetheless, there is considerable diversity in this "wave," not least in the types of illness experiences these writers address. Although cancer narratives remain numerous, writers today equally allow themselves to write about psychological trauma and the shock of bereavement (Berkéwicz, Roche), burnout (Meckel), disability after a stroke (Köster, Schmidt), deafness and life with a cochlear implant (Görsdorf), Alzheimer's disease as well as other forms of dementia (Geiger, Jens), autoimmune diseases and organ transplants (David Wagner), or neurodegenerative conditions such as ALS or Parkinson's disease (Dubiel, Schadek, Sighişorean, Richard Wagner). Within the texts listed above are examples of writing centering on illness that the authors themselves have experienced firsthand but also of "auto/biography," that is "life writing that focuses on the relation between the writer and a significant other."[8] Diez, Jens, and Geiger all offer examples of such texts. Brought about by a parent's suffering from illness, they chart the mother's or father's illness progression (including, often, their dying) from their distinct perspective as sons. Through the prism of that relationship, they thematize generational change and—although to varying degrees—the demands of their conflicting roles as child, carer, and writer.⁹

To explore contemporary German-language life writing and its aesthetics of illness adequately, a corpus of texts had to be selected that could be subjected to closer literary analysis. Because auto/biographical texts require a distinct theoretical approach—one that considers the ethics of writing a story that is another's as much as one's own (in the way that, for instance, G. Thomas Couser's study *Vulnerable Subjects* does)—and because in cases of collaborative writing such as Westerwelle and Wichmann's, authorship is difficult to determine, this study focuses on autobiographical representations of illness. Not aiming to be a thematic study of one particular illness but rather looking for larger, structural similarities and differences across diverse representations of illness (in the makeup of the texts themselves as well as their reception), the selected texts represent a variety of illness experiences. This also reflects the diversity of this wave of illness writings, despite some similarities in, above all, their sociopolitical motivation to share what are still deemed "private" stories with a wider audience, as well as in the writers' preferences for certain life-writing genres and writing strategies as they come out in this book.

Forming the basis of this study are, to list them in the order of their publication, Verena Stefan's *Fremdschläfer* (2007), Kathrin Schmidt's *Du stirbst nicht* (February 2009), Christoph Schlingensief's *Tagebuch einer Krebserkrankung* from April of the same year, Charlotte Roche's *Schoßgebete* (2011), and, lastly, Wolfgang Herrndorf's *Arbeit und Struktur* (first published online 2010–13). They represent a range of life-writing genres, encompassing autobiographical novels as well as autofictional and diaristic writing. The only one of my texts to be translated into English, to date, is Roche's novel; it was published as *Wrecked* in 2014.¹⁰ However, all of the other chosen texts have been translated into at least one other language—and indeed often more than one.¹¹ Each of the illness narratives considered here is analyzed for the narrative strategies, aesthetic forms, and experimentations with genre in this kind of life writing. Chapter 1, dealing with *Schoßgebete* (Lap prayers), begins analysis with the most ambiguously positioned text on the autobiography-fiction continuum; from there, the study moves along this continuum. It closes with an extensive discussion of the diaries by Schlingensief and Herrndorf as representing the most straightforwardly autobiographical texts of those discussed. By grounding my distinctly literary analyses in the field of disability studies, I identify gaps and contortions in the hitherto dominant readings of the selected texts—readings that often effectively disregard the illness experience at their center or contest their literary quality.

On the basis of these five texts published between 2007 and 2013, I examine how illness/disability as an aspect of identity is developed in and beyond narration, between cliché and exceptionality, both in the texts and beyond it, in the wider public realm. Most, if not all, contemporary authors of illness narrative can be presumed to feel the eyes of the public already on them at the time of writing, and the other writers whose texts I deal with in this book have likely felt a similar lack of precursors as has Schlingensief (whom I quoted at the outset). Aware of the ways in which a life writer's "exercise in self-attention" stimulates the readerly imagination,[12] I examine how the authors—who are known authors or artists—are able to create a space within which they can move publicly as they address themes of illness/disability typically still understood as private, sometimes even shameful, matters. This approach draws particular attention to each text's formal features and enables me to explore representations of (altered and altering) selves in illness, as well as to trace authors' attempts to "make sense" of illness, or their refusal to do so, privileging the perspective of personal experience. I explore each writer's motivation to thus share illness in the first place, something linked to both an author's needs when touched by illness as well as to the knowledge gained from the experience of illness. To share the latter with the reading public—against convention and despite the artistic and personal risks this involves—is recognized here as an ethical act.

A political conviction worth emphasizing underlies the inclusion of representations of both psychological and physical illnesses in this corpus. The disability studies stance that I take up as a scholar resists applying the diagnostic gaze of the doctor to the selected material. Instead, determining the perspective of lived experience as central to the analyses, the aim is to open up such medical/diagnostic categories to an extent. The choice of texts challenges a Cartesian body-mind split that is still at work in the popular imagination and that continues to keep the topics of mental and physical health apart, be it on the neatly arranged display tables of bookshops or in scholarly analyses. Cutting across this dualism, I highlight the fact that clear demarcations cannot be drawn between psychological and physical impairments, and that indeed often, if not always, in a person's experience of illness, the psychological and the physical are closely intertwined.

Before delving into the individual literary analyses, the remainder of this introduction provides a brief overview of the history of autobiographical writing as it pertains to this study. I then comment on the "occasion for autobiography" that illness provides,[13] before giving a short introduction to the history and objectives of disability studies, a field I identify with as a literary scholar, myself living with chronic illness. After introducing some of the most relevant terminology from the field, I explain why disability studies constitute a fruitful framework when dealing with illness narratives. I then sketch out the media reactions that arose in the context of the new German illness writings, focusing on the culmination of a feuilleton debate on the (non)place of illness/disability in German literature in 2009. The debate is briefly evaluated from the perspective of disability studies and life writing research. Next I explore how German studies scholarship has so far addressed illness narratives, when it has done so at all. I go on to point out the shortcomings in the approaches displayed in the realm of German-language literary studies and suggest that alternatives need to be found to analyze, in an unbiased, detailed manner, the illness narratives in the corpus of this study (as well as other examples of illness writing in the future). The study as a whole demonstrates what this approach could look like; builds on some fruitful theories from, among others, the fields of autobiography, life writing, and disability studies research; and paves the way for future work in Germanistik from a literary/cultural disability studies point of view.

From Autobiography Proper to the Autobiographical

The emergence of modern autobiography is generally linked to "the emergence of the modern subject,"[14] with the associated rise of notions of individuality and agency across Enlightenment Europe. From this admittedly Eurocentric point of view, one can link the rise of autobiography, philosophically, to "man" becoming "embedded in the world" during the eighteenth century, that is, "no longer simply a subject of knowledge, but also an object of [his own] investigation."[15] The study of human psychology has its origins in that time, branching off from philosophy to become a separate discipline. The introspective self-scrutiny advocated by the Pietist movement grew in popularity from the late seventeenth century—and further contributed to the spread of autobiographical writings; diary writing, for example, was taken up by many Pietists. As being able to read and write in the vernacular languages of Europe became more common and the diversity of the texts in circulation extended beyond religious pamphlets and catechisms, a new appreciation of authorship itself can be observed. The wider sociohistorical context allowing for the advent of autobiography as a genre or writing mode is one of secularization, the rise of literacy, and the development of the book into a mass-produced, more easily affordable commodity.[16]

Although nearly as difficult to define and as large and complex a category as fiction, autobiography typically "is characterized by autodiegetic, i.e. 1st-person subsequent narration told from the point of view of the present. Comprehensive and continuous retrospection, based on memory, makes up its governing structural and semantic principle. Oscillating between the struggle for truthfulness and creativity, between oblivion, concealment, hypocrisy, self-deception and self-conscious fictionalizing, autobiography renders a story of personality formation, a

Bildungsgeschichte."[17] Canonical texts exemplifying this prototype are numerous, with Rousseau's *Confessions* (1782 and 1788) and Goethe's *Dichtung und Wahrheit* (*Poetry and Truth* / Fiction and facts, 1811–33) among the most widely cited. Autobiography, at this point, and in this narrow form, was a form of expression reserved for a select elite of largely white, male figures.

Since then, the autobiographical field has diversified dramatically in authorship, thematic foci, and form(s); originally a highly exclusive genre, autobiography has been destabilized, then rewritten as an inclusive form of expression. It has become what we can aptly describe as a widespread cultural practice. In this process, it has shed much of its certainty about the author's sense of entitlement to self-expression and diverged from the traditional teleological trajectory. Politics, especially the politics of representation, has come to have a strong influence on autobiographical writing.[18]

As they emerge from the diverse rights and protest movements of the nineteenth and twentieth centuries, autobiography's new voices problematize—within the field—some of its founding myths: they question the idea of a unified/coherent self; of authorly autonomy; and of the transparency of language, memory, and history. Additionally, the autobiographical subject can be observed to become reembodied, especially in texts that have as their main foci gender, race, or, of course, illness/disability, or that show these aspects of identity to intersect. In short, autobiography—formerly a self-assured expression of cultural dominance—becomes a highly self-conscious site, a medium for "writing back," to employ a term from postcolonial studies, and thus a "prominent ground for cultural critique."[19]

All this has implications for the form(s) more recent life writing takes: most autobiographical writers of the twenty-first century—especially those previously confined to the margins of the literary field—produce texts that appear open and processual rather than stable or final, just as their content is decidedly intersubjective or "relational."[20] They are rarely easy to subsume under just one genre label. Engaging in the autobiographical without necessarily being autobiographies in the classic sense, these texts tend to focus on aspects or stages of a life rather than any narratable whole. Life-writing scholarship has of course recognized these shifts, and, in academic language, "the autobiographical" today refers to more than autobiographies in the narrower sense.[21] It better grasps this development as well as the general breadth and heterogeneity in the content and form of contemporary writers' endeavors. Life-writing scholarship's growing interest in realms other than the strictly literary, such as the medial, digital, and virtual worlds as other important arenas in which contemporary selves are being negotiated,[22] also is reflected in this more open term.[23]

Even when confining one's focus to the literary world, one must recognize that the autobiographical today has entered much contemporary writing; it willfully ignores genre boundaries and wanders between fact and fiction. The currency that terms like "autofiction" (Doubrovsky) or "autobiografiction" (Saunders) have gained in recent years reflects this development, as well as the need, and difficulty, to find new words to describe such writing, its diversification and hybridization. As Max Saunders explains, in relation to the way modernist writers approached autobiography, a text's "autobiographical dimension can be covert, unconscious, or implicit."[24] Speaking of the autobiographical, then, allows literary scholarship to read texts that position themselves ambiguously between fact and fiction (also) from the vantage point of life writing studies.

In doing so, I bring together texts that at first do not seem to have much in common—yet, significantly, the discourse around them is strikingly similar, as is shown later in this introduction. This indicates that the debate these illness narratives have incited hinges on their relationship, however fictionalized or ultimately unclear it may be in some cases, to an author's own life experience. It also allows me to relate to each other not only different life-writing genres (from the autofictional to the autobiographical novel to the diary genre) but texts by professional authors and first-time writers (whose experience of illness/disability has turned them into authors)—in other words, to relate what is thought of as high literature to products of pop culture.

While it is not the aim of this book to advance the theoretical debate on autobiography's status as a genre,[25] it remains to position this study toward that debate. For my purposes here, I conceptualize the autobiographical as a flexible mode of expression, rather than the more strictly defined genre that it may once have been, and overall to regard "autobiography-and-fiction as a system or set of discursive and formal practices" in the way Saunders does.[26] Saunders makes the pertinent observation that the autobiographical "gains its significance [only] according to its relation to the term 'fiction' (whether opposed or combined),"[27] with writers developing "an increasing awareness of this system" through the centuries.[28] Instead of propagating an either/or position, then, Saunders suggests that "perhaps ... we should speak of the *autobiographic effect*, or the *fictional effect*, and recognize that particular works can produce first one then the other."[29]

The following section deepens these reflections on the autobiographical in combination with a focus on the experience of illness/disability as a crucial motivator—personally, politically, and ethically—for engaging in life writing.

Illness and the Attraction of the Personal

"Die Leute überleben schwere Krankheiten mehr als früher, und dann kann man auch hinterher drüber schreiben."[30] (People are more likely to survive serious illness than they were in the past, meaning you can write about it afterward.) This is author Kathrin Schmidt's terse explanation for the rising number of German-language publications of personal illness narratives. Schmidt is right to correlate the advances of modern medicine and our growing life expectancy to the proliferation of these kinds of texts. Yet there may be more to it, and indeed her remark falls short of explaining the occurrence of autothanatographical writings, which make up two of the five texts dealt with in detail in this book.

Despite its commonness, the experience of illness has not lost any of its shock value in contemporary society. It has not been normalized. As the medical sociologist Arthur W. Frank emphasizes, the experience of a lasting disease or impairment takes most people by surprise—regardless of the age at which they experience it.[31] In Havi Carel and Rachel Cooper's recent philosophical definition,[32] for the individual confronted with it, "illness [or, sometimes more significantly, its diagnosis] disrupts the lived experience of one's body, leading to an overarching existential disruption of the ill person's way of being in the world and their life world."[33] Illness, in other words, creates fissures in one's story of the self, in both the internal narrative and how one presents oneself to the world. It initiates, to echo Woolf, "spiritual change."[34]

Across the disciplines, ill persons thus fundamentally unsettled—thrown back on their messy, mortal bodies, coming up against the limits of their agency that tend to go unrecognized in times of relative health—have been found to evince a storytelling impulse in reaction. Frank, for example, declares, "Illness is an occasion for autobiography."[35] This alone does not yet, of course, give any clues about authors' intentions, hopes, or desires in addressing their illness experience through life writing (or concerning this writing's effect once published). For life-writing scholar Kay Cook, an explanation for the rise in illness narratives lies in our strong identification with our physical bodies and, linked to that, a fundamental discontent of the person-cum-patient with the way they are being treated in the context of modernist medicine. Cook writes, "Clearly, as in no other time in history, the body is the self, and the ill individual's narrative seeks to gain control—or wrest it from the medical establishment—of the illness through creating discourses that counter, among other challenges to identity, the jargon of the medical world."[36] The formulation of illness narrative functions as a reassurance of oneself or one's language, and with that one's agency, in more or less direct distinction to the medical world and its respective language.

In his 1997 book *Recovering Bodies*, G. Thomas Couser highlights the wish to contribute to a condition's destigmatization as a particularly powerful motivating cause for illness narrative.[37] At the time of writing, he specifically (yet not exclusively) had HIV/AIDS narratives and their politics in mind.[38] Published illness writing, as becomes clear, is as much born from the personal as it is politically motivated, and thus outward facing. Thinking across the spectrum of illnesses and disabilities, Couser further writes, "One common purpose [of personal illness narratives] is to invalidate cultural narratives of invalidism."[39] To look ahead, this still seems to match at least some of what the German-language authors read in this study do.

The sociologist Frank understands autobiographical narrative as a "means of repair" for lives disrupted in the way Carel and Cooper describe.[40] Ignoring the mechanistic and slightly simplistic assumption underlying his choice of word of "repair," Frank here (and elsewhere) clearly stresses the therapeutic element of autobiographical work; he values illness narratives for it. When people do turn toward attending to illness autobiographically—and many do not—they are frequently assumed to have such therapeutic intentions by those who take an academic interest in their writing.[41]

The therapeutic interpretation crops up, furthermore, in German literary criticism about autobiographical illness narratives of the 1970s and feuilleton reactions today. Despite its ubiquity, it must be treated with care, I argue, in order to take the texts under examination seriously as valid objects of literary studies, for this topos has the potential to harm a person's story, by restricting its meaning to the writing individual's life. Although from a medically informed perspective, such emphasis on the therapeutic effect of illness narrative is often intended as an entirely neutral, even a positive, point (and out of my authors, as we will see, Charlotte Roche and Christoph Schlingensief in particular invest in the idea of writing as self-healing), the connotations become less positive when the term is taken up by literary criticism. The label "therapeutic" then marks such texts as inward looking, if not narcissistic. This isolates both text and author from the cultural context in which they emerged and closes down avenues of interpretation (especially regarding the cultural work that they do or tracing what has motivated the textualization and publication of someone's experiences), rather than encouraging their intellectual exploration.

Another interpretative model that appears regularly is that of the confessional. It is a paradigmatic subgenre of the autobiographical: Saint Augustine and Jean-Jacques Rousseau's autobiographies, both bearing the genre designation in their titles, are historical landmarks in its development.[42] We read of it in *On Being Ill*, too: illness, according to Woolf, "enhances our perceptions and reduces self-consciousness. It is the great confessional; things are said, truths are blurted out which health conceals."[43] Woolf, from the perspective of a creative writer, sees illness as an enabler of autobiographical writing. She adds a psychological dimension to it when highlighting an element of recklessness in the ill writer's endeavor. Doing so, Woolf promises the reader of personal illness narratives rare, truthful, and potentially provocative insights: the currency in which autobiographical writing trades. At the same time, she undersells the artfulness and narrative strategies of autobiographical writing—the phrasing that truths are "blurted out" instead supports notions of immediacy, intimacy, indiscretion even.

Writers, like Woolf above, do like to play with the idea of the confessional as a mode of relating their experiences. It is one way of generating readerly interest in writing about illness. Traces of this can be seen in Roche's *Schoßgebete*, for example. Yet it may not be as dominant in illness writing as the available secondary literature to date suggests. That the idea looms so large in the critical discourse is both understandable and problematic. It is understandable; in fact, it seems logical to expect autobiographical illness narratives to take a confessional shape "in a society where health is upheld, paradoxically, both as a normative, regulating category and as an ideal state of personal utopia."[44] This applies to both the cultural realm of the United States, on which Einat Avrahami's research focuses, and the Germanic one investigated here, as well as other Western contexts. Avrahami infers, therefore, that "the decision to disclose a seriously debilitating illness is itself transgressive, verging on admittance to a state of sin."[45] However, insofar as it is bound up with the myth that ill people have somehow deserved their illness, on account of behaviors, lifestyle, or attitude (this, it would seem, is what needs confessing), the continued centrality of the confessional model to our readings of illness narratives is problematic. Again, this is because it locates illness so strictly within the individual—in ways that in the past, for instance, the idea of the "cancer personality" did.[46] Furthermore, conceptualizing illness narrative as confession hierarchizes the relationship of author and reader in a manner antithetical to what we find in the contemporary illness narratives examined here. These texts instead stress the equality and similarity of autobiographical author and readership. This is writ large particularly in the poetics of Verena Stefan and Christoph Schlingensief (explored in chapters 3 and 4).[47]

None of this is to deny that narrating illness can be therapeutic (for the author) or confessional (in appearance) in part, but, as published life writing texts, we must consider illness narratives, like any other literature, as multidimensional and complexly motivated. Illness narratives must be expected to be both inward and outward looking. Analyzing the German-language texts at its heart, this study aims to approach them in a way that, with Avrahami, we could call "unpatterned," or open-minded.[48] For the researcher, this means employing "a modest, self-conscious mode of reading,"[49] the kind that is aware of the master plot of personal illness narratives and the most prevalent myths relied upon in storying illness but does not force them onto a text at all cost. Such a reading cannot allow itself a bias toward one type of emplotment at the expense of others, in the way that, for example, Shlomith Rimmon-Kenan finds Frank ends up doing in his work, ultimately favoring, as she sees it, those stories that characterize illness as having induced a kind of learning and that can be relayed in a more or less coherent narrative form. Reacting to the "phoenix narrative" or "quest" stories more generally,[50] the narratologist ends her article titled "Illness and Narrative Identity" with a defense of fragmented and chaotic writing and illness narratives "without epiphanies."[51] Rather than forcing the narratives at the basis of this book into a preconceived interpretative framework, then, the methods employed here foreground the context from which they arose and the complexity of each resulting text while, at the same time, tracing and making sense of the larger cultural patterns negotiated within them.

With *Recovering Bodies*, Couser was the first English-language literary studies scholar to explicitly write against the idea that autobiographical art centering on illness, death, or disability was "undiscussable."[52] In it, he argues that "to refuse even to consider [illness narratives] as potential art seems a form of denial, an arbitrary ruling out of an important, if threatening, aspect of human experience";[53] and, worse, it manifests a disregard for voices—people—relating such experiences. The problem that Couser identified in the US cultural context in 1997 still holds true for the German literary sphere twenty years later. While in contemporary Germany the eyes of the publishing world and the media affiliated with it have very much turned toward illness narratives in recent years—leading to increased opportunities for publication, wider public attention, and boosting sales figures for many of the books but showing only limited understanding of the autobiographical illness experiences at the heart of these texts—literary scholarship has as yet kept at a safe distance from these new personal narratives of illness/disability.

As a work of literary scholarship, this study begins to make up for this negligence. It reads the texts in its corpus unequivocally as literature: by tracing narrative strategies, aesthetic forms, and experimentations with genre in storying illness, it attends to exactly those elements of the texts that are often assumed to lack sophistication in autobiographical writing about illness/disability. What underlies the research presented here is the conviction that much of a text's force of expression is carried by its formal features. It is essential to examine these in connection with and as meaningful for the content of the illness narratives—precisely because of the texts' autobiographical dimensions and the persistent idea of their artlessness or formlessness. Doing so, this study finds that the presence of the implied reader in the mind of the author, or as constructed by the text, influences writing strategies and pushes formal innovation.

The French theorist Philippe Lejeune's work on the autobiographical—from his theorizations on autobiography proper, to his studies on more experimental narratives of the self, popular texts as well as unpublished ones, through to the diary—has triggered much of the critical thinking on the texts discussed here in terms of their genre affiliation and this affiliation's significance. Lejeune's writing is valuable to this study not least because of his relatively early ventures into fields outside of high literature, related to his grasp of our propensity for the autobiographical "as a pervasive social and cultural phenomenon."[54] With Lejeune's work in mind, an important focus of the book at hand is the question of each text's "packaging" in terms of genre. In each chapter, I ask, How is a text's genre designation linked to the issues it negotiates, and to the conflicting wishes of, on the one hand, wanting to speak out and be heard about illness and, on the other, protecting one's vulnerable subject position as one does so? Almost as important is the question concerning the effect genre has on our reading of personal illness narratives.

In academic autobiography studies today, looking for any kind of straightforward truth in autobiographical writing is agreed to be a dated approach and cul-de-sac. However, analyzing truth or truthfulness in a relatively literal/factual sense was a major concern of autobiography studies when it emerged as a field in the 1950s and 1960s.[55] After the deconstruction of such criteria by poststructuralists, there is a consensus within literary scholarship today to see the fictional in any "true" account (think of the necessary step of mediation—that is, the putting into speech or writing—of what is remembered), as well as to assume that any fiction writing is somewhat grounded in life experience. Nonetheless, the lay reader continues to have heightened expectations when a text signals autobiographical relevance.[56] Ideas of truthfulness or authenticity therefore remain relevant in the discussion of autobiographical writing, especially as they influence reception.[57]

Lejeune formulated the "autobiographical pact" in 1975 with all this in mind. The pact describes the special relationship between the writer and reader of autobiographical writing, one that is invested in heavily by both parties. This study contends the pact to still be a productive "hypothesis and . . . working tool" when working on contemporary forms of life writing.[58] Paul John Eakin summarizes the original idea thus: "In effect, the autobiographical pact is a form of contract between author and reader in which the autobiographer explicitly commits himself or herself not to some impossible historical exactitude but rather to the sincere effort to come to terms with and to understand his or her own life [or an aspect of it]."[59] In other words, in the Lejeunian thinking that informs this book, autobiographical texts are positioned, by definition, as resting on ideas of truthfulness, which inform the author's writing as well in that they fundamentally affect the way we read texts marked as autobiographical. The discussions sparked by fake memoirs—Trojan horses that violate the idea of the pact—may best bring this out. Autobiographical writers today, of course, tend to be less explicit and more ambiguous about their "sincere effort." This is mirrored in my corpus too—in the context of which such ambiguity and experimentation is pivotal, as first and foremost enabling the publication of one's negotiations of illness/disability and dying. Authors can be seen to use personal pronouns other than "I," as well as employing alter ego figures and autofictional writing strategies.[60]

Ambiguity plays out on the level of the paratext too. Refining his work on the autobiographical in the 1980s, Lejeune notes, "A book can be presented as a novel, at the level of the subtitle, and as an autobiography at the level of the publisher's blurb."[61] Today this and similar strategies are widely practiced. It is not a coincidence that the covers of *Schoßgebete*, *Du stirbst nicht*, and *Fremdschläfer* all bear the word *Roman* (novel). The designation may have to be taken less literally now than ever before. Yet an "abandonment of a notion of pure genres," as we can currently observe it, "does not mean an abandonment of sensitivity to generic distinctions."[62] The general perception seems to be that "'*writers*' write novels while 'anyone' can write a memoir (or, worse, have one written)," as Couser ironically puts it.[63] Today, labeling a text a novel aims less at assigning it a genre than it does a status: its purpose is to convince potential readers of the fact that these texts are of literary value.[64] The term "novel" promises an enjoyable read, a well-written text that is typically narrative in nature. In this sense, the designation as "novel" is in the interest of publishers. When insisted on by life writers, it is a signal intended to discourage readers from focusing overly on "breaches of contract"[65] in the writing and appears to suggest replacing factual scrutiny with a sensibility for a different kind of truth in the text: one that emerges from the text as a whole and as it communicates the author/narrator's shifts in perspective caused by the events at the heart of the life writing (here: the illness experience).

The texts in my corpus are contemporary expressions of the autobiographical, reflecting the extent to which the genre has evolved and diversified over the past decades, and in ways that were unpredictable, with the texts discussed in the first two chapters stretching in particular the early Lejeunian idea that there must be "identity of the proper name shared by author, narrator, and protagonist" for a text to be considered autobiographical.[66] They are marginal cases and deal with the stuff of a real (empirical) person's life in more experimental ways than Lejeune foresaw at his time of writing. However, and this is where Lejeune's writing has not aged in the slightest, the reader who was central to Lejeune's grasp on the autobiographical—and who looms over the author of illness narrative in the form of anticipated criticism and, worse, dismissal—remains highly important to my work. It was Lejeune who recognized and stressed that autobiography is "a mode of reading as much as it is a type of writing."[67] This study is built on the understanding that authors have "*readerly* knowledge," just as readers can potentially be autobiographers themselves (and can think like writers).[68] This particular feature of autobiographical writing, in which reader and writer may be seen to be on an equal footing, informs my analyses of contemporary illness writings: texts that will be demonstrated at once to trust and mistrust their readership.

(Literary) Disability Studies and Its Concerns

The field of disability studies offers a critical perspective enabling the analysis of ostensibly "normal" or "natural" images and understandings of illness/disability and health or ablebodiedness. According to Lennard J. Davis, "The first task at hand is . . . to see that the object of disability studies is not the person using the wheelchair or the Deaf person but the set of social, historical, economic, and cultural processes that regulate and control the way we think about and think through the body."[69] The field cannot be aligned with a specific academic subject; yet, as becomes clear from Davis's comment, it is firmly grounded in the arts and social sciences, and somewhat opposed to medical subjects (which do focus much more on the physicality or psychology of the disabled person).[70] Sociologists, political scientists, historians, literary/cultural studies and other humanities scholars have all begun to engage with it; the multi- and potential interdisciplinarity of the field certainly is a particular strength. To the literary/cultural scholar, the analysis of representations of illness/disability both today as well as throughout history, in the media, everyday life, low and high culture is of central interest. Literary researchers with a disability studies consciousness are interested in representations of illness/disability as the site of "a . . . dynamic interchange between culture, author, text, and audience."[71]

Advocates of disability studies approaches know that disabilities—in the sense of impairments—are a common (rather than extraordinary), statistically proven given. Beyond that, they see disability in its relationality and recognize its social construction as an important dimension of disabled experience. Someone's impairment as such (especially when it is a stable, manageable disability) does not necessarily have to pose a problem, neither for the individual nor for medicine or society at large. Yet it becomes a problem when the world in which we live posits "health" or "ablebodiedness" as the norm.[72] This impacts, in pervasive ways, upon the world we inhabit: architecturally, economically, and in people's behavior toward and judgment of each other, in the workplace as well as in any other social setting. Ill/disabled people thus become marginalized and are being further disabled as a consequence—in more insidious ways than can be explained by the reality of their impairment alone and the limitations it may bring.

Early disability studies, more directly oriented alongside activism, was steeped in a dogmatic "social model" view of disability (as diametrically opposed to the "medical model" it aimed to free itself from) and neglected to pay adequate attention to experiences of suffering and pain as well as the possibility of an early death that some illnesses/disabilities entail. In a self-reflexive step, the discipline has corrected its own repression of the (suffering) body and overcome early, simplistic argumentation for or against certain explanatory "models" of disability.[73] Critical disability studies today continues to complicate the picture of illness/disability and does better justice to a wider variety of experiences.[74]

Disability studies scholars from across academic subjects reject the conception of illness/disability or health in any absolute terms. They challenge their readership to part with dichotomous conceptualizations of illness/disability on the one hand and a utopian concept of health on the other (as a way of thinking that perpetuates the culturally imagined essential difference between people living with and without illness/disability), and instead posits them as dimensions on the continuum of life that can, and do, intersect. Many disability studies scholars therefore point out that any nondisabled person can find themselves in the place of the ill/disabled other relatively suddenly, for example, through injury, disease, or aging. This is what makes the topic threatening to the nondisabled, or temporarily ablebodied, and in fact a strange "minority" subject. Couser states pointedly that "unlike racial and gender minority status, disability is a minority status that anyone may assume unexpectedly at any time."[75] Social scientist and disability activist Tom Shakespeare calls disability "a universal experience of humanity," and Davis points out that most disabilities are acquired "by living in the world," not congenital.[76] To raise this point serves to highlight the irony of our societal—as well as critical—avoidance of disability.

To engage with disability studies is to politicize one's research. As the last of the civil rights movements to enter the academy, the field has much in common with other minority studies. Having emerged from activists' efforts directed at securing fundamental human rights and demanding participation in the public discourse about dis/ability, ideas surrounding disability rights and disability inclusion first gained traction in the scholarly discourse of the United States and the UK in the 1990s.[77] Disability studies scholars have since demanded the analytical consideration of disability as a marker of identity alongside the more established recognition of class, gender and sexuality, ethnicity and race, and religion. (Post) structuralism and (post)modernism, body theories, and Foucauldian analyses have informed much of the work of the field; critical thinking around stigma, pathology, norms, normality, and deviance is inherent to it.

In parallel to disability activism entering and transforming the academy, in the English-language realm and particularly the United States, a significant number of autobiographical life-writing texts appeared that negotiated illness/disability publicly, some highly critical of the institutionalization their authors experienced (one example is *Girl, Interrupted*, 1993, by Susanna Kaysen), others questioning the rationale of treatment options offered by the medical establishment and their underlying normativity (think of Audre Lorde's *The Cancer Journals*, 1980), or focusing in on the disablism their authors experienced in everyday life and its far-reaching effects on the individual's psyche (Lucy Grealy's *Autobiography of a Face*, 1994). The emergence of such texts coincided with a call, issued by early disability studies scholarship, for a stronger commitment to social realism in disability representation (that is, more accurate depictions of life with disability) and prompted a rising interest in autobiographical narratives among literary scholars.[78]

In Anglo-American cultural and literary studies, disability studies has since established itself as a valid and powerful research perspective. How successfully it has done so may most easily be demonstrated by pointing out the number of available handbooks: the *Handbook of Disability Studies* first published in 2001, *The Disability Studies Reader* (now in its fifth edition), and the *Routledge Handbook of Disability Studies* from 2012 are the three most pertinent to literary studies.[79] Moreover, the field has generated its own journals—with the *Journal of Literary & Cultural Disability Studies*, founded by David Bolt in 2006,[80] being the most relevant for literary disability studies—and dedicated book series, out of which the University of Michigan Press's *Corporealities: Discourses of Disability* is the most notable.

In German-speaking universities, disability studies has not yet established itself to the same extent.[81] Within the arts and humanities, and more specifically within German cultural/literary studies, little identification with the field can be observed so far. One reason why German academia resists the approach so far may lie in disability studies' activist origins, being something that rests uneasily with German academic traditions. Elizabeth C. Hamilton's article "From Social Welfare to Civil Rights: The Representation of Disability in Twentieth-Century German Literature"; Carol Poore's *Disability in Twentieth-Century German Culture*; the Edinburgh German Yearbook's fourth volume, *Disability in German Literature, Film, and Theater*; Pauline Eyre's PhD thesis, "Permission to Speak: Representations of Disability in German Women's Literature of the 1970s and 1980s"; Petra-Andelka Anders's thesis on representations of disability and mental illness in contemporary German feature films; and Allison G. Cattell's thesis on expressionist drama are notable exceptions.[82] With the exception of Anders's work, all of these publications are, however, contributions from English-language German studies. All five have begun to demonstrate forcefully the value of and breadth of thinking in disability studies for Germanistik, and in this, have offered inspiration and motivation for my own research. Despite these exceptions, one can rightfully note a "conspicuous absence" of a literary disability studies within today's German literary studies, to borrow David Bolt's words from 2007. For the UK context, he observed at the time that "the presence of disability is neither denied nor acknowledged. All literary scholars analyze works in which disability is present, yet few engage with the subject on any level, let alone one that's critically informed by the discipline of disability studies."[83] These words are today an apt description of the situation in German literary studies.

Viewing the autobiographical texts at the heart of this book through the lens of disability studies, my research further demonstrates the indispensability of disability studies–informed approaches to representations of illness/disability for contemporary literary studies. As will be demonstrated in the following sections of this introduction, the perspective of disability studies provides an interpretative framework from which to make sense of the "nervousness" displayed by the contemporary literary scene in Germany concerning the centrality of illness/disability in contemporary life writing and the absence of studies into such writing in German literary scholarship to date.[84] Not least, on a practical level, the field offers a precise yet sensitive and carefully considered language for presenting the findings of my analyses.

Terminology

The language used throughout this book is sensitized by disability theory. Commonly employed terms that appear in this book are "illness/disability," "impairment," and "disease" as well as "ablebodiedness," "ableism," and "disablism," some of which have already been used above. I do not tend to use the term "sickness" much, yet, in instances that I do, it is "to denote the social attitudes and perceptions of a disease."[85] As there is significant overlap between illness and disability, I often use the term "illness/disability." Although many disabilities are not illnesses, illnesses do constitute a large proportion of disabilities and are often legally and medically recognized as such. More politicized is the distinction that disability studies scholars make between disability and impairment. Impairment, like disease, is medically loaded terminology. Both encompass recognized diagnostic categories of abnormality and as such describe pathology. "Impairment"—denoting "physical limitation"—is the word that is more closely related to relatively stable, physical disability,[86] whereas "disease"—describing the "biological processes taking place in a diseased organism"—is more closely tied up with illness.[87] Yet disease can also cause impairment.

In this book, "disability" and "illness" are the terms used when discussing the subjective lived experience of medical or medicalized conditions and the way they affect aspects of one's being in the world (including aspects that go beyond one's experience of bodily limitations, if any such limitations are present at all, such as the experience of prejudice and discrimination). Those schooled in the so-called social model of disability rate the limitations imposed by society—encountered by the disabled person in the form of disadvantages (e.g., environmental, cultural, or economic)—as more significantly disabling or debilitating than any impairment. Indeed, they define the term "disability" as meaning first and foremost "social exclusion." It is from this vantage point that Davis writes, "As soon as we use the term 'disabled' we add a political element: suddenly there is a disabler and a disabled."[88] In this book, it is assumed that intrinsic (physical) and extrinsic (social) limitations, that is, both impairment and disability (or disease and illness), are interrelated in complex ways that deserve acknowledging.

As Ato Quayson clarifies, distinctions such as the one between impairment and disability (in the way that the social modelists understand it) seem so clear cut only in theory. In practice, illness/disability and impairment intersect. Quayson reminds us that "it is almost impossible to keep the two [terms] separate, since 'impairment' is automatically placed within a social discourse that interprets it and 'disability' is produced by the interaction of impairment and a spectrum of social discourses on normality that serve to stipulate what counts as disability in the first place."[89] Bearing these definitions in mind and trying to use the terms accordingly nonetheless gives an indication of which aspect of illness/disability is being discussed and fosters analytical precision in the researcher. A challenge for German-language research in the future will be to agree on and establish a similarly sophisticated vocabulary in speaking about illness/disability from a disability studies stance.

In the US context, especially in education research and the social sciences, disability studies advocates tend to make a point of using what is called "person-centered" or "people-first language." By putting the person first syntactically, such as in the expression "people with disabilities" (and as opposed to writing "disabled people"), they seek to stress the fundamental similarities between disabled people and other members of society, that is, to highlight "the shared qualities of personhood," as Alice Hall formulates elegantly.[90] In the British context, on the other hand, many commonly—and consciously—opt for writing "disabled people." Likely influenced by the academic and wider cultural setting in which I completed most of the work on this book, I too predominantly use the adjectival construction. My impression is that doing so, one runs less of a risk of making disability or illness sound like an add-on; this latter phrasing instead emphasizes illness/disability as an important part of people's identity. Although it is important to be aware of the ongoing debate with regards to people-first language, I do not consider it essential to take a firm stance for or against one of these different yet equally legitimate forms of expression.

In instances where "ablebodiedness" is used, it is to be read always as "presumed or imagined ablebodiedness" by those who identify as nondisabled. Many in the field also use the expression "temporary ablebodiedness"—it stresses that at some point over a lifetime most, if not all, people will find themselves disabled. Lastly, David Bolt helpfully distinguishes the relation of ableism to disablism. He marks out a subtle difference between the two terms, both of which are often used, and explains they are "two sides of the same ideological coin: [ableism] renders people who are not disabled as supreme; [disablism] refers to attitudes and actions against people who are disabled."[91] With Bolt, we can think ableism as corresponding to disablism in the way that patriarchy relates to misogyny, or—to add to his another example—heteronormativity to homophobia. The usefulness of "ableism" as a term—and that of all disability studies vocabulary, for that matter—lies in helping "call attention to assumptions about normalcy."[92]

Disability Studies as a Framework for the Analysis of Illness Narratives

This book subscribes to a wide, inclusive definition of disability as encompassing not only what is conventionally taken to be prototypical physical disability but also many mental, chronic, and terminal illnesses. This understanding acknowledges the fact that any definition of disability frays at its edges, and that, rather than fixating on all too strict a category that excludes less obvious circumstances of life, it may be worthwhile maintaining an openness to the term. The lived experience for many is that illness, impairment, and disability can and do all intersect. Crucially, it is this flexible understanding of illness/disability that enables me to interrelate all of the texts in my corpus in the first instance and in a meaningful way and make them speak to each other instead of isolating them by diagnosis or by author. Both my corpus of texts and my definition of disability reflect the fact that there is diversity in disability.

In the public imagination, a rather arbitrary line has been drawn between ideas of illness and of disability, a dividing line that Susan Wendell, for example, highlights as porous when she speaks instead of the "healthy disabled" and the "unhealthy disabled" in an article aiming to raise awareness of the difficult place people with chronic illnesses find themselves in within disability activism and theory.[93] The permanently and relatively predictably impaired who are not on the lookout for any kind of cure and neither want nor need much medical treatment fall into her first category. The second term encompasses the situation of those whose conditions do require medical attention because they are in flux and unpredictable in outcome. The "unhealthy disabled" may suffer pain and may not only have to learn to live with but find themselves dying from illness.

As we will see when turning to the close analysis of life-writing examples in the main part of this study, this complicates the negotiation of illness/disability for the "unhealthy disabled": it is a complex task to incorporate the continuously changing, sometimes life-threatening story of illness into one's life story and reconcile it with one's sense of self. It is less easy to claim illness as a facet of one's identity, with it being a less likely (but not impossible) source of disability pride. Wendell comes to find that "illness is equated with impairment, even by disability activists and scholars, in ways that disability is not; hence there is anxiety to assure nondisabled people that disability is not illness."[94] This, in fact, makes it pressing for disability studies to attend to the complexities of illness, to think through illness and the suffering it (also) brings. This process would further refine the insights gained by disability studies as a field thus far.

Petra-Andelka Anders highlights the usefulness of disability studies in this context: she suggests bringing to bear a disability studies framework on the analysis of portrayals of mental illness/health in film, as the challenges filmmakers find themselves confronted with are effectively the same when representing physical disability as when portraying mental health problems.[95] The stigma that mental illnesses carry is, in her view, also comparable. Anders writes of "die Ängste, die Faszination und der Unterhaltungswert" (the fears, fascination, and entertainment value) that surround both prototypical physical disabilities and mental illnesses and that warrant critical investigation in either case.[96]

Lastly, it is a pragmatic decision to point out how blurred the lines between understandings of illness and of disability are: if literary disability studies is still a rather marginal practice, then a field we could call "literary illness studies" is so far nonexistent.

The Reality of Illness/Disability in Contemporary Life Writing

The texts in my corpus deal with experiences as diverse as suffering from psychological trauma, living with various kinds of cancer, and becoming disabled after a stroke, yet they all take illness/disability "for real."[97] That is, the works covered in this study have one crucial thing in common: illness/disability does not (or not primarily) serve as a metaphor or allegory—as a "narrative prosthesis," in David T. Mitchell and Sharon L. Snyder's sense, that propels a storyline, and in the way that we know it especially from fiction—but is instead dealt with literally and autobiographically, either in retrospect as a liminal experience or in the experience of dying as an existential threat to the authorial self.

The term "narrative prosthesis" emphasizes the fact that disability in literature has traditionally been used as a narrative device, as either a "stock feature of characterization" (think of Achilles, Quasimodo, and Captain Ahab) or else as "opportunistic metaphorical device."[98] In other words, disability in narrative typically serves to mark characters and differentiate them from the "normal" rest. When used metaphorically, it is often employed as a "signifier of social and individual collapse."[99] Consider, for example, the symbolic role of the character Oskar Matzerath in Günter Grass's *Die Blechtrommel* (1959).[100] When using the phrase "narrative prosthesis," literary disability scholars therefore emphasize literature's discursive yet rarely acknowledged dependence on illness/disability.

This narrative crutch upon which authors steady themselves, often without reflecting on the practice, transports ideological convictions and helps bring out the contrast between the normal, good, and (morally) right, and the disabled other. Illness/disability gives stories impetus in a more fundamental sense too: in light of the fact that disability demands explanation in our social climate, one could say that it initiates narration first and foremost. Mitchell and Snyder therefore state that "disability usually provides the riddle in need of a narrative solution."[101] Their criticism does not aim at representation per se but is leveled at the fashion in which illness/disability tends to be dealt with. They observe, "While stories rely upon the potency of disability as a symbolic figure, they rarely take up disability as an experience of social or political dimensions."[102] And if these dimensions cannot be recognized, the social marginalization of people living with illness/disability can hardly move into focus. Similarly, both the literary critics in the media and literary scholars have typically read into or interpreted the representation of illness/disability, rather than taking it (also) as the representation of lived reality—a negligence that in the German academic reception has not yet been made up for even today.

All of the texts in my corpus do recognize the social and political dimensions of the experience of illness beyond the individual meaning illness/disability comes to take on. We have to look no further than to the preface of Schlingensief's cancer diary to find that the sociopolitical dimension is of crucial importance to him, as it is to all of the authors read here. Making this point particularly explicit, Schlingensief addresses a cultural dictum of silence and retreat surrounding illness when he states, "So viele kranke Menschen leben einsam und zurückgezogen, trauen sich nicht mehr vor die Tür und haben Angst, über ihre Ängste zu sprechen." (So many ill people live lonely and withdrawn lives. They don't dare go out anymore and are scared to talk about their fears.)[103] In the preface, the artist further clarifies that his concern is not to produce a polemic against an illness named cancer but to support what he terms the autonomy of the ill. Linked to that, the preface expresses his hope to counter the "Sprachlosigkeit des Sterbens" (speechlessness of dying) that he detects in society.[104] This inclination to speak about the contemporary context outside of literature, however, does not detract from these texts' status as works of literature. While this should go almost without saying, especially from a cultural studies–inflected point of view, this position is not necessarily shared by others working in German literary studies. Before turning to the approaches of scholarship to the topic, I will summarize and evaluate the German media's reaction to the most recent wave of illness narratives of interest here.

The (Non)place of Narratives of Illness/ Disability in Contemporary German Literature

In recently published personal illness narratives, of which this book analyzes a small number, we find an intense actual engagement with illness/disability. This verisimilitude may be precisely the reason the existential stories in my text corpus have produced notably extreme responses in the literary review pages of the German-language press,[105] amounting to a veritable feuilleton debate. The turn this debate took exhibits a societally manifest uneasiness with the topics taking center stage in the contested texts.[106] "Lasst mich mit eurem Krebs in Ruhe. Ich kann es nicht mehr hören. Und lesen"[107] (Please do go away with your talk of cancer. I don't want to hear— or read—another word about it), complains, for example, the journalist Richard Kämmerlings, in an article in the German broadsheet *Frankfurter Allgemeine* in August 2009. He finds himself to be "unpleasantly affected" by what he calls "Boulevardstoff" (tabloid matter).[108] Indeed, a subheading within the article even speaks of literature's "Kontamination mit dem Boulevard" (contamination by the tabloidesque). It is a phrase that introduces a metaphor of medicine, or more precisely epidemiology, that is here bound up with aesthetic value judgments and that situates the topic of illness where most critics believe it belongs: outside the walls and beyond the gateway to the citadel of literary quality.

In strong words, Kämmerlings's reasons that at a time when cancer is all around us, as *Volkskrankheit* touching everyone's life, it need not also be dragged into public discourse. He is convinced that people go into detail about illness (and in particular cancer), whether on TV or in books, merely for sensational effect, as supposedly "jeder weiß, was damit verbunden ist, welche medizinischen Prozeduren, welches Leiden, welches Hoffen und Bangen" (everyone knows what this involves, the medical procedures, the suffering, the hope and worry). This view denies illness narratives any cultural, let alone aesthetic, value. The underlying reproach of Kämmerlings's article is that those who do decide to confront cancer publicly must be attention-seekers and shameless, egotistical people.

The reader of his article is left to wonder why—if, as Kämmerlings insists, there is no notion of taboo, no silence that needs breaking—these new, decidedly personal narratives have the power to provoke him so much that he concludes, "Lasst uns mit eurem Krebs, eurem Schlaganfall, eurer Leberzirrhose, eurer Schweinegrippe in Ruhe. Erzählt von dem, was zählt, und nicht von Tumormarkern. Erzählt vom Leben. Das Ende kennen wir schon."[109] (Leave us alone with your cancer, your stroke, your liver cirrhosis, your swine flu. Tell us about what really matters, and not about tumor markers. Tell us about life. We already know how it ends.) The persistent ranking in the best-seller lists of a large proportion of recent illness narratives stands in contrast especially to his concluding claim and hints at the fact that readers must be reading these texts for experiential value, if nothing more. The popularity of this kind of literature in our current cultural moment reveals that the issues it addresses are central to many.

Critical attention reached a climax in October 2009 when Kathrin Schmidt was awarded a literary prize for *Du stirbst nicht* (You aren't dying / You won't die), a literary reworking of her stroke and subsequent experience of disability (chapter 2). Interestingly, this text, which is labeled a novel, is spared Kämmerlings's wrath, and it is telling that this is because the story of convalescence culminates in what appears to be a happy ending, with the protagonist Helene preparing to leave the space of the clinic.

Michael Angele, journalist with *Der Freitag*, takes a similarly provocative line as Kämmerlings in his article contributing to the discussion, titled "Wer hat geil Krebs?"[110] (So who's gagging for cancer?). Perceiving exhibitionist tendencies in the life writing of authors such as Schlingensief, Leinemann, and Roche, he attests to a lack of humility on their part and alleges that their decision to make their stories public was motivated by financial gain and psychological neediness. In short, there is no understanding on his part for authors of personal narratives about illness, death, and dying. He asks, "Läge wahre Größe nicht ... im Verzicht?" (Wouldn't true greatness be revealed by self-restraint?), and goes on to plead, with biting sarcasm, "Wenn die eigene Krankheit schon öffentlich gemacht werden muss, dann bitte mit dem Anspruch, es nicht unter dem Rang von Kunst zu machen (Merke: es könnte das letzte Werk sein!)" (If you really do feel the need to publicize your illness, then please don't do it with aspirations of creating art [NB: this work could be your last!]). The first person to reply to Angele's article was Schlingensief himself, a day after learning that his remaining right lung has been found to be full of new metastases. He feels compelled to clarify, "mein text entstand ohne literaturanspruch, ohne verleger im nacken! ich habe nachts, wenn die angst kam, alles in dieses band gesprochen." (My text came about without claiming to be literature, without a publisher breathing down my neck! At night, when the fear closed in, I just spoke onto this tape.)[111]

Over the days and weeks that followed, Angele's comment triggered a remarkable 236 online reactions—ergo, receiving a lot of attention of the kind its author denies the writers of illness narratives.

When the tough matter of real life gets too close to literature, German reviewers from across the political spectrum writing for a wide range of media outlets ranging from the conservative *Frankfurter Allgemeine* through to the liberal newspaper *Der Freitag* display surprising agreement. Their deprecatory reactions reveal more about the sociopsychological processes at work in the nondisabled reader/critic than they do about the quality of the individual texts. With sociologist and disability scholar Bill Hughes and especially his research into the affective responses displayed toward ill and disabled people in mind, we can read their adverse words as typical defensive responses. They are "a form of violence bred from our fear of and anguish about our alienation from the human condition."[112] As ableist sensibilities are shaken by authors who address head-on "the harsh inevitable realities of suffering, loss, pain and death" in a form that stresses as central their personal, firsthand experience and that cannot be cushioned, more safely, as fiction, these writers and their texts become "objects of fear and disgust."[113] Othering the authors as they challenge what Hughes terms "the non-disabled imaginary" includes relegating their texts to the margins of literature. Charges of egocentrism and of banality as leveled by the critics turn into something negative the offering of authenticity that all of these personal narratives make, that indeed many make artfully so, as shown in the analyses to follow.

When journalist Tina Klopp in 2015 claims that "für viele westliche Künstler bleibt . . . nur der Rückgriff auf individuelles Leid: Krebs statt Holocaust, Magersucht statt Nachkriegshunger"[114] (for many Western artists, all that remains is falling back onto individual suffering: cancer instead of the Holocaust, anorexia instead of postwar hunger), she relegates the artistic turn toward the public negotiation of illness and of dying into a stopgap. Instead of considering such autobiographically inspired work as a new cultural phenomenon worth investigating more closely, she believes it to originate from a dearth of topics available to a sheltered younger generation of artists, with illness being one of the few topics that can give their work gravitas, as she sees it. The wider sociopolitical context and topicality of these publications—comprising debates around the rising cost of health care, abuse scandals in nursing homes, lack of funding for hospices, and a continuous lack of clarity marking the German legislation on assisted dying (last revised by the Bundestag in November 2015)—is not recognized.

Through my disability studies lens, attempts to fence off the supposedly literary from supposedly subliterary texts become apparent as exclusionist practices. Dismissing the texts as fashionable "Bekenntnisliteratur"[115] (confessional literature), as Klopp and others do, undermines them by questioning their quality and precludes the necessity to analyze them in depth. This study will demonstrate that writers of illness narratives employ a whole range of autobiographical genres and narrative strategies. It reveals these narratives to be sophisticated writing at the forefront of contemporary literature. In this context, it is noteworthy that the German language lacks a category or term, such as "creative nonfiction," that would help to explain the nature and achievement of these personal narratives. Critic Dirk Peitz, while regarding the phenomenon with favor, therefore ends up describing them, in a rather longwinded manner, as "eine Reihe neuer Sachbücher ..., die sehr persönliche Geschichten über [beispielsweise] Krebserkrankungen erzählen"[116] (a range of new nonfiction books ... that tell very personal stories about [for instance] cancer). Indeed, the majority of the texts falls between the two categories *Belletristik* (belles lettres / fiction) and *Sachbuch* (nonfiction) that the *Spiegel*-Bestsellerliste allows for.[117] Being difficult to categorize as writing that finds ways around and, in part, actively deconstructs the fact-fiction binary that traditionally separates nonfictional from fictional writing, many of today's illness narratives sit uncomfortably between these categories and are thus also in their formal features difficult for readers, and maybe especially reviewers, because of their failure to conform.

German Studies Scholarship and Its Attitude toward Illness in Literature

Following on from Woolf's words cited at the beginning of this introduction, one could find it "strange indeed" that the representation of illness "has not taken its place" among the "prime" interests of literary scholarship. Mitchell and Snyder have long proven that images of illness/disability are everywhere in literature (including, even especially, the literary canon), yet these images have circulated within our cultures without attracting much scholarly interest, in German-language academia considerably less so than in the English-language realm. The question is how to approach German-language illness writings, especially those of autobiographical nature, as a literary scholar, despite the persistent critical idea that they are lacking in literary quality—an argument often put forth by those whose notions of privacy or decency are violated by the author's going public with illness, which a priori closes down any in-depth examination of such texts.

In 1989, Thomas Anz published his habilitation dissertation on the usage of *gesund* (healthy/sane) and *krank* (ill/diseased) as normative terms of value judgment in the literary discourse.[118] With the help of Anz's comprehensive work, one can trace the historical development of our tendency toward medical imagery.[119] He delineates the way in which, hand in hand with the medicalization of Western society, the "soziale Autorität" (social authority) of medical knowledge continuously increases.[120] Anz writes, "Medizinische 'Wahrheiten' und Begriffe entfalten verstärkt seit dem 18. Jahrhundert eine normative Kraft, von der kaum eine Entscheidung über den Wert menschlicher Verhaltensweisen, Einstellungen und Lebensformen unberührt bleibt"[121] (Increasingly since the eighteenth century, medical "truths" and terms unfold a normative power from which hardly any decision about the value of human behaviors, attitudes, and lifestyles remains untouched). At its most basic, health is "Basiswert" (base value), and illness "ein Übel" (an evil / a malady), with which one is cursed for wrong (e.g., immoral, irrational, criminal) conduct.[122] Over the course of his book, Anz highlights the fact that literary and metaliterary discourses are as little able to evade the effect of this as ethical, political, or judicial discourses. Beginning with what may have become the most influential medical case study in literature, the descent into madness of Jakob Michael Reinhold Lenz as first described by Johann Friedrich Oberlin,[123] the examples Anz analyzes demonstrate the persistent use of *gesund* and *krank* as ideological figures of thought, shape-shifting throughout the centuries but carrying lasting argumentative potency from the age of Goethe to late modernity. Peaking under National Socialism, such loaded rhetoric remains in use through to the 1980s, when Anz was writing, and, I would add, beyond.

Anz examines, among other aspects, the close association of the terms "illness," "morality," and "guilt" (tracing it in Büchner's *Lenz*, Goethe's *Werther*, Susan Sontag's writing), "illness" and "society" (Nietzsche, Freud, Otto Gross), as well as "madness" and "femininity" (the paradigmatic example here being Wolf's *Kassandra*). In metaliterary terms, he is particularly interested in those moments in literary history in which certain connotations can be noticed to change, for example, when the stigmatization of mental illnesses gives rise to the glorification or idealization of these illnesses, as can be observed in the context of the Neue Subjektivität and Antipsychiatrie. Importantly, however, Anz does note that in such cases of inversion, the dichotomy within which illness and health are conceptualized remains.[124]

Yet it becomes apparent that Anz cannot escape the impulse to which the critics of the feuilleton pages have more recently succumbed. This is shown in the way he deals with the autobiographical literature of the 1970s, with which our contemporary wave of illness narratives can most obviously be aligned: over the course of the decade during which "die kulturelle Produktion von Theorien, Metaphern und Geschichten über Krankheiten geradezu mythische Qualitäten erhalten"[125] (the cultural production of theories, metaphors, and stories about illness were endowed with quasi-mythical qualities), certain conventions of writing and speaking about illness take shape and solidify. Observing this, Anz goes on to characterize the literature as having a clear "Authentizitätsanspruch" (aspiration to be authentic), which may indeed not be surprising for life writing, yet is used by him to suggest that this is at the cost of writing artfully.[126] He then takes the texts to be "Verständigungstexte" (roughly: texts that seek mutual understanding, or texts that assume a shared social or cultural understanding) in search of like minds,[127] that is, self-help books rather than literature, and claims that what guided the production of this type of text was above all "das soziale Prinzip gegenseitiger Hilfe in einer Leidensgemeinschaft"[128] (the social principle of mutual support within a community of suffering). In a very practical sense, he asserts, this autobiographical literature was intended by its authors "als Lebenshilfe und Therapie" (as counseling and therapy), which he exemplifies through a discussion of Karin Struck's *Klassenliebe* (Class love, 1973).[129] From a disability studies stance, the determination that the writing of the period was above all therapeutic must be recognized in its double-sidedness: suggestions of inwardness and an overstated emphasis on suffering and victimhood go hand in hand with it, and disable the texts' functioning as literature, that is, writing that would contribute to a wider public conversation on the universal issues of illness/disability and dying, rather than—isolated from it—circulating among the hands of a readership of like minds only.

Anz does observe that these texts, focusing on the experience and meaning of illness in unusually personal ways, cannot easily be classified as novels or reports, literature or record.[130] He even notes that, for many who work professionally with literature and who are "über die Differenzen zwischen Dichtung und Wahrheit, Literatur und Dokument zu wachen gewohnt"[131] (used to watch over the differences between poetry and truth, literature and document), a provocation lies in exactly these genre crossings.[132] Yet, ultimately, Anz passes judgment on this type of literature as he targets especially a young, not yet established generation of authors including Maria Erlenberger, Fritz Zorn, Claudia Storz, Peter Schneider, and Karin Struck. He concludes in unequivocally derogatory words:

> Viele der hier genannten Bücher werden vermutlich bald völlig vergessen sein oder nur noch als Zeitdokumente überleben. Manche dürften in ihrer literarischen und intellektuellen Anspruchslosigkeit nur deshalb einen Verleger gefunden haben, weil ihre Inhalte als marktgängig eingeschätzt wurden. Krankheit und Tod . . . wurden jedenfalls in den siebziger Jahren für die nachrückende Generation zu den beliebtesten Einstiegsstoffen in die literarische Praxis.[133]

> [Many of the books named here will most likely soon be forgotten entirely or only survive as documents of their age. In their literary

and intellectual simplicity, some will have found a publisher only because their content will have been marketable. In any case, illness and death became one of the most popular topics in the 1970s for the next generation to break into creative writing.]

For Anz, this is sufficient assessment, and he then moves on to those texts that seem to be of more interest to him—a few select examples of autobiographical literature by more established writers as well as fictional texts. Despite having set out with his monograph to examine value judgments—the mission statement reading, "Zeigen wollte und will ich in erster Linie, wie bestimmte, historisch variierende Vorstellungen von Gesundheit und Krankheit eingehen in verbale Akte der Wertung und Normvermittlung" (I want to show above all how certain, historically varying ideas of health and illness influence verbal acts of judgment and the mediation of norms)—he himself in the end cannot resist the temptation to take a judgmental position against the autobiographically motivated illness narratives that were central to the New Subjectivity of the 1970s.[134] By doing so, he suggests that a more in-depth examination of these particular texts is not merited, at least not from a literary studies stance.

We observe that autobiographical approaches to the topic of illness provoke unease in the literary scholar, which leads to their rejection on the grounds of such approaches' alleged literary inferiority. Anz's reaction, then, is eerily similar to those displayed in the feuilleton discussion from around 2009 (a whole twenty years on), in the sense that he declares the autobiographical writing of illness that arose in the 1970s to be subliterary. Corina Caduff's 2013 book *Szenen des Todes* (Scenes of death) demonstrates that this cultural bias against personal narratives of illness and dying persists among literary scholars even today, even among those who, like Caduff, take a firm interest in the proclaimed "neue Sichtbarkeit des Todes" (new visibility of death) in contemporary culture.[135] In a chapter titled "Schreiben über Sterben, Tod und Tote" (Writing about dying, death, and the dead), Caduff finds contemporary authors and publishers disinhibited in disseminating personal cancer stories.[136] She commends those texts that, in her view, display "Diskretion und Zurückgenommenheit von personaler Darstellung" (discretion and restraint in personal representation) above the rest, and, overall, she thoroughly denies life writing about illness any literary value.[137] This recurring critical impulse within German literary criticism of policing the borders of literature where the representation of illness and the personal mode converge may be part of the reason the texts of the New Subjectivity (many of which Anz mentions in his 1989 book) did not achieve canonization and have instead largely been written off by scholarship. That, in turn, may explain why Schlingensief could not find any personal illness narratives to read in the new millennium.

For this study, the consequence to be drawn methodologically from the observations above is to approach the selected contemporary personal illness narratives in a decidedly scholarly manner, from as objective a stance as possible: where Anz suspects opportunism, as a disability studies scholar, I see a considerable number of individual contributions amounting to a cultural phenomenon worth examining more closely. Exactly because of their autobiographical relevance, this book takes an interest in questions of genre and in writers' formal strategies. (Authors' experimentations with different genres is an aspect that Anz raises yet does not delve into.) In other words, it approaches its text corpus as literature, not as an isolated kind of minority writing appealing exclusively to ill/disabled people, a collection of self-help books, or titillating confessions. The texts are read for form as much as for content, and the picture that emerges from this is certainly not one of simplicity or uniformity; instead, the texts examined here appear concerned with accessibility, very much with the reader in mind—but this does not preclude writerly accomplishment.

Academic Nervousness in the Face of the Real?

When illness moves into the focus of Germanistik, scholars tend to display either a historic interest (often in the representation of a specific condition, typically in fiction),[138] or they focus on an individual and typically canonized author whose own illness experiences have influenced their oeuvre.[139] As important as such studies are, it is notable that, generally, autobiographical illness narratives are shied away from. When they are being dealt with—and this is an impression that contextual analyses of the reception of the texts in my corpus confirm—the autobiographical element is suppressed. The result is that illness is read allegorically; that is, it is abstracted from and taken as "really" standing in for something else that the literary scholar then goes on to illuminate, to the detriment of the text and neglecting the wider discussion to be had about illness/dying. As Cattell agrees, when academics in German literary studies deal with representations of illness/disability at all, they tend to focus their analytical efforts on "the ways in which disability is used to represent abstract concepts."[140] In a similar way to authors' historically largely symbolic use of illness/disability,[141] then, German-language scholarship traditionally fails to consider stories of illness/disability (be they fictional or not)—also—as (potential) depictions of the reality of lived experience. It is an oversight that this book addresses.

The edited volume *Krankheit schreiben: Aufzeichnungsverfahren in Medizin und Literatur* (Writing illness: Recording methods in medicine and literature) is a case in point.[142] The volume has a clear historic focus; it keeps its distance from our present age. Instead, it centers on specific conditions, historical figures, and associated cases from around 1900. In those chapters that deal with literature at all, the book addresses only the work of canonized (male) authors. The "recording techniques" it takes a major interest in are those of the medical professionals; the way literature writes or rewrites illness is subsidiary to the volume's composition.

This publication is representative of an area of research called "Literatur und Medizin" that has gained considerably more traction in German-language academia than literary disability studies has (and more than it may ever do).[143] Led by figures such as Bettina von Jagow and Florian Steger,[144] the field is rooted in the history and ethics of medicine more than in literary studies, albeit aspiring to speak across subject disciplines. Researchers working from this perspective stress medicine as a practiced art[145] and tend to take an interest in potential exchanges between the practices and knowledges of medicine and literature. Those taking up this stance often work from a historical perspective, read with the syllabi of medical schools in mind, and suggest utilizing literature as a means to give medical education a more reliable ethical grounding. They analyze the representation of medicine in the literary and artistic worlds or examine the genres of medical writing with the tools of literary studies. Many engaging with the field do, however, ultimately display one-sided interests. Privileging the doctor's perspective—already endowed with power and authority—over that of the ill, such scholarship tends to turn to the writing doctor for insights.

By contrast, this study does not limit itself to the investigation of a particular illness/condition but explores the work of several authors writing the ill self publicly across a range of experiences and mediations. Tracing writers' politics of patienthood and authorship in a cultural context that still gives only little of its attention to the inside, lived perspective of illness/disability, this study consciously focuses its attention on what in German literary studies is an underresearched area, despite an increasing amount of contemporary literature coming out that addresses illness from a personal stance.

In the course of this, the work presented here furthermore hopes to widen disability studies' focus beyond the borders of the English language, as Pauline Eyre calls for in a recent article, in which she writes that "the predominantly Anglophone world of disability studies has thus far been impaired by a lack of engagement with the literature and culture of Europe where English is not the first language."[146] Methodologically situated between Anglo-American and German literary studies, it hopes to mediate the value of a disability studies approach from this position. Just as it may be time for literary disability studies to look beyond English-language cultures, as Eyre suggests, it is, I contend, high time for German literary studies to open up to methodological approaches informed by disability studies and pay the texts examined here the critical attention they deserve.

Overview of the Chapters

Sensitized by readings in disability studies, this book recognizes the cultural significance of the work the individual primary texts do in their negotiations of illness/disability, self, and society. What is more, it naturally understands these texts to be literature, in an unqualified sense, and as such of interest to literary scholarship—especially as they have recently come out in such short succession. Recognizing the texts' relationality, that is, their being in dialogue with both literary history and popular culture, as well as their place within our contemporary world and within an author's previous work, this study's methodology is one of careful contextualizations of each examined text. Instead of isolating the illness experience and the writing to which it led, it contends that answers to questions such as why and how an author decided to confront illness publicly can be explored adequately only by reading each text decidedly in its context.

Certain types of response, some of which I have drawn out from media reactions and comments of scholars above, surface time and again. Such responses can be suspected to be "socially conditioned, politically generated."[147] One example is the (at times unwitting) expression of feelings of repulsion toward the ill/disabled or dying person; on a societal level, Davis suggests, such negative feelings translate into "actions such as incarceration, institutionalization, segregation, discrimination, marginalization, and so on."[148] The disability studies reading of my corpus offered here therefore further combines the findings of close readings with observations concerning readerly reactions to the texts.

Instead of presenting the texts in the chronological order in which they were published, the progression of this book is guided by the question, How explicitly is the relation of the portrayal of illness to the author's own life experience being made? The analysis begins with the most ambiguous text in this respect, Charlotte Roche's *Schoßgebete*, a text that I identify as an autofiction, and from there moves on to Kathrin Schmidt's *Du stirbst nicht* and Verena Stefan's *Fremdschläfer*. Both are autobiographical novels, but Stefan's book is the more classic life writing text, its protagonist sharing the author's name.[149] Lastly, in a comparative chapter, analysis turns to the two diaries by Christoph Schlingensief and Wolfgang Herrndorf, which—as indicated by their genre designation—take up the most explicitly personal and immediate stance of the five texts, and were written directly at the time of their author's experience of illness and of dying (not retrospectively).

Charlotte Roche's *Schoßgebete*

Charlotte Roche's popular novel *Schoßgebete* tells the story of the everyday life challenges of Elizabeth, who is portrayed as suffering from a complex psychological trauma caused by the death of her brothers. It is this tragedy that forms the narrative's nucleus, and it is through this crucial aspect of the story line that the novel is indelibly linked to Roche's own life experiences. Reading Roche's second book publication as a narrative that traces and articulates the author's personal trauma of multiple bereavement, two strategies employed in *Schoßgebete* are examined more closely: the first is the use of an autofictional narrative mode, which, I argue, undermines the assumed referentiality of the much-talked-about novel at the same time as establishing it.[150] This grants Roche poetic license, which enables agency and helps the author/narrator to evade traumatic passivity and silence. It allows her to belatedly take control of this part of her life story as a celebrity, inevitably in the media limelight, and thus to reclaim it from the tabloid newspaper *Bild*, which reported extensively on the accident in 2001, exploiting it for sales. Autofiction emerges as a mode of writing eminently suitable for the storying of illness and traumatic loss.

The second focus of the chapter, intertwined with the first, is Roche's employment of an aesthetics of disgust in *Schoßgebete* and what this suggests about the relationship between the text and its readership. Thinking back to disability scholar Bill Hughes's article "Fear, Pity and Disgust: Emotions and the Non-disabled Imaginary," we recall the role affect plays in the negotiation of such taxing themes as illness/disability and death and, what is more, the role of disgust specifically as a reaction that invalidates the ill/disabled as other.[151] Roche, more than aware of this, incorporates and preempts potentially negative reactions by readers in her subversive aesthetic representation of the "sickness" of her protagonist's mind and lifestyle in *Schoßgebete*.

As both a physical and an emotional primal response, disgust typically finds expression in an open-mouthed face, with the tongue protruding,[152] and can, at its most extreme, cause retching and feelings of nausea. Disgust at its most archetypal or typical is encountered when one is confronted with what is considered dirty, poisonous, or otherwise dangerous, abnormal, or diseased. Disgust can often also take on a moral significance and in this is less instinctive (as a form of built-in self-protection) but similarly visceral. In my analysis of Roche's writing, disgust is of interest as "a physical, visceral aversion that becomes a culturally powerful—and manipulable—aesthetic response."[153] My approach to it is informed most noticeably by the work of Mikhail Bakhtin on the grotesque and Julia Kristeva's theory of abjection.[154] I speak of an aesthetics of disgust to stress that disgust is created deliberately in literature (and other art), purposefully complicating the writer-reader relationship. The term "aesthetics"—in this chapter, as in the overall book—is used in its most neutral (contemporary) sense, denoting "the distinctive underlying principles" of a text,[155] rather than encompassing only philosophies or representations of the beautiful and sublime as worthy of artistic, and scholarly, attention.

Together, the autofictional mode and the aesthetics of disgust Roche employs in telling this highly personal story help her to position herself and her text ambivalently toward, yet just out of reach of, publicly voiced reactions to its publication. Often stressing the fact that she does not regard herself an author,[156] which rhetorically in fact heightens claims of authenticity, Roche remains unperturbed by criticism of her writing as nonliterary. The writing and publication of *Schoßgebete*, for Roche, appears to have served the function of formulating trauma in her own words and communicating the experience to a readership willing to empathize with its narrator figure across difference. Yet, as this fruitful analysis underlines, it does not diminish the text's literariness (its constructedness and its inherent value as writing of its individual and cultural moment—regardless of readers' tastes or sensibilities), or indeed its complexity.

In relation to wider genre discussions, this first chapter finds that, in German literary studies, the term "autofiction" is still strongly indebted to the French tradition. Yet, as scholars are beginning to recognize more and more German-language literature as autofictional, this is starting to have an effect on the understanding of the theory.[157] Generally, one would hope that autofiction studies will not develop the same elitist tunnel vision that marked the initial history of autobiographical research as well as trauma studies. Instead, it should from the start read the marginal and the new, draw upon popular literature (such as Roche's *Schoßgebete*) as well as the canon.

Kathrin Schmidt's *Du stirbst nicht*

Disability often is, as Davis phrases it, "a specular moment."[158] In the chapter on Kathrin Schmidt's "Erinnerungsroman" (novel of memory), as the blurb of *Du stirbst nicht* describes it, the physical act of staring that occurs between the visibly ill/disabled person and the onlooker constitutes the main focus of the analysis, and it is probed for its effect on both the diegetic level (that is, between characters) and beyond (namely, between author and readership of illness/disability narrative). If not because of one's noted functional limitations, disability—from the outside—is determined visually, on the basis of one's appearance: "The missing limb, blind gaze, use of sign language, wheelchair or prosthesis is seen by the 'normal' observer."[159] Davis stresses the dominance and violence this gaze can exert on the visibly disabled person—and the "powerful emotional responses" this gaze is accompanied by.[160] To understand ideological constructions of disability and normalcy (his term), Davis stresses that "attention must be paid to the violence of the response [of the supposedly 'normal']—in a way more than to the object of the response [i.e., the disabled person]."[161] Studying normality is therefore key to understanding disability—and Schmidt's text addresses questions of ab/

normality most directly out of all texts included in my corpus, and most didactically so.

This chapter, in order to approach the narrative device of staring in Schmidt's novel, adapts Rosemarie Garland-Thomson's theoretical considerations of "staring" for literary analysis.[162] Building on previous scholarship on manifestations and effect of the gaze and the discourse about the gaze within disability studies (as exemplified in Davis's notion rendered above), Garland-Thomson broadens our understanding of visual encounters in her work on staring as a natural impulse and social necessity. She does so by focusing attention on the stare as inducing an interchange of looks and triggering identity work in those involved. Garland-Thomson stresses that "who we are can shift into focus by staring at who we think we are not."[163] I contend that this idea widens interpretative possibilities for cultural/literary studies and may be an especially valuable approach when working on autobiographical literatures, as Garland-Thomson's framework allows us to recognize agency in the position of those typically confined to the position of objects.

The close analysis reveals the visual in *Du stirbst nicht* to be the dominant plane of protagonist Helene's subjective experience and consciousness; possibly because her vision remains unimpaired by the stroke she suffers, just as her creator's had. Her ways of seeing are found to be closely linked to issues of self-image or self-perception and externally determined image, as well as attitudes toward the disabled other—which, as Helene awakens from a coma at the onset of the narrative, is also found within the self. In its frank appraisal, staring is found to be a crucial means for the author's alter ego to reflect upon the situation she finds herself in. It enables the character to reassemble an image of her self over the course of this narrative. The novel takes the shape of an *Entwicklungsroman* and can be taken to "provide the public with controlled access to lives [or a life] that might otherwise remain opaque or exotic to them"—thus fulfilling a major function, at least in Couser's view, of disability life writing.[164]

In fact, Schmidt's text does not stop there. It invites but simultaneously troubles the reader's stare and the emotional repertoire of responses the encounter with impairment/disability brings to the fore. The use of staring as storytelling technique by Schmidt again raises profound questions about the relationship of the autobiographical author of illness narrative and its readership, the media and scholarship included (as did Roche's use of autofiction and disgust in *Schoßgebete*). Beyond providing a revealing close reading of the text itself, the chapter therefore investigates what the effect of normative reading practices is on a text that has the lived experience of illness/disability at its center, once it is exposed to a large, mainstream readership in the way *Du stirbst nicht* has been since winning the Deutscher Buchpreis in 2009. With Jürgen Link and his theory of normalism in mind, we recognize that the prize confers upon it the status of exception, and that this is a strategy that reels in the stretched boundaries of "normal"—reestablishing an essential difference between Helene and those she interacts with on the level of story who see themselves as ablebodied, and between Schmidt and her readers in the extra-textual world.[165] It is in this context that Schmidt's vehement rejection of her book as therapeutic—and as *Betroffenheitsliteratur*, that is, as belonging to a group of texts of interest to a small section of the reading public only, written by those concerned for those concerned (in both senses of the word)—must be understood.[166] The hasty assumption on the side of reviewers that illness writing is always (only) therapeutic writing is found to be disabling, as it confines Schmidt's novel, against its ambitions, to the sidelines of contemporary literature.

Verena Stefan's *Fremdschläfer*

The restrictive label of *Betroffenheitsliteratur* that Schmidt so vehemently rejects is one all too familiar to Verena Stefan. Her 2007 book *Fremdschläfer* (Alien sleeper) is the third text analyzed in this study. It deals with the life writer's breast cancer experience as a mature woman, alongside and in connection with other themes such as migration and personal relationships. The issues that labels such as *Betroffenheitsliteratur* create for authors will be explored further in the chapter on Stefan's illness writing. Monique Wittig's theorizations of the struggle for recognition maintained by the minority author in the literary field are helpful in doing so—and can further elucidate Davis's remarks concerning the "violence" done to the ill/disabled person in society, which I above transferred to the situation of the author of illness/disability life writing whose work is being denied access to the realm of literature.[167] For the study as a whole, what can be drawn from Wittig's essay is encouragement, methodologically, to read each of the texts in my corpus in the context of its individual production, its author's work thus far, and the literary field it moves in; thus, precisely not reducing its complexity to one "minority" issue. This enables me to respect the complexity of each piece of writing analyzed in the book, even when it is analyzed with specific view to the representation of experiences of illness/disability.

Like Schmidt in 2009, Stefan too had once been exposed to the full force of normative reading practices, in fact more aggressively so. In one review from 1976, for example, Stefan's autobiographically inspired debut *Häutungen* (*Shedding*; the text with which she rose to fame as an author) was attacked as the "Krankengeschichte einer schweren Neurotikerin" (case history of a severe neurotic), its author labeled "ein zutiefst verstörter Mensch"[168] (a most deeply disturbed person). In contrast Anne Betten, more recently, has called it a "Kultbuch"[169] (cult book). Both reactions reveal that it clearly hit a nerve at the time of the "Neue[] Frauenbewegung" (new women's movement) and "Neue Subjektivität,"[170] to name the two related movements—one social, one literary—with which *Häutungen* is typically associated. More than thirty years later, the life writer then indeed tackles illness autobiographically in *Fremdschläfer* (published in 2007). In Stefan's own words, the book and its interwoven strands deal with "(im)migration, dislocation and connection to place and space viewed from inside the body, its visceral and cultural codes."[171]

Again, as in previous chapters, the analysis of *Fremdschläfer* too centers on questions of narratability. It traces the narrative strategies and aesthetic forms that allow Stefan to write of cancer personally and, what is more, explores what traditions writers can build on, which texts they can engage with, when there is no real tradition, at least not a recognized one, of writing illness autobiographically, as is the case in the Germanic cultural realm. The focus in analyzing Stefan's breast cancer narrative *Fremdschläfer* lies on how she—today a resident of Canada—writes breast cancer "from beyond the border," literally and metaphorically. By means of intertextuality she situates herself and her text in a tradition of Anglo-American writings above all, and, by referencing texts by Virginia Woolf, Susan Sontag, and Audre Lorde, among others, Stefan distances herself from the German-language literary circuit and its critics. The chapter demonstrates that, for the second-wave feminist, it is typical that only the written word has the power to trace and make fully real the experience. Assessing Stefan's position on the international stage as a writer today, she is found consciously to take up what I call a transnational stance with *Fremdschläfer*.

Starting from her feminist position, with this text she "work[s] to reach the general";[172] in other words, she writes it to address numerous social topics, touching on the experience of various sections of society. Knowingly writing from a privileged position, Stefan thus produces a deeply political and ethical text that we could call multidirectional in the way it addresses the intersecting themes of illness, im/migration, and more, finding the universal in the individual and familial life story, and vice versa. Consequently, *Fremdschläfer* is a text that offers itself up to a wide and diverse readership.

Christoph Schlingensief's and Wolfgang Herrndorf's Cancer Diaries

The final, comparative chapter returns to a specific autobiographical genre: that of the diary. It is an important form of expression for illness writers—particularly when there is severe uncertainty as to how much longer one has to live. Both Christoph Schlingensief and Wolfgang Herrndorf broke new ground for their artistic work by turning to the diary genre. This raises the question, What promises does the diary form specifically hold for the self in (terminal) illness? In addition to addressing previously formulated research questions, this concluding, longer analysis traces the particular investment made by the dying author in end-of-life writing.

The comparative analysis of the two diaries brings out both parallels and differences in each writer's motivation behind writing illness, his practice of doing so, and each diary's reception. Beyond that, the chapter contributes to contemporary diary research by doing ground work in exploring its suitability—and provocative potential—as an outward-facing genre for writing the ill and dying self. Building above all on the work of Philippe Lejeune, as collected in the edited volume *On Diary*, and identifying with contemporary research approaches such as Kylie Cardell's,[173] this chapter recognizes the diary as simultaneously a mode of writing and of living.

So schön wie hier kanns im Himmel gar nicht sein! Tagebuch einer Krebserkrankung (It can't possibly be as beautiful in heaven as it is here! A diary of cancer) was published in 2009—one year before Schlingensief died from the illness that he began documenting in it. The first half of the chapter shows that the genre ascription of diary was a deliberate one and, what is more, is reflective of Schlingensief's beliefs in his artistic life and absolute commitment to his work. For Schlingensief, the desire to record and disseminate his own experience of illness in diary form seems to have overridden the risk of a potentially hostile reception. Even so, the relevance of the artist's turn to the diary form was missed by the majority of critics and scholars commenting on Schlingensief's late period. The diary, as representative of a marginal literary form, has in fact been neglected altogether in the otherwise large and growing scholarly interest in Schlingensief's late work. The work presented here rectifies this omission in Schlingensief scholarship, arguing that his diary, crucially, sets the direction for the artist's subsequent prolific late work.

The analysis of Schlingensief's diary like that of Herrndorf's, which follows on from it, investigates how the diary as a form is suited to the task of writing the dying self publicly and in which ways the use of the diary as an exploratory space maps onto, or departs from, either author's previous work. In each case, the analysis takes into account the effect that the terminally ill author's nearness to death has on the contemporary as well as posthumous reception of each author's end-of-life writing. It pays particular attention to the material transformations that each text undergoes as their author's illness unfolds and the different media that both Schlingensief and Herrndorf experiment with.

With an analysis of Wolfgang Herrndorf's diary/blog *Arbeit und Struktur* (Work and structure; 2010–13), the second part of the chapter complements the observations made about Schlingensief's published diary. Like Schlingensief, Herrndorf has begun to attract considerable scholarly interest. Although there was little scholarship available on Herrndorf's texts when I worked on *Arbeit und Struktur* (and none concerning the diary/blog), it is striking how fast the body of work on the author's textual legacy is currently growing.[174]

In my analysis of *Arbeit und Struktur*, I trace why and how Herrndorf, in a prolonged state of "livingly dying" that we can observe to become more and more common in the twenty-first century,[175] writes cancer in the everyday genre of the diary. Additionally, his choice of publication via the blog is discussed,[176] and the transformations (material and otherwise) that the evolving diaristic text undergoes over time are examined. In a way that can be compared to Schlingensief breaking out of and questioning the medium of theater in his *Tagebuch*, Herrndorf critically thinks through the relation of *Arbeit und Struktur* to other literature, of both the canonized and popular kind. Besides anticipating posthumous reading practices, the author makes a last literary point with *Arbeit und Struktur*: in it, Herrndorf demonstrates the kinship of the fictional and the nonfictional in a way that only life writing, and maybe particularly end-of-life writing, can do. *Arbeit und Struktur* thus chips away at the demarcation of low and high literature that traditionally operates in German culture.

Both authors display a wariness of cultural elitism in their diaristic illness projects and set out to reach a diverse audience. Their autothanatographies are not merely therapeutic for them, as is commonly assumed, implying an inwardness. My analysis reveals each diary is put to a multitude of uses by its creator, as outward-facing, complex texts daring to engage in a wider societal conversation about illness, death, and dying in the twenty-first century. In contrast to similar illness writing from the 1970s and 1980s (much of it in diaristic form),[177] which was typically published after the author's death, Schlingensief and Herrndorf bring their readerships into their present, knowingly overtaxing them when confronting them with their suffering and dying. The Internet as a place of publication helps such more prompt publication, which in turn heightens the illness diaries' provocative effect.

To summarize, the analysis offered in this book examines how different authors rise to the challenge of writing illness at once personally and publicly. It does so by tracing which aesthetic strategies and narrative forms or genres the authors consider in storying illness, and explores how they use, stretch, and, at times, redefine them. Doing so, this study provides an important literary/cultural disability studies perspective on contemporary German literature—especially that which arises from autobiographical experience—dealing with themes of illness, disability, and dying, and demonstrates ways in which literary scholarship can read these texts more adequately.

1: Autofiction, Disgust, and Trauma: Negotiating Vulnerable Subject Positions in Charlotte Roche's *Schoßgebete* (2011)

> *The conflict between the will to deny horrible events and the will to proclaim them aloud is the central dialectic of psychological trauma.*
>
> —Judith Lewis Herman, *Trauma and Recovery*

"Dieser Roman basiert auf einer wahren Begebenheit. Darüber hinaus ist jede Ähnlichkeit mit lebenden oder toten Personen sowie realen Geschehnissen rein zufällig und nicht beabsichtigt."[1] (This novel is based on one true event. Beyond that, any similarities to people living or dead as well as to any real events are purely coincidental and not intended.) The reader encounters this legal statement on opening Charlotte Roche's 2011 novel *Schoßgebete*, before turning the page to start reading what has been another huge success for its author after her debut *Feuchtgebiete* (*Wetlands*, 2008), which is said to have sold around two million copies.[2] While such disclaimers today seem fairly standard, upon finishing this text, which bears the description "novel" on its cover, the reader is struck by the necessity, but also the inapplicability, of the legal disclaimer that refutes the close and complicated relationship of fiction and fact as presented in *Schoßgebete*.

This chapter focuses on exactly this intertwined relationship by reading the narrative as an autofiction, as coined by literary theorist and author Serge Doubrovsky when describing his own experimental text *Fils* (Son/Threads, 1977).[3] Historically, the concept emerged "at a time of severely diminished faith in the power of memory and language to access definitive truths about the past or the self," as Johnnie Gratton points out.[4] In literary scholarship, the term has been applied widely since, generally describing a "variante de l'écriture autobiographique . . ., qui tend à abolir la frontière entre la fiction et la non-fiction"[5] (variation of autobiographical writing . . . that tends to remove the border between fiction and nonfiction). My understanding of autofiction is informed by the psychoanalytic connotations the term has for Doubrovsky. It recognizes an element of play—and within that opportunities for cross-media performance—in the autofictional mode, which authors such as Roche today consciously exploit. Autofiction here is seen as a form of life writing that proves aptly contemporary, being much more fluid and harder to grasp than other forms of (more conventional) autobiographical writing. Isabelle Grell, a leading literary scholar of autofiction, speaks in this context of autofiction's "transparence énigmatique."[6] Beyond merely identifying *Schoßgebete*'s autofictional qualities, my analysis formulates reasons for Roche's use of this narrative mode and probes its intersection with a bold aesthetics of disgust that is employed to narrate this equally personal and fictional story. Disgust is understood as "a physical, visceral aversion that becomes a culturally powerful—and manipulable—aesthetic response."[7] Consequently, this chapter reads disgust as a figure for a problematized author-reader relationship. It is here that the autofictional writing mode and disgust find common ground. Finally, this chapter suggests autofiction as a mode of writing eminently suitable for the storying of illness, death, and trauma.

Schoßgebete portrays three days in the life of the homodiegetic narrator. Accordingly, the chapters are titled "Dienstag," "Mittwoch," and "Donnerstag." These three days are representative of first-person narrator Elizabeth Kiehl's everyday life: she and her husband Georg have sex, she cooks dinner at night, and they watch porn when their daughter Liza is away. On the Thursday, Elizabeth and Georg visit a brothel. Elizabeth narrates daily appointments with her psychotherapist and thus introduces the reader to her troubled psyche. Her fears and suicidal thinking, her many neuroses, and her sexual desires loom large throughout these three ordinary days. They are all linked to the tragic event at the heart of the novel, which is the death of the protagonist's brothers in a car accident. Central to the narration are Elizabeth's reflections on her difficult relationship with her mother, who was the driver but survived the accident, and her thoughts on her near-symbiotic relationship with her husband. Overall, *Schoßgebete* in many ways reads like a confession or apology—it is a minutely detailed account of Elizabeth's struggle with life.[8]

The accident is the one true event to which the book's paratext refers; it is central not only to Elizabeth's but also to Charlotte Roche's life. Because of the author's high public profile, when picking up the book the majority of Roche's readership will know that her own brothers died in a car accident on the way to her wedding in 2001. This complicates any straightforward reading of *Schoßgebete* as a novel; at the same time, as is explored below, its fictional dimension should be respected. Throughout the analysis, the narrator is therefore called Elizabeth, even if many readers might be tempted to take her name as standing in for Roche herself. In keeping with the fictional name for the largest part of my discussion, the analysis hopes to show appropriate respect for both the author and the narrative she created, and grant it the space it demands. In my reflections on this, I, as a reader, am already unmasked by the effect of autofiction.

This chapter approaches the novel as an autobiographically motivated illness narrative, or more precisely a trauma narrative. *Schoßgebete* has not yet been adequately recognized as such,[9] partly because initial readings of Roche's second book publication were skewed by expectations of continuity between it and her first novel. This is to be attributed, at least partly, to the choice of the book's title, which through rhyme makes a deliberate connection to Roche's first publication, *Feuchtgebiete*.[10] Marketing strategies employed in the advertisement of the text reinforced such ideas of similarity, for instance, by matching the design of the book jacket for *Schoßgebete* with that of Roche's debut. Furthermore, both book titles play with allusions to the genital area. Since *Feuchtgebiete*, the media likes to call Roche "Sexautorin," her books are branded "Sexromane," and the language she employs has been attacked by literary critic Ruthard Stäblein as "Schrumpfdeutsch" (shrunk/stunted German), to give just one example. Just like *Deutschlandfunk*'s critic, Denis Scheck, Stäblein finds Roche's literary language too colloquial and contracted. The unanimous critical verdict seems to be that her novels are trivial, verge on the pornographic in content, and are stylistically weak.[11] Roche's self-presentation as not being an author (in the sense of literary author) willingly adds to this, yet this must be noted to in fact heighten readers' perceptions of Roche's texts as authentic.

The little scholarship there is to date that deals with *Schoßgebete* does not focus on the text in its own right. Instead, in the case of Hester Baer's article, for example, attention is directed to the way it contributed to public debates in Germany around 2011 concerning the state of feminism.[12] Emily Spiers takes the more historicizing approach, examining "intergenerational feminist relations" from Alice Schwarzer to Roche and other "new" feminists, on the basis of Roche's and others' books.[13] With Baer and Spiers thus engaging in discourse analysis rather than in-depth analysis of the text itself, *Schoßgebete* is not analyzed as a piece of literature or stand-alone text. Spiers insinuates that such analysis is not worthwhile when she writes that "apart from the narrative strands that deal with the familial trauma . . . the novel's general aesthetic is pornographic kitsch."[14] This reaction dovetails with the feuilleton critics' verdict, and, by stressing its aesthetic as simple and unappealing, in short, as substandard, an academic engagement with Roche's second novel and the difficult topics of illness, death, and loss that it negotiates is foreclosed. My analysis will recenter attention to the text itself and these main themes. Through "unpatterned" close reading and in contrast to previous scholarship, I pay particular attention to the mediation of the protagonist's psychological trauma and preoccupation with the body, sex, and death, and find a number of complex narrative strategies and forms of aestheticization at work in *Schoßgebete*.[15]

The neologism *Schoßgebete*, literally translating as "lap prayers," bears strong associations with the female body and sexuality.[16] Yet, besides these sexual connotations, the word evokes religious connotations too: it is a dark-humored pun on the German noun *Stoßgebet*—a quick, short, last-minute prayer uttered in a situation of sudden danger.[17] Therefore, the novel's title already alludes to the more complicated, existential meaning sex takes on for the protagonist of *Schoßgebete* and the differences between Roche's debut and its successor. The autobiographical dimension of *Schoßgebete* is distinct and presents a major development in comparison to Roche's less personal, more programmatically feminist first novel.

What unites both publications, however, is a sociopolitical commitment underlying Roche's writing that few reviewers or cultural critics recognize, which expresses itself in a sustained interest held across both texts in exploring the repressive potential of culturally prevalent ideas about health and illness and, linked to this, notions of hygiene and norms. Doing so openly in her books, Roche's writing upsets powerful cultural notions of decency and privacy concerning the physicality of the body as well as our vulnerability to illness (mental and physical illness alike). When Tony Paterson writes that *Feuchtgebiete* unfolds into "an at times excruciating account of how a young woman systematically goes about breaking almost every sexual taboo,"[18] this may be true, yet—as is symptomatic of many of the book's reviews—he seems to miss the fact that *Feuchtgebiete* first and foremost is the story of a girl who is hospitalized for an injury sustained through self-mutilation and who is portrayed as suffering from a childhood trauma (nor does he ask himself how the text's sexual explicitness relates to that narrative).

The following discussion of *Schoßgebete* as an autofictional trauma narrative is written with these important resonances across Roche's writing in mind.

Trauma in Literature, and *Schoßgebete* as Trauma Narrative

In the late 1980s and early 1990s, literary scholars began to theorize the characteristics of trauma as displayed in literary writing by tracing and making sense of its transformation into aesthetic textual representations. Cathy Caruth's working definition of trauma from 1991, which served as the basis for her influential works on trauma theory throughout the decade, is still a useful starting point: "In its most general definition, trauma describes an overwhelming experience of sudden or catastrophic events, in which the response to the event occurs in the often delayed and uncontrolled, repetitive occurrence of hallucinations and other intrusive phenomena."[19]

This definition reflects now generally accepted assumptions Caruth drew from earlier findings in psychology and neuroscience, as well as the 1980 definition for posttraumatic stress disorder in the *Diagnostic and Statistical Manual of Mental Disorders*, the *DSM-III*.[20] Departing from this, she has shaped what is still the most influential understanding of trauma in literary studies. Central characteristics of trauma can be deduced from this definition: the event that causes it is understood in some way to be "overwhelming," for example, because of its suddenness or scope, which overtly challenges the unprepared victim (and it is therefore "catastrophic"). The delayed response with accompanying symptoms is central, as this response constitutes the actual trauma. This had already been observed by French psychologist Pierre Janet and his contemporary Sigmund Freud, who borrowed the term "latency" or *Nachträglichkeit* (literally: belatedness) from medical discourse on infectious diseases, in relation to the incubation time Freud perceived it took until trauma manifested itself in symptoms.[21] The phenomena, lastly, are "uncontrolled," "repetitive," and generally "intrusive," because they come to haunt the traumatized person over and over again, against his or her will. The victim in Caruth's view is doomed to passivity and has to endure these repetitions. Caruth further explains that trauma "is always the story of a wound that cries out, that addresses us in the attempt to tell us of a reality or truth that is otherwise not available."[22] She sees the main task of an ethical literary studies approach as listening to these attempts to tell of a traumatic reality.[23] Nevertheless, Caruth's emphasis constantly lies on the paradoxical side of this endeavor: just as trauma demands "our witness,"[24] at the same time it defies such witness, because traumatic testimony is always "enigmatic testimony."[25] Trauma—in her understanding—"resists simple comprehension,"[26] which is why it can always only be an attempt to tell us.

In relation to this, it has often been said that trauma is unspeakable. Judith Lewis Herman clarifies what this means: "Certain violations of the social compact are too terrible to utter aloud: this is the meaning of the word *unspeakable*."[27] Understanding the nuanced use of the adjective here is important—it helps illuminate the theory, as well as potentially giving an answer to the question of why literature, especially from the twentieth century onward, has become the primary site to attempt a storying of trauma. The fact that one might hardly bear speaking aloud about traumatic experience might be exactly what prompts so many to try to put their experiences into written words first, shutting out all awareness of a later audience or readership, and at least in the process of writing trying to concentrate on the self, in an attempt to gain a sense of control. Interestingly, Charlotte Roche details that she does exactly this: "When I write, I try not to think about that this is going to get published—obviously this does not completely work. But I want to be brave when I write.

Because I write about things I feel embarrassed about and have issues with."[28] Yet we must be aware that simultaneously, in the act of finding words for trauma, the writing subject takes up a precarious position and, in a struggle for words, constantly fears for his or her inadequacy.

Peter Gasser highlights the fact that autofictional writing consciously addresses the gap between a life's experience and the writing thereof,[29] in contrast to more traditional autobiography, which aims for a smooth, teleological narrative. Gasser's observation holds true, too, for trauma narratives, at the center of which is a gap or—to use a term more widespread among trauma theorists—a void, and this constitutes a first significant parallel between the writing of trauma and the autofictional mode.

The event that triggers the traumatic reaction can be a commonplace event, like, for instance, Freud's example of an accident, which Caruth also uses for illustration.[30] What is decisive is that, subjectively, the event is considered overwhelming. This has often been misunderstood: in the 1980s, the *DSM* edition that Caruth, like others, referenced deemed it "essential" that an event triggering the trauma be "outside the range of usual human experience."[31] Considering that, for instance, rape or domestic violence are tragically frequent rather than extraordinary isolated cases, this unfortunate wording was criticized by feminist therapists like Judith Lewis Herman or Laura S. Brown until its revision by the American Psychiatric Association in the mid-1990s. Importantly, Brown highlighted that women run a higher risk for trauma due to the social realities in which they live.[32] Brown specified that the then dominant notion of what constitutes traumatic stressors supported the social and political status quo, which discriminated against women as well as people from minority groups. It is generally accepted among scholars today that such tragically common events (that members of disadvantaged sections of society are disproportionately exposed to) can be at the source of a person's trauma. Additionally, and this constitutes another shift of opening up in the professionals' grasp on trauma, psychotherapist Jeffrey Kauffman in *The Shame of Death, Grief, and Trauma* outlines how mourning and grieving in consequence of a loved one's death have been found to be more frequently traumatic in the last few decades.[33]

That the traumatic truth, to return to Caruth's definition, is "otherwise not available" alludes to an understanding of traumatic memory that can again be traced back to Janet: traumatic memory is separated from regular or narrative memory and cannot actively be retrieved or dominated (by narration).[34] While "the images of traumatic re-enactment," for example, in the form of flashbacks or nightmares, remain absolutely literal, "accurate and precise,"[35] paradoxically, as Caruth stresses, the victim of trauma at the same time may suffer from amnesia—a manifestation of the fact that conscious or active retrieval of the traumatic memory is impossible.³⁶ Literality of repetition and dissociation of the memory of the event at the root of the trauma thus form a paradoxical pair.

On the whole, therefore, Caruth views the structural elements of trauma as defining, which becomes apparent when she states that "[the] pathology [of trauma] consists . . . solely in the *structure of its experience* or reception: the event is not assimilated or experienced fully at the time, but only belatedly, in its repeated *possession* of the one who experiences it. To be traumatized is precisely to be possessed by an image or event."³⁷ Because of its belatedness, in Caruth's line of argument, trauma "is fully evident only in connection with another place, and in another time." It is therefore not locatable, appearing "outside the boundaries of any single place or time."³⁸

The outlined perspective highlights trauma's structure as one of paradoxes that underlie all traumatic symptoms: a traumatizing event is perceived as overwhelming, yet this is realized only belatedly. Trauma is incomprehensible yet demands a listener. It is there, in the form of flashbacks or nightmares, yet not there, as is expressed in the symptom of amnesia, or present only in leaving a void; and it therefore dominates a person's life. Not fully understanding it, not having been able to work through it, the trauma dominates a person's present and is anything other than past, even while—in a distorted way—referring to a past event.³⁹

In *Schoßgebete*, Elizabeth tries to describe the effect of trauma on her life: "Ich bin gefangen in den Tagen, in denen das passierte, ich komme einfach nicht drüber hinweg. Der Film im Kopf spielt sich immer wieder von Neuem ab. Vielleicht hört das ja mal auf. Glaube ich aber nicht." (*SG*, 116; I am trapped in the days in which it happened, I simply cannot get over it. The film in my head plays itself over and over again. Maybe sometime that will stop. But I do not think so.) The feeling of being trapped in time perfectly matches the notion that trauma invalidates any temporal limits. It also dooms Elizabeth to passivity, against her will. The traumatic memories are indeed uncontrolled. Furthermore, the "film" she sees in her mind's eye is repetitive and intrusive. With trauma theory in mind, the use of the film metaphor for unprocessed traumatic memories seems particularly apt, because the memories of the phone calls she receives on the day of her family's accident and the events they trigger, as well as the images of the accident, remain absolutely literal to Elizabeth. They have become indelible in the process of traumatic inscription. One might object that this cannot be true, as she was not at the scene of the accident when it happened, therefore has no real images of it, yet, through not only empathy but indeed identification with everyone in the crashed vehicle, she has imagined these images for herself. The quotation above gives an indication of the nightmare in which the narrator of *Schoßgebete* lives. From her perspective, surviving in a traumatized state is worse than death (*SG*, 108–9, 115, 238). It matches, too, the narrator's recurring suicidal thinking.

Schoßgebete writes the symptomatology of Elizabeth's trauma of bereavement, which manifests itself in the protagonist's suffering from multiple fears and neuroses as well as clinical depression. The opening lines of the first chapter serve to illustrate this and set the scene for what is to come: "Wie immer vor dem Sex haben wir beide Heizdecken im Bett eine halbe Stunde vorher angemacht. Mein Mann hat ganz hochwertige Heizdecken gekauft, die reichen auf beiden Seiten vom Scheitel bis zur Sohle. Für mich muss man da etwas mehr investieren. Ich habe wahnsinnige Angst, dass so ein Ding anfängt zu glühen und ich nach dem Einschlafen bei lebendigem Leibe verbrenne oder am Rauch ersticke." (*SG*, 7; As always before having sex, we switched on both electric blankets in the bed half an hour before. My husband has bought high-end electric blankets; they reach from top to toe on both sides. To please me, you must spend a little extra. I am terribly scared that such a thing will start to smolder and I will burn to death after falling asleep, or suffocate in the smoke.)

The novel is a minutely detailed protocol of Elizabeth's everyday life and thoughts. The apparently trivial—here, the electric blankets—has its place in the narrative and is aligned with serious insights into the narrator's psyche in a stream-of-consciousness style. This method of describing her every move and thought is her only way to slowly approach and access the memories she fears so much, those she can only indirectly allude to in between the lines of this opening paragraph. "Das, was passiert ist" (*SG*, 80; That which happened) is encoded, and Elizabeth evades it for as long as possible. Looking for a language to talk about the unspeakable, the trauma at the center of the novel, the narrator feels compelled to narrate herself from every possible angle. It is significant that she confesses to the first of her many phobias—her fear of fire or smoke—in these early pages of the novel, although the reader will not yet understand its purport. It stems from her brothers' burning to death in the wake of the crash, yet the reader can only make this connection more than a hundred pages later. First, it seems, the narrator's main concern is to confide her everyday survival struggles. This begins with a detailed fifteen-page description of sexual intercourse with her husband, which is followed by a graphic account of a visit to the bathroom and includes the equally extensive description of her every move in the kitchen when preparing dinner. Elizabeth clearly feels the compulsion to tell, maybe more so to display herself, that is, both her psyche and her body.

Foregrounding the Unsexy, Sick, and Oozing Body

After a long stream-of-consciousness passage in which she shares her thoughts about anal sex, the narrator of *Schoßgebete* confesses, "Ich hasse es, alleine zu sein mit diesen Gedanken, immer so ekelhafte Gedanken, entweder Tote oder anal, was anderes gibt's wohl nicht in meinem Kopf?" (*SG*, 274; I hate to be alone with these thoughts, always these disgusting thoughts, either dead people or anal, there does not seem to be anything else in my head?) It is insinuated that Elizabeth's obsession with sex is, to a degree, a symptom of her trauma, providing a way to block out—however temporarily—any thoughts of her dead brothers, or fears of the premature death of any more of her loved ones, or her own suicidal fantasies. Distracting herself by consciously thinking of sex and thus preventing an anxiety attack, the narrator determines wryly, "Das funktioniert wenigstens" (*SG*, 197; At least that works). But sex does not offer salvation. Instead, sex as represented in *Schoßgebete* has the qualities of a drug, functioning almost as a kind of tranquilizer. The time of day when Elizabeth and her husband have sex is "der einzige Moment am Tag, wo ich richtig durchatme" (*SG*, 7; the only moment of the day that I can breathe freely), she observes. For once, the physical gains advantage over the psychological, overlaying her multiple fears: "Nur wenn ich die Angst mit Hypersexualität überlagere, bin ich angstfrei" (*SG*, 107–8; Only by blanketing the fear with hypersexuality am I free from fear). And it works, temporarily, as in a Bakhtinian reversal this narrator's emotional center is located in her "Gedärme" (*SG*, 199; guts) and thereby in the body's lower stratum. Instead of displaying attempts to transcend corporeality, Elizabeth's bodily needs and functions, sexual and otherwise, reassure her in a way that says, "Ich bin auch noch da, wenigstens ein bisschen" (*SG*, 160; I am still here, at least a little).[40]

This is what makes sex so central to Elizabeth's life and consequently to the narrative. Sex is valued for the temporary relief it brings, yet it has no lasting healing effect: after the sex act, death returns. The reader learns from Elizabeth that her sleep at night is "Leichenschlaf" (*SG*, 123, 237; the sleep of a corpse). Night after night, to fall asleep, she needs to take up this pose, with her folded hands resting on her chest (*SG*, 123). With Julia Kristeva's *Powers of Horror* in mind, we instantly read the human corpse as epitomizing abjection. It is the self turned to waste[41] and emblematic for what most of us, barring Elizabeth, cannot easily accept: the fact that the dead body's corporeality is ours, too, that the self is, after all, an embodied and therefore mortal self.[42] Elizabeth knows from her extraordinary experience that death is as unavoidable as it is uncontrollable, and at times death truly tempts her, as it promises "a relief from the burden of individual selfhood."[43] In its materiality and concreteness, the corpse posture Elizabeth takes on bears the potential to deeply disturb its onlooker, including *Schoßgebete*'s reader, while for her it has a calming effect. Elizabeth is constantly, maybe overly, aware of the fragility of life. She is thus clearly positioned as different from the implied reader.

The unreliable, mortal, and unclean body, which, as Kristeva's *Powers of Horror* shows, is often equated with the female body, is the ultimate site of abjection in Western culture. The abject, to put it in a nutshell, makes its subject aware, above all, of its "relation to death, corporeality, animality, materiality—those relations which consciousness and reason find intolerable."[44] Yet necessarily these relations take center stage when it comes to dealing with topics of illness, disease, and bereavement, and they are consequentially not repressed by Elizabeth.

Schoßgebete and the Autofictional Mode

Shirley Jordan's review article on the state of research in French literary studies on autofictional writing in general and that by female authors in particular makes clear that there is yet much scholarly work to be done on the nexus of autofiction and trauma.[45] For German writing, no parallel survey article exists at all. Much groundwork is needed, not only to pay women's autofictional writing choices and strategies the attention they deserve but also to address trauma narratives (maybe especially those by women) in the autofictional mode.[46] Johnnie Gratton tentatively connects the upsurge of published autofictions to the traumatic experiences of the twentieth century in his entry "Autofiction" in the *Encyclopedia of Life Writing*. However, in-depth analyses of the relation of autofiction and trauma are hitherto desiderata, particularly outside of French literary studies.

What we can observe in contemporary literature is that the boundaries and connotations of factual truth (as signifying authenticity) and fiction (as inauthentic) are actively being dissolved by authors. This goes hand in hand with the growing interest of literary scholarship in the theory of autofiction and scholarship's attempts to understand whether and how it translates into practice.[47] While the notion of a dichotomy of fact and fiction has a long tradition,[48] particularly those with an interest in autofiction begin to dismiss it as "irrelevant" to contemporary literary studies, with Martina Wagner-Egelhaaf leading the way within German literary studies.[49] Concerning the terminology within German-speaking academic discourse, one notices that scholars follow the French labeling of such literatures as "autofiction," the term that Doubrovsky coined and that, for instance, Gérard Genette, Vincent Colonna, or Philippe Lejeune have come to use, rather than trying to find new terms for it, as is the case in the American realm with the neologisms "surfiction" or "factual fiction," to name just two.[50]

Conventionally, an autofictional text must make a highly ambiguous offer to the reader in order to position itself as referential and fictional in equal measure.[51] Certain elements in *Schoßgebete* accordingly seem to authenticate the story to a lay reader, signaling a high degree of factuality: besides the car accident, real people's names and lives too have found their way into the stream-of-consciousness-style narration, "rein zufällig" (purely coincidentally) so, if we are to believe the opening legal statement. Most notable among them is Alice Schwarzer, an iconic figure of second-wave feminism in Germany.[52] The story is further authenticated by organization of the stream-of-consciousness narration into three chapters titled after the three days of the week that *Schoßgebete*'s plot covers, a structure that invokes the diary genre's immediacy. The novel's style then is decidedly colloquial, suggesting thoughtless spontaneity and thus again authenticity. Lastly, the novel's first-person narrator, Elizabeth Kiehl, is designed in recognizable biographical proximity to Charlotte Roche herself: at the time of publication, Roche was thirty-three years old, exactly Elizabeth's age in the novel. Not only are both the author and her heroine of mixed German-English background but they both are mothers, stepmothers, and daughters of divorced parents. Roche's celebrity status ensures that most German readers would notice these similarities—and they may have chosen to read the book because of them in the first instance.

Other elements position the narrative much more ambiguously between the autobiographical and the fictional: above all, with the cover of the novel clearly stating "Roman," any hastily assumed referentiality of the book's to the empirical world is undermined.[53] Roche's and her heroine's un/likeness is carried into the choice of name for the protagonist, which—at least according to more traditional understandings—would exclude *Schoßgebete* from the realm of autobiographical writing, as the protagonist's and the author's name do not match exactly. Going by the name of Elizabeth (spelled the English way, i.e., with a *z* rather than the more German *s*), Roche's character does, however, evoke the author's second name (her full name being Charlotte Elisabeth Grace Roche)[54] and thus bears a name that, with Lejeune, can be said to be "at the same time similar to the name of the author and different."[55] This prevents the reader from making Lejeune's alluring autobiographical pact too easily while simultaneously remaining open to it.

With autofiction being a writing mode that abandons or transcends the idea of any boundaries between fiction and nonfiction, ultimately it cannot be sufficient to list and weigh against each other the fictionalizing and authenticating strategies of any one text. To truly identify *Schoßgebete* as an autofictional text, I will therefore demonstrate how it transgresses the limits of fiction and nonfiction on the level of the text, thereby—to an extent—dissolving them.

One of autofiction's main characteristics, as expressed in prototypical texts like *Roland Barthes par Roland Barthes* (1975), is its programmatic self-reflexivity as a linguistic construct aware of its mediality.[56] Self-conscious use of language and the recognition and exploitation of language's performativity is highly typical of autofictional writing. Furthermore, crucial, I would add, is the autofictional mode's awareness of its "effects on the world outside the text."[57] In *Schoßgebete*, this reflexivity is particularly acute in its media awareness and is expressed in the text's cutting depiction of the workings of the tabloid press.

As an alias or stand-in for the German *Bild-Zeitung*, a tabloid paper and top-selling newspaper in Germany, Roche's novel features the *Druckzeitung*, hardly veiling its real-life reference point. Its fictional name is a sarcastic pun: while *drucken* as a verb is "to print" in German, the noun *Druck* can also mean "pressure." It is known that alleged *Bild* journalists terrorized Roche after her family's fatal car accident in 2001 and tried to blackmail her into granting them an interview about the accident.[58] In *Schoßgebete*, Elizabeth is similarly threatened by *Druckzeitung* reporters, reexperiencing, almost reenacting what Roche went through: a journalist calls her about the accident, believing he is the first person to speak to her and thus the one to deliver the harrowing message of her relatives' deadly accident. From a trauma studies perspective, this revisitation of the experience is highly significant.

On pages 136–39, Elizabeth minutely narrates her feelings toward the *Bild/Druck*-newspaper, personified as "diese Bestie, das Böse" (*SG*, 136; this beast, the evil). She expresses an anger beyond words about the methods they employ: "mich am Telefon für eine Geschichte, für Auflage, in dem schwächsten Moment meines Lebens zu vergewaltigen" (*SG*, 137; to rape me on the phone for a story, for sales, in the weakest moment of my life). Full of revenge, she swears, switching into English, to "*track them down and smoke them out of their holes*" (*SG*, 137). While one might argue that any autobiographical text is more acutely aware of its extratextual consequences than is "pure" fiction, it is crucial to note that this passage from *Schoßgebete* culminates in advice directly and urgently addressing the reader, advice that is as valid in the fictional world as it is in the real world it blatantly references: "Es gibt nur was zu drucken, weil zu viele noch mit ihnen reden. *Haltet alle dicht!* . . . Mach den Mund auf, und du bist selber schuld." (*SG*, 138; emphasis mine; There only are stories to print because too many people still talk to them. *Hold your tongue, everyone!* . . . If you open your mouth, it's your own fault.) The provocative rape metaphor is repeated several times in this context (*SG*, 163–66), and Elizabeth again addresses the reader directly when condemning the tabloid press's output as "Emotionsporno" (*SG*, 166; emotional porn), stressing, "Jeder hat die Wahl: zu den Anständigen gehören und so was vermeiden oder zu den Unanständigen gehören und die Sensationsgier befriedigen, tatsächlich, nachweislich auf Kosten anderer!" (*SG*, 166; Everyone has the choice: to be one of the decent people and avoid that stuff or to be one of the indecent people and satisfy one's desire for sensation, in actual fact and demonstrably at the expense of others!)

The narrator thereby transgresses all boundaries between fact and fiction, mirroring the factual in the fictional and vice versa. In its seeming artlessness and straightforward, often colloquial language, the textual construct that *Schoßgebete* nevertheless is reverberates with questions to the reader: Do we give in to *Bild*-like voyeurism and read the text as "really" autobiographical in nature, thereby applying an almost pornographic gaze of pleasure, or at least amazement, to the sight of the traumatic other-that-cannot-be-me? If so, does one take part in the metaphorical rape of the narrator and, by extension, the author and her family? Or shall we instead avert our gaze, attempting to console ourselves it is only fiction—yet is it? Lastly, the question is, can we transform our gaze into empathy, regarding the other, however temporarily, as someone who could (also) be me? Whichever path a reader chooses, *Schoßgebete* manages to make the reader feel highly self-conscious and more than just uneasy as he or she becomes a witness to this text, or story, or life.

An in-depth engagement with the text pivots on such questions as these. *Schoßgebete*, despite its confessional qualities, its stream-of-consciousness style, its minutely detailed description of Elizabeth's life and the tragedy that is at the center of it, aims precisely not to be "emotional porn." The aesthetics of disgust employed by Roche underlines this further. As the following section shows, the text's use of disgust serves to test its readership's capability for empathy.

Schoßgebete's Aesthetics of Disgust and Its Alienating Effect

Roche commences the novel with an elaborately described sex scene that is above all a gatekeeping scene, preventing an all-too-easy identification with the narrator/protagonist: "Ich rutsche langsam mit dem Gesicht in seinen Schritt. Und rieche seinen männlichen Geruch. Ich finde, der ist nicht sehr weit weg vom weiblichen. Wenn er sich nicht direkt vorm Sex geduscht hat, und wann macht man das schon, wenn man so lange zusammen ist wie wir, hat der eine oder andere Urintropfen schon angefangen zu gären zwischen Eichel und Vorhaut. Es riecht wie in der Küche meiner Oma, nachdem sie auf dem Gasherd Fisch gebraten hat. Augen zu und durch. Es ekelt mich ein wenig, gleichzeitig aber erregt mich dieser Ekel." (*SG*, 8; With my face I slowly slip into his crotch. And smell his male odor. I think, it is actually not so far off the female one. If he does not shower right before having sex, and when, if ever, do people do that when they've been together for as long as we have, then one or two drops of urine will have started fermenting between glans and foreskin. It smells like it does in my nan's kitchen after she has been frying fish on the gas cooker. Take a deep breath and get to it! It disgusts me slightly, while at the same time this disgust arouses me.)

The author presses every button to elicit disgust in the reader—having her narrator talk about smells, sex, urine, decay, and foods. This detailed description of the sexual intercourse between Elizabeth and her husband, Georg, goes on for fifteen pages in total and, following the passage quoted here, is—seemingly randomly—interspersed with thoughts about her relationship to Georg and their age difference, among other topics, introducing the reader to her realm of thought and how she copes with everyday life. The reader is neither spared "Schmatzgeräusche" (*SG*, 9; squelching sounds) nor "Spucke" (*SG*, 9; spittle) and must bear with the protagonist contemplating her urge to gag when attempting to swallow sperm (*SG*, 10). As a reader, one has to submit oneself to Elizabeth's descriptions of sexual preferences or techniques that, of course, may not be for everyone and that, in this detail, deliberately provoke repulsion in the reader. By being thus confronted with an aesthetics of disgust from page 1 of the book, the reader is guided to feel an exhaustion similar to that of Elizabeth, who admits, "Das ist auf Dauer ganz schön anstrengend: ein Bein im Leben, ein Bein im Grab, die ganze Zeit auf dem Sprung, ich kann mich nicht entscheiden, weder für das eine noch für das andere" (*SG*, 279; In the long run, this is pretty exhausting: One foot in life, one foot in the grave, the entire time on the hop, I cannot make up my mind, neither for one thing nor for the other).

Disgust is an appropriately complex and demanding aesthetics. It is an ambivalent feeling,[59] and in this it is comparable to Elizabeth's subject position, torn between life and death—not able to commit to either. In this, it is a serious emotion, one that puts the reader in the protagonist's shoes, at least in terms of her stress levels, yet is also confrontational, potentially asking much of its reader when confronted with passages such as "Wenn Menschenfleisch brennt, riecht es nach gegrilltem Bauchspeck, hab ich mal gelesen" (*SG*, 274; I once read that when human flesh is burning, it smells of barbecued pork belly). The confusion of the categories human/animal within this statement and its allusion to the taboo of cannibalism transgresses moral boundaries and thus elicits disgust. Elizabeth equates the human body to meat, which after all it is, a thought that—precisely because of its truth value—we collectively suppress.

Schoßgebete takes seriously the demand originally raised by Doubrovsky that autofiction be absolute, that it is ruthlessly candid, intimate, and revealing, instead of all too preselective in what it narrates (as classic autobiography is).[60] Roche's strategic use of disgust guides the reader in understanding: this book is trying to be anything but kitsch, which the narrator defines as "die Verneinung von Tod und Scheiße" (*SG*, 131; the denial of death and shit). Instead *Schoßgebete* is brutally frank about these potential sources of disgust. It is all about death, shit, and sex, and focuses in on these matters along with Elizabeth's troubled psyche.

In order to disable self-consciousness, embarrassment, and shaming mechanisms as much as possible for her to be able to tell her story in the first place (a story which in extensio may be seen as Roche's), the narrator figure Elizabeth—informed by her daily therapy sessions—almost seems to apply a medical gaze to herself, analyzing her behavior as if it were someone else's. An aesthetics of disgust lends itself to this taking up of the more objective medical gaze, as, to a degree, it others the self. And in Elizabeth's case it helps her view her actions and thoughts as if from the outside, from a distance that enables both Bakhtinian laughter where others are long repelled and a lingering at the brink of abjection without completely losing control.

With this in mind, Elizabeth's description of herself preparing dinner early on in the novel must be taken as poetological commentary: "Aus dem Kühlschrank nehme ich den Wirsingkopf, das schönste Gemüse überhaupt. Mit einem großen, sehr scharfen Messer schneide ich den Wirsing in der Mitte durch und gucke mir die Schnittfläche genau an." (*SG*, 24; From the fridge I get the savoy cabbage, the most beautiful vegetable ever. I cut the savoy right through its center with a large, very sharp knife and inspect the cut surface thoroughly.) In a Kristevan reading, this violation of tenuous boundaries placed toward the beginning of the novel attunes the reader to what is to come. Elizabeth acts as her own surgeon and fearlessly tries to operate on the open wound that is the traumatic experience of her brothers' deaths. While this might seem an individual matter, a blow of fate, she does not refrain from putting her suffering, her marital life, and the expectations that she is confronted with as a mourner, patient, woman, mother, and lover into societal contexts (*SG*, 71). For example, she discusses her pronounced atheism (*SG*, 274) or discloses secret fears like that of the "virtuelle Gefahr des sexuellen Missbrauchs" (*SG*, 177; looming danger of sexual abuse), which she believes women and children are exposed to. She thereby denaturalizes the darker mechanisms of Western society and draws attention to what—like Kristeva in *Powers of Horror*—she sees happening "under the cunning, orderly surface" of civilization, as well as under the surface of the self that encounters abjection, as is metaphorically expressed in the image of cutting open the cabbage.[61] The implied reader is invited along to watch the operation but will have to expect to see some bloody entrails.

Autobiographical Writing in Suspicion of the Self

According to Martina Wagner-Egelhaaf, critical reflections of autobiographical narcissism are another programmatic feature of the autofictional mode.[62] Possibly in anticipation of reviewers' uncompromising attitudes to the publication of her second novel as a writing celebrity, so again arising from an evident media awareness, Roche has her narrator figure

Elizabeth reflect on exactly this narcissism, as is expressed in the following, to quote just one example: "Ich rede über den Unfall, all die blutrünstigen Details, *kann mir aber selber kaum glauben, dass das wahr ist, was ich da erzähle*. Es erzählt aus mir raus. Ich werde das Gefühl nicht los, dass ich alle *anlüge* mit dieser Geschichte. . . . Ich bin eine Hochstaplerin. Eine Wichtigtuerin. Will mich nur mit einer *erfundenen* Geschichte in den Mittelpunkt oder Vordergrund oder was auch immer drängen." (*SG*, 121–22; emphasis mine; I am talking about the accident, all the gory details, *yet can hardly believe myself that what I am saying is true*. It narrates itself out from inside of me. I cannot rid myself of the feeling that I am *lying* to everyone in telling this story. . . . I am a fraud. An exhibitionist. With an *imaginary* story I simply want to take center stage, or push myself to the fore, or whatever.)

Prior to the quoted passage, the narrator describes being on the phone to her father, who tells her the shattering news of the accident. This is a key passage as Elizabeth expands on her obsessive-compulsive need to talk about the event that is at the heart of much of her suffering, while simultaneously critically portraying herself as an attention-seeking "liar." If lying is the telling of imaginary or fabricated stories (that is, fiction making), yet the story could not possibly be any more real, then *Schoßgebete* could not tell this paradoxical story of trauma in any mode other than the autofictional. In other words, the autofictional mode and the space it creates, an in-between zone of fact and fiction, facilitates, if not primarily enables, the transformation of death and trauma into story.

When first-person protagonist Elizabeth states that she can hardly believe the truth of what she then must relay to the relatives surrounding her, this is simultaneously an expression of trauma. In these reflections of Elizabeth on the first time she put the accident into narration, the reader learns that she cannot in that moment process the information given to her by her father; it is marked by belatedness. It remains to be ever-present as traumatic memory that cannot be organized into the mind's schemes[63] and therefore hovers over the rest of her life "like an intruder or a ghost," as Sigmund Freud and Joseph Breuer had already suggested at the turn of the twentieth century.[64]

If in contemporary times "the writing of the self is suspicious,"[65] as Armine Kotin Mortimer puts it—a circumstance that can be seen as one reason for the observable upsurge in publications of autofictions in a shift away from more straightforward autobiographies—then it must be stressed that the writing of the shattered, traumatized self is all the more self-conscious or "suspicious" of itself. The writing of the traumatized self might indeed best be written under the guise of fiction, where one can dissociate the narrator from oneself, as Charlotte Roche did in her creation Elizabeth. While dissociation as well as reenactment are two symptoms of trauma we have traced for Elizabeth Kiehl in relation to Charlotte

Roche in *Schoßgebete*, Suzette A. Henke, who has looked into trauma in women's life writing from a perspective informed by psychoanalysis and scriptotherapy, nonetheless comes to the conclusion that what she calls "veiled autobiographical narrative" can effect a therapeutic recovery from trauma.[66] Autofiction therefore is both risk and promise: it entails the risk of again having to relive one's trauma but also promises to empower its writer, to help conquer the trauma and tame it in the process of putting the unspeakable into words and thus give it narrative structure.

Performing the Self

When considering Roche's media appearances (which may more aptly be called performances), it is worth noting that Roche was mainly known for her work as a television presenter before publishing her first novel *Feuchtgebiete* in 2008. In interviews and videos from around the time of *Schoßgebete* in 2011, Roche has taken her autofiction beyond the written text, thereby truly merging a reality and fiction that, she seems to imply, should not be separated. In an online video produced by her publishers to promote the book, Roche declares her intentions for writing the book as primarily self-centered, playing down the effect that critics' and readers' feedback could have on her.[67] It is first and foremost she who must find the book funny, extreme, honest, and truthful.[68] In the video, she further emphasizes that the novel is a full-blown soul striptease on her part: "ein kompletter Seelenstriptease meinerseits," as she puts it. This once more perfectly conforms to Doubrovsky's dictum not to hold back but to reveal everything—a dictum Roche appears to have followed intuitively. Crucially, in this performance, Roche confirms the emotional/psychological proximity between herself and her protagonist extratextually by stating that, now that *Schoßgebete* is published, all that is left for her to do is to sit at home and await death—a sentence readers might expect from Elizabeth, who regularly imagines her suicide or otherwise premature death (*SG*, 65, 168, 108–9, 115, 238).[69] In performances such as these, Roche truly embodies the autofiction, moving in a space opened up by the text and going beyond the real and imagined life contained therein. While she thus underlines the resemblances between herself as author and her character Elizabeth Kiehl in the novel, even toys with the idea of their inseparability, she uses other public performances to complicate any simple autobiographical readings of the text.

In a talk show hosted by Markus Lanz in August 2011, Roche again alluded to a high degree of congruence between Elizabeth and herself by speaking in her character's voice, stating, for instance, that she is reliant on sex as a means to help her relax.[70] The narrator of *Schoßgebete* is found to make this kind of comment on pages 7, 14, and 107–8 of the book. After Lanz reads aloud a passage of the novel, however, Roche thwarts the audience's imagination by countering, "Nur um das jetzt noch mal zu sagen: Man veröffentlicht ja nicht seine intimen Details, das ist ja falsch, es ist ja nicht so, dass man keine Geheimnisse mehr hat" (Just to say this one more time: you don't publish your intimate details, that isn't correct, it's not as if you don't have any secrets any more). And she stresses a few minutes later, "Damit muss man erst mal klarkommen, dass jeder denkt, alles was in dem Buch steht ist hundertprozentig echt. Das ist nicht so." (For starters, you've got to be able to deal with the fact that everyone thinks all that is written in the book is a hundred per cent true. That isn't the way it is.) But, of course, she does not detail "the way it is"—thereby keeping up the tension constitutive of the autofictional space in which she writes and acts. The word "tension" here is to be understood decidedly positively: in the autofictional realm, it enables agency, opens up avenues for dealing with issues otherwise "unspeakable," and provides a protective mask for an author negotiating vulnerable subject positions in the public arena. Identification of author and narrator simultaneously is and is not encouraged. As a text violating common notions of boundaries between the private and public, *Schoßgebete* reveals as much as it conceals.

The question why Roche felt the need to address her trauma in such an ambivalent manner and in the public realm can possibly be answered by thinking back to the *Druckzeitung* allegory: to prevent others from further exploiting the story of the accident, as a public persona she must mark this story as her story and be the one who eventually, after ten years, puts it into words in the form of *Schoßgebete*.

Anticipating the Media as Regulatory Body

The media response to Roche's second novel has been extensive and—as both provoked and foreseen by its autofictional mode and use of an aesthetics of disgust—echoes a wide-ranging array of reactions. In two of the largest German newspapers, *Stern* and *Süddeutsche Zeitung*, two male reviewers condemn *Schoßgebete*: unable to recognize or place any of the book's narrative strategies and experimentations within any one genre, Thomas Steinfeld calls the book "unerheblich" (insignificant), "trivial," and even "verlogen" (mendacious)—mainly because he openly dislikes its sexual explicitness and because he perceives the relation of author and narrator figure negatively as confused, literally speaking of "Verwirrung."[71] Carsten Heidböhmer's article in *Stern* carries as subtitle: "'Schoßgebete' dreht sich vor allem um die Autorin—die ihr Familienunglück zur Schau stellt" (*Schoßgebete* above all revolves around its author—who puts on display the calamity of her family), thereby accusing Roche of exactly the kind of egocentrism and narcissism that the novel, as an autofiction, is trying to avoid. Heidböhmer deems the novel's content as not appropriate for publication, even wondering whether it was morally right of Roche to do so. And he ultimately passes judgment, more on the author than on the book: "So bleibt der schale Nachgeschmack, dass Roche—um den Erfolg ihres Debüts zu wiederholen—bereit ist, alles zu tun. Und dabei nicht einmal auf ihre von schrecklichem Unglück heimgesuchte Familie Rücksicht nimmt."[72] (Thus one is left with the sour taste that Roche—to repeat her debut novel's success—is willing to do just about anything. And in doing so, she has no regard at all for her disaster-stricken family.)

In this, he disregards the fact that her family's tragedy is essentially her tragedy, too, hence denying her any kind of agency. I read reviews of this kind—grounded in their author's conviction of moral superiority rather than in an argument formed on the basis of engagement with the text—as incidents of policing, if not of discrimination. Steinfeld and Heidböhmer's reviews exemplify the media's regulatory structure with its tendency to dismiss the abnormal or heterodox, to police new discourses about sex or death or illness, and to defend the societal—and literary—status quo.[73] Yet, because of the novel's inherent autofictional self-reflexivity, reproaches like these, of inauthenticity and immorality, cannot be taken fully seriously, as they have been anticipated and countered within the novel itself before they even occurred (e.g., *SG*, 121–22). Reproaches that could otherwise have harmful potential are thus weakened in their effect and are already rebutted in the self-conscious genre that is autofiction.[74]

As someone who believes in the benefits of reclaiming and potentially working through her experiences in narration, Roche knowingly risks hostile readings such as these. The following section demonstrates how autofictional detachment enables narration in the first place and how it can provide a way for dealing with the intrusion of the traumatic real.

Autofictional Detachment

It takes *Schoßgebete*'s narrator a long time to address the source of her trauma. The reader follows Elizabeth drawing closer to it over more than a hundred pages. Yet the accident and its horrific outcome again and again infest her thoughts, and consequently the narration as it unfolds—demanding a listener. While the main plot from "Dienstag" to "Donnerstag" is in decidedly chronological order, the narration of the car accident is anything but. In the face of trauma, this logical order breaks down. Instead, it is narrated in snatches, which Elizabeth alternately tries to block out (*SG*, 122) or dwells upon obsessively to assure herself it "really happened" and until she feels as if she, too, had been there (*SG*, 151): "Mein Mann denkt, ich gucke fern, aber ich grübele wieder mal heimlich über den Unfall nach, ich lasse den immer gleichen Ablauf Revue passieren, als wäre ich dabei gewesen. Um mir immer wieder zu sagen: 'Ja, Elizabeth, so war das, damit musst du jetzt klarkommen, das ist die Wahrheit, das ist wirklich passiert.'" (*SG*, 110; My husband thinks that I am watching TV, but yet again I am secretly brooding over the accident, reviewing the ever-same course of events as if I had been there. To tell myself over and over: "Yes, Elizabeth, that's how it was, you better deal with it now, this is the truth, this really happened.") The unassimilated traumatic experience simply does not seem "real"; it is indeed outside the range of Elizabeth's experience. Yet, eight years after the accident, the urge to take on this nightmare "jetzt" (*SG*, 99; now) in the narrative present seems more pressing than ever.

Only after narratively revisiting phone calls she had to make on the day, the subsequent trip to the site of the accident in England, the call she received from the *Druckzeitung*, and so on, the narrator begins to reconstruct the events of the accident themselves. They truly possess her; not having been there, the narrator cannot really know any of it for sure. In the reconstruction that Elizabeth attempts regardless, she depends on fictional strategies to fill the gaps as much as on the facts she has been gathering ever since from survivors and from police files, as is made clear to the reader (*SG*, 141). Twice detached, that is, through creating a narrative alter ego and by having Elizabeth only indirectly know the course of events of the day of the accident, the autofictional mode gives Roche the necessary space to build a story of her family's accident that is both real and is not real—and that, in this mode, finally no longer resists narration.

Through short sentences, sometimes consisting of just one word, the reader becomes immersed in the story. In the present tense, Elizabeth, in this narration, shows a level of detail that complements her wish to have been there, to truly know what has happened (articulated, e.g., *SG*, 151, 153–54). She pictures her mother taking her shoes off like she always does when driving on a hot summer's day (*SG*, 141), thereby implying knowledge from experience. Based on the police reports, she can describe the traffic—"Es ist viel los auf der Autobahn, aber der Verkehr fließt" (*SG*, 142; It is busy on the motorway, but traffic is moving)—as well as the moment of the accident in which a truck driver on the other side of the motorway crashes into a traffic jam ahead. He does so "ungebremst" (*SG*, 142; without braking), she tells the reader, which in turn is knowledge she gathered from eye witnesses. The moment her mother drives her car into the crash, with the sons on the back seats, Elizabeth believes, "Im Radio im Auto meiner Mutter läuft 'Lucky Man' von The Verve" (*SG*, 142; On the radio in my mother's car they play "Lucky Man" by the Verve). Tracing this intertextual reference, one finds that this 1997 song by the Britpop band culminates in the line "Gotta love that'll never die." This imagined detail of the circumstances of the accident is a declaration of Elizabeth's love for her dead brothers.

Her sentences become even shorter, turning into ellipses, as she attempts to imagine what the moments after the crash must have been like for Rhea, the girlfriend of one of her brothers: "Stille. Lange. . . . Rauschen im Kopf. Alles in Zeitlupe." (*SG*, 142; Silence. For a long time. . . . Noise in the head. Everything in slow motion.) Narrating how her mother and Rhea can escape the deadly vehicle, Elizabeth draws a striking comparison to another indelible image, one that she carries with herself since childhood: "[Rhea] robbt sich wie die kranken Gorillas im Nebel aus dem Film, den wir viel zu jung gucken mussten, damit wir Tierforscher werden oder wenigstens Umweltschützer, mehrere Meter weit vom Auto weg" (*SG*, 142; Rhea crawls away from the car for several meters, like the sick gorillas in the mist in that film we had to watch way too young, so that we would become animal researchers or environmentalists at least). Elizabeth says of her mother, awaking from unconsciousness: "Sie sitzt und sitzt und sitzt. Und wundert sich über die Stille im Auto. Sie dreht sich *nicht* um. Sie guckt *nicht* ihre Kinder an. Sie ist *keine* Mutter mehr, die sich um ihre Kinder kümmern kann. Sie kann sich *nicht* mal selber retten. Sie ist wie ein schwer verwundetes Tier." (*SG*, 143; emphasis mine; She sits there, and sits there, and sits there. And wonders at the silence in the car. She does *not* turn around. She does *not* look at her children. She is *not* a mother anymore who can take care of her children. She *cannot* even save herself. She is like a seriously injured animal.)

In Elizabeth's fantasy, they emerge from the tragedy as wounded animals. Rhea, just functioning and with animalistic survival instinct, can save herself from the ensuing fire. The mother is not in any state to do so. The multiple negations indicate that her mother is not the mother Elizabeth knew any more. She lost her ability to be that person under these circumstances, to be someone who can take care of her children. She is reduced to her wounded shell. Crucially, at the end of this detailed reconstruction of the accident, Elizabeth confesses, "Für mich, in meinem Kopf, ist das Schlimmste: dass wir alle nicht wissen, ob meine Brüder, als sie in Flammen aufgegangen sind, noch gelebt haben oder ob sie von dem Aufprall schon tot waren. . . . Das verfolgt mich täglich. Tagsüber und nachts in meinen Träumen. Ich werde es nie rausfinden." (*SG*, 144; To me, in my head, the worst is: that none of us knows if my brothers were still alive when they went up in flames, or if they were already dead from the collision. . . . That haunts me daily. In the daytime and at night in my dreams. I will never find out.) Despite all her research, nobody was able to give her this crucial bit of information. The one thing she does not dare imaginatively reconstruct is what haunts her most. How much did they have to suffer? This is the missing piece, the source of her lasting pain.

Missing also are the brothers' bodies. There are no corpses, as they were consumed by the fire. The narrator yearns for them, believing the tragedy would be easier to understand, somehow more straightforward and simpler to integrate as a memory if not for this circumstance that she perceives as unnatural and therefore all the more cruel: "Ich beneide jeden, der jemanden verliert, wenigstens aber einen toten Körper hat, zum Anfassen. Zum besseren Begreifen. Damit das lahme Gehirn verstehen kann, diese Person ist jetzt tot. Das Leben kommt nicht wieder in diesen toten Körper zurück. Niemals. Guck, fass ihn an. Er ist steif und läuft gelb an und ist kalt wie ein totes Hühnchen aus dem Kühlschrank." (*SG*, 151; I envy everyone who loses someone, but at least has a dead body—to touch. To better grasp things. So the sluggish brain can understand, this person is now dead. Life will not return to this dead body. Never. Look, touch it. It's stiff and turning yellow and cold like a dead chicken from the fridge.) Elizabeth's belief that "anfassen" (to touch) would provide opportunities to "begreifen" (to grasp/understand) indicates that, for the narrator, words in themselves are not enough to begin to understand the deaths of her loved ones. Visual and kinesthetic cues are needed to literally grasp a message as drastic and indeed outside the range of comprehension as the message of the simultaneous, premature death of all of one's siblings. While it might be a false hope that things would be easier to process if only there were dead bodies to prove the facts, Elizabeth will never find out.

Out of this lack emerges what is by far the most striking passage of the novel: Elizabeth reveals to the reader a figment of her imagination that stands in for the missing bodies of her brothers in a story within the story that can in many ways be said to bear magic realist traits (*SG*, 151–54). She sets the scene thus, imagining a second life for the three of them: "Sie leben jetzt im Wald von Belgien, bei all den Tieren, die noch nicht von uns brutalen Fortschrittswirtschaftswachstumsautofahrern überfahren wurden. Der Unfall hat sie natürlich sehr mitgenommen, sie sind seitdem verrückt, können sich an nichts erinnern." (*SG*, 151–52; They now live in the woods of Belgium, with all the animals that have not yet been run over by us brutal progress-economic-growth-drivers. The accident of course has had its effect on them, they have been insane since then, cannot remember anything.) She embellishes this story subsequently, creating a parallel world for her brothers in which, secluded from most influences of the modern world that Elizabeth criticizes by means of the neologism *Fortschrittswirtschaftswachstumsautofahrer*, they almost live happily ever after. Having introduced the animal simile when describing Rhea and her mother and having carried it forward in the image of human corpses as dead chickens, it turns up again here as the brothers in this story are likened to forest animals, forever "unschuldig, klein, natürlich" (*SG*, 155; innocent, small, as nature made them), as the narrator's faith in humankind is irretrievably lost. This "Land, in dem sie wohnen" (*SG*, 153; land in which they live) is complete with a functioning societal structure—her oldest brother is the leader of this community of three—and a currency to facilitate trade among them.

They have all they need in life (*SG*, 152), Elizabeth stresses. Time passes as it does in the "real" world, and, over the years, the fractured skull of one of the younger brothers heals well, his pain ceases. Nonetheless, the reality of the accident even breaks into this fantasy, and, just as Elizabeth cannot let go of it, neither can her brothers free themselves of its grip: "Durch seine langen, dreckigen, verfilzten Haare spürt mein Bruder noch den Knochenhubbel von damals" (*SG*, 154; Underneath his long, dirty, matted hair my brother still feels the bony bump from back then), Elizabeth, omniscient narrator of this story within a story, knows about one of them. The most significant consequence of the accident is this: "Alle drei haben . . . ihre Sprache verloren und verständigen sich nur durch Blicke. Sie verstehen sich eigentlich blind, denn sie sind Überlebende." (*SG*, 152; All three of them have lost their language and communicate solely via eye contact. In actual fact, they understand each other blindly [i.e., intimately], for they are survivors.) The effect of trauma has freed them not only of their memories but also of language. Understood positively, this relieves them from remembering the actual incident. Read more pessimistically, however, it forever binds them to the accident: the only time that something like communication through language occurs between them is in their joint humming of "Lucky Man" in moments of distress (*SG*, 153), with the accident being the zero hour of their wildlife existence.

Imagining her brothers' afterlife is similarly tainted for Elizabeth, as it both consoles her and continues to distress her. This can be inferred from the way she closes the story: "Ja, so ist das da in dem belgischen Wald. Und niemand kann mir das Gegenteil beweisen. Weil mir niemand die toten Körper zeigen kann. Weil nichts mehr da ist zum Beerdigen." (*SG*, 154; Yes, that is the way it is in that Belgium forest. And no one can prove me wrong. Because no one can show me the dead bodies. Because nothing's left to bury.) This striking tale, featuring her dead brothers in animal form, can in some sense be regarded as a fable; yet it is one, poignantly, without a "useful lesson,"[75] providing no sense of closure for Elizabeth. Trauma will not lessen its grip on her, but the autofictional detachment the narrator displays here helps her to cope with the intrusion of the real. The autofictional mode initiates, at least in the case of *Schoßgebete*, a "continual leaving" of the site of trauma,[76] made possible by the poetic license it grants narrator and author.

Narrating Vulnerability

This chapter has pursued a twofold objective: to highlight why *Schoßgebete* as a trauma narrative might be best represented in the autofictional form it takes and to explore the effect of a striking aesthetics of disgust employed by Roche to tell this personal story publicly. In more than one way, *Schoßgebete*'s form has thus been substantiated as contingent on its content, the story of trauma it begins to tell.

In *Schoßgebete*, disgust helps to expose the myth of our bodies as clean and proper, as controllable by us transcendental beings. As an author, Roche generally writes against the idea that women—and indeed also men, yet to a lesser degree—are a "sexy presentation space," as she has suggested in an English-language interview.[77] Probably derived from the German term *Präsentationsfläche*, this German-English hybrid word is telling, beyond what Roche literally intended to say: it directs readers who have proven themselves worthy to see through the novel's surface.[78] Elizabeth's body is central to the narrative that *Schoßgebete* tells, but only insofar as the external—that is, her body as space or canvas—leads the way to the internal world of the novel's protagonist and guides us to reading *Schoßgebete* as the story of a wounded mind.

Access to the more personal aspects of the novel, then, is granted only to those readers who withstand the initial impulse to turn away and put the book down—who instead show a willingness to accompany the narrator/protagonist into a world of pain and illness that is, by its nature, likely to be at times disgusting and disturbing. Elizabeth deliberately does not make it easy for the reader to like her, still less to identify with her, constantly marking herself as the disgusting and sick other, displaying grotesque behaviors and reasoning. In a 2011 TV interview from around the time of the book's publication, Roche made a significant comment on her writing strategy: "Ich will, dass die Leute sich an den ekligen Sachen vorbeigraben. Und dahinter, da ist die Charlotte."[79] (I want people to dig past the yucky stuff. And behind all that, there is Charlotte.) The author favors clearly those who are willing to put up with the demanding aesthetics of disgust, those who are capable of empathizing, if not sympathizing, with Elizabeth—vis-à-vis this challenge—at the same time she baits them with the promise of insights into her own psyche. The fear of being rejected plays into the complex aesthetics of the book and matches the narrator's panicky behavior, her innermost fears, and feelings of self-disgust and shame. Evocative of Elizabeth, in yet another autofictional move, Roche in the same interview also stated, "Ich möchte so wahnsinnig gerne geliebt werden. Ich will, dass die Leute mich mögen!" (I want to be loved so badly. I want people to like me!) As a celebrity writer borrowing so heavily from her own experiences, Roche is highly aware of the gaze of others she exposes herself to and complicates this gaze via disgust. Her use of autofictional strategies adds to this problematization of the reader's gaze onto the personal tragedy of which the book tells, a gaze that is at once invited and challenged.

Autofiction, we have seen, can—to an extent—enable those in vulnerable subject positions to speak. By undermining any readily assumed referentiality of the novel, the mode creates the necessary space to accommodate the paradoxes and contradictions that define the traumatic experience at the center of *Schoßgebete*. It helps disable both external and internal mechanisms of censorship[80] and thus first and foremost enables the transformation of death and trauma into story. The dialectic of the autofictional mode, unintentionally yet fittingly expressed in *Schoßgebete*'s legal disclaimer, perfectly mirrors the central dialectic of trauma: "the will to deny horrible events," as Judith Lewis Herman highlights in her work, is as strong as "the will to proclaim them aloud."[81]

In an interview with *Der Spiegel*, Roche phrased her motivation to write about the accident thus: "Weil ich das Gefühl hatte, das muss jetzt raus. Ich habe bis heute nicht getrauert, kein bisschen."[82] (I had the feeling that I had to get it out now. To this day I've still not grieved, not a bit.) This kind of "formulation" can be a first step toward recovery from trauma.[83] Work like Henke's confirms literature as a platform able to initiate communication and healing, and psychotherapists such as Herman moreover emphasize the importance of an understanding listener and healing relationships for a continual leaving of the site of trauma. Ultimately, this therapeutic relationship is what Roche—through the novel's publication and encounters with readers—seems to be looking for. Fittingly, the reading tour was the most important aspect to her of the publication of her second novel. She expressed hopes that it would enable her to show her wound ("Hier ist meine Wunde!"), connect with people, and start a healing process (literally: "Heilung").[84] This is both a brave and risky business. Theorists' claim that writers of autofiction can fulfill for themselves the "Traum der literarischen Selbsterschaffung" (dream of literary self-creation) and can create "eine neue Existenz" (a new existence) may be daring, but it is also an incentive for writers to try to do so.[85] Yet the achievements of Roche's text do not stop here.

Beyond its personal importance for the author, the wider social critique offered in this "disgusting" novel is apparent: the isolation and marginalization of the main character as woman, mourner, and patient in the medical system demonstrates plainly the consequences that ensue when everything to do with the body, every deviation from utopian norms in society is hushed up and continues to be surrounded by taboo. It is precisely the unruly, unsanitized body that is the site where issues of femininity, illness, and death converge. It is therefore at the center of this novel and all its entangled themes, as it is the body, as Bakhtin put it, that "fecundates and is fecundated, that gives birth and is born, devours and is devoured, drinks, defecates, is sick and dying."[86]

* * *

Turning to Kathrin Schmidt's *Du stirbst nicht*, the next chapter deals once again with a text that was written and published with considerable temporal distance from the author's own experience.[87] Commenting on the years that lapsed between her stroke and the book publication inspired by it, Schmidt stresses she had never planned to write about it at all. Yet, with the encouragement of a friend, she stuck with it, having one day put into words the extraordinary experience of awaking from coma: "Eines Tages war es einfach über mich gekommen, mal aufzuschreiben, wie ich aus dem Koma erwacht war, und ich habe 30 Seiten in Ichform geschrieben. Einer Freundin gefiel das gut, und die sagte: 'Mach doch die erste Seite zur letzten!' Auf der ersten Seite riss die Gehirnarterie, und so hatte ich den langen Weg vor mir, die Heldin zu diesem Anfang zurückzuschicken, dass sie sich erinnert, wie dieses Aneurysma geplatzt war."[88] (One day it just came over me to write down how I awoke from coma, and I wrote thirty pages, in the first person. A friend liked it a lot and said: "Why don't you make the first page your last!" On the first page the brain artery ripped, and so I had ahead of me the long way of sending the heroine back to this beginning, in order for her to remember how this aneurysm burst.)

Like Roche, Schmidt employs an alter ego–protagonist with a fictive yet recognizable name, and in doing so borrows a narrative strategy from autofictional writing. The book is, however, best described as an autobiographical novel. This is, above all, because its autobiographical and its fictional elements remain relatively clear cut—they are clearly distinguished by its author in interviews, for example. As much as she too grapples with the reader's gaze, Schmidt's means of complicating the relationship with her readership are different from Roche's; they are reflected in practical narratological decisions made from the point of view of professional authorship. Exactly which narrative devices and strategies Schmidt employs in the text and what narrative work the more fictional and the more directly autobiographical strands do in this very personal novel is the focus of the following analysis.

2: Looking Beyond the Self—Reflecting the Other: Staring as a Narrative Device in Kathrin Schmidt's *Du stirbst nicht* (2009)

und aus dem spiegel steigt / der erste schrei.

—Kathrin Schmidt, "ob sommer, ob winter" (*Blinde Bienen*)

DU STIRBST NICHT (You aren't dying / You won't die) won Kathrin Schmidt the Deutscher Buchpreis in 2009 and attracted more media attention to her person than any of the poetry and novels for which she had won several prizes previously in her career. It is the writer's second novel after suffering a brain hemorrhage in 2002 that put her in a coma from which she regained consciousness after two weeks, at the age of forty-four finding herself hemiplegic, having undergone major surgery, and—suffering from Broca's aphasia—unable to speak.[1] The narrative begins with Schmidt's alter ego–protagonist Helene Wesendahl waking up to find herself in exactly this state. The author bestows much verifiable biographical data onto her protagonist,[2] and, by giving her the surname Wesendahl, she creates a name that is literally "close to home," Wesendahl being a district of Altlandsberg, which lies to the northeast of the author's home city, Berlin. In a complimentary step, the reader of *Du stirbst nicht* confirms the resemblance of author and protagonist that is thus suggested through their crucial contextual knowledge of Schmidt's own stroke, which—not unlike in the case of Roche's trauma writing—may indeed haven driven them to pick up the text in the first instance.

Despite this resemblance—or perhaps precisely because of it—Schmidt closely guards her professional identity as an author, especially once having won the *Buchpreis* for *Du stirbst nicht*. Against the backdrop of an increasing number of publications of autobiographically inspired illness narratives, Schmidt insisted her book was different, effectively arguing for it to be considered as real or proper, that is serious, literature.[3] Indeed, for Schmidt, the majority of illness texts do not qualify as literature (in a traditional sense). The author is frank in her explanation of why she dissociates herself from writers such as Christoph Schlingensief, Georg

---

Epigraph translation: and from the mirror the first cry rises.

Diez, or Jürgen Leinemann,[4] all of whom also published in 2009, and in conjunction with this rejects an understanding of her novel as an example of writing as therapy: "Ich habe das nicht als Therapie angesehen. Ich wollte einfach wieder schreiben; ich wollte einfach keine Rente. Schreiben als Therapie, das würde ich nicht unterschreiben. Ich verstand mich ja auch als professionelle Schriftstellerin. Schreiben als Therapie ist behaftet mit Möchtegern-Schreiben. Ich wollte nicht um jeden Preis wieder schreiben, sondern richtig schreiben können."[5] (I didn't regard it as a therapy. I simply wanted to write again; I simply didn't want retirement. Writing as therapy, I wouldn't subscribe to that. Because I took myself to be a professional author. Writing as therapy is tainted with "wannabe" writing. I did not want to write again at all costs, I wanted to be able to write properly.)

This statement reveals Schmidt's acute awareness of the fact that, in the Germanic realm, both reviewers and academic readers often still dismiss writing that is too closely based on autobiographical experience as "bloßer Verarbeitungsversuch" (mere attempt at working through [a blow of fate]) in a distinctly derogatory sense.[6] What this furthermore shows is that, in contemporary public perception and discussion, autobiographical writing continues to be equated with non-aesthetic (ergo, naïve and even trivial) forms of writing. The specific narrative strategies Schmidt employs in representing her personal illness experience in novel form, which will be explored in this chapter (most notably that of staring as a narrative device), are conscious of and somewhat haunted by this discourse. At the same time, their complexity and accomplishment exposes the logic of that discourse as inconsistent.

Possibly because of Schmidt's concern for literary value, *Du stirbst nicht* is labeled, unconventionally, as "ein Erinnerungsroman ganz eigener Art" (unique novel of memory) in the publisher's description. On the back of the book it is advertised in large font as "die atemberaubende Geschichte einer Heilung" (the breathtaking story of a healing). Noticeably, we are dealing here with an illness narrative that, to be taken seriously on the literary book market, is not explicitly marketed as such.

Another aspect of the reception of *Du stirbst nicht* that Schmidt feels the need to contest is some critics' allegorical interpretation of the autobiographical illness experience at its center. Contemplating her resistance to the label *Ostschriftstellerin* (author from the East) and the fact that she tends to be pigeonholed as one, Schmidt states, "[Es gibt] Rezensenten . . ., die diesen ganzen gesundheitlichen Zusammenbruch als Metapher für die Wende in der DDR lesen. Das finde ich schrecklich, und ich weiß überhaupt nicht, wie die darauf kommen. Und ich werde auch gefragt, warum ich denn auch in diesem Roman viel über die DDR geschrieben habe. Ich finde nicht, dass ich viel über die DDR geschrieben habe, und ich habe ja nun mal kein anderes Leben. Ich kann ja kein anderes Leben erfinden."⁷ (There are reviewers . . . who read this whole breakdown in health as a metaphor for the "turnaround" [i.e., German reunification] in the GDR. I find that terrible, and have absolutely no clue how they come up with that idea. I also get asked why I have written so much about the GDR in this novel, too. I don't think I have done that, and, after all, I have no other life. I cannot possibly invent another life for myself.)

This statement is crucial for two reasons: first of all, Schmidt explicitly calls for *Du stirbst nicht* to be read in its own right as an illness narrative, discouraging too much abstraction from it. Her request matches that of literary disability scholar Pauline Eyre, whose guiding concern is to ask both academic and lay readers to "look beyond the impaired values of hegemonic reading practices [of reading disability as a trope] toward the empowering possibilities of reading disability for real."⁸ Eyre thus concludes an article on Libuše Moníková's 1983 novel *Pavane für eine verstorbene Infantin* (Pavane for a dead infanta), which she reads—against the normative grain—as an investigation into the lived reality of disability, highlighting her unwillingness to limit the depiction of disability in the novel to the metaphorical realm. Polemically, the disabled scholar thereby turns the tables and calls normative readings "impaired," outraged precisely by their tendency to not lend sufficient weight to the depiction of disability in literature.

Second, Schmidt in this statement explicitly identifies the book as highly reliant on her own life experiences ("ich habe ja nun mal kein anderes Leben"), with much in there that is "real." This applies to both her life in the GDR as well as the complex experience of becoming ill and living with disability that informs Schmidt's writing in (and since) *Du stirbst nicht*. It clearly places the book on one shelf with other autobiographical writing. Accordingly, the author gives herself little artistic freedom in writing the main character's biography: "Ich habe lange überlegt, welchen Beruf sie haben könnte. . . . Aber es ging nicht anders. Sie musste Schriftstellerin sein, auch auf die Gefahr hin, dass mich nun alle Leser mit ihr verwechseln"⁹ (I have contemplated for a long time which profession she might have. . . . But there was no other way. She had to be an author, despite the risk of now having all my readers confuse her with me.) In conversation with the magazine *Psychologie Heute*, she stresses that, had she not made Helene a writer, "hätte sich die Schere zu weit geöffnet zu meinem eigenen Erleben"¹⁰ (the gap to my own experience would have widened too far). Notwithstanding this, strikingly, she also says in the same interview that she sent her protagonist "auf eine Reise weit von mir weg"¹¹ (on a trip far away from me). And in another interview, Schmidt admits that she could not help but share with Helene many of the crucial features of her own biography, concluding elusively, "Die Geschichte . . . ist biografisch grundiert, aber doch eine andere Geschichte. Das ist komisch verschränkt."¹² (The story . . . has a biographical basis, but is nonetheless another story. That is strangely interlaced.) In these careful considerations, a tension inherent to the author's public negotiation of the book's reception comes to the fore: there is both the need to mark it as authentic in its representation of the author's life experience (and, above all, the far-reaching experience of illness) and the urge to ensure the autobiographical novel is perceived as substantial and meaningful beyond the author's individual life, that is as a piece of writing worthy of being called literature—rather than *Betroffenheitsliteratur*.

Schmidt, we note, understands her role as that of the professional writer—whereas Roche (whose writing I discussed in the previous chapter) explicitly does not: "Ich fühle mich nicht als Schriftstellerin, auch wenn ich jetzt zwei Bücher geschrieben habe"[13] (I do not consider myself to be an author, even though I have written two books by now). While, for Roche, *Schoßgebete* is a means to formulate trauma as well as to connect with others and in this way functions as a step toward recovery, Schmidt seems to reject both of these more personal intentions for her text. Moreover, Schmidt's appraisal by critics is wholly different, since not one accused her of the commodification of her illness experience. Certainly helped by winning the Deutscher Buchpreis, reviewers and scholars instead draw parallels between Schmidt's Helene Wesendahl and Kafka's Gregor Samsa (both wake up to an alien body, isolated from the world that surrounds them), and they assess Schmidt's writing in its eloquence as reminiscent of, for example, Günter Grass's style, thus elevating her to the rank of an author who will make a lasting impact on the literary landscape of Germany.[14]

In contrast to the default first-person voice that, if we agree with Schmidt, the "wannabe writers" would conventionally take up, her novel, in its published form, is narrated in the third person and predominantly internally focalized.[15] This unusual combination of narrative voice and perspective produces a noteworthy tension as a detached voice narrates the highly intimate thoughts, feelings, and memories of Helene (and, as the reader speculates, in extensio, Schmidt). This gives the impression that she has stepped outside her own body, spinning her "Erinnerungsfaden" (thread of memory) or "Halteleine" (guiding rope) from an emotional distance, with the ultimate aim of recovering her memory and language competency.[16] Analogous to the nature of the impairment Helene finds herself with on awakening, conversations (other than remembered ones) take up little room in *Du stirbst nicht*; much of what the reader learns Helene herself cannot communicate, at least not in conventional ways.

The protagonist's linguistic recovery from aphasia is reflected in the vocabulary and grammar of the narrating voice, mirroring Helene's very limited ability to stay conscious or even open her eyes at the beginning of the novel. Gradually, from there, the language used to tell Helene's story becomes more complex as her memory returns, her awareness of her surroundings increases, and her body and mind recuperate. Longer paragraphs as well as more diverse and sophisticated vocabulary are introduced as the novel progresses.

Making her way hand over hand along the thread of memory, thus regaining knowledge of her life before the aneurysm burst, Helene discovers that she and husband Matthes were living through a major marital crisis. One reason was her feelings for Viola, who was born male (formerly named Viktor) and transitioned to female.[17] Schmidt identifies the love triangle she portrays as "frei erfunden" (purely fictitious) but equally emphatically asserts the depiction of the illness experience as accurate: "Ich habe mich aber natürlich ganz exakt erinnert an die Zeit des Aufwachens und an die ersten Schritte im Krankenhaus"[18] (But of course I remembered the time of waking up and my first steps in the hospital most accurately). The author thus asserts one of the defining criteria of autobiographical writing from a general reader's point of view, that of truthfulness or authenticity.[19] Both the fictional and the more closely autobiographical strands of *Du stirbst nicht* will be analyzed in the main body of this chapter.

On a technical level, authenticity, directness, and immediacy are reinforced, for instance, through the frequent use of free indirect discourse, smudging further the already fine line between narrator and protagonist and, as such, feed into the production of experientiality.[20] From time to time, however, this is resisted, and the narrator's voice becomes surprisingly overt, which then disrupts the illusion of sharing in someone's perception or consciousness. Examples of both immersive and distancing narrative strategies are given in the close analysis to follow.

The main part of this chapter, therefore, brings together the different aspects of the story Schmidt tells by analyzing the ways of seeing presented in *Du stirbst nicht*. These are closely linked to issues of self-image or self-perception, and externally determined image, what I would call *Selbstbild* and *Fremdbild* in German, as well as attitudes toward the disabled other. Seeing, or more specifically staring, in its frank appraisal, is a crucial means for Helene to reflect on the situation she finds herself in upon awakening at the start of the novel and enables her to reassemble an image of her self over the course of *Du stirbst nicht*. My findings from the close analysis inform my assessment of extratextual aspects of the novel, with which I conclude.

Conceptualizing Staring

In her 2009 publication *Staring: How We Look*, cultural critic and leading disability scholar Rosemarie Garland-Thomson tackles the stare as a physical response.[21] While offering no precise definition, she approaches the stare from a number of perspectives: she traces its cultural history (understanding it as having emerged in parallel with modern diagnostics and medicine), explains how it initiates a social relationship between a "starer" and the person being stared at (whom she calls "staree"), and under which circumstances staring can be a form of knowledge gathering—thus attempting to free it from its condemnation as being entirely negative and above all voyeuristic (as it is portrayed, for instance, in Sartre's prototypical keyhole example). Indeed, the driving force behind the book is to highlight staring's more positive aspects. Garland-Thomson's exploration relies, to a large extent, on examples (mainly from the US context) of disabled people as presented or displayed through history, in art, and the media, from being forced to participate in circuses or freak shows, being exhibited on the marketplace, to more contemporary and positive examples such as their recent role in fashion photography.

The underlying assumption is that, as a natural bodily impulse and social necessity, staring can hardly be suppressed. Garland-Thomson stresses that staring is "fundamental to our survival as social beings" and emphasizes that "to navigate the . . . social landscape of modern life, we need to read others."[22] Visibly impaired people, in this cultural climate, are bound to attract stares. Even those who do not voluntarily expose themselves to the public gaze must envisage being made the object of others' quasi-automatic—and potentially disabling—stares in public.[23] They must plan for this imperative to represent the self, be prepared to react to others' stares that they incur for the simple reason that they live as extraordinary bodies.

Garland-Thomson's book is written in contrast to traditional understandings of the act and effect of staring, such as that of Susan Sontag, which condemns staring as voyeuristic and intrusive per se and which informs her last book, *Regarding the Pain of Others*.[24] Garland-Thomson redefines the staring act as an opportunity "to rethink the status quo," and she further stresses, "Who we are can shift into focus by staring at who we think we are not." Staring begins "when ordinary seeing fails," in other words, "when unfamiliar people take us by surprise."[25] The starer is not mastering the situation but rather failing to meet the social demand to stay in control of one's eyes, to be able to avert them.[26] Despite the discriminatory damage this can do to anyone whose physique or body language is perceived as deviating from the norm, the involuntary response of staring can be used to good effect, so it is claimed, and ideally turns into a conscious act of connection with another (that of "beholding"). It is for this reason that Garland-Thomson characterizes the stare as "both impersonal and intimate"—it "makes things happen between people," as it is a two-way encounter.[27]

Overall, the stress is on the dynamic, engaging aspects of this interchange of looks, which, for those involved, can be uneasy and illuminating in equal measure. In all this, Garland-Thomson wants the stare to be understood in difference to the much-theorized gaze, because the stare is less predetermined in its effects. The scholar puts it in a nutshell: "We may gaze at what we desire, but we stare at what astonishes us."[28] The gaze, to her, is only one type of stare, closely associated with the objectification or colonization of an other. *Staring* does not reject previous academic insights into visual culture or how we regard the other, as explicated by those investigating it from feminist/psychoanalytic (Laura Mulvey), Marxist (John Berger), or postcolonial perspectives (Frantz Fanon, Edward Saïd).[29] But *Staring* departs from former examinations of our visual behavior in that it is open to a wider range of interpretative possibilities: traditionally, for example, masculinity is seen as occupying the active role in theorizations on the gaze, with femininity accordingly signifying passivity. To transfer these assumptions into the realm of dis/ability, one would assume an unimpaired or ablebodied viewer as the active subject (i.e., being the one who initiates the looking), the disabled person as passive "spectacle" and at the receiving end of others' stares (as object). Be it women, minority groups, or disabled people, starees are not only in positions to-be-looked-at (Mulvey's term) but it is inherent to Garland-Thomson's concept of staring that it ascribes them agency too.[30]

Acknowledging disability, according to Garland-Thomson, is "one of the best opportunities to understand how we stare."[31] The effects of our staring can be manifold, and, importantly, they are not only negative. They include domination (as in the case of the asymmetrical gaze), stigmatization, disgust, and shame, yet Garland-Thomson contends that they can also elicit curiosity, adoration, and a sense of allegiance with another person.[32] Ultimately, Garland-Thomson suggests that the often so negatively connoted act of plain staring bears the potential to turn into the positive act of complex beholding (as mentioned briefly above): an engaged self-consideration on the part of the starer at the sight of the other that also results in recognizing the other more fully, and as an individual. In Garland-Thomson's words, the starer thus "bring[s] visual presence to another person."[33]

It is striking that neither *Du stirbst nicht*'s discussion in the press nor any of the academic work on Schmidt's novel to date acknowledges the crucial role sight has in it. Instead, the vast majority of reviews and interviews focus on the protagonist's (and often the author's) loss and subsequent reclamation of her extraordinary linguistic abilities. Scholarly articles on the text go in a similar direction. Sonja E. Klocke, being one scholar who has published on *Du stirbst nicht* so far, explores the interplay of body, memory, and language in the novel, reading it as "a woman's quest for agency and positionality."[34] Deirdre Byrnes in her 2013 article examines memory, language, and identity in *Du stirbst nicht*, highlighting as crucial an understanding of the hospital as a transformative liminal space—a "space of possibility"—from which, as Byrnes sees it, the protagonist writes herself "back to life."[35] Besides that, what gets little attention in the published work on *Du stirbst nicht* so far is the autobiographical dimension of Schmidt's illness narrative—one that is crucial to my reading of the book. Klocke and Byrnes instead both emphasize that the novel is, in Klocke's words, "much more than a tale of illness and recovery."[36] In Byrnes's article, we find the assertion that "the novel clearly offers itself as an allegory for political transition,"[37] which likewise has the effect of reassuring an academic audience that *Du stirbst nicht* is not merely, as it seems, an illness narrative, implying that such a text would not deserve the kind of scholarly attention the article goes on to grant it.

In the following close reading of the text, I apply Garland-Thomson's understanding of staring to Helene's ocular behavior in *Du stirbst nicht*, as it reveals hitherto unnoticed facets of her interaction with others (largely visual) in grappling with her self. Her exposure to others' stares also becomes relevant. I am thus testing out a focus on the stare as a potentially fruitful framework for analysis in literary disability studies. To begin with, I concentrate on a few selected passages in the novel in which the protagonist displays fears of having lost her "image," and those striking episodes where she feels compelled to behold her image in front of a mirror.

Staring at the Mirror Image—Searching for a Sense of Self

From the first chapter, while still hardly conscious, the protagonist is strikingly concerned with her "image," that is, her physical appearance and the impression she gives others. Not being able to speak to her sons standing at her bedside, Helene wonders how they might be reading the facial expressions that she assumes she is displaying. She realizes "sie hat kein Bild von sich" (*DSN*, 13; she has no image of herself). The worried thoughts that follow revolve around an ominous "they" who Helene believes to have stolen her image: "Die haben ihr das Bild von sich geklaut!" (*DSN*, 13; They have stolen her image of herself!) The situation is fundamentally frightening. Her "image" that she feels she needs to see will occupy the protagonist's mind throughout the novel. As Garland-Thomson states, drawing on Lacanian psychoanalysis and phenomenology, "We stare to know, and often we stare to know ourselves. Perhaps, as Jacques Lacan (1977) suggests, our first . . . stares are at ourselves."[38]

Garland-Thomson here is alluding to Lacan's psychoanalytic formulation of the mirror stage: the stage in childhood development in which, according to Lacan, one begins to gain an understanding of oneself as an individualized embodied subject, and object to others. Naming the register in which these identificatory developments take place "the imaginary" stresses "the importance of the visual field" in this.[39] If we follow

Lacan, children enter this phase of development between six and eighteen months of age. They are then able to recognize themselves and identify with their ("ideal") image as interpreted from the reflections of the "mirror," in this way for the first time "establish[ing] a relation between the organism and its reality—or . . . between the *Innenwelt* and the *Umwelt*."[40] They are thus prepared to enter next the symbolic systems of language and culture, in other words, a larger social order. However, this sense of mastery over an imaginary "I" the child has now begun to acquire remains illusory, because it is premature (if not entirely unattainable), as he or she wants to see a unified self "where there is [only] a fragmented, chaotic body."[41] This rift between one's self-perception and reality causes the subject to henceforth be "an alienated and paranoid construct—always defined by/as the other."[42] Against the background of Lacan's culturally pervasive conception of the mirror stage, I choose to speak only of a "sense" of self that Helene is striving for in relation to her quest for an image. The protagonist of *Du stirbst nicht* noticeably negotiates *Innen-* and *Umwelt* throughout the novel, striving to harmonize *Selbst-* and *Fremdbild(er)*. From a Lacanian perspective, this may seem a virtually impossible endeavor, yet it can equally be understood as an inherently human one.

On awakening in her hospital bed, Helene senses a conspiracy, imagining the hospital staff to be making an attempt on her life. Hardly in control of her bodily movements when responding to an itch on her head, she manages to raise an arm and scratch, only to find, "Aber da, wo es juckt, hat sie keine Haare. Was ist mit den Haaren passiert? Deshalb haben sie ihr Bild von sich geklaut! Ha, sie wird es zurückerobern, das verspricht sie sich. Mit aller Kraft beginnt sie, die Finger über die Kopfhaut zu ziehen. Sie kommen nicht weit. Kleine metallene Panzersperren stecken im Schädel, sie versucht, zwei oder drei herauszubrechen. Plötzlich spürt sie die Flüssigkeit an den Fingern. Sie kostet. Das ist Blut!" (*DSN*, 17; But there, where it's itchy, there is no hair. What happened to her hair? That's why they've stolen her image of herself! Ha, she will reclaim it, that she promises herself. With all the strength she possesses she begins to pull the fingers across the scalp. They don't make it very far. Little metallic tank barriers are plugged into her skull, she tries to break off two or three. Suddenly she feels the liquid on her fingers. She tastes it. That's blood!) Employing free indirect discourse, the passage conveys an immediacy that makes the events described so vivid and tangible that disgust is elicited in the reader, who is made to witness her doing harm to herself. But, for Helene, this is a crucial moment. It is her first attempt to regain—against the odds—the image of herself she feels she is lacking. The tone is set, as she pledges resistance. Her senses of touch and taste enable her to get a first impression of the changes that her body has undergone as a consequence of the burst aneurysm—of which, at this point in the novel, she is not yet fully aware.

Overall vaguely surprised to be still alive yet also strangely detached from what is going on, Helene discovers what she assumes is a photo of herself on the table in the corner of her room. Bits of it she can see clearly; others, like her eye color that she cannot make out from the distance, she instead has to imagine, letting her gut feeling guide her to believe it is blue (*DSN*, 20). Helene's relief at having thus reassembled a provisional image of herself in her mind becomes obvious: "Sie ist so froh, dass sie ihr Bild wiederhat" (*DSN*, 20; She is so glad that she has got her image back). Amalgamating fact and fiction, her creativity helps her to achieve this.

Weeks later, having long left the intensive care unit, a mirror helps Helene to get a clearer picture of what is happening to her:

> Heute hat man die Panzersperren aus dem Schädel gezogen. Sie hat nichts gemerkt. Es waren gar keine Panzersperren, sondern Metallklammern. Man scheint sie am Kopf operiert zu haben. Warum? Keine Ahnung. Als sie sich auf die Toilette schieben lässt, ist sie begierig auf einen Blick in den großen Spiegel. Bislang hat sie den nicht einmal bemerkt! Darüber wundert sie sich. / Das ist sie. Nichts zu deuteln. Auf der linken Schädelhälfte fehlen die Haare. Nein, das stimmt nicht ganz: Zwei, drei Millimeter sticht das neue Haar hervor. Eine feine rote Linie zieht sich vom Haaransatz in der Stirn in hohem Bogen bis vors Ohr. Beidseits der Linie von vielleicht fünfzehn Zentimetern Länge sind dicke rote Punkte zu sehen. Sie rühren von den Klammern her und erinnern an abgehackte Alleebäume, deren Stümpfe nur knapp aus dem Boden ragen. Ein Stumpf hat sich entzündet, er schmerzt. / Interessant, muss sie denken. / Broca-Aphasie, denkt es sie plötzlich. (*DSN*, 30–31)

> [Today the tank barriers were pulled out of her skull. She has not noticed a thing. They weren't tank barriers after all but metallic staples. It seems she has been operated on the head. Why? No idea. When she has someone wheel her to the toilet, she is eager to catch a glimpse in the large mirror. Up to now she has not even noticed it there! That surprises her. / That's her. No doubt. On the left half of her skull the hair is missing. No, that is not quite true: two or three millimeters long, the new hair sticks out. A fine red line runs from the hairline on her forehead up to her ear, in a wide arc. On both sides of that line of about fifteen centimeters length big, red dots are visible. They are from the staples and remind her of an avenue of felled trees, the stumps of which only just protrude from the ground. One stump is inflamed, it hurts. / Interesting, she cannot help but think. / Broca's aphasia, it thinks her (*sic*; in the sense of "occurs to her") suddenly.]

Presenting the first of many encounters with mirrors in the novel, this passage is significant, as it enables Helene to recognize herself, but also to register changes. Lacking information about her condition, the mirror image helps her to examine her body in more detail. Enabling her to scrutinize her looks and new circumstances more closely than before, she thus gains an idea too of how others must see her. At the same time, in its use of war imagery, the passage, with its references to tank barriers and avenues of felled trees, conveys how she feels about herself. Her body, the implied reader is to understand, has become a battleground. Her mirror image further enables Helene to identify one of these "stumps" as "inflamed." She feels this pain only once she visually registers the inflammation; as Lacan might say, the visual (and the linguistic too) here constructs the bodily. While this indicates that her overall numbing has begun to vanish, it seems that, still, her body is more physical shell (*Körper*) to her than lived body (*Leib*), to put it in the phenomenological nomenclature.[43] Finally, she can synthesize from the observations made in the mirror, and, by skill of interpretation, it strikes her that she is suffering from aphasia. Grammatically, the sentence that conveys this sudden realization is interesting, as, unusually, the active agent in it is the personal pronoun *es*. This serves to highlight the unexpected manner in which this shred of memory returns to Helene. The medical term comes unbidden and surprises in its precision. With her language skills and memory severely impaired, such visual cues are what Helene is dependent on. They anchor her in an experience that is otherwise overwhelmingly disorienting.

Negotiating the Disabled Self

Having gained a rough understanding of her situation, her image as externally determined by others—her *Fremdbild*—starts to concern Helene more as time goes on and she starts receiving more visitors. Seeing her sisters, for instance, she is worried they might think she is as crazy as the "zwei verrückten Alten" (*DSN*, 38; two crazy oldies) she shares a room with. In a particular moment of crisis, Helene's mind again focuses on her physical appearance. This is after a visit by her husband leaves Helene feeling infantilized, shamed, and misunderstood. Contemplating her anger, which stems from her helplessness toward him, she reflects on her appearance and the feelings this triggers:

> Furchtbares Gefühl, dämlich (und vor allem offen) lächelnd anderen ausgeliefert zu sein. Jetzt erst glaubt sie zu bemerken, dass sie tatsächlich über Gebühr lächelt: Die kleinste Freude zieht sofort den Mund breit, sie merkt es inzwischen daran, dass Speichel läuft. Und die Freude hört damit so leicht nicht auf. Sie ist ein

Breitmaulfrosch. Sucht das Gesicht im Spiegel der Waschnische auf. Nein, Glupschaugen sind ihr noch nicht gewachsen. Die Finger sind nicht trommelschlegelförmig verändert, ebenso wenig die Zehen. Ein bisschen grün sieht sie aber aus. Siehst du, Helene: grün vor Wut. Sie lächelt, und da überkommt es sie auch schon wieder, das rauschbrausende Wüten. Hilflosigkeit . . . (*DSN*, 81)

[A terrible feeling, to be at others' mercy, grinning stupidly, and so openly. Only now does she believe to notice that she is indeed smiling excessively: the smallest pleasure pulls her mouth wide, she notices this by now because saliva is dripping. And the pleasure does not stop at this. She is a wide-mouthed frog. Searches for the face in the mirror above the sink. No, she did not yet go goggle-eyed. The fingers are not deformed to little drumsticks, nor are her toes. But she does indeed look a little green. See, Helene: green with rage. She smiles, and there, it overcomes her yet again, toxically roaring rage. Helplessness . . .]

Her disabled state both shames and angers her—because she cannot keep pace with (and thus feels inferior to) the ablebodied and because of a lack of control over her own embodied self. At first the reader finds Helene blaming what she perceives as—and worse, what she believes must appear to others as—her grotesque bodily (re)actions: the smile is too wide, saliva trickling from her mouth. However, searching for her image in the mirror makes her realize she is not yet quite the monster she fears herself to be. By finding her mirror image, Helene creates a dialogic situation (in her mind, addressing her opposite as *du*)—one in which various senses of self, old and new, are negotiated through attentive looking. The mirror helps her to focus on herself and to forget about others. If only for an instant, it means she can be kinder to her body, which, as is becoming clear, plays a significant role in her self-conception.

Helene's struggle with the different aspects of her self that account for a sense of identity is at the fore of *Du stirbst nicht* and is negotiated throughout the text. "Wenn sie jetzt eine *Behinderte* ist?" (*DSN*, 112; [What] if now she is a *disabled person?*) is the central question the talented writer and formerly eloquent intellectual dwells on. Unsure about how to feel about this label, she soon realizes that the answer to this question is not in her control. The eyes of others posit people like her as either within the realms of the "normal" or else as a disabled spectacle, regardless of how able or limited one might feel in a given moment and context, instead depending on how visibly the deviation from the "healthy" norm manifests itself.

Another significant narrative setting besides that in front of mirrors is in the communal spaces of both the hospital and—later in the novel—the rehabilitation center in which Helene learns to take her meals. At one of her first breakfasts in this semipublic realm, she sits opposite a young man with spasticity. She observes him struggling to have his meal and is disgusted particularly by the saliva that is dripping from his mouth. This ableist (even disablist) reaction to the young man is interrupted by her catching a glimpse of herself in a reflection on a wall unit, which makes her realize, "Ach ja, ihre rechte Hand kann ja auch nichts mehr halten! Sie wird nicht mehr Klavier spielen können, nicht nähen oder stricken, und das Gesicht sieht auch anders aus als noch vor einem Monat. Hoch ausrasiert links, wächst erster Haarflaum nach, sie sieht seltsam aus, und, da!, auch aus ihrem Mund tropft Speichel." (*DSN*, 45; Oh yeah, her right hand can no longer hold on to anything either! She won't be able to play the piano, or sew or knit, and her face, too, looks different to how it did a month ago. In the high shaved patch on the left, a first bit of fluff is growing again, she looks weird, and, there!, from her mouth, too, saliva is dripping.) The literal reflection triggers an intellectual one, abruptly bringing her judgmental train of thought to a halt. Having him sit opposite her, he becomes a mirror image to her, too, much more so than she would like him to be. Initially condemning him as an incapable, repulsive other, she is forced to realize that they have more in common than separates them.

Staring at ourselves is always, to an extent, staring at a stranger. The view in the mirror offers, as Garland-Thomson phrases it, "a sight we at once doubt and trust."[44] For Helene, at a time of limited agency, these encounters with her mirror image are particularly intense, sometimes threatening. At the sight of the disabled other within the self, protagonist and reader alike have to reassess their accustomed assumptions about human variation and "normality."

Staring at Others—Learning through Empathetic Engagement

In parallel to an analysis of Helene's self-reflections vis-à-vis mirrors, then, her staring at other disabled, ill, or otherwise extraordinary people around her is illuminating. These other "deviants" (such as fellow patients) become physical, and visual, reference points for Helene. I argue that for the protagonist, moments of beholding other extraordinary bodies trigger a learning process about what it means to be human, enabling her to reflect on her own changing identity as she shares in their disabled experience.

A highly significant character in the novel and an important point of reference in the protagonist's routine in the clinic is "der Schadhafte" (the defective man), as she dubs him in her mind.[45] About their first encounter on the hospital corridor, we read:

Vor ihr ein *schadhafter* Mann—kann man so sagen? Von der Kalotte fehlt links ein großes Stück, wie eingeschlagen sieht der Schädel aus, es pulsiert heftig unter der rosa Haut, sie spürt keinen Ekel, eher will sie ihn fragen, was ihm geschehen ist, da sieht sie, dass ihm ein Arm fehlt, und um den Kohl fett zu machen, fehlt ihm auch ein Unterschenkel, hat man ihm etwa einen Fuß ans Knie genäht? Nun wird ihr doch übel, aber der Schadhafte sieht es nicht, er dämmert, seine Augen sind nur einen Spaltbreit geöffnet, und was dahinter schimmert, ist weiß. Wenn sie jene Hälfte seines Kopfes anschaut, die ganz geblieben ist, kommt sie zu dem Schluss, dass er sehr jung sein muss und gut aussehend. Gewesen. / Gepfriemelt in der Flickschusterei. / Sie schämt sich auf der Stelle. . . . Wahrscheinlich hat sie es noch gut getroffen mit dem, was ihr zustieß. (*DSN*, 117)

[In front of her a *defective* man—you could say? A large piece on the left of his cranium is missing, his skull looks as if has been bashed in, it pulsates eagerly under the pink skin, she does not feel any disgust, rather she wants to ask him what happened to him when she sees that he is missing an arm, and—this takes the biscuit—he is missing a lower leg, too, did they sew a foot onto his knee? Now she does feel sick after all, but the defective does not see it, he is dozing, his eyes only slits, and what shines through from behind is white. When looking at the half of his head that remained intact she concludes that he must be very young and good-looking. Used to be. / A botch job from the tinker's workshop. / She immediately feels ashamed of herself. . . . She has probably been lucky with what happened to her.]

Helene stares overtly, not able to restrain herself. She is certainly not in control of this impulse, taking in every distressing detail of the body she finds herself confronted with, such as the throbbing under his scalp. This is emphasized stylistically by the extensive use of subordinate clauses and commas. Her thoughts, just like her eyes on his body, are racing. Taken by surprise, Helene's eyes demand a narrative that can make sense of the sight of the young man—"ihn fragen, was ihm geschehen ist"—to be able, to an extent, to normalize the sight he presents. When eventually she is overcome by feelings of disgust due to being confronted with excessive, Frankensteinesque abnormality, she feels guilt and the urge to check, crucially, whether he notices that he has been made the object of her stare and thus become a grotesque attraction. The man himself, however, is barely conscious and not aware of Helene, who does draw a lesson from this one-sided encounter. For her, indeed, it serves as "an occasion to rethink the status quo,"[46] as she comes to assess her own situation in comparison to his. Previously feeling isolated in the unfamiliar medical environment, as if enclosed by a glass sphere ("gläserne Kugel um sich herum," *DSN*, 123), she begins to find a way out of isolation both through her unimpaired ability to see as well as through her explicit efforts to train her memory.

Helene's need for a narrative concerning "der Schadhafte" is satisfied only much later in the novel, when she comes across a newspaper article about the man, complete with a photo in which a baseball cap and leather jacket disguise the worst of his injuries. This is her opportunity to learn about his life before. She finds out that he had been the victim of the "U-Bahn-Schubser," as the local paper calls the perpetrator who pushed people into the path of underground trains. Comparing him to her son Bengt, as they are both musicians, it hits her "wie unglaublich es war, auf diese Weise um sein Leben gebracht zu werden und doch am Leben bleiben zu müssen" (*DSN*, 289; how unbelievable it was to be cheated of one's life that way but still have to remain alive). The article makes her empathize much more strongly and more easily with him than when they had their first encounter—the freak she initially saw in the "defective man," as Helene's later realization suggests, could well have been her son.

However, this realization on Helene's part is not an ad hoc one; it develops over the course of several staring encounters between the two. One takes place in the rehabilitation center, with Helene and the "defective man" sitting on opposite sides of a table over dinner, each mirroring the other. Surprised to see him again, Helene notices that "seine Augen dämmern nicht mehr unter der fehlenden Kalottenhälfte, sondern schauen Helene an. / Füllen sich mit Tränen. / Na, prost Mahlzeit." (*DSN*, 170; his eyes aren't dozing anymore below the missing half of the cranium, instead they're looking at Helene. / They fill up with tears. / That's just great.) This second meeting, involving—importantly—an exchange of looks, is much more intimate than the first, yet not one word is said. The only communication they have is of a visual/physical nature. Helene, still openly curious about him,[47] imagines various scenarios of how to console him, how she could help him eat—all the while ceaselessly staring at his face and hands in particular. Realizing she is no more dexterous in her bodily movements than he is and at a loss as to how to put her arm around him without touching any of his severely wounded body parts, the situation becomes unbearable for her, and she abruptly breaks off the intimacy of the relational stare: "Auf einmal hat sie keinen Appetit mehr. Sie lässt alles stehen und liegen und flieht." (*DSN*, 170; She has suddenly lost all appetite. She drops everything and flees.)

Another intense scene highlights just to what an extent his presence and the pain he goes through demand Helene's attention. Sharing the sports hall in their physiotherapy sessions, Helene cannot help but stare continuously at the young man's efforts to try walking one-legged and do other exercises that emphasize the permanence of the injuries that, to him, are still shockingly new. Surprised, she notices that she psychosomatically feels his pain (*DSN*, 180). Reencountering and closely observing him during a swimming lesson they each have with their therapists, she comes to the conclusion "dass ihm der Lebensmut fehlt, soll er ein toter Mann sein für eine Weile" (*DSN*, 183; that he is lacking the will to live, let him be a dead man for a while).[48] While never having communicated in an ordinary way, she believes she has a "Verbindung" (*DSN*, 183; connection) with him. The stare has established a relationship. Eventually she does learn his name—Wojziech Kostrzynski—and notices his continuing refusal to speak, which, although deliberate on his part, matches her difficulties with speech (*DSN*, 200–201). Like her, he has a preference for silently watching what is going on around him, missing nothing (*DSN*, 201). It is left to the reader to recognize these characteristics of Helene's behavior in the "defective" other as traits that they share.

Naming this character Wojziech is a way, for Schmidt, to relate *Du stirbst nicht* to the high literary canon: that she is thus alluding to the Georg Büchner play *Woyzeck* (written 1836/1837) is obvious. It constitutes an ambiguous reference considering that, in the play, the eponymous hero takes part in a doctor's dubious medical experiments, which have serious effects on his mental health. Later on, Schmidt's text makes explicit reference to *Lenz* (1839) and thus to a second work by Büchner that deals with the "madness" of its protagonist (or, indeed, that of society around him), maybe even more distinctly so than *Woyzeck*. Toward the end of the novel, the reader encounters Helene drafting an opening speech for a friend's public reading of the novella. This provides an opportunity, for Schmidt, to slip into her text a metaliterary commentary on its place within contemporary literature and its relationship to literary history. Within this draft, Helene highlights the fact that Büchner's literary case study of Lenz was based on a medical one, that is, on true events that fascinated the author so much he reimagined them. Helene then goes on to emphasize, "*Nicht fiktional, ist die Geschichte doch eine der modernsten Erzählungen der deutschen Literatur*" (*DSN*, 344; *Albeit nonfictional, the story is one of the most modern narratives of German literature*). Via the author figure Helene, the novel's actual author Schmidt can thus be seen to make a statement on using her own illness experience for *Du stirbst nicht*; the fact that she writes autobiographically, for Schmidt, does not contradict her literary ambitions for the novel. Any literary references we encounter in *Du stirbst nicht* must be read as highlighting these ambitions.

In relation to the important mirror figure of Wojziech, Helene displays the sort of staring Garland-Thomson wants to see emphasized, demonstrating the full range of complexities in our ways of seeing. On the basis of his experience more than that of her own, Helene comes to fully realize "the truth of our body's vulnerability to the randomness of fate."⁴⁹ It may be a rare kind of staring, yet Helene can transform the plain impulse to stare into active empathetic engagement with the young man, and she thus begins to depart from the normalist/ableist attitudes that pervade Western culture. What is more, via Helene's staring at him and others on the diegetic level of the novel, the implied reader gets the valuable opportunity to share in this in/sight alongside her.

Seeing Viola

Only a third of the way into the book does Helene recover some memories of Viola (*DSN*, 125),⁵⁰ her former lover, which from then on dominate her world of thought. She recollects the first time they met, in a café, for an article the writer was working on. Helene's memory of their first meeting is dominated by a tense interchange of looks:

> Der Kerl in Viola faszinierte sie, sie empfand Scham darüber, wie sie vorhin Schuld empfunden hatte, Scham und Schuld, geschwisterliche Verfühlungen. ... Viola schaute zum Fenster hinaus. / Wahrscheinlich litt sie an Rosazea. Um den Mund herum zeigten sich stecknadelkopfgroße Eiterpusteln, die auf der entzündlich aufgetriebenen Haut residierten, als wüssten sie, dass ihnen nur schwer beizukommen war. Wenn diese Situation hier Stress war, würde sich die Hautreaktion vermutlich verstärken. Zu Scham und Schuld gesellte sich Mitleid. ... Unangenehme Konstellation. Viola trug das Kinn hoch, die Augen blickten so in der Tat von oben herab auf das platte Volk ringsum, und dass ihnen nichts entging, schien Helene eine mühselig erlernte Fähigkeit zu sein. Die Violaaugen huschten. Flitscherten. Flitzten. Schwirrten. Hasteten. Holten aus. Schlugen zu. Solch einen Schlag bekam auch Helene zu spüren, als sich ihr Blick wider Willen an Violas Brüsten aufhielt, die nicht groß, aber wirklich da waren, sogar einen BH konnte man an der rückseitigen Einkerbung erkennen. Wenn sie solch intuitives Gestarre immer aushalten musste, verwunderten weder Rosazea noch Kinnhaltung. Sie hätte sich ohrfeigen können. (*DSN*, 134–35)

> [The guy within Viola fascinated her, she felt shame about it, just like earlier she had felt guilty, shame and guilt, the siblings of mis-sentiments. ... Viola looked out of the window. / Probably she was suffering from rosacea. Around her mouth pus-filled spots the size of pinheads showed up, residing on inflamed and chafed skin, as if they knew they were hard to defeat. If this situation here was stressful, the skin reaction would probably become worse. Shame and guilt were joined by pity. ... An unpleasant constellation. Viola held her chin high, the eyes were thus indeed looking down onto the common

people all around, and that they did not miss a thing, to Helene, seemed to be a learned skill. The Violaeyes darted. Flitted. Raced. Bustled. Scurried. Reached back. Struck. Such a blow, Helene, too, had to endure when her eyes, against her will, stopped at Viola's breasts. Which weren't large, but truly there, even a bra was to be identified by the indentation on her back. If she always had to endure such intuitive staring, neither rosacea nor chin posture were surprising. She could have slapped herself across the face.]

Being a trans woman and thus an experienced staree, Viola gives Helene an initial opportunity to look at her while she gazes into the distance. Helene avails herself of the moment and scrutinizes Viola's outward appearance. Fascinated, she cannot avert her eyes, all the while going through various awkward emotions. The longer Helene stares, the more her observations gain in depth. Helene's stare dominates at the beginning, but, in her curiosity, she, too, is vulnerable. Viola signals this by bluntly catching her out in the staring process—indicating that it is time for Helene to avert her eyes. Understanding this, Helene ultimately comes to feel empathy for Viola—realizing what violence she must have been doing to her by staring at her for so long. Thus, the first of many powerful lessons from Viola is learned.

As Helene recalls it from the hospital bed, Viola's story—that of a transgender person deciding to undergo treatment for a male-to-female sex change, being forced to divorce her wife, and ultimately tragically falling in love with Helene—unfolds in symmetry to Helene's day-to-day experiences in the confinements of hospital and rehabilitation center. Helene only fully understands Viola's life in the public eye and the difficulties she had accepting herself, as well as being accepted by others, in retrospect, from the position of disability, and after Viola has died in what might have been a suicide. Rather than equating transgender identity with disability, the novel utilizes the similarities of the marginalized positions both transgender and disabled people find each other in when in public. In her attempts to evade the constraints of culturally dominant bigenderism, Viola had faced issues not unlike Helene's in the narrative present of the novel. Helene, at this point, needs to reassess all she had taken for granted—her relationships, professional identity, physical and intellectual capabilities included. As an unruly patient, unwilling to identify herself as incapacitated other, Helene tries to evade static, incongruous labels like *behindert* in a similar way in which Viola longed to evade rigid ascriptions of gender norms.

Throughout the novel, Helene can be found to creatively experiment with various terms she makes up for herself, such as "Invalidin" (*DSN*, 337; invalid) or "Schadhafte" (*DSN*, 337; defective), as she begins to work out how the aneurysm and its consequences impact her identity.

The protagonist cannot seem to find satisfactory words to describe her altered subject position—but this should not be put down to her aphasia. Much rather, Helene must be taken as wary of the negative effects of calling someone disabled in an ableist world. Trying to grasp linguistically what she comes to think of, tentatively, as her "Zustand" (*DSN*, 313; state) or "Unvermögen" (*DSN*, 313; inability), one notes that neither illness, accident, nor stroke of fate seem quite adequate terms to her. For this reason, that which lies at the heart of Helene's struggles to reassemble an image of herself is referred to as "es" in what is a key passage (*DSN*, 90–91). *Es* is all of the suggested—a blow of fate, the cause for her lapse into coma, her physical dysfunction—and more: it is a higher power at the mercy of which Helene finds herself, signifying a void in her memory and holding Helene in its tight grip, having assaulted her, as she sees it, so suddenly and unexpectedly.

Just as Viola had learned to negotiate others' stares, Helene now finds herself in a position in which the discrepancies between her *Selbst*- and *Fremdbild* have become apparent, and problematic. Both characters submit themselves—more or less voluntarily—to the power of medical institutions, despite being uncertain of the outcome. Helene now too is a sight to be stared at as she violates normative expectations, albeit in a different (less voluntary or proactive) way from Viola: dribbling, in a wheelchair, with limited agility, her head shaved and marks of her operation all over her body.

Remembering how she got to know Viola better, Helene realizes anew, "dass Viola nicht allein dastand, obwohl sie, Helene, sie bislang angestaunt hatte wie einen dreibeinigen Kometen, der mitten unter ihnen niedergegangen war. Ein Sonderfall, eine exzeptionelle Singularität! Aber das stimmt nicht, sie hatte nur keine Augen für sie, bis sie eine von ihnen kennenlernte" (*DSN*, 186; that Viola did not stand alone, despite her, Helene, so far having gaped at her as if she was a three-legged comet which fell amid them. A special case, an exceptional singularity! But that wasn't true, she simply had no eyes for them until she met one of them). The narrative strand revolving around Viola continues to bring to the fore the productive side to staring—Helene comes to correct her gender binarism,[51] and, finding herself positioned as extraordinary, develops her own sensitivity to the extraordinary in others. It is for exactly this reason that this fictional narrative strand is included in the autobiographical illness narrative, the authenticity of which Schmidt otherwise vouches for. Learning to behold Viola as the individual she is, as someone not too dissimilar from herself (and by no means extraterrestrial, as likening her to a comet implies), Helene learns much from having stared at her initially. Just as this and other passages of the book criticize thinking of gender in absolute binaries and suggest, in a literary way, that the reader acknowledge gender as a "variable construction of identity,"[52] *Du stirbst nicht* as a whole criticizes dividing the healthy and unhealthy, the ablebodied and disabled, into two diametrically opposite categories with no gradation in between. Viola becomes a belated ally for Helene, so much so, in fact, that Helene dreams up Viola's consoling presence and imagines her making supportive comments in a moment that her own speechlessness threatens to frustrate her (*DSN*, 285).

In literary form, Schmidt thus calls for what Garland-Thomson in the article "Integrating Disability, Transforming Feminist Theory" asks for as a scholar: that disability studies and gender studies be allies and integrate one another's findings in their inquiries.[53] In this respect, *Du stirbst nicht* indicates an expansion of the sociocultural themes that have been at the heart of Schmidt's previous publications. While the body, gender, and sexuality have been subject to literary exploration by Schmidt before (she tackled them from a distinctly feminist stance), these themes and their relation to "normality" are recognized as transferable in *Du stirbst nicht* and are hence integrated into the autobiographical novel as they are found to support the illness experience's insights.

While Helene is strangely detached from her body, perceiving it as a kind of faulty machine or apparatus for most of *Du stirbst nicht*, Viola brings back emotions into Helene's life. Vacillating among happiness, pain, and grief when thinking of Viola, the narrating voice therefore comes to conclude about Helene: "Sie lebt noch in ihrem Körper, eines hängt mit dem anderen zusammen, trotz der sich mehrenden Metallteile in Kopf und Brust" (*DSN*, 238; She is still alive in her body, one is connected to the other, despite the multiplying metal pieces in head and chest).[54] In this way, the memories of Viola that return to Helene significantly contribute to the protagonist's convalescence and her ability to create a coherent image of her self poststroke.

Transcending Binary Thinking

The "primacy of vision" that Garland-Thomson points out as an uneasy one in today's social world is neatly encapsulated in a short paragraph describing Helene's visit to the opticians.[55] Matthes takes Helene there to get her new glasses: "Der Optiker hat einen Spiegel wie einen dreiflügligen Altar. Darin kann sie sich von der Seite sehen. *Was sieht sie?* Der Haarwuchs auf der linken Seite ist noch spärlich, vielleicht einen knappen Zentimeter lang. Er ist völlig grau. Silbern stehen die Borsten zu beiden Seiten der Narbe vom Kopf ab. Sie dreht den Kopf: Auf der anderen Seite glänzt es kastanienbraun. Sie stellt sich vor, wie es aussähe, wären die Haare wieder gleich lang: links grau, rechts braun, der Gedanke beginnt ihr zu gefallen. Sie dreht einige Male den Kopf." (*DSN*, 166; emphasis mine; The optician has a mirror like an altar triptych. In it she can see herself sideways. *What does she see?* On the left, hair growth is still sparse, maybe just short of a centimeter. It's completely grey. The bristles on both sides of the scar, silver, protrude from the head. She turns her head: On the other side it glistens chestnut brown. She imagines what it might look like if her hair was back to one length: grey on the left, brown on the right, she begins to like the thought. She turns her head a few times.)

Being publicly confronted with a mirror in this scene, at the altar of vision, which society collectively worships, Helene can be found to consciously reassess her appearance. While she still is an unusual sight, she comes to like the two colors her newly growing hair displays, as her turning her head—the classic movement of self-admiration—indicates. The new and old senses of self may not be entirely reconciled, but, so this signals, they do find their space in the same body. Employing this image, Helene, or, for that matter, Schmidt, acknowledges the "dual citizenship," to echo Susan Sontag's eloquent metaphor, that she holds "in the kingdom of the well and in the kingdom of the sick."[56] What is striking about this passage on a technical level is the disruption of the narrative flow caused by the narrating voice overtly asking, "What does she see?" Rather than sharing in Helene's perspective or consciousness at this point, the implied reader is placed in the role of external observer, similar maybe to that of Matthes or the optician on the diegetic level, or indeed that of the author during the novel's conception extratextually. Thus disturbing the reader's immersion in the text for the moment, the implied reader is thrown back on him- or herself—confronted with the question, What do *you* see in Helene?—and is left to contemplate possible answers. This and other passages demonstrate the novel's didactic intentions.

Overall, the book's trajectory is that of an *Entwicklungsroman*. Toward the end of the novel, the reader can observe Helene in an unfamiliar role. It is that of staree, negotiating two elderly women's stares at the bus stop, when Helene's scar and the fact that she cannot stop dribbling attract their attention: "Eine schaut sie mitleidig an, die andere ist bemüht, wegzusehen. Schade. Dass sie noch immer ein seltsamer Anblick für andere ist, vergisst Helene wieder und wieder. Dabei trägt sie die Schädelnarbe unter der Mütze verborgen, es kann also so schlimm gar nicht sein, aber wahrscheinlich sind die beiden alten Dünnen noch leichtfüßig zugange, und es fehlt ihnen die Vorstellung, eben das nicht zu sein. Jetzt bemerkt sie aber doch den Speichel, der sich vor ihrem Mund abgesetzt hat, und kann die Alten besser verstehen." (*DSN*, 320; One of them looks at her with compassion, the other is careful to look away. [What a] Shame. Helene forgets time and again that she is still a strange sight for others. And that despite keeping the scar that covers her skull hidden under a hat, so it really can't look that bad, but these two slender old women are probably still light on their feet, and they can't imagine what it would be like if they weren't. But now she does notice the saliva around her mouth after all and she can understand the two oldies better.) Still getting used to this new role of hers, Helene displays a fair amount of understanding toward the starers. Not too long ago, she was one of them, with a much more restricted way of seeing. "Lack of imagination" narrows their view of others, and of life; this is Helene's, and, we may speculate, Schmidt's conclusion. Less poetically, one may identify an impulse to avoid, out of fear, the abnormal sight Helene presents, an impulse that seems to override any capacity for empathy in the two women of this passage.

Helene, on the other hand, begins to be more comfortable in her skin. Gradually, she rediscovers composure and contentment despite her new restrictions (*DSN*, 319, 330). What is more, she begins to believe in her physical recovery, to the extent that she imagines herself to be able to physically sense it happening: "Plötzlich nimmt sie ein neues, unbekanntes Ziehen im Kopf wahr, eigentlich sitzt es genau an der Stelle, an der sie den Titanclip verortet, sie muss an einen seltsam schmerzfreien Wadenkrampf denken, der sich nach oben verlagert hat, ins Hirn. Es heilt, denkt sie begütigend, es heilt. . . . Es ist, *als nehme sie das Fitzchen Metall endlich als zu sich selbst gehörig wahr*, als fühle sie seine Existenz." (*DSN*, 333; emphasis mine; Suddenly she picks up on a new, unknown tugging sensation in her head, in actual fact residing exactly in the place where she locates the titanium clip, it makes her think of a strangely pain-free cramp in the calf muscle that has shifted upward, into the brain. It's healing, she thinks placatingly, it is healing. . . . It's *as if she were finally accepting the shred of metal as part of her self*, as if she were feeling its existence.)

Although one may note, critically, an element of magical thinking here, Helene's optimism as displayed at this point illustrates the overall spirit at the conclusion of the novel. *Du stirbst nicht* ends with an emphasis, maybe an overemphasis, on reconciliation—Helene and Matthes's married life improves, the protagonist becomes reconciled with her body and starts being kinder to herself. To some extent her self-image, as conflicting and multidimensional as it may be, is restored. In fact, it may be yet more fitting to say that as a result of the illness experience, her self-image has expanded over the course of the novel, and with it her capacity—or her imaginative faculties, in keeping with the narrator's words—for seeing and understanding others.

Through engaging in acts of staring and experiencing what it means to be both on the giving and the receiving end of a hard look, Helene has grown as a person and has come to question culturally pervasive ideas of "normality": "Wie hatte Matthes gesagt, als sie ihn auf sprachliche Defizite ansprach, die sie immer wieder bei sich bemerkt? *Ach Helene, du bist doch nur endlich normal geworden*. . . . Das war ein Satz, der einerseits vermutlich seine Hochachtung vor ihrem Sprachvermögen ausdrückte. Andererseits fühlte sie sich durch ihn seltsam bedroht, ohne dass sie genau sagen konnte, warum." (*DSN*, 287; ellipses in original; How did Matthes put it when she addressed the linguistic deficits she noticed in herself again and again? *Oh Helene, all that happened is that you finally became normal....* As a sentence, on the one hand, this presumably expressed his deference to her language competency. On the other, she felt strangely threatened, without exactly being able to say why.)

The idea of a return to normality is illusory, as the highly talented writer was never "normal," if normal is taken to mean "average." Matthes's statement underlines pervasive sociocultural assumptions about disability as abnormal, which—from a disability studies' perspective at least—have been shown to be ideological constructs, most notably by Lennard J. Davis in his seminal publication *Enforcing Normalcy* (1995).[57] What Matthes says is threatening because it implies a disregard of her personhood in illness. Lastly, as a societal ideal and impossible prescriptive goal, and by devaluing alternative visions for a possible future, Matthes's notion of normality is confining and regressive. The text makes the complexity of the challenges involved for Helene in negotiating a new identity clear and portrays its protagonist—in contrast to her husband—as someone who has begun to outgrow such simple modes of binary thinking.

Seeing the Bigger Picture

While most autobiographical writing today subverts rather than adheres to the criteria formerly deemed typical of the genre, it retains a crucial difference from fiction: as a writer's "exercise in self-attention,"[58] it creates or elicits a stronger response in the reading public. Each of the writers I deal with in this book has experienced this, but—as is demonstrated in each chapter—what is more, each of the authors already prepared for it in the writing process.

Kathrin Schmidt finds an explicitly literary way of dealing with the great resonance that she, to an extent, anticipated as an author writing illness autobiographically. Among other strategies, such as deciding against a first-person voice (which, in a first draft, she had experimented with) and making use of an alter ego–protagonist under a fictional name, Schmidt's key strategy in *Du stirbst nicht* is to address the human stare. Beyond their intradiegetic functions, the stares and their reflections cannot be confined between the book's covers. Extratextually, they function as commentary on its author's exposure to the public eye. Words, as Schmidt has her protagonist claim, can indeed be "seltsam nackte Lemminge" (*DSN*, 130; strangely naked lemmings), generating uncontrollable meanings beyond their writer's intention, leaving one dangerously exposed and vulnerable. *Du stirbst nicht* therefore holds up a mirror to all of us both as readers and as starers who desire some kind of insight into an "authentic," near-fatal illness experience. In so doing the text may make us uncomfortable, but it can also encourage us to reflect on our own normative behaviors and assumptions as we accompany Helene in the process of reassessing old certainties, as well as Schmidt in revisiting the illness experience creatively. Subtly but effectively, the implied author as staree thus ultimately deflects attention away from herself, eliciting an introspective response from the reader. In this, *Du stirbst nicht* bears the potential to unsettle our confidence in the validity of the images we form of others.

In hindsight, one knows that Schmidt did not have much to fear in daring the step into the autobiographical narrative realm by publishing *Du stirbst nicht*. Critical appraisal of the book was generous, and, since winning the *Buchpreis*, Schmidt's reputation and renown have only increased. However, it seems that in the wake of its success, *Du stirbst nicht*'s story is already being recast, smoothed out, and generally made more harmless than the text suggests. Both its author and the press have participated in this normalization process that occurred postpublication, but for diverging reasons. When the press praised *Du stirbst nicht* as the story of a healing, taking the book as a "testimony to her success,"[59] talking of a rebirth or a miracle, they situated Schmidt as the "exceptional singularity" (*DSN*, 186) she would not want to be—at least not for her illness (or the relative recovery from it). In general, the reviews legitimized the book as a strong candidate and later deserving winner of the book prize on the basis of the experience's authenticity and alleged difference. Many a critic praises the overall tone of the book, particularly because, as they read it, its protagonist is "nie verzweifelt, nie deprimiert" (never desperate, never depressed).[60] Schmidt, in interviews, then added to this process, by stressing how quickly and easily she adapted to the situation she found herself in, thus drawing a line under the experience, and under the text that has arisen out of it. One can find evidence that she did so to keep the public focus on her writerly achievements rather than drawing it to the details of her personal history with illness.[61] It is up to the attentive reader to assess the experience of illness/disability in this book in its full complexity and thus to find what the text is actually communicating by stripping it of the heroic gloss that it has already gained since its publication.

* * *

The stereotyping that Schmidt struggles with in relation to *Du stirbst nicht* is all too familiar to the life writer Verena Stefan, author of the third text analyzed in this study. The Swiss-German writer herself was once exposed to the full force of normative reading practices of the kind I have been tracing in relation to Schmidt's text. The issues that labels like that of *Betroffenheitsliteratur* create for authors will be explored further in the next chapter. Indeed, like Schmidt, Stefan in her 2007 text *Fremdschläfer* prepared for certain critical reactions in explicitly literary ways.[62] Whereas *Du stirbst nicht* deflects the reader's gaze through the thematization of staring (and its use as narrative device), Stefan's breast cancer narrative prepares for publication in a different way: its intertextual references become a strategic means of preempting the anticipated judgment passed on *Fremdschläfer* by German cultural critics. The text can be said to contribute to Stefan's loosening of ties with the realm of German-language literature.

First rising to fame in the 1970s, Stefan emerged as a published author, at twenty-eight years old, with a book that became one of the most widely read texts of the "Neue[ ] Frauenbewegung" (new women's movement) and "Neue Subjektivität" (New Subjectivity),[63] to name the two movements—one social, one literary—with which her debut *Häutungen* is typically associated.[64] Much of the often heavily autobiographical writing that arose from this context in the 1970s, in particular that published by female authors, was (and sometime still is) referred to derogatorily as *Betroffenheitsliteratur*.[65] Undeterred by such strategies of exclusion (including personal attacks), Stefan continued to publish auto/biographical texts ever since, as well as becoming versed in other nonfiction and fiction writing. With *Häutungen*, the foundation had been laid for a writer's life.

Out of the texts discussed so far, then, Stefan's breast cancer / migration narrative *Fremdschläfer* is also the most straightforwardly autobiographical text—yet, as should go without saying, it is no less artistic for it. As in previous chapters, the analysis to follow traces questions of narratability. Which narrative strategies and aesthetic forms allow Stefan to write cancer at once personally and publicly? Additionally, in turning to this early example of contemporary illness narratives, it explores what traditions a writer can build on, which texts one can engage with, when there is not much of a tradition—at least not a recognized one—of writing illness autobiographically in the cultural realm within which one's books appear (here, the Germanic world). In contrast to Schmidt, who through intertextual references can be observed to align *Du stirbst nicht* with the canon of German literature, Stefan's use of intertexts in writing illness autobiographically is diametrically opposed to any such localization. Lastly, it is worth noting that *Fremdschläfer* is not Stefan's first work dealing with illness and death through literature. Already in 1993, Stefan published an auto/biographical account about her mother's dying in the form of *Es ist reich gewesen: Bericht vom Sterben meiner Mutter*, inspired by and in response to her mother's diaries.[66]

3: Intertextuality and the Transnational in Verena Stefan's *Fremdschläfer* (2007): Writing Breast Cancer from beyond the Border

> *After many years as a rabid separatist another need took over in my life: to be present, visible, audible in society at large; in brief, to be generally human.*
>
> —Verena Stefan, "We Live as Two Lesbians"

At the Solothurner Literaturtage in 2008, Verena Stefan publicly recalled her first encounter with the strange and striking word *Fremdschläfer* (alien sleeper), which a friend had read to her from a newspaper. The term's strangeness resonated strongly with Stefan, and its potential polysemy tempted her to use it as the title of the book she was working on at the time.[1] As the author takes care to explain in a postscript inserted in the back of the 2007 publication, it is originally a Swiss bureaucratic term denoting asylum seekers who are caught staying overnight at a place different from the one they have been assigned.[2]

Most readers will know the author for her debut text *Häutungen* (*Shedding*, 1975)—simply described as a "buch[ ]"[3] (book) by Stefan herself in the foreword accompanying it and, equally loosely, labeled "autobiografische Aufzeichnungen Gedichte Träume Analysen" (autobiographical notes poems dreams analyses) on its first page. In 1975 and the following years, in the wake of the second-wave feminist movement, *Häutungen* became a best seller, and Stefan's name has since been closely associated with the radical autobiographical turn of the time. Considering its impact, one could rightfully call it the *Feuchtgebiete* of its time.[4] As is indicated by the fluid genre labeling, the text combines diary-style passages with essayistic and poetic writing. *Häutungen* did two things: first, it denounced all-too-common sexist and abusive behavior toward women and the patriarchal societal structures that render women powerless. And, second, from a highly personal perspective, the book described Stefan's path to lesbian love, beginning with her renunciation of men[5] and leading to the gradual rediscovery of her "verloren gegangene eigenkörperlichkeit" (*H*, 17; roughly: lost familiarity with and lacking agency over one's own body). The reader witnesses the self-realization of the protagonist as an independent woman; toward the end she finds herself able "to 'shed' the constraints of patriarchal heteronormativity."[6]

In recounting these experiences, *Häutungen* memorably experiments with language, searching for what Stefan calls "eine weibliche sprache" (*H*, 4; a feminine language) to tell her story adequately. She does so in the hope of being able to use this female language as a corrective to the ways in which the societal status quo was (and, one may argue, still is) perpetuated in German everyday expressions. While its sales figures alone prove just how strongly the slim volume resonated with many contemporary women's experiences,[7] the publication also attracted criticism, some of it quite aggressive: Dieter Bachmann, reviewing *Häutungen* in the Swiss magazine *Die Weltwoche* in 1976, calls it a "*Krankengeschichte einer schweren Neurotikerin*" (*case history of a severe neurotic*), emphasizing he believes its author is "*ein zutiefst verstörter Mensch*" (*a most deeply disturbed person*).[8] From today's perspective, it is striking that Bachmann was able to use allusions to mental health issues as an insult and apparently legitimate basis to dismiss the work.[9]

Thirty-two years later, *Fremdschläfer* takes as its topic Stefan's experience of immigration into Canada and works into it the discovery, subsequently, of a lump in her breast. At first sight ostensibly ignoring all risk in writing illness autobiographically, Stefan in *Fremdschläfer* narrows her focus to her life with cancer, "um nah heranzuholen, was unerreichbar ist, lautlos, schwerelos" (*F*, 121; to bring closer what is out of reach, soundless, weightless). In contrast to *Häutungen*, *Fremdschläfer* was labeled and marketed as a novel.[10] It could equally, and indeed maybe more adequately, be referred to as another volume of "autobiographical notes poems dreams analyses," as, over the course of her writing career, Stefan has remained committed to the principles of life writing and faithful to her personal poetics as first taking shape in *Häutungen*. Sharing this impression, Ruth Klüger refers to Stefan's writing in *Fremdschläfer* as "Prosagedichte" (prose poetry).[11]

The diagnosis of breast cancer along with the ensuing treatment to combat what feels like a foreign body inside her cause a new sense of dislocation for the author just as she was settling into Canadian life. Yet another layer of meaning is given to the overarching motif of the "alien sleeper" through Stefan's retrospective assessment of a piece of family history: making use of documents from the Swiss Federal Archives in Bern and merging them with childhood memories, she integrated into the book the story of her father's displacement and life as a Sudeten-German in Switzerland after the Second World War. Categorized as Austrian, then Czech, and eventually German in Switzerland, he remained a foreigner—"Ausländer" (*F*, 70)—for the rest of his life, readily identifiable by his non-Swiss accent and always threatened with deportation by the Swiss authorities. He thus is the original alien sleeper to whom the title refers, although his experience precedes the coinage of the term in the 1980s (*F*, 218). Freeing the term of its specific legal context, Stefan herself too, with a little poetic license and taking the unusual compound noun literally, identifies as a *Fremdschläfer*, having moved to Canada primarily to be with her lover, whom she gives the fictional name Lou in the book. The fact that Lou is a woman also informs this self-designation; a little tongue-in-cheek, it may be a way of highlighting the lesbian author's, and with it her narrator's, awareness of being different from the hetero norm.

In Stefan's own words, the book and its interwoven strands deal with "(im)migration, dislocation and connection to place and space viewed from inside the body, its visceral and cultural codes";[12] in other words, it meditates on questions of belonging and estrangement / being an outsider, and it does so by focusing on life experiences that have troubled and intensified Stefan's identity work at different points of her life. She revealed that the breast cancer experience—constituting the main focus of this analysis and being such a central and prominent theme of the novel in its published form—was not meant to be included originally. The author's decision ultimately to incorporate it into the manuscript was based on her realization that the illness represents, as she puts it, "yet another experience of dislocation in which one has to emigrate temporarily to the country of illness."[13] We realize that illness in *Fremdschläfer* is at once a trope and a powerful and painful reality.

Stefan's initial doubts about including the illness in her narrative are reminiscent of comments made by Kathrin Schmidt about her hesitation to write illness autobiographically (see previous chapter). Monique Wittig's essay "The Point of View: Universal or Particular?" is helpful in understanding such doubts about including personal illness experiences in one's work.[14] Wittig, in the essay, reflects on the decisions "minority writers,"[15] as she calls them, are confronted with in regard to their texts and their anticipated reception.

Writing in the early 1980s, the French writer and theorist sets out the situation an author finds herself in when homosexuality is a theme in a piece of literary writing. As a risky subject, and in this way comparable to the representation of personal experiences of illness or disability in literature, it may come to "monopolize the whole meaning" of a complex piece of work, with readers focusing on just this one aspect. Through such biased reception, if read as "symbol" or "manifesto" of one position rather than a multilayered piece of writing, a text's potential productive ambiguity comes to be disregarded, alongside its literary value and its "relationship to other past or contemporary texts." If we accept Wittig's presupposition, however, an author's more complex and ambitious aim is to "[want] above all [to] create a literary work" with which "to change the textual reality within which it is inscribed." This fails when the text is read, in a limited way, as merely the social commentary it may—also, but not exclusively—convey. According to Wittig, the consequence of such a discriminatory reading practice is such that one's readership is reduced to the small group of people who share the minority identity of the author. Ultimately, the reading public determines what gets read. Biased reading thus turns these texts into *Betroffenheitsliteratur*, limiting their relevance to those whom it may directly concern.[16] The text then disappears from the wider public's sight through what Anita Konrad describes as "Ausgrenzung durch Anerkennung" (exclusion through acknowledgment)—getting "the silent treatment," as Wittig puts it.[17]

By including her personal illness experience in *Fremdschläfer*, Stefan exposes herself to the risks outlined by Wittig; at the same time, it can be argued that she uses her personal experiences of migration and illness as starting points from which she "work[s] to reach the general."[18] The "polysemy" of the word *Fremdschläfer* makes it possible for Stefan to address universal issues through the medium of her particular experience.[19] For this study, which of course has an explicit thematic focus on the representation of experiences of illness and disability, what can be drawn from Wittig's essay is encouragement, methodologically, to read each of the texts in the corpus in the context of its individual production, the literary field it moves in, and, not lastly, in its own right as literature.

This chapter, in exploring Stefan's representation of her cancer experience, accordingly centers on three interrelated aspects: the role of intertexts in *Fremdschläfer*, the authorial/narratorial positioning its intertextuality enables, and Stefan's assumptions about her readership as manifest in the autobiographical text.[20] I first situate *Fremdschläfer* within the tradition of breast cancer narratives in which it stands and without which it would not have been written in the existing form. I discuss in particular how, through citation, Stefan aligns her account with those by female pioneers of illness (often cancer) narratives, to what ends this is done, and in which ways she departs from these precursory texts. I demonstrate that, for Stefan, writing is the only possible way to confront the disease, as only the written word has the power to trace and make fully real the illness experience—both for herself and for her readership. I conclude by assessing Verena Stefan's position on the international stage as a writer today: thirty-two years after *Häutungen*, this chapter shows how and why she consciously takes up what I describe as a transnational stance with *Fremdschläfer*.

Women and Cancer—Cultural Connotations

When the narrative voice in *Fremdschläfer* comes to state, "Mit Krankheit kennst du dich aus. Von Krebs weißt du nichts" (*F*, 103; You are familiar with illness. Of cancer you know nothing), she alludes to cancer's exceptional status as "more" than a "normal" disease. With its particularly frightening connotations, of presumed and real effects on the body and on female identity, breast cancer especially is symbolically laden. It therefore stands out even from the range of cancer types. It bears all the common cancer connotations—that of a body turning against itself, killing from the inside, quietly. Additionally, however, breast cancer largely affects women; it therefore is "Frauenkrankheit" (*F*, 28). Up until the recent past, receiving a diagnosis of breast cancer entailed social stigmatization and marginalization for the women inflicted with it.[21] In some cases (and places), this still pertains today.

For the Western context, Thatcher Carter reminds us of the shame that historically went along with any physical examination of a woman's body by a (typically male) doctor: "For centuries, female patients refused to show their breasts to their doctors without a layer of clothing between them."[22] This modesty women displayed, while conforming to social expectations, made diagnosis difficult, if not impossible. Residues of it as well as additional effects of persisting gender biases in the doctor-patient relationship affect the accuracy of diagnoses and the options for treatment subsequently offered to this day.

On the one hand, thanks to the widening of schemes for preventive screening as well as medical advances in diagnosis and therapies, the number of breast cancer deaths in Europe has been falling since the 1990s (after peaking in that decade). Nonetheless, in 2013, breast cancer was still the primary cause of cancer deaths in women, although culturally, at the same time, attitudes toward breast cancer seem to have begun to shift toward the condition being perceived as one you can live with.[23] Writing in 2010, Brenda L. Blondeau and Eva C. Karpinski, editors of a special issue of *Canadian Woman Studies* titled "Women and Cancer," note with relief that the stigma around cancer "has been lifted and a new public discourse has developed in response to its epidemic proportions."[24] On the other hand, Blondeau and Karpinski also still find that "we often neglect to investigate the environmental causes of this epidemic, its social determinants, its alternative treatments, and the different methods of its prevention."[25]

In the cultural imagination, breast cancer remains more emotive than uterine and ovarian cancers because it affects a more visible—and displayed—body part. Its origin and center sit squarely in the female breast, a highly symbolic body part, the place that contains, as Stefan puts it, "das ganze Leben" (all of life): "Erotik, Stolz, Scham, Begehren, Lust, . . . Stillen, Nähren, Genährtwerden, Fürsorge, Gewalt, Belästigung, Verletzung, Konkurrenz, Neid, Liebe, Trennungen, Kinder, Attraktivität, Altern, Angst" (*F*, 29; eroticism, pride, shame, desire, lust, nursing, nourishing, being nourished, care, violence, harassment, injury, rivalry, jealousy, love, separations, children, attractiveness, ageing, fear).

Fremdschläfer, as this quotation indicates, is a text that is highly aware of these discourses surrounding the female chest and sketches them out in a few concise yet evocative words.

In between doctor's appointments, Verena (that is, the narrative persona in the text) notices in passing, "Das Leben ist ganz zu Körper geronnen. Mit Stumpf und Stiel bist du aus dem Ideenparadies vertrieben worden." (*F*, 29; Life has been completely reduced to the body. You have been expelled root and branch from the paradise of ideas.) Instead of leading to self-transcendence, she finds, cancer does the opposite. Stefan echoes Susan Sontag here, who stressed in *Illness as Metaphor* that, as a particularly aggressive yet often insidious illness, cancer "attacks" the body and "reveals that the body is, all too woefully, just the body"—rendering the illness scandalous.[26] Breast cancer as a specific form of cancer remains a troubling condition and for many women poses a severe threat to their identity, because undergoing treatment and most likely losing one's hair, plus possibly part or all of one's breasts, can feel like losing one's femininity.

Traditions in Breast Cancer Writing and Their Diversification

Cancer stories arguably form the largest and most established subgenre of illness narratives today. Susan Sontag's famous essay—tellingly more a sociocultural polemic than a personal narrative—constitutes one of the early interventions in the way cancer diseases were discussed in public, its author wary of the harmful effects of the metaphors that ran through this discourse on people living with a cancer diagnosis. In the 1970s and 1980s, when breast cancer narratives (together with other cancer narratives) first emerged to form a genre in their own right, most mainstream autobiographical literature dealing with the difficult topic followed a chronological master narrative dictated by the medical regimes of diagnosis and treatment; these accounts were often set almost exclusively in the space of the clinic. In terms of their style, the available scholarship tends to perceive the publications as reminiscent of self-help books,[27] classing them as documents of psychological "self-healing."[28] Considering their depth, Ulrich Teucher claims that "many of these narratives remain on a linear, descriptive level."[29]

Narratives of this kind usually end on a positive note, as, for instance, Couser, DeShazer, and Herndl have observed, that is, with the recovery of the subject from cancer.[30] Herndl, in the context of making this observation, rightly asks, "But are such narratives [of recovery and healing] unproblematically true? What are their political consequences?"[31] As Teucher highlights, writing in 2007, more crafted and poetic accounts too are to be found among what we might want to call first-wave cancer narratives, which—at least according to the scholarship—otherwise adhered to a societal imperative for optimism. Teucher himself picks out Maja Beutler's *Fuss fassen* (Gaining a foothold) from 1980 as one such clearly literary, partly fictionalized, and less conciliatory account that, as he stresses, does not strive for closure but complicates the cancer experience by remaining "open-ended."[32]

From the mid-1990s, and there are more prominent examples of this in the Anglophone literature than in the German-language realm, the trend toward publication of personal breast cancer stories intensified. DeShazer attributes this to the success of the women's movement, the general increase in both diagnoses of and deaths from breast cancer, and the rising media presence of cancer as a topic.[33] More and more women have since come to express their illness story in writing, claiming for themselves the sovereignty to represent and interpret their experiences with cancer as they see fit.[34] The types of cancer stories continue to diversify accordingly, as does their plotting. Autothanatographies like those by Maxie Wander (published posthumously in 1980) or Ruth Picardie (1998) now as a matter of course form part of the range of cancer narratives and stand alongside those that end with the authors' thematization of their survival.[35]

The contemporary literary scene has most recently seen online narratives added to the now-diverse spectrum of (breast) cancer literature (typically published in blog form but also in the realm of social media). Additionally, new ways of representing breast cancer (and other illness experiences) are sought in the form of the graphic novel; just two examples of graphic breast cancer memoirs are *Cancer Made Me a Shallower Person* (2006) and *Cancer Vixen* (2006).[36] However, as Teucher points out, "The ready availability of cancer narratives, whether published or unpublished, should not be allowed to obscure the fact that many patients choose, for good reasons, not to talk or write about their experiences."[37] This pertains until and beyond today. As scholars and as readers, we must be all the more respectful of the relatively small group of those affected by cancer who, against all difficulties, have put their experiences into words, and sometimes images, for others to share.[38]

In writing her cancer experience, Stefan too makes use of typical motifs recurring in breast cancer narratives. Naturally, the reverberating shock of discovering a lump in one of her breasts leaves Verena feeling betrayed by the body she thought she knew so well. Questions like the following are repeatedly asked in the text: "Wie ist es gewachsen, unsichtbar, im Inneren, was spielt sich jetzt, grade jetzt im Inneren ab, innen im Körper?" (*F*, 24; How did it grow, invisibly, inside her, what is happening now, right now, on the inside, the inside of her body?)—an urgency and disquiet spread in the protagonist's anticipation of her self as failing body.[39] In *Fremdschläfer*, we read both of the moment Verena first discovers the lump as well as of her increasing alienation from her body that ensues with the medical treatment she subjects herself to. But *Fremdschläfer* goes beyond the portrayal of these stages of illness and treatment. Fears of the total disintegration of her life and the life writer's thoughts on death are given intense expression. Stylistically, the text breaks with some of the most conventional storytelling practices: it neither aims to narrate strictly chronologically, nor does it portray the breast cancer experience in isolation. In terms of the illness topic, the experience intersects with that of the author's migration to Canada and the process of settling in there and is furthermore interwoven with memories of Stefan's upbringing in Bern; it thus provides a way to reassessing family history too. Altogether this makes *Fremdschläfer*—though the oldest text in my corpus—a multidirectional and so very contemporary narrative.

Fremdschläfer is aligned with the illness writings of literary predecessors such as Virginia Woolf, Susan Sontag, and Audre Lorde in multiple ways. Stefan draws on and builds upon these prominent early counterhegemonic examples of illness narrative, each of which took issue with an aspect of the dominant sociocultural ideology informing attitudes toward illness/disabilities. Woolf's text *On Being Ill* aims to give illness its rightful place in literature, and begins the search for an adequate language to express the experience of medical conditions in literary ways.[40] Sontag in *Illness as Metaphor* takes on the task to expose what she saw were harmful stereotypes surrounding the person suffering from cancer (as expressed in culturally disseminated myths and metaphors).[41] With *The Cancer Journals*, Lorde became the trailblazer for any woman with breast cancer who wanted to resist the silence imposed on her with diagnosis and who doubted the use and need for a prosthesis postmastectomy.[42] And in *Autobiography of a Face*, Lucy Grealy confronts the ablebodied with the discriminatory ways in which they treat people with visible differences (in her case, the result of numerous facial operations) by telling her own illness narrative that began when she was still a child—in some ways suffering from others' behavior toward her more than from the facial bone cancer she was afflicted with and the treatment that came along with it.[43] I show how Stefan both references and departs from these Anglophone forerunners, finding her own unique way of portraying her illness experience in literary form.

The Writer as Reader—Stefan's Self-Positioning in a Female Genealogy

Fremdschläfer clearly engages with other representations of illness that predate it. All of the works thus taken up in the book are by female writers, and, like Stefan, a number of their authors identify as lesbian. The influence of and engagement with these intertexts in *Fremdschläfer* underlines the importance that must be ascribed to them in having paved the way for Stefan's own 2007 publication. As a contemporary approach to writing breast cancer autobiographically, it can operate in the way it does only because of its "relationship to other past or contemporary texts," as Wittig had theorized with regard to so-called minority literature,[44] and as especially feminist writers like Stefan are aware. For my reading of Stefan's book, it is therefore significant exactly which authors and texts the Swiss-German writer adopts as her literary foremothers.

Stefan cites the preface to Susan Sontag's influential essay *Illness as Metaphor* explicitly, picking up on words that resonate with her own decision to draw parallels between the illness experience and her migration to Canada. On pages 104–5 of *Fremdschläfer*, a German translation of the following sentences from the English original is given: "Illness is the night-side of life, a more onerous citizenship. Everyone who is born holds dual citizenship, in the kingdom of the well and the kingdom of the sick. Although we all prefer to use only the good passport, sooner or later each of us is obliged, at least for a spell, to identify ourselves as citizens of that other place."[45] Sontag in turn may have taken inspiration from Virginia Woolf, who at the outset of *On Being Ill* uses a similar image when musing about "the undiscovered countries" disclosed to the ill.[46] Stefan contends that, like moving from one country to another, cancer has a disorienting effect. Aware of the cultural baggage the word "cancer" carries, in *Fremdschläfer* she expresses it thus: "Man sieht, daß das Wort Krebs eine Flut von Ängsten und Gefühlen auslöst, so daß man Begriffe, Regionen, Gebiete verwechselt, sobald es im Raum steht. Man ist sofort topografisch und räumlich verwirrt." (*F*, 104; One sees that the word cancer triggers a flood of fears and emotions, to the effect that one mixes up terms, regions, territories, as soon as it appears. Immediately, one is topographically and spatially confused.) She has only ever been similarly confused or disoriented in the initial period of her time in Canada. The self in cancer is once again hit by foreignness: "Wie heißt das Land, die Gegend, in die es dich jetzt verschlagen hat? Wie bist du hierher gelangt? Niemals würdest du Postkarten abschicken aus diesem Land. Ein Land ohne Briefkästen, ohne Tauben. Die Flüsse fließen vom Meer weg" (*F*, 103; What is the name of the country, the region where you have ended up now? How did you get here? Under no circumstances would you ever send postcards from this country. A country without postboxes, without pigeons. The rivers flow away from the sea)[47]

Looking for points of comparison in her life preceding the breast cancer diagnosis to the experience of the illness, Stefan, the life writer, aestheticizes cancer in *Fremdschläfer* in ways that were "unimaginable" to Sontag.[48] In *Illness as Metaphor*, however, while written to eradicate metaphorical uses of the word "cancer," Sontag herself notes the strong topographical element circulating in the discourse about cancer: "Metaphorically, cancer is not so much a disease of time as a disease or pathology of space. Its principal metaphors refer to topography (cancer 'spreads' or 'proliferates' or is 'diffused'; tumors are surgically 'excised'), and its most dreaded consequence, short of death, is the mutilation or amputation of part of the body."[49]

Stefan picks up on the pervasive topographical/spatial imagery and adapts it to her own circumstances in *Fremdschläfer*. It is a means of, retrospectively, integrating the illness experience as well as the story of her migration into her life narrative, in a manner that makes both manageable. For Stefan, it is a natural step to seek such similarities and relate various life experiences in the echo chamber of her personal memory. In a self-reflexive manner, the book's narrative persona Verena expresses this belief—albeit in a different context—when she observes, "Man ist ja stets versucht, die Dinge, die man zum ersten Mal sieht, mit Dingen zu vergleichen, die man kennt, damit man nicht von zu viel Unbekanntem überwältigt wird" (*F*, 21; One is always tempted to compare things one sees for the first time to things one is familiar with, so as not to be overwhelmed by too much of the unknown). When taken as poetological commentary, these words gain immense significance. For her own cancer writing but also in the place of others', by pointing out the psychological benefit of our tendency toward comparative thinking, the statement offers an explanation for the appeal and continuous use of metaphors in grasping and communicating illness.

With Woolf's 1925 essay *On Being Ill*, lines of which form the epigraph to the second part of Stefan's book,[50] the author shares the conviction that illness cannot be regarded in isolation. It changes everything for the life writer, giving a whole new perspective when "all day, all night the body intervenes," as Woolf puts it. And Woolf goes on, expounding the conviction that mind and body are inseparable, as "the creature within can only gaze through the pane—smudged or rosy; it cannot separate off from the body . . . for a single instant."[51] The ill in *On Being Ill* are the "refuseniks."[52] As their lives are slowed down, they begin to see differently than the people who surround them, "able, perhaps for the first time for years, to look round, to look up—to look, for example, at the sky."[53] In Stefan, this sentiment reads, "Ich darf leben wie eine Wildblume" (*F*, 126; I can live like a wildflower). In illness, the writer can capitalize on this deceleration of perspective and draw creativity from the experienced intensification of being. Stefan, from a standpoint recalibrated by illness, takes the liberty of working creatively around the curious term *Fremdschläfer* to approach, and rewrite, her life story so far. Like Woolf's own text, *Fremdschläfer* is as much about the process of lifelong reading and writing as it is about being ill.

Woolf's influence further makes itself felt in the form of a stylistic decision Stefan took for *Fremdschläfer*: she adapts the English writer's habit of finding alternatives to using the personal pronoun "I" for herself.[54] *Fremdschläfer* accordingly vacillates between *du* (you), *man* (you/one), and—though less often—*wir* (we) instead of speaking of an *Ich* (I). It indicates that the text can be read as a retrospective dialogue of the writer with her self in illness, as well as signaling Stefan's awareness of the representative status of her breast cancer narrative. Stefan writes not from the position of exceptionality but as one of many women being confronted with breast cancer at some point in their lives. *Fremdschläfer* thus offers itself up to appropriation by its readers, and, by not exclusively speaking from the stance of "I," reduces the dominance of the autobiographical narrator figure.[55]

Unlike *On Being Ill* or *Illness as Metaphor*, *Fremdschläfer* is much more explicitly steeped in its author's own personal history and life experience; it makes this public. This may well be the biggest difference from Woolf's and Sontag's guarded authorial positions that, by talking about being ill in the abstract rather than relating it to, and thus unveiling, their personal lives with illness, aim to keep separate their immediate, personal confrontations with the difficult topic from their intellectual grappling with it.

It was Audre Lorde who wrote about cancer as personally and poetically in *The Cancer Journals* as Stefan does in *Fremdschläfer* and who first stressed the fact that her diary excerpts represent shared, not unique, experiences. One can only guess how much of a role model Lorde, as a strong lesbian woman writing breast cancer autobiographically, was for Stefan in the decision to use the cancer experience productively. The poet, activist, and academic believed that only by speaking up as a myriad of voices could the silence and isolation that surrounded women with breast cancer diagnoses in 1970s America be broken. *The Cancer Journals* crucially voices Lorde's firm belief that there is not one uniform correct or "normal" response to the experience of breast cancer. The slim book holds an important place in the history of breast cancer narratives for thus addressing and critically assessing the normalizing discourses surrounding mastectomy and the pressure exerted on women to opt for reconstructive surgery, exposing the gender normativity behind societal images of the ideal female form. Throughout her life, Lorde saw herself perceived as "other in every group I'm part of,"[56] and she lived and wrote from that stance: "Growing up Fat Black Female and almost blind in america [*sic*] requires so much surviving that you have to learn from it or die."[57] Stefan similarly always found herself assigned the place of the other: "Vor vierzig Jahren sagten wir, Frauen sind die Fremden im Patriarchat. Als Lesbe wird dieses Fremdsein verstärkt, manchmal auch unter Frauen." (Forty years ago we said women are the others in patriarchy. As a lesbian this feeling of being alien is amplified, sometimes also among women.)[58]

Contrary to what some might expect from Stefan against this background, the experience of marginalization finds entrance into *Fremdschläfer* not in the form of a separatist attitude; instead, the text shows its protagonist longing for community with others, especially other ill women. The support provided by the various women in her life—Selma (an old friend from home); her partner, Lou; and their joint circle of female friends in Montréal—occupies an important place in the narration. For it, Verena is grateful. But, ultimately, it does not lessen the desire to be with others who, like her, know of illness firsthand, for "die Kranken reden untereinander ohne zu stocken" (*F*, 145; the ill talk among themselves without halting). Yet overall, in the demanding routine of examinations and treatment cycles she too enters, moments of connection with others are rare. And so the author Stefan conjures up a sense of community in writing about the hospital space, drawing attention in *Fremdschläfer* to the presence of physical objects related to breast cancer treatment that surrounded her as a patient and that surround every patient, whether or not they are aware of it—paraphernalia, at first sight of little meaning, that are indicative of something larger. Each individual's experience of illness and treatment forms part of a collective experience: "In den Umkleidekabinen der Röntgenabteilungen steht jeweils ein Plastikbecher, der sich im Lauf des Vormittages mit kleinen runden Aufklebern aus blauem Plastikmaterial anfüllt. Sie sehen wie große Druckknöpfe aus und werden auf die Brustknospen geklebt, um diese bei der Röntgenaufnahme zu schonen. *Ein Behälter voller Brustknospenschoner, die man nach der Mammografie ablegt wie den hellblauen Krankenhauskittel, den man in den Behälter für Schmutzwäsche wirft*. Aus der ganzen Stadt, aus allen Himmelsrichtungen kommen Frauen jeden Tag zum Röntgen und klauben hinterher die blauen Plastikaufkleber von ihren Brüsten und werfen sie in den Behälter." (*F*, 160; emphasis mine; The changing rooms in x-ray departments each have a plastic cup in them that over the course of the morning fills up with small round stickers made from some kind of blue plastic. They look like large snap buttons and they are stuck on the nipples [described in the German as the breasts' buds] in order to protect them during the x-ray. *A container filled with nipple protectors, which you take off after mammography like you take off the light blue hospital gown that you throw in a container for dirty laundry*. From all over the city, from all the points of the compass, women come to get x-rayed every day and afterward pick the blue plastic stickers off their boobs and throw them into the container.)

The rhetorical emphasis put on the full plastic cups through use of repetition and ellipsis indicates the emotional importance of the tangible evidence they hold. In the spirit of Lorde, Stefan's text here dwells on the existence of women within one's close proximity who are undergoing the same procedure, as well as their large number. Both authors are aware of the solace and strength this number can give others. Its realization bears emancipatory potential. To maintain visibility in society as a breast cancer survivor was Lorde's main reason for refusing to wear a prosthesis. It lay the foundations of her political activism in the wake of illness. In their writing about breast cancer, Lorde and Stefan strive to increase public awareness of the illness's omnipresence and the effect it has on countless women's lives—what is more, they point toward sources of unnecessary suffering in the context of a patient's medicalization and social pressures.

Beyond building upon the discussed intertexts in such literary and political ways, we note that Stefan relates to their authors on a personal level. The memory of Lucy Grealy halts the narrative voice of *Fremdschläfer* in a moment of self-pity: "Man hat *Anatomy* [*sic*] *of a Face* gelesen. Dieses Kind hat zwei Jahre Chemotherapie überlebt, viermal pro Woche. . . . Man hat vier Behandlungen vor sich, alle drei Wochen eine, das scheint lächerlich dagegen." (*F*, 134; You have read *Anatomy* [*sic*] *of a Face*. This child has survived two years of chemotherapy, four times a week. . . . You have four treatments scheduled, one every three weeks, that seems laughable in comparison.) As this shows, Verena Stefan the writer is also, and equally importantly, a reader, crucially connecting herself with selected female authors of earlier illness/cancer narratives. She builds on them emotionally and intellectually as she pays homage through citation, incorporates and carries forward their ideas and observations. In this context, it is significant to note that Woolf, Sontag, Lorde, and Grealy are all authors from the Anglophone cultural sphere. No discernible lines of reference to German-language or indeed European authors are drawn: as an author/reader crossing borders, literally as well as intellectually, Stefan appears to be looking for new connections.[59]

An Illness Narrative with an Awareness of a New Audience

The genealogy of feminist writing on illness, disability, and prospective death suffuses Stefan's text. Knowing her literary foremothers to be behind her helps the narrator fulfill a need she at times feels as a cancer patient undergoing treatment: "Du spürst das Bedürfnis, kahl und knochenfarben auszusehen, du möchtest sichtbar machen, was sich im Unsichtbaren abspielt" (*F*, 117–18; You feel the necessity to appear bold and bone colored, you want to make visible what is taking place inside you). Her medium of expression to make these changes apparent is the written word—the writer's most natural territory. In *Fremdschläfer*, Verena grasps her metaphorical migration into cancer country thus: "Du beginnst, einen Pfad zu treten, fußbreit, einen Fuß vor den anderen. Es ist *nicht* abenteuerlich. Du fragst dich, ob der Pfad, den du trittst, in die Unterwelt führt. Du spürst *kein* Verlangen, das Terrain auszukundschaften. Du kommst dir *nicht* wie eine Heldin vor" (*F*, 118; emphasis mine; You begin to tread a path, only as wide as your foot, placing one foot in front of the other. It is *not* adventurous. You wonder if the path you are treading leads into the underworld. You do *not* feel any desire to explore the terrain. You do *not* see yourself as a heroine) Feeling particularly close to death at this moment in the narrative, the desire to be visually identifiable as a cancer patient stems from wanting to bring in line her outward appearance with her inner feelings. At the same time, the author Stefan knows that her subject matter—describing her "journey"—does not make for a classic story, in the sense of being entertaining, as the negations in the above quotation indicate. All the more important, then, are considerations of her readership in writing *Fremdschläfer*. These considerations are influenced by Stefan's own role as reader, as well as other experiences of being part of an audience: living through the ordeal of chemotherapy, Verena remembers a visit to the museum, seeing exhibited "jenes Objekt, von dem sich alle schnell wieder abgewandt haben, als sie in die Glasvitrine auf ein Konglomerat aus Haut, Knorpel, Fettgewebe spähten, das wie ein Stück Pansen zwischen zwei Plexiglasscheiben eingeklemmt war. Eine Fotografin hat ihre amputierte konservierte Brust ausgestellt. Wie abstrakt dieses Objekt anmutete, damals, wie es tatsächlich ein weit entferntes ausgestelltes Objekt war, sicher hinter Glas verwahrt" (*F*, 155; the object from which everyone turned away again quickly after they had peered into the glass cabinet at the conglomeration of skin, cartilage, fatty tissue, which was squashed in between two panes of perspex like a piece of tripe. A photographer had exhibited her amputated conserved breast. How abstract this object appeared to be, back then, how it really was a distant exhibition piece, kept safely behind glass)

Her own change of perspective could not be communicated more drastically than with the aid of this memory. What seemed so far removed from her own life at the time of the museum visit—the touch of cancer, a potential amputation of part of her breasts—has come precariously close. This further makes clear the challenge *Fremdschläfer*'s narrator—and author—sees herself confronted with in sharing her personal illness in writing: remembering how quickly people turned away from the museum piece, the question that surfaces is how to gain an audience or readership, how to connect across diverging lines of experience in the first place, so as to make real for those not afflicted with breast cancer the experience that may seem as vague and distant to them as the exhibited breast did to her back then.

Even in facing such difficulties, the firmly held belief underlying *Fremdschläfer*'s conception is that there is something in the experience that would attract a readership, including those who may identify as healthy or ablebodied. I believe this comes through clearly in the narrative. Observing birdwatchers, Verena notices, "Die Menschen stellen sich mit Ferngläsern und Kameras mit lang ausgezogenen Objektiven auf, um nah heranzuholen, was unerreichbar hoch ist, lautlos, schwerelos" (*F*, 121; The people position themselves with binoculars and cameras with long lenses, to bring closer what is out of reach, soundless, weightless). The narrator here ascribes to people an innate curiosity, if not a potential for sympathy that draws them toward imagining others' lives and experiences. And if it was not for autobiographical narratives like *Fremdschläfer*, one might wonder, narratives that originate from a willingness to share and make accessible an experience that is otherwise "out of reach," in the sense of not being lived experience for at least part of the readership, what else would have the power to bring closer and make a little more comprehensible the "soundless, weightless" experience that is cancer?

Gaps of experience may exist between an author writing from a perspective of, for instance, illness, and readers as yet untouched by such an experience, yet *Fremdschläfer*'s reflections on the turbulent life story of the author's father further illuminate the belief Stefan holds that such gaps can be narrowed. His life story strongly informs Stefan's views on *fremd sein* (being foreign) and *Heimat* (home country), and her understanding of her own—however privileged—status as an immigrant in Canada. On the story of his displacement, and its presence in the family's communicative memory, Verena states, "Wie oft hat man das erzählt bekommen, hat zugehört, weggehört, nachgefragt, wieder vergessen, wieder nachgefragt, zugehört, wieder nicht alles verstanden, die Reiseroute, die Himmelsrichtungen nicht verstanden, wohl aber die Angst" (*F*, 78; Many's the time one has been told this, has listened, failed to listen, asked for details, has forgotten again, and asked again, has listened, and again not fully understood, the travel route, one has not understood the directions, but the fear was understood)

The teller-listener or author-reader relationship, as it comes across here, is one that is certainly not without challenge. True understanding of another's extraordinary experience requires a consistent engagement with that person's story. It necessitates repeated retelling of painful personal histories and repeated attentive listening. An active role is demanded of both parties. More important, for Stefan, than fully understanding the facts of the story of another is to try to grasp the experience of the other emotionally—to get an idea of how that person must have felt, if only for a moment. Consequently, in *Fremdschläfer*, precise communication to the reader of the feelings of the person with cancer is paramount: "Hinter den Wörtern, den gefühlten Wörtern, steckt die eine wirkliche Angst, ausgeliefert zu sein an eine Übermacht, gegen die man nichts ausrichten kann, die mitten im Leben einfach Hand anlegt" (*F*, 61; Behind the words, the felt words, there is the real fear of being at the mercy of a greater power, against which you cannot do a thing, which grabs hold of you in the midst of life).

Fremdschläfer emerges to be a highly crafted retrospective assessment of Stefan's breast cancer in the light of her life story that uses the moment of illness to meditate on the motivation for and power of writing (as a form of speaking) and reading (listening) in general.

Writing Her Way Home

The tactics Verena employs to make Canada home, to find her way around, geographically as well as linguistically, fail her in her transition to the "country of illness." Linguistically, the jargon of the clinic she finds herself confronted with is a foreign language all over again: "Du mußt neue Wörter lernen, *ganglions, lymphnodes,* oder alte Wörter vergessen, dir Namen merken, weil sie plötzlich in den Körper eingeschrieben sind, Orte aufsuchen, an die du nie für dich selbst gedacht hast. *Cancer station. Oncology.* Krebsstation. *Centre du sein.* Breast center. Die Brust hat ein eigenes Zentrum." (*F*, 29; You must learn new words, *ganglions, lymph nodes,* or forget old words, remember names because suddenly they are inscribed into your body, frequent places you have never thought of for yourself. *Cancer station. Oncology. Centre du sein.* The breast has its own center.)

The "ungebetene" (*F*, 42; unbidden) medical terminology invades her life without her consent and, unprepared as she feels, overwhelms her with its consequences, "allen voran das Wort bösartig" (*F*, 42; above all the word malignant). In the face of the situation, the eloquent writer denies herself any talent with words: "Bin ich zur Analphabetin geworden? Ja." In the same breath, however, she dedramatizes, "Lerne ich schlichtweg, ein unliebsames Wort in meinen Text einzufügen? Ja." The text that is her life will henceforth contain the word "cancer." Without a doubt, this signifies a break for her and induces changes in how she goes about her life and her writing: "Muß ich ein Hurenkind einbringen? Ja." (*F*, 123; Did I become illiterate? Yes. Do I simply learn to insert a disagreeable word into my text? Yes. Will I have to integrate a widow line? Yes.) But that she must and will write is beyond question.

Expressing her fundamental confusion with a geographical metaphor, the narrative voice notes, "Auf dem Parkplatz vor einem Krankenhaus ist auf keine Achse, keine Linie mehr Verlaß" (*F*, 74; In the car park in front of a hospital there is no relying on any axis, any line). Her sense of direction, literally as well as metaphorically, is lost in the space of the clinic. The treatment regime a young doctor draws out for her on a straight and strict timeline, however, does not present a valid alternative. Instead, grasping her individual experience in writing, working to make language meaningful again and by doing so shaping her "eigene[] Wahrheit" (*F*,

73; own truth), is a means of resistance for Stefan. Alongside reading her feminist predecessors and walking the streets of her new home Montréal, life writing is a tactic, in Michel de Certeau's sense of the word, that is actively employed to regain a degree of orientation and a sense of agency in her life with cancer.

Stefan's affinity to de Certeau's sociophilosophical writings and, in particular, to his key work *Arts de faire* (1980) shines through here.[60] It is appealing for the weight it lends to the practices of the "ordinary man" or "common hero,"[61] that is, the ordinary person, consumer, or, for that matter, the faceless patient. De Certeau recognizes an individual's agency when seeing subversive potential inherent in one's often overlooked everyday decisions, without denying people's being bound into the dominant and at times repressive systems of power and thought of their contemporary society. As Ian Buchanan puts it, de Certeau in *Arts de faire* is "looking ... for ... subtle movements of escape and evasion,"[62] and he finds them in the acts of reading, talking, walking, dwelling, and cooking, which he highlights as "tactics" utilized by us all: means of creatively resisting, or at least bending, the power structures we find ourselves moving in (and as opposed to the "strategies" employed by institutions). Buchanan, on these grounds, praises de Certeau for having valuably complemented Foucauldian theorizations to provide us with "an adequate account of the other."[63]

The important connection of Stefan's thinking to de Certeau's, and its appeal to her as she engages in "writing from below," is established from the very beginning of *Fremdschläfer*. Using a quotation from *Arts de faire* as the epigraph to the first of three sections that together make up the book, Stefan opens her story with his words: "Die Geschichte beginnt zu ebener Erde, mit den Schritten" (Their story [i.e., the story of pedestrian movements] begins on ground level, with footsteps).[64] Where this story ends or leads to—as opposed to where it begins—is not at all clear at the outset. In a nutshell, this epigraph contains Stefan's poetics of writing illness, one that in many a sense could be called Certeaudian: it is processual, creative writing, unfolding to both writer and reader (between whom there is no hierarchy, as they both start walking "on ground level") as it is written. It is a writing that underlines that everyone's ordinary yet individual story is worth being heard. This kind of storytelling values the micro over the macro perspective. Exploring her experiences on equal terms with the reader by writing the experimental text that became *Fremdschläfer* expresses the wish to regain a kind of familiarity over her own recent past, striving toward a "kartografierte Vertrautheit" (*F*, 13; roughly: mapped/charted familiarity). Word for word, or step by step, Stefan's narrator regains the desired sense of orientation in the process of tackling the challenge that is writing illness and the question of how to incorporate it—effectively and appropriately—into her life writing.

That this is no simple task she sets herself is made transparent in the shape the final text takes. It is interspersed with meta-passages about the difficulties of the writing process. Furthermore, we find repeated expressions of the fear that she may lose the thread of the narrative that is her life: "Jetzt aber entgleitet dir alles, das Manuskript, der Sommer, das Leben. Ich weiß den Text nicht mehr, denkst du, betäubt, wo bin ich stehen geblieben, was ist gerade dran?" (*F*, 49; But now everything is slipping away from you, the manuscript, summer, life. I don't know the text anymore [less literally: I can't remember my lines], you think, dazed, where did I stop, what is next?)[65] Knowing her lines, or knowing how to write, equals knowing how to live. This provides insight into how existential and innate a matter life writing is for Stefan. It is nothing less than a lifeline for the author.

As a consequence, only in and through writing can she face up to illness and reorient herself when all other guidance seems lost. Key to the book is its opening sentence, the one that, in an interview on Swiss radio,[66] Stefan herself called the most important sentence in *Fremdschläfer*: "Du kennst dich aus, abgeschirmt, mit geschlossenen Augen, im Dunkeln" (*F*, 7; You know your way around, shielded, with your eyes closed, in the darkness). This is a statement that identifies the realm of the written word as a well-known, safe space, one that the writer can navigate under the most limiting circumstances. Half asleep, the narrator seems to hear "eine Stimme, die ... um ein Zuhause weiß" (*F*, 7; a voice that ... knows of home), and, upon awakening, she has conceived, indeed simply "sees," a beginning to her text: "Du siehst durch einen schmalen Spalt am unteren Rand der Augenbinde, wie der Text beginnt" (*F*, 7; Through a slim crack at the bottom edge of the sleep mask you see how the text begins). Stefan has made explicit the fact that is only alluded to here in a different interview, stating, "Sprache, das geschriebene Wort ist tatsächlich meine wichtigste Heimat, eine, die mir immer geblieben ist" (Language, the written word is indeed my most important homeland, one that has always remained with me).[67] Other kinds of *Heimat*, this implies, have turned out not to be so reliable.

The Transnationality and Reach of Author and Genre

Even the small wooden house from which the narrator composes the final part of her story is not meant to last (*F*, 177). Situated on a hillside, surrounded by Canadian woods, we learn early on that Verena feels "das Haus könnte jederzeit den Hang hinabrutschen" (*F*, 177–78; the house could slide down the hill anytime). It is a magical place, close to nature, from where she can cast her mind back to the story of her father, whose right to reside in Switzerland always remained provisional. Eventually, upon anticipating her partner asking, "wie es weitergeht" (how it will go on), the storyteller decides, "*At this point of the story*, . . . beginnt das Haus, den Hang hinunterzurutschen" (*F*, 214; the house begins to slide down the hillside). The magic realist ending that ensues from this sentence demonstrates once more, via narration itself, the power of the written word, not least the power of Stefan's own capabilities as storyteller. It is the only unambiguously fictional part of the "novel" and an assertion of her agency as (life) writer. In opting for this ending, the author skillfully evades following the cancer script—of recovery and closure—some readers might still expect. As an open ending, it departs from the illness experience but comments on cancer's lasting and unpredictable effects nonetheless—if only via the narrative voice's satisfaction with the transitoriness of life that leaps from these final, light-hearted pages.

As someone so rooted in text, that is, in both her own and others' writing, Stefan can do away with material homes. Moreover, she can be seen to emancipate herself from any all-too-narrow, static national affiliation. Thirty-two years after *Häutungen*, she renounces the German-language literary and cultural context of her debut.[68] Instead, Stefan has turned into a strength the homelessness that has marked her identity from birth[69] and that was reinforced by the vociferous critical reactions to *Häutungen*. As a feminist and lesbian writer who for the longest time has found herself placed paradoxically in- and outside the canon, she not only accepts but embraces her liminal status in the German-language literary scene—and orients herself instead toward a much more international, feminist scene.[70] Thus, her experience calls to mind Virginia Woolf's dictum that "in fact, as a woman, I have no country. As a woman I want no country. As a woman my country is the whole world."[71] Stefan might, with Woolf, have discovered an element of freedom in her marginalization as a writer. This at least comes through in statements such as the following, in which Stefan reflects on her peculiar standing as an author since the 1970s: "I have since added geographical dislocation to that already ambiguous status when I moved to Montreal in 1998."[72] Note how Stefan phrases this in active rather than passive terms. The publication of *Fremdschläfer* marks her transformation into a writer who actively takes up a transnational stance.

From this stance, she can carry forward the work begun by Audre Lorde (and continued by other female writers, scholars, and activists worldwide since) of bringing into question the normalized breast cancer discourse as it presents itself today and of diversifying this discourse by adding her own experience and literary voice to it. Carter highlights its lack of diversity as a major shortcoming of the popular breast cancer discourse in Western societies today, still finding—with regret—"only limited types of representation in the public arena."[73] She identifies "the public breast cancer patient" today as "almost exclusively heterosexual, white, married, middle class, thin, and thirty."[74] Even though the silence that surrounded breast cancer in the past has been broken, we realize that certain stories are still privileged over others. *Fremdschläfer* or *D'ailleurs*,[75] as it was published in French, as the life writing of an aging woman in a same-sex relationship and an immigrant to Canada at that, provides readers with an alternative to the mainstream in more than one respect.

Remembering the divided responses *Häutungen* received, ranging from euphoric to hostile, Stefan, somewhat sarcastically, summarizes what she sees as the wrongs of the German literary circus: "Einige sagten: Aber das ist keine Literatur, das ist ein Bekenntnis, ein besseres Tagebuch. . . . Für mich war es ein literarisches Experiment, ich habe mit Sprache und Form experimentiert. Ich bin sicher durch die feministische US-Literatur beeinflusst gewesen. Im deutschen Literaturbetrieb gibt es immer Aufpasser und Aufpasserinnen, die dir sofort sagen, was du falsch gemacht hast. Man ist nicht sehr experimentierfreudig. Man gesteht einer Frau nicht zu, ein Experiment zu machen. Das ist auch sehr deutsch: Darf man das? Ist das richtige Literatur? Nein, das ist falsche Literatur."[76] (Some said: But that is not literature, that's a confession, an elevated form of diary. To me it was a literary experiment, I experimented with language and with form. One influence was certainly US feminist literature. In the German literary scene there are always watchdogs who tell you right away what you've done wrong. People there do not like to experiment. They do not grant a woman the right to experiment. That's very German too: Is that allowed? Is that proper literature? No, that's not proper literature.)

With *Fremdschläfer*, another literary experiment, this time from the margins because of illness, she tactically places herself out of reach of that kind of criticism—and beyond the border. From her transnational standpoint, German critics' assessment of the books she writes loses significance. It frees her from having her texts classified as right or wrong, labeled as a success or failure. This particular position Stefan finds for herself, which strengthens her in her continuous autobiographical/creative work, may go some way toward explaining why, chronologically, her 2007 book was among the first to be published in this new wave of illness narratives that can be observed to have washed up on the German literary shore. Orienting herself toward the Anglo-American literary scene, Stefan was able to find many examples of personal illness/disability narratives there.

The increase, internationally, in the number of breast cancer narratives has brought them a larger and more diverse readership than ever before. It must therefore be stressed that this readership no longer consists exclusively of "vulnerable readers," as Herndl suggests.[77] Nor does Couser's claim in *Recovering Bodies*, that "breast cancer narratives are written primarily for an audience at risk, especially perhaps for women struggling to comprehend and to cope with their diagnoses," seem plausible anymore when considering newer publications such as Stefan's.[78] This limited (and, worse, limiting) view on breast cancer or any other illness narratives as therapeutic or *Betroffenheitsliteratur* is, I believe, now obsolete. My suspicion is it may have always been too short sighted—yet this remains for another study to explore adequately.

Today, there is certainly a wider public interest in illness narratives, in Germany as elsewhere. As this chapter has shown, Stefan is aware of both the subjectivity as well as the commonality of the illness experience that she portrays in *Fremdschläfer*. While far from aiming to be a bestselling author, she accordingly reaches out for a larger and more diverse audience than ever—writing for readers from across the spectrum of dis/ability, with varying degrees of personal experience with illness (including, but not limited to, forms of cancer). In her experimentality in approaching breast cancer in personal narrative, Stefan writes on a par with contemporary Anglo-American autobiographers and others around the globe who approach cancer through life writing and try to find new forms for it. Verena Stefan thus significantly contributes to the continuing development of the growing genre of personal illness writing—a genre that, one could speculate, in its universal topic and fundamental, "generally human" concerns intrinsically disregards national boundaries themselves.[79]

* * *

Having previously analyzed texts written from a position of relative health by their authors and with some distance from the time of acute illness, the following chapter has at its center two examples of writing about what turned out to be terminal illness.[80] More precisely, both texts—Christoph Schlingensief's *So schön wie hier kanns im Himmel gar nicht sein!* (It can't possibly be as beautiful in heaven as it is here!, 2009) and Wolfgang Herrndorf's *Arbeit und Struktur* (Work and structure, published online 2010–13)—are diaries.[81] Rather than suggesting an absolute difference between the two kinds of writing, it seems more adequate to point out only a difference of degree between illness narratives like those discussed in chapters 1–3 and what may be labeled end-of-life or autothanatographical writing. This difference can reflect in a stronger focus on death and dying in the latter (and, linked to this, may mean a more obvious engagement with ideas of leaving a legacy). Typically, however, it is a difference that is created in the posthumous negotiation of a text; it is from a later readership's position of hindsight that illness writing that ends with the death of the author is marked as having been on a relatively clear trajectory toward death seemingly all along.[82]

The effect is a disregard for the ambiguity and uncertainty so typical of living with serious illness. It runs the risk of producing reductive readings because it does not recognize the volatility of the writer's situation and effectively irons out the ever-changing circumstances of living with illness; circumstances that make it such a challenge to try to write illness as it unfolds in the first place. At worst, such a reading practice establishes a clear-cut difference between a readership that self-defines as healthy or ablebodied on the one hand and the writer who is constructed as having been doomed to die all along on the other.

As literary scholars of illness narratives (and as disability studies scholars all the more so), we have to reflect on this effect and remain sensitive to our position in time with regard to the genesis and development of the particular text we analyze. This is especially important when researching autothanatographical diaries, as most such research is carried out after the author's death, from a retrospective point of view, a position from which it can be all too easy to neglect the diary's daily rhythm. Apart from gaining a deeper understanding of someone's writing in the light of his or her fluctuating health/illness, with this awareness it becomes possible to analyze critically a text's history of reception, which in turn can reveal a great deal about the cultural place that a text has been, or is being, assigned. I demonstrate what such a detailed and time-sensitive approach may look like in the following, final chapter of this study.

Life writers' choice of medium for artistic expression seems influenced, to a degree, by their sense of how much time remains to them. It is conspicuous that writers and other artists who, upon diagnosis with a potentially fatal illness or in relation to their impending death, feel more distinctly pressed for time, tend to employ short or more instant forms of expression such as poetry (Robert Gernhardt), photography (Hannah Wilke, Jo Spence), blogging, or diary writing. In chapter 4, I analyze the diary genre and its media, and consider what it offers autothanatographers.

4: Confronting Cancer Publicly: Diary Writing in Extremis by Christoph Schlingensief and Wolfgang Herrndorf

Ich halte das Tagebuch wie einen Kompass vor mich hin.

—Wolfgang Herrndorf, *Bilder deiner großen Liebe*

CHRISTOPH SCHLINGENSIEF (1960–2010) and Wolfgang Herrndorf (1965–2013) have produced what in the German-language context are two of the most widely read illness narratives of recent years.[1] It is no coincidence that both their texts are more specifically diaries. I will argue that part of the reason each author with his respective book and blog has caused such a stir is to be found in this choice of genre, or writing mode. The diaries make accessible their suffering and their thought-world in medias res, and in the mode of the everyday. As a genre rooted in the mundane, being a widespread cultural practice as much as a literary art form, the diary is provocative because it brings difficult topics closer to readers than they might like, magnifying, in the cases at hand, the transgressive nature of narrating the experiences of serious illness and of dying. The following examines in which respects the diary form may be particularly suited to the task of writing the ill and dying self. In doing so, the diary will, however, be identified as a challenging format too—for both author and reader alike.

There has been little exploration to date of the diary as a genre for writing the ill and potentially dying self. To be sure, Philippe Lejeune and others have pointed out that the activity of keeping a diary is one often taken up in times of crisis or pain and suffering.[2] However, as Kathryn Carter also asserts, what exactly it is in the diary form that suits autothanatographical expression has not yet been subject to detailed consideration.[3]

The diary holds a special place on the margins of not only the literary field generally but also life writing more specifically. From this outsider position, it can represent the most controversial kinds of autobiographical subject matter, using to its advantage the fact that throughout history and up until today, the diary form has been employed when "writing

---

Epigraph translation: I am holding the diary up in front of me like a compass.

back" from a disadvantaged position. It is closely tied to readers' expectations of immediacy and intimacy, oftentimes conveying an impression of authenticity and confession. Charges leveled against diarists have included narcissism, while their readers have been belittled as voyeurs. The scholarly discourse is not immune to such preconceptions, and literary scholars especially have long avoided the diary.[4] A persistent misconception about the diary is that it is formless and therefore artless. Hand in hand with this belief, common in popular and scholarly understanding alike, goes the assumption that the diary is a monologic and private text type. Only in recent years has a growing number of literary researchers started to question the simplistic and prejudiced view with which diaries have been regarded, when they have been analyzed at all.[5] Beyond addressing the immediate research question of Schlingensief's and Herrndorf's motivation for deciding to share their experiences of illness and nearing death publicly, and investigating their choice of genre, this chapter therefore adds to the scholarship that takes the diary form seriously as an object of investigation in literary studies.

In contemporary literary scholarship, there is some engagement with the aesthetics of the diary, in an endeavor to revise the superficial picture so many have of the text type. This work has not only revealed the genre to be a more complex and artful one than previously thought, but it also uncovers the diary's heterogeneity in form and use across time and place. Scholars like the contributors to *@bsolut? privat! Vom Tagebuch zum Weblog* call into question assumptions about the diary form as used either for intimate confessions of a self, deemed private and unintended for others' eyes, or—to name the other extreme—as exhibitionistic ego narratives.[6] They point out, too, the inherent dialogic nature of the diary that has long gone unremarked: at the very least, a diary is a form of dialogue with oneself across time.[7] Furthermore, it is difficult to imagine the diaries of better-known figures, in particular, to have been written without a potential readership in mind. However, any concerns over such a readership—imagined or real—fade into the background compared to what Lejeune identifies as "the real problem" for diarists: "The real problem is less the danger posed by the gaze of the outsider than that of writing in the face of tomorrow, in the face of emptiness, in the face of no one, in the face of death."[8] This rings particularly true for end-of-life diarists such as Schlingensief and Herrndorf, and suggests there is more to the link so casually established in the quotation of the diary writing practice to death and dying. It raises the question of whether diaries are in fact outward facing, anticipating publication.

Rachel Cottam calls the diary "a capacious genre,"[9] as defining features and generic conventions are notoriously difficult to pin down for this protean form. Possibly with this in mind, Lejeune offers a minimal definition (of a structural, not historical or thematic nature) with his succinct observation: "A diary is a *series of dated traces* [série de traces datées]."[10]

Martin Lindner suggests a more extensive, but equally formal definition: "*Ein Tagebuch besteht . . . aus einer Reihe (1) von graphisch und inhaltlich klar voneinander abgesetzten Teiltexten (2) ohne direkten Adressaten, (3) die explizit oder implizit datiert und chronologisch geordnet sind, (4) die explizit oder implizit auf Ausschnitte einer außertextuellen 'Wirklichkeit' verweisen (5) und in denen das schreibende Subjekt, das durch den 'diaristischen Pakt' mit dem Autor identifiziert wird, explizit oder implizit präsent bleibt.*"[11] (*A diary consists . . . of (1) parts of text that are clearly separated from each other both in layout and in content. It is (2) without a direct addressee, and is (3) dated explicitly or implicitly, and ordered chronologically. (4) The diary's parts explicitly or implicitly refer to an extratextual "reality." (5) The writing subject remains present either explicitly or implicitly, and is identified with the author through the "diaristic pact."*) Yet even a definition like Lindner's, aiming to be descriptive and impartial, may not achieve consensus easily: the point about the addressee is made to delimit the diary from correspondence such as letters; however, counterexamples such as Anne Frank's addressee, Kitty, come to mind. Even though she is fictional, the addressee Frank constructs in her formative diary writing matters, in the sense that it informs both her writing process and our reading of it.

When investigating autothanatographical diary writing, the diary's close ties with a particular construction of time appear to be a particularly important factor in shaping texts and also their reception. No other genre is so sensitive to time passing, or records and incorporates it quite like the diary. As Lejeune indicates, "The main thing is how the diary relates to time and supports truth-seeking,"[12] emphasizing his view that the act of dating diary entries should be read as a pseudo-legal assurance of authenticity. It is a legacy of Lejeune's work on autobiography.[13] As explained in the essay "The Diary as 'Antifiction'" that the quotation stems from, he comes to find that such authorial signals of commitment are taken to the extreme in diary writing. (Lindner, raising the notion of a "diaristic pact" in the quotation above, is obviously influenced by these findings too.) In relation to his definition of the diary as a "*series of dated traces,*" lastly, Lejeune makes a point of stressing the diary as an evolving, dynamic text. Indeed, he understands it to be an occupation more than anything static or complete: "Like correspondence, the diary is first and foremost an activity. Keeping a diary is a way of living before it is a way of writing."[14] In other words, the diary is or becomes text from a reader's point of view only. For its author, it always remains a mode of writing/living, which is highly relevant in the context of autothanatographical diary writing.

Schlingensief's *Tagebuch einer Krebserkrankung*

Christoph Schlingensief, a director of film, theater, and opera as well as a performance and installation artist, had a firm reputation as the enfant terrible of the German arts scene. It is a label that reflects public reactions especially to his early films and art actions like *Mein Filz, mein Fett, mein Hase—48 Stunden Überleben für Deutschland* (1997), during which he was temporarily taken into police custody for putting up a poster asking to have Helmut Kohl killed ("Tötet Helmut Kohl"). Schlingensief, always out to attack complacency, testing the limitations of artistic freedom, continued to challenge the public over the years to come: through his satirical lens, he questioned the harmonious official narrative of German reunification (in *Das deutsche Kettensägenmassaker*), the veracity of German *Vergangenheitsbewältigung* (coming to terms with the past; *Terror 2000*), as well as the effectiveness of the work of the United Nations (*United Trash*) and the absurdity of political election campaigns (*Chance 2000*). By having prostitutes, drug addicts, and homeless people take center stage in his art actions and theater productions, as well as featuring ill/disabled people such as Angela Jansen (*Kunst und Gemüse*) or his *Freakstars*, asylum seekers (*Bitte liebt Österreich*) or ex-neo-Nazis (*Hamlet*), Schlingensief created a public space for those at the margins of society. However, by the time Schlingensief was asked to direct the Wagner opera *Parsifal* at the Bayreuther Festspiele 2004–7, a major feature of German high culture, the dubious label enfant terrible had begun to appear out of date. The invitation arguably serves as proof that Schlingensief and his work had become an established part of German "Hochkultur" (high culture).[15]

The artist had always invested much of his person into his work and vice versa, including appearing on the theatrical stage in all of his plays since spontaneously doing so in a performance of *100 Jahre CDU—Spiel ohne Grenzen* (1993) as replacement for Alfred Edel, lamenting the actor's death on stage. In the words of Klaus Biesenbach, "Von diesem Moment an war der Filmemacher Schlingensief als Performer Schlingensief in einen einzigartigen Real-Theater-Künstler mutiert"[16] (From this moment onward the filmmaker Schlingensief as performer Schlingensief had mutated into a unique artist of real-world theater). This made it increasingly difficult to speak meaningfully of any kind of separation between the spheres of supposedly (personal) life and (public) work. When diagnosed with cancer in 2008, for Schlingensief the question thus was not whether it would be appropriate to incorporate the experience, and the diary material it yielded, into his work but rather when and how to do so. As someone whose work, especially his early performances, often relied on media interventions and the involvement of audiences or reactions of passers-by to gain momentum, Schlingensief anticipated a mixed public reaction and charges of commodification. In the diary, which is a transcribed selection of audio recordings from his first year with cancer,[17] he reflects at an early stage on the appropriation of his personal illness experience for his work. He questions the artistic productions he had made about his father's death the year before,[18] referring to himself as "Verwertungsanlage Schlingensief junior" (*So schön*, 152; Schlingensief Jr. recycling plant). For dealing with his own serious diagnosis, he realized he had a moral obligation to process his experience publicly—just as he had "used" other people's stories in his art: "Wenn es jetzt um mich geht, dann darf das nicht fehlen, schon aus Gerechtigkeitsgründen nicht. . . . Aber es darf eben auch nicht zu einem Zeitpunkt stattfinden, wo die Verwertungsanlage noch gar nichts kapiert hat von dem, was sie erlebt hat." (*So schön*, 152–53; Now that it's about me, this [i.e., using his illness experience for his art/work] must be included, out of fairness alone. . . . But then it can't take place at a point in time when the recycling plant has not yet understood any of what it has been experiencing.)

The period in which Schlingensief received his first intensive treatment, covered in the published diary from January to April 2008, can be considered a time of incubation, metaphorically speaking. The act of diary keeping was a crucial part of beginning to grasp the reality of his diagnosis, with all its possible consequences, and fostered the kind of introspection revealed in the quotation above. The diary looks inward, however, to prepare its author for stepping out of the role of passive patient and back onto the stage and screen, to become more present and harder to ignore than ever. It launched his late work, which had a great impact on German cultural consciousness because of the artist's deliberate reframing of his work in the light of his experience of illness.[19] Schlingensief had grappled with illness, disability, and death before as he addressed individual and societal wounds. Concerning his own life and death and the threat of cancer from within, however, he observes that his confrontation with these issues is different, perhaps more authentic: "Jetzt ist es anders" (*So schön*, 159; It's different now).

Against this backdrop, it is all the more striking that scholarship on Schlingensief's late work hitherto seems largely to ignore *So schön wie hier kanns im Himmel gar nicht sein!*[20] This, to some extent, fits in with a widespread lack of engagement with this text type or genre as outlined in this chapter's introduction. The first half of this comparative chapter begins to redress this omission by investigating how Schlingensief turned to the diary form as suited to the task of writing the dying self and how the use of the diary as exploratory space maps on to his previous work or departs from it. In the analysis, *So schön* will be identified as central to the creative period of the artist's final years.

As outlined in more detail in the introduction to this book, German literary criticism dismisses illness narratives, and particularly autothanatographies, as *Bekenntnisliteratur* (confessional literature) or as *Boulevard* (tabloidesque);[21] both terms are employed in a derogatory manner and indicate that critics struggle with the content of these new narratives about illness/disability and dying as much as with their documentary yet highly personal mode, which is still generally deemed artless. In contrast to that stance, this chapter (as well as this study as a whole) is built on the conviction that contemporary autobiographical narratives, including those with illness as their focus, can do cultural work of similar importance to that achieved by fiction.

While Schlingensief's diary shows features of the confessional, in that its subject is speaking to himself but also to an implied readership that may pass judgment on him, it is reductive to read it solely as that. Close reading of Schlingensief's published diary entries reveals that the recordings serve a variety of purposes: in documenting his hospital days, test results, and treatment decisions, the records are empowering, as they enable the patient to go over new developments as they unfold each day. They also help him to anticipate and manage his own death from an early stage, by registering thoughts on his will and ideas for a comprehensible legacy. Recording his feelings on a daily, and sometimes hourly, basis furthermore helps manage the author-subject's immediate emotional reaction to this confrontation with a serious diagnosis, and the gradual realization of what this may mean for his life and his work. The act of speaking into the dictaphone therefore can be said to be therapeutic, too—yet it certainly cannot be limited to this or any other single function.

Going Public with Cancer: Risks and Reasons

If in the twenty-first century, in a post-postmodern setting, autobiographical endeavors of any kind seem to pose a challenging task, writing in the face of illness and near death amplifies dramatically the issues one deals with in life writing. Especially in the adverse cultural climate outlined in the introduction to this book, autothanatographers are rightfully paranoid, haunted writers. A large number of people diagnosed with cancer remain silent about their physical, psychological, and emotional condition; the medical progression of their disease; and their experience of social exclusion from a seemingly ablebodied society. This not only creates a burden of representation for diarists like Schlingensief but also exposes these writers to the danger of being known primarily for their illness. And it leads to situations such as the one faced by Schlingensief in Munich in September 2009. At the restaging of *Mea Culpa*, it pains the director to receive furious final applause, which he interprets as an audience bidding him farewell prematurely. He notes the situation with irony: "Klar, ich tue ja auch selbst alles dafür: Gefühlte zehn Krebsbücher hab ich geschrieben, alles Bestseller, dazu sechzig Theaterstücke, Krebsopern, auch alles Bestseller. . . . Es ist schon eine Selbstentfremdung, die da stattfindet."[22] (Sure, I encourage this myself: I have written what feels like ten cancer books, all of them bestsellers, on top of that sixty plays, cancer operas, again all bestsellers. . . . It is indeed [a process of] self-alienation that is taking place.) Given the risks involved in taking up such a precarious subject position in the public eye, the question that needs to be addressed is why Schlingensief not only recorded but also disseminated his cancer diary so widely.

The decisive impetus for beginning the recordings, and for returning to the dictaphone night after night, seems to lie buried in the self-critical suspicion: "Vielleicht habe ich auch nicht richtig gelebt, vielleicht habe ich nur sehr viel Hektik verbreitet" (*So schön*, 30; Maybe I haven't lived right, maybe I have just caused [literally: spread] a massive fuss). It is a torturing thought and initiates a search for meaning. In various subsequent entries, the author returns to this nagging concern: "Mein Problem ist, dass ich nicht genau formulieren kann, was ich in meinen Arbeiten getrieben habe, was mich in meinem Leben geritten hat. . . . Ich weiß nicht, was ich den Leuten erzählen soll. Ich weiß auch nicht, was ich mir selbst erzählen soll." (*So schön*, 42; My problem is that I can't exactly put into words what I strove for in my works, what has driven me in my life. . . . I don't know what to tell people. I also don't know what to tell myself.)

Schlingensief at this point knows that some sort of narrative will be requested of him as a public figure, but he also needs one for himself, and the recordings offer a testing ground for this narrative. The lack of clarity, or "Klarheit" (*So schön*, 31), he perceives is a driving force behind the recordings and the plotless diaristic form he chooses to adopt allows for this challenging search. It enables him to follow a circular rather than linear movement, revisiting thoughts he develops in earlier entries, discarding some, repeating and developing others.

The diarist, captured on tape in his own recording, declares his failure: "Ich bin nicht mehr der, der ich bin. Bin nicht der, der ich war. Ich bin nicht der, der ich werden wollte." (*So schön*, 68; I am no longer who I am. I am not who I was. I am not who I wanted to become.) What underlies this triple negation, suggesting a Nietzschean influence,[23] is the painful insight that he might not be granted the necessary time to yet attain self-realization. However, in recognizing this failure lies the chance of recasting himself in his role as artist and public figure. Schlingensief therefore calls this opportunity for a change of course a "schmerzhaftes Geschenk" (*So schön*, 163; painful gift). Addressing himself as *du* and by name, which signals his accountability, Schlingensief sets himself a challenging task: "Du musst aus dem, was du jetzt hast, Fülle spüren, aus dem Weiterwurschteln und Basteln. . . . Vielleicht schaffst du es ja, Christoph." (*So schön*, 234; You must make the most out of what you have now, out of muddling on and being creative. . . . Maybe you will make it after all, Christoph.) In some sense, the illness experience can be said to have repoliticized Schlingensief's creative work, having given him a cause to fight for from a distinctly personal stance and thereby reinvigorating his interventions in contemporary sociopolitical discourse.

In rethinking his approach to this "life/work," his engagement with Joseph Beuys, who had been a constant reference point throughout his career,[24] crucially serves to give direction. Referring to Beuys's installation piece *Zeige deine Wunde* (*Show Your Wound*, 1974–75) in a recorded entry dated "Donnerstag, 21. Februar" (*So schön*, 194),[25] Schlingensief explores the place of sorrow and suffering in contemporary society. He speculates that because *Leid* (suffering) has lost its value and is conventionally not shared but silenced, being confronted with his potentially terminal illness causes people to be extremely uneasy around him. He wonders, "Diese Leute haben doch auch alle ihre Einschnitte, ihre Wunden. Warum zeigen wir sie uns nicht gegenseitig? Beuys sagt: 'Zeig mal deine Wunde. Wer seine Wunde zeigt, wird geheilt. Wer sie verbirgt, wird nicht geheilt.'" (*So schön*, 197; These people all have their own incisions, their wounds. Why don't we show them to each other? Beuys says: "Go on, show me your wound. Those who show their wound will be healed. Whoever hides theirs will not be healed.")

Schlingensief applies this to his own situation thus: "Ja, das ist es vielleicht: Wer seine Wunde zeigt, dessen Seele wird gesund. Denn der Krebs ist weg, aber der Einschnitt bleibt." (*So schön*, 197; Yes, maybe this is it: The soul of those who show their wound will heal. Because the cancer is gone, but the incision remains.) Appropriating Beuys, and via Beuys citing the wider "Topos der Ostentatio Vulnerum" (topos of the *ostentatio vulnerum* [the showing forth of Christ's wounds]),[26] he thinks beyond the personal, too: "Einschnitte" (caesuras), as Schlingensief makes explicit, may constitute anything from the breakup of a relationship to the loss of a loved one, an accident as well as a serious diagnosis like his own (*So schön*, 196). He thus explicitly opens up the conversation that he believes needs to be had, instead of closing it down. "Zeige deine Wunde" becomes a maxim Schlingensief vows to act on in the space of the diary. Like a mantra, this belief in admitting and sharing one's wound publicly guides his processing of his being ill and dying, both on and off stage, from then on.

As Nancy K. Miller and Jason Tougaw observe,[27] when giving testimony, be it of the AIDS crisis or the Holocaust, and also when publicly recounting the experience of cancer, "we bear witness individually for ourselves, our own sake, but always in relation to others (again, both individually and in the name of a community). In that process, the act of testimony also becomes a speech act and draws meaning from its effects on the listener . . ., whose empathic response can be palliative, if not curative."[28] In Schlingensief's case, the act of testimony is quite literally a speech act. Resuming an active role by speaking, recording, and listening back to one's own voice can be assumed to afford some initial relief to the cancer sufferer. There is no denying that autothanatography is very much about the "auto," the self that finds itself literally and possibly very suddenly in extremis and has to deal with this. The autothanatographical endeavor often starts out as a form of self-care. Accordingly, finding a means of expressing the ill and potentially dying self through the recordings is indeed consoling for Schlingensief: "Wenn ich noch denke, wenn ich noch aktiv bin, dann leide ich nicht. ... Und wenn ich über die Ausrangierten, die Weggesperrten nachdenke, dann leiden vielleicht auch sie nicht mehr. Das ist das Grundprinzip: Solange ich über mich und andere nachdenke, leide ich nicht. Und umgekehrt: Solange man über mich nachdenkt, leide ich nicht." (*So schön*, 60; While I still think, while I am still active, I do not suffer. ... And when I think about those who are outcast, who are incarcerated, then maybe they don't suffer anymore either. That's the basic principle. As long as I think about myself and others, I do not suffer. And vice versa: as long as someone thinks about me, I do not suffer.)

In his own words, the artist grasps intuitively what research into psychic trauma confirms. The self cannot be regarded in isolation from its social context, especially when knowing there are others out there suffering just the same. The healing of the Beuysian—or traumatic—wound can only truly begin once it is shared, via publication, not only with other ill people but also with a wider public. This act of sharing, and the response it triggers, has the potential to endow the experience of illness and dying with particular significance. The role of mediator between the terminally ill and the ablebodied, which Schlingensief assumes over the course of the diary, lends a moral purpose to his act of confronting his personal illness so publicly. The private and the public function of keeping and disseminating a record of illness and dying are thus intricately linked.

As autothanatographer, Schlingensief discloses on several occasions that his thoughts on his own work are being recalibrated by the life-threatening illness: "Vielleicht muss ich Sachen machen, die sich noch stärker auf die Gesellschaft beziehen. Am Ende, egal wann, will ich sicher sein können, dass meine Arbeit einen sozialen Gedanken hatte. Dass meine Projekte der Frage nachgegangen sind, warum manche Systeme Zwänge brauchen und andere nicht, wie diese merkwürdigen Zwänge funktionieren, und vor allem, warum manche Leute in diesen Systemen nicht vorkommen." (*So schön*, 32–33; Perhaps I have to do things that are even more relevant to society. In the end, no matter when, I want to be certain that a social dimension underlies my work, in the sense that my projects questioned why some systems need coercion and others do not, how these strange coercions work, and, above all, why some people do not have a place in these systems.)

He brings to the fore a desire to continue the social concerns of his creative work but now with renewed vigor, despite the uncertainty of how this will affect it (*So schön*, 146). His cancer diary becomes a repository for visions of how his work could be reshaped: his "Afrika-Idee" (*So schön*, 204) that will develop into the Operndorf Afrika in Burkina Faso[29] and his reflections on whether and how well other ill or traumatized people out there cope (*So schön*, 87–88, 104–5), which eventually initiate his setting up of the *Geschockte Patienten* forum,[30] must suffice as just two examples. Both these projects leave the theatrical stage and are sociopolitical as much as artistic endeavors.

In rethinking the trajectory of his work, Schlingensief also begins to question whether theater is the best medium for it. On April 1, 2008, after visiting the ensemble rehearsing *Jeanne D'Arc* at the Deutsche Oper, Schlingensief records the following entry: "Überlege, ob und wie ich diese Arbeit unter den neuen Bedingungen weitermachen und das Erlebte sinnvoll für die Bühne transformieren kann. Vor allem frage ich mich, ob die Bühne der richtige Ort ist, um Begegnungen zwischen Menschen zu erzeugen." (*So schön*, 213; Thinking about whether and how I can continue this work under the new circumstances and if I can transform this experience for the stage in a meaningful way. Above all I am wondering if the stage is the right place to generate encounters between people.) It seems fitting that this radical questioning of the social relevance of the theatrical world is voiced in a new medium. If theater, at its worst, can be ephemeral and socially exclusive, the diary—although initially seemingly private and "of the moment"—signals inclusivity and can function as a lasting repository of ideas, once it is shared with the wider public in book form. Both characteristics of the diary genre match the artist's desire to expand his sphere of action into the wider social realm, as is explored further below.

The Diary Form and Its Suitability for Autothanatography

Committing his thoughts to tape and later publishing them as text, Schlingensief remained accountable to the radical alterations of his perspectives through cancer. His entry from March 3, 2008, demonstrates this when it ends in the promise, to both himself and the implied reader: "Eins ist klar: Wenn die Sache hier gut läuft, dann werde ich alles dafür tun, nicht zu vergessen, wer ich in den letzten zwei Monaten gewesen bin. Das darf ich nie mehr vergessen. Amen." (*So schön*, 201; One thing is clear: if this goes well, then I will do everything I can in order not to forget who I have been for the past two months. I must never forget that ever again. Amen.) Spelling it out in this way works against the risk of forgetting, or abandoning, his commitment. Concluding that day's entry using the Judeo-Christian formula "Amen" (so be it) affirms his intentions.

Like any diarist, Schlingensief is concerned with conveying truthfulness and sincerity, underlining his authenticity by dating and thus validating each entry. The author of a diary, as writing subject, therefore can be said to become "auf eine Weise Teil des Textes, wie es bei den anderen literarischen Formen (ausgenommen den Brief) nicht der Fall ist" (in a way part of the text that is not the case with other literary forms [except the letter]), as Lindner writes.[31] Nonetheless, the diary is not unmediated reality, and, in writing, a diaristic persona is created. In the case of Schlingensief, this persona maps onto his public persona already familiar to his readers. With every entry anew, the diary puts special emphasis on the tacit agreement of trust that necessarily exists between author and reader. The writer endows the diaristic text with signs of authorial intention, and the reader picks up on these in combination with the author's "proper name" on the cover of a book or manuscript.[32] The diarist's unique presence—as author-narrator and protagonist—is thus constantly in the foreground. It may appear fitting, therefore, that the cover of *So schön* shows a section of a black-and-white portrait photograph of its author, who can be seen looking directly at the beholder. All in all, the choice of medium seems to suit Schlingensief as an artist who had always sought ways of stressing his full commitment to his work—a tendency that intensifies in his late period.

Highly conscious of its limits, the diary never claims greater validity than for the moment in which the entry is composed. In this sense, it may be the most humble form of autobiographical creativity. It does not attempt to be more than a collage of impressions or snapshots and resists any larger narrative arc. When Susanna Egan notes that the diary form "replaces chronology and teleology with a continuous present tense," she rightly finds this form apt for autothanatography.[33] For Schlingensief, to go beyond the moment often seems impossible: "Das Schlimmste ist, glaube ich, dass alles Fiktive, alles für die Zukunft Erträumte ausgeträumt ist. Im Moment ist alles endlos real und damit komme ich nicht klar." (*So schön*, 188; Worst of all is, I think, that all that's fictitious, all the dreams for the future have been vanquished. At the moment everything's endlessly real and I can't cope with that.) His diary writing is bound to always be provisional and vulnerable to being overrun by the progression of disease that the writing subject knows he cannot in any way control or foresee. This is part of what Egan has in mind when she stresses the difficulties autothanatographers face: when writing in extremis, she believes, "the adequacy of linguistic (therefore linear) narrative breaks down, the body provides no familiar (therefore readable) signs, and the positioning of the individual in time lacks a forward trajectory."[34] In this regard, the gaps between the recordings are as significant as the content of the autothanatographical diary entries themselves, standing in for all that may resist formulation.

While Schlingensief's writing, then, is bound to the moment both in (diaristic) form and in (autothanatographical) content, the decision he makes every single day to record an entry in itself expresses what to many must be an astounding hopefulness (or simulation of it) in the face of a life that has become "endlos real." Every diary entry posits a "wager on the future,"[35] as Lejeune puts it; in other words, the entries are wagers on being read and reread, at least by one's own older self. In the case of the autothanatographical diary, this creative expression of hope is especially significant; once the writing subject has no more future, there is, consolingly, hope for a future embodied by an anticipated readership.

Lastly, in this context it is important to note the diary's accessibility, increased not least by Schlingensief's use of ordinary, spoken language. The closing sentences to many of the chapters illustrate this. They read, "Schon anstrengend alles" (*So schön*, 35; It's exhausting, all of it), "So eine unendliche Kacke" (*So schön*, 39; Such bullshit, and no end in sight), or they end in Schlingensief bidding, "Gute Nacht" (*So schön*, 131, 156; Good night), in cases when he recorded late at night. Not unimportantly, sharing such detail about the recording situation, that is, the time of day in the last case, only heightens the intimacy between the diarist and his audience. It invites readers to imagine Schlingensief's present retrospectively and marks the text as true to his spoken words and thus authentic. The diary is an inclusive form that aims at minimizing the gap between the author and his readership. After all, all readers could potentially be or become diarists themselves. For the artist who had always insisted that his work had to bear relevance to people's lives or, in his own words, "an der Trennung von Leben und Kunst kratz[en]"[36] (chafing at the separation of life and art), the diary form in which "life and literature meet" seems a natural choice.[37]

A logical step, in this light, also is the decision to have the diary recordings transcribed. While accepting the loss of "Lebensspuren" (signs / traces of life) such as the tone of Schlingensief's voice,[38] what is gained through this change of medium is the wide reach of a book which can be mass-produced and easily circulated. Printed and bound as a book, the *Tagebuch einer Krebserkrankung* forms a lasting, widely available, and durable way of documenting and circulating Schlingensief's first intense months with cancer.

The Reader—Implicated beyond the Page

The relationship between the diarist and his or her readership is a highly charged one; the reader ultimately shares in the vulnerability—that is, the mortality—of the author. Confronted with their own fears and anxieties, readers can, however, employ "self-protective forms of resistance that say 'not me,' 'not really,' 'not yet.'"[39] This type of reaction, at its most extreme, can break into more aggressive expressions of rejection too, as has been exemplified par excellence in the feuilleton reviews discussed in this book's introduction.[40] Writers such as Schlingensief therefore find themselves in an unfavorable position that requires them "to persuade a reading public that this profoundly disturbing experience is not obscene."[41]

It follows that, without the prospect of any consolation, the implied reader of this diary is the opposite of an ideal reader. Consequently, Schlingensief can be found to elaborate on certain points, trying to win over the imagined reader with his arguments. This reader is often referred to in the collective as "die Leute": "Ich höre die Leute schon reden: Der wilde Schlingensief, der Provokateur, das Enfant terrible . . . natürlich wahnsinniger Überlebenswille . . . wahnsinnige Anstrengungen . . . hat bis zum letzten Atemzug gekämpft . . . am Ende dann doch in der Klinik soundso . . ." (*So schön*, 49; ellipses in original; I can already hear the people talk: that crazy Schlingensief, the provocateur, the enfant terrible, . . . incredible survival instinct, obviously . . . such amazing effort . . . fought until his last breath . . . but in the end then in the clinic blah blah . . .) Obvious discontent is expressed in anticipation of his suffering from cancer being turned into a clichéd narrative. Schlingensief fears yet simultaneously dares to envisage a "news story" that he may not identify with. Elsewhere too, especially when he comes to talk about intimate topics such as his relationship with his partner Aino, his faith, or extreme emotional states of anxiety or depression, this critical reader figure is conjured up to be argued against: "Das mag für viele Leute furchtbar klingen, aber ich kann nur sagen: . . ." (*So schön*, 168; This may sound terrible to many people, but all I can say is: . . .) Variants of this rhetorical structure reappear several times in the text (e.g., *So schön*, 177, 200).

Self-consciously, Schlingensief assumes that his reader will outlive the author and have the last word. This is what the vulnerable writer, as autothanatographer, has to accept when setting out as diarist. Schlingensief does so to bear his own approaching death, which he can only imagine being able to do in "ein[em] Akt von Arbeit, Schmerzen, Produktivität, Leiden, Erzählen" (*So schön*, 63; an act of work, pain, productivity, suffering, narration). Planning to keep his voice in the public discourse, he declares defiantly, "Ich finde, das muss ich mir erlauben dürfen" (*So schön*, 63; I think I have to allow myself that much). The autothanatographer as endangered subject is both highly sensitive to the critical readership he anticipates and assertive in insisting on his right to direct his demise on the public stage, even instrumentalizing it for purposes close to his heart, such as the Operndorf Afrika.

The Impossibility of Ending the Autothanatographical Project

The printed *Tagebuch* stops dramatically, in the midst of a situation of extreme uncertainty for its author/subject. In the last three entries from December 2008, which are preceded by a significant gap from April 20 to December 3, Schlingensief reacts to the discovery of new metastases in his remaining right lung. Nearing the last few pages of the published diary, the reader is suddenly confronted with the following lines: "Guten Morgen. Es ist halb neun, und das Logbuch von Mister Spock tut jetzt hier Folgendes kund: Was bisher geschah, ist nicht wichtig, aber was heute geschehen wird, das ist wichtig." (*So schön*, 251; Good morning. It's half past eight, and Mr. Spock's log announces the following: what happened so far is not important; but what will happen today, that is important.)

Talking of himself in the third person and mockingly taking on the role of the otherworldly *Star Trek* character Spock is Schlingensief's attempt at injecting some humor into the way he delivers this grave piece of news. It is also a distancing strategy that enables him to make the announcement in the first place. Fashioning himself ironically as the half-human, half-alien character famous for his logic and stoicism highlights the diarist's own lack of wisdom with regard to the situation he finds himself in that morning. The statement supersedes all that came previously and demonstrates once more the challenges involved both in writing and reading Schlingensief's autothanatographical diary, as well as the volatility of the autothanatographical project as a whole, which constantly threatens to overwhelm both its author/subject and the empathetic reader. These dramatic lines belie any assumption that publication could offer a sense of closure to the complicated and constantly evolving story of illness and dying.

Recorded before setting off to the hospital for a further CT scan, the book's final words are: "Und jetzt fahren wir gleich los" (*So schön*, 255; And now we are about to set off). They mark the beginning of an even more precarious phase of Schlingensief's life with cancer, as its writer is well aware. The way the *Tagebuch* breaks off recalls the crisis that provoked it and broke into Schlingensief's life just as abruptly. Although this particular volume of diary entries stops when the recordings are prepared as a product for the book market, what is signaled to the reader, importantly, is that Schlingensief's crisis of nearing death—and hence his diary-keeping activities—continues. At around this point, he begins to use his personal *Schlingenblog* as a diaristic space, thus breaking out of the medium of the book into a more immediate way of sharing material.[42] The last diary entry collected in *So schön* is dated December 27, 2008; from then on, the blog takes over as the sole vehicle for publication of diaristic material.

Schlingensief's relentless end-of-life writing practice seems to confirm what Lejeune stresses in his theoretical work on the diary: "It is as diary that autobiography is unfinishable."[43] Lejeune's standpoint here is that as autobiographer, "I am always at the endpoint of my story,"[44] that is, writing with a conclusion in mind, however artificially construed it may be. More distinctly looking back than the diarist, autobiographers review their life up to the point they begin the writing process, dealing less with the present (though potentially writing up to it) and more with the past: "If something escapes you, it's the origin, not the ending."[45] To draw a line under a certain stage of one's life is something the diary as a genre makes difficult. The diary can only break off but never be concluded. It ends in abandonment of one's writing or in death. Activity on the *Schlingenblog* consequently ceases only once its author/producer dies, with the last entry dating only two weeks before Schlingensief's passing in August 2010.[46]

The move to the blog has several advantages for the end-of-life writer. First, it provides a more immediate way of sharing an entry with an online community. Second, its electronic form makes it easy to keep for Schlingensief, who now increasingly works on it alongside other projects, as much as it makes it easy to follow, from any location, at any time. Finally, the blog enables its author to keep a diary that incorporates the use of many media, in a way that would not be possible in book form. This suits Schlingensief, who takes to using the space as a kind of multimedia scrapbook, adding pictures, scanned newspaper clippings, and what he calls a "Video-Tagebuch" (video diary) function over the course of the blog's existence as a live site. The *Schlingenblog* accompanies its author's rehearsals for *Mea Culpa* and provides a realm in which the artist continues to push himself to critically evaluate his own belief systems. It also serves as a place where he can commemorate friends' deaths by posting obituaries for actor Achim von Paczensky, for instance, or for Wolfgang Wagner. The blog, like the audio recordings previously, is a tool serving various concerns: it enables Schlingensief to continue to participate in contemporary debates, such as the Helene Hegemann plagiarism scandal but also, in the light of his declining health, to develop his thoughts on an afterlife and to continue to confront squarely his own dying beyond the book publication of his *Tagebuch einer Krebserkrankung*.

In the later memoir *Ich weiß, ich war's* (I know, it was me / I know, I did it, 2012), a collage of material that looks back on his work/life more explicitly and along thematic lines, Schlingensief remarks, "Man kann so einen ersten Bericht nicht so stehen lassen, das geht nicht. Das erste Buch kommt mir inzwischen wie eine zwar völlig ehrliche, aber auch wie eine sich selbst blendende Aufzeichnung vor."[47] (You can't have such a first account as a stand-alone piece, that's impossible. Looking back now, the first book seems to me to be an entirely honest, but equally self-deceptive account.) The autothanatographical diary does not age well, as Schlingensief's own subject position as dying author continues to alter dramatically as time passes. Yet its "errors," as the diarist perceives them later, are valuable in the sense that they were true to his perspective at the time; *So schön* remains an important document testifying to Schlingensief's first year of living with cancer.

The blog post that came to be Schlingensief's last bears a striking equation in its convoluted title: "07-08-2010- DIE BILDER VERSCHWINDEN

AUTOMATISCH UND ÜBERMALEN SICH SO ODER SO !—'ERINNERN HEISST : VERGESSEN !' (Da können wir ruhig unbedingt auch mal schlafen!)"[48] (07-08-2010- THE IMAGES DISAPPEAR AUTOMATICALLY AND OVERWRITE THEMSELVES ONE WAY OR ANOTHER !—"TO REMEMBER IS : TO FORGET !" [In which case we can certainly go to sleep for a change!]). In the post, the diarist touches on the wide gap between this and his previous entry, regretting this silence. He goes on to admit that he has just deleted a recently posted video, wondering, "Wen soll das das [sic] interessieren?" (Who is supposed to care about this?) As readers we do not know what news the author has had that day—we learn only that there were "wieder infos zu neuen dingen" (again info on new things)—but a deeply felt sadness and disillusionment are expressed in the short post.

"Erinnern heißt vergessen" had already played a role in the printed *Tagebuch* (*So schön*, 146). In a long entry dated "Dienstag, 5. Februar," Schlingensief discusses this phrase. It is a leitmotif that guided his work for quite some time, for instance, when directing the opera *Parsifal* in Bayreuth in 2004 and in creating the exhibitions *18 Bilder pro Sekunde* (Eighteen frames per second) and *Querverstümmelung* (Cross-mutilation) not long after his father's death in 2007. Schlingensief is fascinated by the insight that—if every act of remembering is unique, never quite the same as before—this means "dass jede Erinnerung eine Übermalung des Ereignisses ist und je nach Übermalung eben auch viel vergessen wird" (*So schön*, 146; that every act of memory overwrites the original event and that much is forgotten accordingly). This paradox stays with the artist as he confronts first his father's and then his own illness and dying. He actively grapples and experiments with it. At the very beginning of the autothanatographical process as documented in *So schön*, he therefore wonders, "wann und wie ich die Übermalung meiner eigenen Guillotine in Angriff nehmen kann" (*So schön*, 146; when and how I can begin the task of overwriting my own guillotine).

Bridging the Gaps

The first half of this chapter has demonstrated why the diary form provided Schlingensief with the most clear-sighted way of expressing himself autobiographically as life-threatening illness and ultimately the reality of his own death encroached upon him. It highlighted the publication of selected diary entries in *So schön wie hier kanns im Himmel gar nicht sein!* as constituting the beginning of a new creative period, rather than an end to Schlingensief's artistic achievements. With the diary, Schlingensief entered into a new phase of engaging in the politics of the personal.

In one respect especially, this contrasts with the situation in the late 1970s and early 1980s, when the German-language literary scene last witnessed a similar upsurge in intimate writings on illness and death, many of them composed from a diaristic stance. Generally, these were published posthumously, such as Brigitte Reimann's diaries and her exchange of letters with Christa Wolf toward the end of Reimann's life (edited by Wolf's reader at Aufbau Verlag, Angela Drescher) or Maxie Wander's diaries and letters, published for the first time in 1980 on the initiative of her widower, Fred Wander, a fellow writer who edited the material himself. Publication often depended on the material left behind having such literary guardians. It was Adolf Muschg, for example, who solicited Helmut Kindler for the publication of Fritz Zorn's *Mars* (1977) and provided a foreword. Another Swiss author, Max Frisch, made sure that his friend Peter Noll's *Diktate über Sterben & Tod* (*In the Face of Death*, 1984), composed by Noll after making the controversial decision to refuse medical treatment for his cancer, were published posthumously.[49]

While all of these writers, in a more or less direct way, would have had a future readership in mind when they began their autothanatographies, Schlingensief brings his readers into his present, knowingly overtaxing them when confronting them with his suffering and dying as it unfolds: "Ich will in dem Zustand, in dem ich jetzt bin, jemand anderem begegnen und sagen: Schauen Sie, hören Sie! Und der autonome Betrachter reagiert, indem er vor allem mit sich selbst umgehen muss. Dann ist das nicht Christoph Schlingensiefs Leidensweg, sondern viel mehr. Ob das dann noch richtiges Theater ist—wen interessiert's? Und wenn die Leute das nicht wollen, wenn sie sagen, ich sei ein Terrorist, der ihnen zu nahe tritt, dann ist das eben so. Dann ist das auch eine Reaktion." (*So schön*, 243; I want to encounter another person in the state that I am currently in and say: Look, listen! And the autonomous viewer reacts by primarily having to deal with himself. This then makes it so much more than Christoph Schlingensief's via dolorosa. If this is still proper theater—who cares? And if the people don't like it, if they tell me I'm a terrorist, offending them, then that's the way it is. Then that's also a reaction of some sort.) The "terrorist" writer holds the power to challenge previous certainties as held by the reader, and as such presents an external menace. He can fundamentally unsettle them by bringing about a feeling of internal terror. This may take readers to the limits of what they can bear.

Ensuing from the diary recordings, the contemporary observer saw Schlingensief carry his experience of living with illness and nearing death beyond the printed page into talk shows as well as back onto the theatrical stage, doing readings and interviews, all to reach out to as diverse an audience as possible. In doing so, he willfully ignored any boundaries of high and low culture, any distinction between what is art or life, to open up the public conversation he thought needed to be had about illness and dying. As much as he managed his own illness and dying on the public stage, by entitling his final blog post "Erinnern heißt vergessen," however, Schlingensief did pass the baton on to others. It is up to others to interpret his oeuvre as a whole, as well as his late work in particular. It is up to others, too, to keep the conversation going about illness and death, its place in society, culture—and in literature.

Wolfgang Herrndorf's *Arbeit und Struktur*— Creative Productivity in Extremis

Wolfgang Herrndorf took up the project of the autothanatographical illness diary where Christoph Schlingensief left off, having received his own cancer diagnosis in the year of the artist's death. Herrndorf, too, refused to die "still, lautlos, wortlos und handlungslos" (*So schön*, 241; silent, without a sound or word or action), as the Catholic *Die Tagespost* had suggested Schlingensief should do instead of discussing his suffering in the public sphere.[50] While there is only one explicit reference to *So schön wie hier kanns im Himmel gar nicht sein!* in Herrndorf's online diary,[51] important parallels can nonetheless be drawn between the two authors. Both Schlingensief and Herrndorf carried on with their creative work until they died, and by making use of the defiant diary format each asserted his right to participate in the contemporary cultural scene, rather than letting himself be forced into taking up any kind of sick role as demanded by the *Tagespost* article, a request that is indicative of widespread social attitudes toward the ill. What is more, both Schlingensief and Herrndorf clearly dealt with their experience of (terminal) illness in their work from then on. Finishing two novels and starting a third alongside keeping his diary, *Arbeit und Struktur*, Herrndorf too exhibited remarkable drive and productivity in relation to impending death. By comparing Schlingensief's and Herrndorf's cancer diaries through the prism of their genre, common concerns shared by the two autothanatographers and their writing become clear—in their initial motivation for turning to the diary form to process their experience of illness and of dying, their decision to go public with cancer in this form, and the "rhetorical stance" they adopt as diarists.[52]

Herrndorf, a painter by training and self-professed "Behelfsschriftsteller" (*AS*, 115; amateur writer) started his online diary in the wake of his admission to a psychiatric hospital for hypomania, which he had developed in reaction to receiving diagnosis of an aggressive type of brain tumor, a glioblastoma. Over the first part of *Arbeit und Struktur*, the cancer diagnosis, in fact, appears secondary to the psychological fallout caused by it, and its circumstances are narrated only once, more than half a year into the diary.[53] This sets the tone for the text that—without downplaying or glossing over the physical effects of cancer on Herrndorf's body—is in large part a study of the human mind in extremis. In this, *Arbeit und Struktur* reflects a markedly contemporary dilemma, that in this form was unknown to previous generations: the ability of medicine today to diagnose terminal illness relatively early on and to manage it over a significant period has led to a prolonged phase of what can be termed "livingly dying."[54] From the inside perspective, Herrndorf in *Arbeit und Struktur* explores whether it is at all possible to adjust to living with the concrete knowledge of one's own imminent extinction. In doing so, the diarist-author was his own experimental subject. Making use of the chance—and challenge—to document his life with illness on a daily basis, the novelist rendered productive a situation that he neither wanted nor had planned for.

Arbeit und Struktur, as the then relatively unknown author programmatically named his diary, soon attracted the attention and imagination of an ever-growing readership.[55] It was edited posthumously as a book by Kathrin Passig and Marcus Gärtner, who quote Herrndorf's description of brain tumors as the Mercedes of illnesses and his specific glioblastoma as the (yet more exclusive) Rolls-Royce. Herrndorf concluded the provocative statement self-consciously, and not without irony, thus: "Mit Prostatakrebs oder einem Schnupfen hätte ich dieses Blog jedenfalls nie begonnen" (*AS*, 444; If I'd had prostate cancer or a cold, I would have never started this blog). The severity of his diagnosis certainly gave the diary impetus and endowed it with a certain kind of status. In a diary entry reflecting on a telephone conversation with a friend, Herrndorf insists that there is something essential he believes they share as people suffering from a terminal illness: "Man wird nicht weise, man kommt der Wahrheit nicht näher als jeder. Aber in jeder Minute beim Tod zu sein, generiert eine eigene Form von Erfahrungswissen." (*AS*, 227; One doesn't become wiser nor does one come closer to any kind of truth than anyone [else]. But to be with death every single minute generates its own form of empirical knowledge.) To share some of this knowledge appears to be one reason—a deeply caring and ethical one—that drove Herrndorf to write about cancer publicly.

The title *Arbeit und Struktur* points toward what became Herrndorf's self-prescribed antidote to the mental and physical suffering he had to endure living with the glioblastoma. In the time the diary spans, the world he created in *Tschick* especially becomes his refuge; the labor of writing this book for adolescents and then *Sand* and *Bilder deiner großen Liebe* (Pictures of your great love)—which remained unfinished—bound him to and structured his life in the present.[56] Yet it was with the diary that Herrndorf explored new creative avenues, and the illness was central to this writing: *Arbeit und Struktur* came to be his only published life-writing text. This late turn to an autobiographical genre at a time when the author was seeking to express himself in illness warrants investigation in itself.

As a professional author, Herrndorf was highly conscious of the (writerly) conventions and (readerly) assumptions associated with literary genres. Accordingly, the author addresses his diary's relation to other cancer narratives by inserting poems made up entirely of the titles of published cancer books (*AS*, 47, 199, 314, 408). Texts referred to in this playful manner range from fellow sufferers' published diaries to parents' memoirs of their children's untimely deaths and include Schlingensief's *So schön wie hier kanns im Himmel gar nicht sein!* (*AS*, 199). Herrndorf's own eponymic mantra *Arbeit und Struktur* concludes each composition, not unlike the final lines in a Shakespearean sonnet. Hinting at the large number of such texts in circulation, what becomes clear is that the urge to write about one's personal experiences of illness and dying is as strong in unknown, first-time writers as it is in people with some kind of public profile and, in the case of Herrndorf, a distinct sense of authorship. In G. Thomas Couser's terminology, both "somebodies" and "nobodies," but maybe particularly the latter, as Couser speculates, produce autobiographical writing about "some body."[57] Herrndorf's title collages point to the popularity of such texts with a general readership. His correlation of these titles with his own suggests a sameness among the texts, at least superficially. Yet Herrndorf's diary does not entirely fit in with the others he appropriates as lines in these wry poems: six of the titles he uses contain the word *Himmel* (heaven). Those that do not mention heaven still have Christian connotations, referring to paradise or employing ideas of rebirth, angels, and images of rainbows. With the comparatively barren and concise formulation "Arbeit und Struktur" concluding each of the assemblages, Herrndorf consciously makes his cancer diary stand out from and contrast with the rest. Even though he places his work among the ranks of this kind of illness writing, we may conclude, he also struggles with the association. One reason is that his text does not share the sentimentality that the others' titles seem to suggest nor the Christian values or concern with religious faith that they imply.

Conceived as a blog and published in hardcover book form only posthumously, *Arbeit und Struktur* has undergone a medial transformation exactly opposite of that of Schlingensief's diaristic activity, which moved into the blogosphere only once the book was published. Despite putting different media to use at different times, however, upon closer examination it becomes clear that the development of both texts is actually very similar when one considers their gradually growing reach. We saw that for Schlingensief, having started out with voice recordings made when alone in his hospital room, the book publication of selected recordings was an intermediate stage, a way to cement his commitment to his work when he found himself in the midst of treatment regimes. It was an effective way of addressing audiences that might not have necessarily been familiar with him previously—something that was important for the artist with a view to his works' desired social relevance. In Herrndorf's case, a private and at first access-restricted blog intended originally as nothing but a "Mitteilungsveranstaltung für Freunde und Bekannte in Echtzeit" (*AS*, 405; way of notifying friends and acquaintances in real time) was made available to a wider online public only in a subsequent step, before eventually reaching out into the offline sphere after the author's death. The motivation to thus incrementally widen access to the diary for an interested readership has its roots in the belief that there is value (literary and otherwise) in the diary that goes beyond the personal. Without this growing conviction Herrndorf would not have publicized the text, a point I explore further below.

From early on Herrndorf's blog carried features that, in its aesthetics, moved it close to the manuscript for a book publication, a manuscript that, however, was soon tried out on an online public, as a work in progress, rather than being kept under wraps. Although each entry was labeled with a date and time of writing, they were grouped into chapters from the start. Even when it was available solely in blog form, *Arbeit und Struktur* had already been furnished with a preface. Furthermore, from the point that the evolving text was first made available, on the blog's landing page there was an indication, too, as to where to begin reading: "Um das Blog in Gänze zu lesen, beginne man bei dem Eintrag Dämmerung" (In order to read the blog in full, start with the entry dawn). For the reader's convenience, the author hyperlinked the comment so that it would lead directly to the preface.

Herrndorf maintained the diary/blog for three and a half years, up until a few days before his death on August 26, 2013, when—understanding he would not have much longer to live—he committed suicide with a pistol. He first considered this option soon after learning of his diagnosis and repeatedly returned to it in the diary as his "Exitstrategie" (e.g. *AS*, 50, 79, 87). During this time, and unlike Schlingensief in the final years of his life, Herrndorf decided to withdraw from the media and public in all but one way. *Arbeit und Struktur* became the sole channel through which he communicated publicly. The blog was his principal means to engage with news reports or comment on current debates, both those of an intellectual/literary kind as well as those concerning sociopolitical issues such as the liberalization of German law on assisted dying that he pressed for. In what was both a self-protective and time-conscious manner, the author channeled all of the energy and time that remained to him into his writing.

Chronicling the Ill Self Online

Like Schlingensief before him, Herrndorf puts the diary form to a multitude of uses. Besides the blog being a platform for Herrndorf's observations of daily life from the radically altered perspective of terminal illness and becoming his only medium of communication, it is also a free, impartial space for developing his "Exitstrategie" and—linked to that—a way of managing impending death. In a very practical sense, *Arbeit und Struktur* becomes an extension of Herrndorf's "Patientenverfügung" (*AS*, 334; living will). More personally, the writer memorializes the things and people he loves through it, sharing memories of his childhood or those that put in a nutshell the nature of a friendship, as well as posting short death notices for others—not unlike the obituaries that can be found on the *Schlingenblog*. *Arbeit und Struktur* frequently celebrates moments of connection with nature and the author's love for the city of Berlin. It functions furthermore as Herrndorf's reading log as he runs "Projekt Regression" (*AS*, 39), rereading his favorite books from when he was younger, and it becomes important, not least, as a platform for his poetology.

With life having forcefully demonstrated its finite nature, it is Herrndorf's declared aim to finish the half-written novels that now haunt him in their incompleteness (*AS*, 104–5). Narrating retrospectively his experience of the days after his first operation in what he terms flashbacks, he asserts that he had the ambition straight away: "Ich werde noch ein Buch schreiben, sage ich mir, egal wie lange ich noch habe" (*AS*, 107; I am telling myself that I will write another book, no matter how long I have got left). When Herrndorf spells out the task he sets himself in the space of the diary, and he does so more than once, he displays his commitment in a form not dissimilar to a contract or "pact" in Lejeune's sense: "13.3. 2010 11:00 / Gib mir ein Jahr, Herrgott, an den ich nicht glaube, und ich werde fertig mit allem. (geweint)." (*AS*, 22; Give me one year, oh Lord, who I don't believe exists, and I will finish it all. [crying].) It is not a coincidence that this short entry from early in the blog is among the most cited from *Arbeit und Struktur*. It allowed the reader of the diary/blog as much as Herrndorf himself to check in real time whether the author was achieving the goals he had set himself. In this regard, the blog becomes a tool to track the progress he is making during his cancer years. This particular usage of the blog points back to the cultural practice of bookkeeping that contributed to the development of the practice of diary writing as we know it today.[58] It reminds one of similar tendencies of making the self accountable that I observed in Schlingensief's *Tagebuch* and that pervaded the artist's late work generally. Their creative work is integral to both diarists' sense of identity.

Considering the writerly milieu Herrndorf frequented, one can see reasons it may have been a fairly obvious choice for him to write and publish *Arbeit und Struktur* online. Herrndorf was close to the capital's so-called digital bohemian scene and a member of the creative network Zentrale Intelligenz Agentur (Central Intelligence Agency).[59] Previous to the inception of his personal blog, Herrndorf had contributed to the communal literary blogs *Wir höflichen Paparazzi* (We, the polite paparazzi) and *Riesenmaschine* (Megamachine).[60] Lastly, he was a great admirer of Rainald Goetz, who as early as 1998/1999 wrote and published the experimental diary *Abfall für alle* (Garbage for all) online, becoming the first high-profile German-language author to close in a radical fashion the gap between production and reception of his daily writing in this way. Goetz kept *Abfall* until, after the course of one year, he announced—with characteristic grandeur—that he had achieved self-realization: "Schließlich war, ein Traum, der wahr geworden ist, das Buch entstanden, das ich bin"[61] (At last, a dream come true, the book that I am came into being). Among contemporary authors, Goetz was one of Herrndorf's main inspirations. Goetz's *Abfall*, indeed like Schlingensief's *Schlingenblog*, is an example of an author writing the self online that preceded (and, in the case of Goetz, can be seen to have directly influenced) the genesis of *Arbeit und Struktur*. What unites all three blog authors is a radical approach to their artistic work that deliberately extended its reach into their lives as a whole. Each artist/writer, in the space of his respective blog, self-reflexively and daringly questioned and measured the private/public self against all-encompassing principles, openly probing current projects for their value, taking their own poetology as rules to live by.

In relation to other, more traditional forms of writing and publishing, however, literary or artists' blogs—despite and including the above-mentioned high-profile examples—are still niche products, catching the eye of only a small section of the reading public. It was only from the time of its publication in book form that a wider reading public engaged with Herrndorf's autothanatographical diary. In this sense, keeping a diary online blurs the lines of presumed privacy and publicity all the more.[62] Linguistically, too, the medium of the blog in particular offers itself up as a platform for keeping a diary, as the personal tone adopted by most bloggers comes very close to that of the diarist.[63] The Internet, as a virtual space, epitomizes a private/public space into which, in fact, all diaries are written. Publication in this realm therefore seems apt when dealing with delicate subject matter such as personal illness.[64] The large number of personal blogs and online diaries by ill and dying people of all ages and from all walks of life available on the Internet today seems to confirm that impression. Their number also demonstrates that a widespread desire to speak and be heard is felt by many ill people, most of whom do not lead lives in the public eye. Although Herrndorf, as a writer with a public profile, was the first online illness diarist to reach a larger audience in German, he should be read in the context of both a multitude of lesser-known illness blogs, therefore, and as standing alongside other professional writers who have confronted illness in this way, such as Ivan Noble and Tom Lubbock in the UK, for instance.[65]

In the diary's early phase, the medium of the Internet gave Herrndorf—as the blog's author/producer—crucial independence from

Rowohlt, the publishing house to which he was contracted, helping him keep the diary separate from his other writing. This separation between the diary/blog as his more personal pursuit on the one hand and his fiction writing as his professional occupation on the other dissolved over time. Yet, as Herrndorf started out on *Arbeit und Struktur*, it seemed particularly relevant to the professional author that the online diary does not have to meet the same normative expectations, concerning style or "literariness," as does the classic book. It can be a freer, looser, more experimental text—never completed, always ongoing, as long as its author is alive. As much as the diary/blog has endless potential, though, it too is a text of the present, for two reasons: on the one hand, each post is available online for an audience to retrieve within split seconds of uploading it; on the other, its ephemeral URLs, and with them all content, can be moved or deleted in the blink of an eye.

The blog's ultimate rootedness in the present fits in with the drastic change of perspective the glioblastoma brought about for Herrndorf, as can be assumed for many others confronted with a terminal diagnosis. Only by consciously refocusing on the present can the author keep his fear of death in check, he reports, asserting that "in der winzigen Sekunde der Gegenwart" (in the tiny second that is the present) he is "unantastbar" (*AS*, 110; untouchable). Laconically, the diarist proclaims, "Es beginnt: Das Leben in der Gegenwart" (*AS*, 111; Now launching: life in the present). For the terminally ill author, who cannot rely on an imagined future any longer, the immediacy and independence offered by both online self-publishing and the present-tense genre of the diary correspond to his needs as autothanatographer. Lastly, the diary form's inherent lack of plot proves to be an advantage as illness progresses and Herrndorf becomes less and less physically able to keep the diary regularly, ultimately relying on friends to help him upload new posts, posts that become shorter and sparser, before the blog as a whole falls silent just days before its author's death.

Herrndorf's Self-Positioning as Natural Diarist in "Dämmerung"

Although at first just a sideline to his fiction writing, contemporary readers soon observed Herrndorf's diary/blog transforming into a literary project all of its own—growing in importance and itself becoming "work" for the author. From the blog's outset, the author strives to demonstrate his choice of the diary form as a natural one. Close reading of its preface as a site of authorial self-reflexivity reveals the crucial importance the diary had for him from the start, indicating the central position it would take up in Herrndorf's oeuvre as a whole. Titled "Dämmerung" (dawn), the preface relates Herrndorf's earliest memory, or "erste Erinnerung an diese Welt," as the writer declares, from around the age of two. It provides *Arbeit und Struktur* with what in German I would call an *Urszene*, a scene of origins, as it celebrates the intensity of sensory impressions experienced when waking up and literally coming to one's senses. Herrndorf describes how, as a toddler, he experienced this feeling in perfect harmony with his surroundings—a blank slate: "Mein Körper hat genau die gleiche Temperatur und Konsistenz wie seine Umgebung, wie die Bettwäsche" (My body has exactly the same temperature and consistency as its environment, the same as the bedding). Metaphorically, this memory can be read to extend to a description of the birth of the author, as well as hinting at his return to the bed as deathbed.

The description of this particular morning conveys a feeling of having fallen through the cracks of time. Despite the author programmatically positioning himself as a nostalgic writer in the second paragraph—"Mein Blick war von Anfang an auf die Vergangenheit gerichtet" (From the beginning, my gaze was directed at the past)—neither the past (that he cannot remember) nor the future (that he cannot yet imagine) comes close to the significance of the child's vivid present, his being in the moment as described in these opening lines. According to the adult Herrndorf, the sensation of waking up is one that he consciously relished despite his young age: "Ich wünsche mir, dass es immer so bleibt" (I wish for it to always stay this way). The final words of the one-page preface stress the consistency of this life-affirming desire over time: "Und immer wollte ich Stillstand, und fast jeden Morgen hoffte ich, die schöne Dämmerung würde sich noch einmal wiederholen" (And I always wanted everything to come to a halt, and almost every morning I hoped for the beautiful dawn to break one more time). It seems to predestine Herrndorf as diarist and explains his motivation for returning to the blank page (even if it is a virtual one), time and again. Lastly, the image of dawn and the daily recurrence of that in-between time, being neither night nor day, is one heavy with meaning in relation to the act of diary writing from the in-between place that is terminal illness, the fleeting dawn being a cipher for the transience of life.

The (momentary) being outside of time that the autothanatographical diarist programmatically strives for also signifies a coming to life in text. In "Rückblende, Teil 8: Fernando Pessoa" (*AS*, 135–40), the author recounts a psychotic episode (that eventually leads to his hospitalization) in which he is trying to recover a text he imagines having written, and in his frenzied, manic state he believes he has found "die Weltformel" (the theory of everything). Slipped into the middle of this account—easily missed—we find the following lines: "Aber vielleicht ist es ein literarischer Text? Ja, natürlich, das ist die Rettung: *Ich* bin in meinem eigenen Text." (*AS*, 136; emphasis mine; But maybe it is a literary text? Yes, of course, that's the salvation: *I* am in my own text.) In the face of the absurdity of having knowledge of one's impending death, writing *Arbeit und Struktur* becomes a truly existential—or existentially metafictional—task. The author himself lends strength to my argument here when he closes his flashbacks and returns to the day-by-day mode of the diary thus: "PPS: Überflüssig zu erwähnen, daß der bei Holm von mir verzweifelt gesuchte Text später doch noch aufgetaucht ist: Es ist dieser Text" (*AS*, 149; PPS: Needless to say that the text I so desperately looked for at Holm's did appear later on: it's this text).

There are several other passages in the diary that mention Herrndorf's struggles to say "I" (*AS*, 272–73, 290, 331), in times of emotional crisis, as a consequence of depersonalization, and as he goes on to lose certain abilities that he had always considered to be almost innate. Keeping the diary that is *Arbeit und Struktur* helps consciously "ich zu sein und zu sagen" (*AS*, 331; to be me and say I). In this light, it is unsurprising that the diary would become central as the illness progressed. Indeed, it becomes a major focus of Herrndorf's late creative work; it comes closest to the idea of an author living, breathing, being in the text and is aptly described by Herrndorf as "Roman in Form einer Endlosschleife, . . . Text, der mich so glücklich und verzweifelt macht und der sich selbst und alles andere und die ganze Welt erklärt" (*AS*, 139; novel in the form of an infinite loop, . . . text that makes me so happy and so desperate and that explains itself and everything else and the whole world).

The Diary Develops a Dynamic of Its Own

Over time, as Herrndorf comes to invest more time and creative energy into *Arbeit und Struktur*, the promise of personal as of writerly autonomy that the diary form has initially held for him proves to be an illusion. This is a gradual realization that the author/narrator makes and feeds back into the continuously evolving text, exploiting the fact that he can react so speedily in the medium of the blog. Along with Herrndorf himself, the diary's growing readership was thus confronted with at least some of the dangers the author recognized in his public confrontation with cancer.

A first example is the early commodification of Herrndorf's blog by his publisher Rowohlt, which used it for marketing purposes and did so without the author's consent or knowledge (*AS*, 96). It is a violation of boundaries for the author at a time when he is far from deciding whether and how the diary texts will ever be published outside the online sphere. And it constitutes the first of a number of incidents that bring home to Herrndorf his exposure and vulnerability as the author of an ongoing illness narrative of which he is also the protagonist and therefore—almost unavoidably—the ultimate tragic hero, whose nearness to death has a profound effect on the reader's imagination.

Rightly anticipating some interest in his person from when he first set up the blog, Herrndorf from the start had restricted ways for his readers to make contact with him. In the site notice, he specified, "Keine Anfragen, keine Interviews, keine Lesungen, keine Ausnahmen. Bitte schicken Sie mir keine Bücher, keine CDs und nichts, was über Briefformat hinausgeht."[66] (No inquiries, no interviews, no readings, no exceptions. Please do not send me any books nor CDs and nothing larger than a standard letter.) This message was supported by Herrndorf disabling the comment function that is built into most blogging software when setting up *Arbeit und Struktur*, leaving no opportunity for readers to directly reply to any of Herrndorf's entries.

In parallel to his shooting to fame as the author of *Tschick*, by November 2010, Herrndorf nonetheless notes, "Bekomme jeden Tag Briefe und Karten, die ich nicht mehr beantworten kann. Grüße an dieser Stelle." (*AS*, 156; Every day I receive letters and postcards that I cannot reply to anymore. Saying hello here instead.) More than once, Herrndorf does use the blog to signal receipt of and thanks for the letters sent to him by other cancer sufferers, old acquaintances, and schoolchildren (who share with him their opinion of *Tschick*). In an indirect way, his carrying on with the blog, post by post and day by day, is a reply to these letters in itself and testimony to the encouragement that, although Herrndorf may not admit this explicitly, he draws from many of them.

As the illness progresses and the diary grows in content and in popularity, the pressure grows for the celebrity patient to be on guard concerning his privacy and sense of self. In November 2011, an outraged Herrndorf therefore repeats his terms of noncommunication: "Keine Anfragen, für alle, die Schwierigkeiten haben, das zu verstehen, bedeutet: Keine Anfragen" (*AS*, 270; For anyone who has trouble understanding this, no inquiries means: no inquiries). This warning precedes an eloquent diatribe about the homeopathic treatment regimens or religious belief systems forced upon him by the "mad" out there, as he calls them. They get in touch, unsolicited, via "Brief, Mail, Telefon" (*AS*, 312; letter, e-mail, telephone), and have a serious impact on the programmatic "Struktur," emotional and otherwise, that Herrndorf yearns for and hoped to establish for himself by taking up the regular writing practice that is the diary: "Und wieder ist mein Tag unterbrochen, wieder ist meine Arbeit unterbrochen, wieder stehe ich in meiner Wohnung und weiß nicht, wo ich war" (*AS*, 312; And yet again my day has been interrupted, again my work has been interrupted, again I am standing in my flat and don't remember where I was up to). He had not planned for these disruptions, had underestimated the desire for contact the blog would instill in so many of his readers. Ironically, it is his success as a writer and diarist in engaging a readership so imaginatively that we see backfiring here. The imagined intimacy that prompts so many to get in touch must be directly attributed to *Arbeit und Struktur*'s diary form, depicting life as it happens in all its banality and detail. A portrayal such as Herrndorf's minimizes the gap between reader and writer, bringing into the everyday sphere the experience of terminal illness that is unimaginable for a large section of the readership and that for those themselves suffering from cancer or another serious illness evokes memories of comparable experiences. For Herrndorf, the scope of the intrusions he experiences is unexpected. As an effect of keeping the illness diary in real time and so publicly, they infringe on his selfhood, or sense of autonomy, with each incident causing him to become more "paranoid" (*AS*, 390).

The media reports from that time, casting Herrndorf as a hardworking hermit and terminally ill prodigy, add to this pressure and skew his self-representation by focusing upon the ill health of the author more than on his writerly achievements. His productivity continued to be hailed and admired, yet a certain fascination with the severity of the glioblastoma in his head in many cases diverted journalists from discussing Herrndorf's new publications in much depth.[67] The reasonable fear of the writer in this context is that he will become famous for his illness instead of his literature, reminiscent of Schlingensief's conflicted feelings at the raging applause for him at the restaging of *Mea Culpa* in Munich. As a friend remarks with dry wit that Herrndorf enjoys and therefore shares in an entry, "Die Sensation überwiegt die Konzeption, sagt Julia über Leben und Blog" (*AS*, 253; The sensation is larger than its conception, says Julia about life and blog).

All in all, this culminates in recurring entries expressing thoughts of abandoning the online diary; as they are rendered, they hint at the extreme emotional struggle involved in keeping a diary in the face of impending death: "23.2.2013 14:47 / Würde die Arbeit am Blog am liebsten einstellen. Das Blog nur noch der fortgesetzte, mich immer mehr deprimierende Versuch, mir eine Krise nach der anderen vom Hals zu schaffen, es hängt mir am Hals *wie mein Leben wie ein Mühlstein*. Ich weiß aber nicht, was ich sonst machen soll. Die Arbeit an 'Isa' tritt auf der Stelle." (*AS*, 392; emphasis mine; Would love nothing better than to end my work on the blog. The blog [is] only the continued, more and more depressing attempt at ridding myself of one crisis after the other. *It is a millstone round my neck just like my [own] life*. Yet I don't know what else to do. Work on "Isa" is stagnating.)[68] At a point where its effectiveness as a means of self-empowerment is exhausted, the remedy becomes a burden in itself, and—as a "millstone"—Herrndorf likens the diary to his life generally. Yet he sees no alternative to it, especially as he has vowed to work until the end. At this point in time, the diary project has superseded all other writing projects.

Elsewhere, Herrndorf repeats his severe doubts about the blog: "19.4.2013 17:26 / Den ganzen Tag lang über nichts anderes als darüber nachgedacht, das Blog einzustellen, nicht zum ersten Mal, die mühsame Verschriftlichung meiner peinlichen Existenz." (*AS*, 405; Spent the whole day thinking about nothing but finishing with the blog, and not for the first time. The arduous textualization of my awkward [or, in an older sense of the word, painful] existence.) This time, however, and not coincidentally, another author/diarist's words sound through these lines. They are those of Thomas Mann, who noted a year before his death, "Ich sollte aufhören, dies nutzlose, leere Tagebuch zu führen, aus Scham vor meiner gegenwärtigen elenden Existenz" (I should stop keeping this useless, empty diary, for I am ashamed of my current miserable existence).[69] A sense of disillusionment and exhaustion comes through both Herrndorf's and Mann's reflections on their nonetheless tireless diaristic activity, reflecting each writer's state of mind at a bleak point in his life, marked by illness and by old age, respectively, both nearing death. Herrndorf practically paraphrases Mann, albeit substituting the pivotal shame (in Mann) with the sense of tribulation that he feels and replacing Mann's misery with his own awkwardness and pain. The citation establishes a connection between the two authors, neither of whom could imagine a life without writing.[70] Furthermore, it indicates Herrndorf's wider knowledge of diary literature, from which a reading of *Arbeit und Struktur* cannot be separated.

Herrndorf's threats of ending the blog fit in with the more drastic impulse that overcomes him irregularly to destroy diary material, along with other items of his creative past (drawings and paintings as well as unpublished written work). This, too, links him to other diarists from literary history as well as the late Schlingensief deleting at least one video from the *Schlingenblog*. Although present in many diarists, the urge to destroy the memory archive that is the diary at the same time as one expands it may be particularly strong in autothanatographical writers. Herrndorf's actions as documented in *Arbeit und Struktur* in a sense echo Schlingensief's forlorn words asking, "Wen soll das das [*sic*] interessieren?" (Who is supposed to care about this?) Partly to record, partly to make clear what did or did not fall prey to his destructive frenzies, and maybe to boast about them, Herrndorf tends to report about these acts of destruction afterward in his blog (e.g., *AS*, 232). In the face of his own anticipated death, he cannot bear the thought of leaving older diaries or copies of personal letters behind. As the author's outlook on life, work, and the blog changes, so too does his assessment of his past life and his previous work—many a time, the self-declared nihilist finds nothing is worth keeping. From the perspective of illness, his old diaries and letters especially make Herrndorf despair for his younger self's melancholy and aimlessness as he was drifting through life, until settling in Berlin. As can be gathered from the fragments published in the appendix to the book version of *Arbeit und Struktur*, about his Berlin years, the author states emphatically: "Hier bin ich der Mensch geworden, der ich bin" (*AS*, 430–31; Here I became who I am). We notice that Herrndorf too references

Nietzsche's *Ecce Homo* here, but in stark contrast to Schlingensief—who does so in the context of mourning the loss of a future previously imagined safe—Herrndorf recalls Nietzsche to assert that he has found his true self and calling in the city. The tragedy, for Herrndorf, lies in having found his place so late in life.

Intellectually, Herrndorf somewhat anticipates that the diary will develop a dynamic of its own in the way outlined above. He is aware of what he succumbs to when setting out on *Arbeit und Struktur*: "die sich im Akt des Schreibens immer wieder einstellende, das Weiterleben enorm erleichternde, falsche und nur im Text richtige Vorstellung, die Fäden in der Hand zu halten" (*AS*, 292; the notion, which regularly sets in during the act of writing, of holding the reins; a wrong assumption that massively helps with surviving, although it is right only within the text). The illness diary as a whole demonstrates the author's essential interconnectedness with others and remains ever aware of life's ultimate uncontrollability. It makes a mockery of illusions of autonomy so dear to us from the perspective of twenty-first-century individuality and hegemonic ableism—illusions that the writer Herrndorf too nonetheless indulges in. This comes out, for example, in the consolatory poem he thinks up one night in the first months with cancer: "Niemand kommt an mich heran / bis an die Stunde meines Todes. / Und auch dann wird niemand kommen. / Nichts wird kommen, und es ist in meiner Hand." (*AS*, 111; No one can get hold of me / until the hour of my death. / And even then no one will come. / Nothing will come, and it is in my own hands.) The verse is designed to reassure the atheist author of his independence and agency. He recites it to himself whenever feeling overwhelmed, exactly because he, being subject to illness, knows himself to not at all be in control of the course of events. Closely tied to this poetic assertion of autonomy are flash-forwards, as imagined by the author, of his suicide by firearm.

That Herrndorf as cancer sufferer is not exempt from ableist ideas—and that indeed these may have influenced the point in time at which he decided to take his own life—comes across when, in reaction to an epileptic attack, he attempts to define the limits of a life worth living: "Menschliches Leben endet, wo die Kommunikation endet, und das darf nie passieren. Das darf nie ein Zustand sein." (*AS*, 224; Human life ends where communication ends, and that must never happen. That must never be the state of affairs.) This statement's danger lies in its generalization beyond the fears of the individual author. It relies on vague concepts: What, for instance, is meant by communication? Does it include touch and its perception? We can assume that Herrndorf defined communication much more narrowly, thinking primarily of his own ability to express himself, and eloquently so, both orally and in writing. In the diary, Herrndorf actively negotiates and develops his views on difficult issues, thus engaging in public discourse, yet he does so from a position of radical subjectivity, in the light of his own constitution.

In writing *Arbeit und Struktur*, Herrndorf relinquished the powers he had as a novelist, over a cast of characters, the plot, and the end of a story. Instead, as diarist he had to accept, as Lejeune describes it from the inside perspective, that "we are writing a text whose ultimate logic escapes us; we agree to collaborate with an unpredictable and uncontrollable future."[71] This highlights the experimental nature of all diaristic texts, as well as the vulnerability of their authors—and gives an idea of the immense difficulties (psychological, physical, and emotional) involved for the autothanatographical diarist. *Arbeit und Struktur* was a tightrope walk for its author/subject. Herrndorf could not bear the thought of leaving any work behind unfinished, yet he knew that, by its nature, he would do exactly that in the case of the diary. Emotionally, this stretched Herrndorf to his limits as he wrote himself closer to his death, tracking his own decline, a day at a time.

Herrndorf's Literary Sensibility

The magical power of literary words is addressed in *Arbeit und Struktur* when Herrndorf writes about a significant change that he notes in himself when beginning to read again in hospital, in the days after the first operation:

> Ich bin Schriftsteller, und man wird nicht glauben, dass Literatur mich sonst kaltgelassen hätte. Aber was jetzt zurückkehrt beim Lesen, ist das Gefühl, das ich zuletzt in der Kindheit und Pubertät regelmäßig und danach nur noch sehr sporadisch und nur bei wenigen Büchern hatte: dass man teilhat an einem Dasein und an Menschen und am Bewusstsein von Menschen, an etwas, worüber man sonst im Leben etwas zu erfahren nicht viel Gelegenheit hat, selbst, um ehrlich zu sein, in Gesprächen mit Freunden nur selten und noch seltener in Filmen, und daß es einen Unterschied gibt zwischen Kunst und Scheiße. Einen Unterschied zwischen dem existenziellen Trost einer großen Erzählung und dem Müll, von dem ich zuletzt eindeutig zuviel gelesen habe. (*AS*, 104)

> [I am an author, and you won't believe that literature would have left me cold in the past. But what returns now when I read is the feeling that I last had regularly in my childhood and in puberty, then only very sporadically, and only with very few books: the impression that one shares in an existence, in being human, and in the consciousness of other people. That is something that you don't have much chance to experience otherwise in life, only rarely, if we are

honest, in conversations with friends and even more rarely when watching films. And the realization that there is a difference between art and crap. A significant difference between the existential solace of a great narrative and the rubbish that I have recently been reading too much of.]

Rediscovering his readerly enthusiasm for literature inspires him to confront his own unfinished projects as a writer. In an indirect way, the above passage explains much about his own aims as author and why literature became his medium of choice for artistic expression. Within the imaginative space of the written word, Herrndorf hopes to enable his readership to have that special experience that he so values as a reader himself, aiming to make it possible for others to share in a character's consciousness and lifeworld. To him, a text qualifies as *Kunst* (art) when it succeeds in offering such an experience upon interplay with a receptive reader's imagination. For the reader, the engagement with art thus defined presents a rare and precious opportunity for experiencing empathy and immersion across difference. Herrndorf himself, for example, finds it in Charlotte Brontë's *Jane Eyre*: "Meine Lieblingsstelle immer noch ihre einsame Wanderung. Wie sie fast verhungert, wie sie übernachtet zwischen Felsen und Heidekraut. Wo man sieht: ein Mensch. Und auch 150 Jahre nach ihrem Tod ist es immer noch: ein Mensch." (*AS*, 59; My favorite passage still her lonely walk. The way she almost starves, and spends the night between rocks and heather. Where you realize: a human being. And even 150 years after her death it still is: a human being.)

Remarkably, in his role as reader, Herrndorf here blurs the lines between the image he has of the historical figure Charlotte Brontë and the fictional heroine she created: from praising the text's ability to bring to life its eponymous heroine—"sie"—and her struggles, he swiftly moves to assert the novel's longevity as a work of art by pointing out "her" death so long ago as not having had an effect on *Jane Eyre*'s literary potency. It is Charlotte Brontë's death, however, and not Jane Eyre's, which he refers to in making that point. We can infer that, to Herrndorf, it appears secondary if a character is fictional or, as is indeed the case in *Arbeit und Struktur*, if he or she finds a real life referent in the author as life writer. This is consistent with Herrndorf's radical belief system that he develops during his illness. In various diary entries, he asserts "dass dieses Universum nicht existiert. Oder nur in diesem Bruchteil dieser Sekunde." (*AS*, 57; that this universe doesn't exist. Or merely in this fraction of this second.) And in a similar vein: "Es gibt uns nicht. Wir sind schon vergangen." (*AS*, 421; We do not exist. We have already passed on.) Herrndorf thus further relativizes any distinction between any kind of text-external reality and that contained in literary writing. Ultimately, it is a consoling thought for the ill author that time did not take a toll on *Jane Eyre*'s literary power or its popularity. In Charlotte Brontë, Herrndorf finds an author who—in her readers' imaginations—in some sense "lives on" through her literary legacy. Not least, this points forward to potential workings of the posthumous reception of Herrndorf's own writing.

Herrndorf's criteria for what kind of writing is of literary value, we note, are markedly different from the criteria of the mainstream critics, who seem so intent against considering illness narratives as literature: his are certainly not divided along deceptively clear-cut boundaries of fictional and nonfictional genres, nor do they have to do with the subject matter of a text. Much more relevant, to Herrndorf, are a text's accessibility or readability and a thought or an emotion's validity over time; in other words, a piece's potential—both in form and in content—to remain relevant beyond its specific moment.

Herrndorf has, however, no illusions about the difficulty of conveying something of one person's *Bewusstsein* to another relying solely on the medium of language. He thinks this through in relation to himself, writing—and waiting, moribund—as a dying man. As he attempts a definition of this key term in his poetics,[72] the near-impossibility of realizing what he strives for as diarist, recording and sharing some of his own inner landscape, is acknowledged: "5.7.2011 20:26 / Warten. Wenn man stirbt, stirbt das Bewusstsein. *Was ist das Bewusstsein?* Man spürt es nicht. Um es zu spüren, fehlt das Organ. Ein paar Gedanken, die sich vergeblich selbst untersuchen, ein paar Ideen vielleicht, zu weiten Teilen ein Ramschladen, das meiste secondhand. Irgendwo ein *Buchhalter*, der die Inventarliste schreibt, die immer wieder angefangene und nie vollendete Sicherungskopie des ganzen Unternehmens, flüchtigen Medien, *Tagebüchern*, Freunden, Floppy Discs und Papierstößen anvertraut in der *Hoffnung*, sie könne eines Tages auf einem ähnlich fragwürdigen Betriebssystem wie dem eigenen unter Rauschen und Knistern noch einmal abgespielt werden." (*AS*, 214; emphasis mine; Waiting. Your consciousness dies when you die. *What is consciousness?* You can't feel it. We lack the organ to feel it. A few thoughts, which analyze themselves to no avail, a few ideas maybe, but in large parts a junk shop, most of it secondhand. Somewhere there's a *bookkeeper* who is making an inventory; the backup copy of the whole enterprise that is started again and again and never completed; fleeting media, *diaries*, friends, floppy discs, and stacks of paper are entrusted with it in the *hope* that in among the background noise and crackling they could one day be played back again, on a similarly dubious operating system as one's own.)

As the subject of ongoing debate in the sciences and in philosophy, the question of the nature of consciousness that he puts to himself must by necessity be approached creatively. And this is, of course, exactly where the author's—and generally literature's—strengths lie. For the dying man, it soon turns into the more pressing question of whether and how one's consciousness and individual perspective on the world can "outlive" a person's (physical) death. Strikingly, when considering the traces one leaves, Herrndorf is quick to see the act of diary writing as a way of preserving and sharing at least a fraction of one's elusive mental landscape. What is more, he mentions not only the diary verbatim but also his role as diarist: he is that bookkeeper taking the inventory, producing the faulty backup copy—all in the hope of finding readers willing to engage with the self-reflexive product of one man's short-lived consciousness vis-à-vis death. We are familiar with this hope the autothanatographer puts in the readership from Schlingensief's words in *So schön*.

In light of Herrndorf's hardened nihilism, any such expression of hope (to connect with a readership, potentially creating something of lasting value to people) cannot remain uncontested. However tentatively the feeling is expressed in *Arbeit und Struktur* in the first place, its optimism is immediately qualified by the author pointing out the absurdity of the diaristic project, considering the grand scheme of things: "Der Versuch, sich selbst zu verwalten, sich fortzuschreiben, der Kampf gegen die Zeit, der Kampf gegen den Tod, der sinnlose Kampf gegen die Sinnlosigkeit eines idiotischen, bewusstlosen Kosmos, und mit einem Faustkeil in der erhobenen Hand steht man da auf der Spitze des Berges, um dem herabstürzenden Asteroiden noch mal richtig die Meinung zu sagen." (*AS*, 214; The attempt to administer the self, to continue writing it, the battle against time, the battle against death, the pointless battle against the pointlessness of an idiotic, nonsentient cosmos, and with a hand axe held high one stands on the top of a mountain to give the asteroid that comes crashing down a piece of one's mind.) Approaching the end of his life, Herrndorf must convince himself of the use of the craft of writing and the powerful effect reading can have all the more, as against the odds, he employs the primitive tools at his disposal: the hand axe that self-mockingly stands for the writer's pen or the blogger's keyboard.

Despite the difficulties for the autothanatographer outlined here, Herrndorf rejects concerns over voyeurism and reverence that are so typically and readily proffered, recognizing them as leading to exclusion from social and cultural life. From the perspective of the terminally ill author, these concerns appear hypocritical and are merely a way of policing discourse: "Denn warum nicht hingucken?" (*AS*, 254; Why shouldn't we look on?) Herrndorf asks in October 2011 in the context of having watched a documentary about André Rieder,[73] a man living with manic depression who comes to end his life with the organization Exit in Switzerland. Discontent with the fact that the film declines to show the man's actual death, the rhetorical question the author poses reveals part of his motivation for having made his own diary available to the online reading public. It is his attempt to minimize the gap the documentary leaves as it refrains from showing the moment of Rieder's death.

In its eschewal of screening such images, ultimately circumnavigating the controversial core of its subject matter, the documentary's structure demonstrates the force of the cultural taboos that surround the act of killing oneself as well as representations of the moment of dying and the showing of corpses. Himself more and more concerned with, indeed fascinated by, the "Darstellung der unbegreiflichen Nichtigkeit menschlicher Existenz" (*AS*, 255; representation of the inconceivable futility of human existence), Herrndorf, by making his diary freely available online, explicitly invites "the gaze of the outsider" and offers anyone willing to read it a glimpse into life with progressive illness and approaching death.[74] Doing so connects back to Herrndorf's literary ideals, precisely aiming to enable the reader to get an idea of "etwas, worüber man sonst im Leben etwas zu erfahren nicht viel Gelegenheit hat" (*AS*, 104; something that you otherwise in life don't have much chance to experience). It makes him a "terrorist writer" very much like Schlingensief.

Reacting to the panel discussion that follows the program, Herrndorf notes, "Pietät mein Arsch. Wenn mit Lebenden einmal so pietätvoll umgegangen würde wie mit Toten oder Sterbenden oder wenigstens ein vergleichbares Gewese drum gemacht werden würde." (*AS*, 255; Piety my ass. If only the living were treated with as much piety as the dead or dying or at least were made a similar fuss about.) Beyond being a comment on the Rieder case, it is a comment too on the irony the diarist sees in his own soaring fame as celebrity patient as well as on the brutality of societal power dynamics more generally. We note, however, that such social concerns overall feature less prominently in Herrndorf's end-of-life writing than they do in Schlingensief's.

The Diary as a Means of "Touching Time"

Time becomes a precious resource for Herrndorf, its passing a major problem. Keeping the diary at once displays an obsession with time and provides a way of writing the self in what could be called suspended time. *Arbeit und Struktur*'s preface and the image of dawn that the author conjures up in it suggest as much, and so does the text's growing importance for Herrndorf as he is approaching death.

In June 2012, Herrndorf logged his thoughts after reading the diary of Anne Frank, the best-known diary of our time.[75] Reflecting on how, as a child, German history to him was "vergangenste Vergangenheit" (*AS*, 333; a bygone past), his reading of Frank's diary now, as an adult, gives rise to the exact opposite impression: "Jetzt zum ersten Mal die zeitliche Dimension bemerkt: 23 Jahre liegen zwischen dem ersten Tagebucheintrag und meiner Geburt, eine Generation, mehr nicht, ein Wimpernschlag" (*AS*, 333; For the first time I have consciously noticed the temporal dimension: twenty-three years lie between the first diary entry and my birth, one generation, that's all, the blink of an eye). The fact that Frank chose the diary form and duly dated her entries is exactly what, to borrow the words of Lejeune, paradoxically "immunizes it against ageing,"[76] in the sense that it gives Herrndorf, and any reader, the opportunity to pick up on and relate to a specific historical date from his position in the present. Even more so, it enables "the feeling of *touching time*."[77] It is above all for this, its potential for reaching out across differences (temporal, among others), that Frank's diary qualifies as literature when measured against Herrndorf's literary ideals. And it explains why Herrndorf himself chose the diary genre for what many would soon see as "sein eigentliches Hauptwerk"[78] (actually his most important work).

The effect of touching time is precious when it occurs; Herrndorf also writes about the frustration of failing to achieve this, when he himself brushes up against the limits of his imagination. In an entry from November 2010, pervaded by suicidal thoughts, two other historical figures crop up. These are Albrecht Dürer and the life model for Dürer's 1493 drawing "Female Nude (with Headcloth and Slippers)": "Ich denke an Dürer, der tot ist, warum ausgerechnet Dürer, ich weiß es nicht, an einen seit 500 Jahren toten Maler, der seine Badefrau gezeichnet hat, der ihr gegenübersaß und sie zeichnete, der mit ihr redete, kein Mensch weiß, worüber, und sie waren glücklich oder unglücklich, verschämt oder aufgekratzt, verliebt oder gleichgültig, für ein paar Minuten oder Stunden, waren einmal *reale* Wesen in einer *realen* Welt, was man sich *nicht vorstellen* kann. Ich kann es mir *nicht vorstellen*. Und die Absurdität macht mich verrückt." (*AS*, 160; emphasis mine; I am thinking of Dürer, who is dead, why Dürer out of all people; I don't know. A painter who has now been dead for five hundred years, who drew his woman before the bath, sat opposite her and drew her, talked to her, no one knows what about, and they were happy or unhappy, coy or in high spirits, in love or indifferent, for a few minutes or hours, once were *real* people in a *real* world, which you just *can't imagine*. I *cannot imagine* it. And the absurdity of it drives me insane.)

His thinking of Dürer is, of course, not quite as random as Herrndorf makes out, the painter being one of the old masters he so admired when studying art in Nuremberg, Dürer's hometown. Albeit able to visualize the drawing, a work of art that has outlasted centuries, what remains distant is an understanding of the artist and his model as people, who once were living, breathing humans just as the diarist himself in this moment. Unlike in the case of Anne Frank's daily life and thoughts as rendered in her diary, Herrndorf fails at imagining the couple alive on the basis of the image that has remained of their encounter. As a consequence, the sketch to him remains enigmatic, hollow, lifeless. The repeated use of the adjective "real" and the successive negations of the verb *vorstellen* (to imagine) indicate the extent to which this bothers him. It drives him insane, as he puts it, because it is exactly what he writes against in *Arbeit und Struktur*: "Die Unmöglichkeit, sich ein nicht selbst erlebtes Vergangenes vorzustellen, die Unmöglichkeit, sich in ein anderes Lebewesen hineinzudenken, die Unmöglichkeit, sich das Nichtsein vorzustellen" (*AS*, 160; The impossibility of imagining a past you haven't yourself experienced, the impossibility of knowing what is going on inside another creature, the impossibility of imagining not existing). The autothanatographical diary is the author's attempt to chip away at these bounds of the human imagination, counting on the power of literature as a site where memory comes alive—very much with his own readership in mind.

Fact, Fiction, and the Faculty of Imagination—Reaching beyond Genre

In *Arbeit und Struktur*, human inventiveness (expressed both in the form of Herrndorf's admiration for all kinds of inventions and scientific knowledge, as well as his pleasure in his own and others' literary creativity) comes up against humankind's limited agency in times of illness. Worst of all, for Herrndorf, is to have to endure not knowing any definite facts concerning the course his life with, and death from, illness will take; he receives conflicting prognoses from the various doctors who treat him (*AS*, 30–31) and comes up with contradictory findings when searching the Internet for medical research on the type of brain tumor he suffers from. The only way the diarist can bear the severe uncertainty he faces is through creative play. His rendering of a walk to the practice of "Dr. Fünf" (*AS*, 397; Dr. Five) on a snowy morning exemplifies what this entails: "Im Laufen mache ich einen Schneeball und werfe ihn mit einer halben Drehung nach einem Laternenmast, an dem ich gerade vorbeigegangen bin, um herauszufinden, ob ich zu den 0,5 Prozent Zehn-Jahre-Überlebenden gehöre. Ein Meter vorbei. Man hat nur einen Versuch, oder? Oder darf ich nochmal? Nein, wie im richtigen Leben, immer nur einmal." (*AS*, 398; As I am walking I form a snowball in my hands and, doing a 180-degree turn, I throw it back at the lamppost I just walked past, in order to find out whether I belong to the 0.5 percent ten-year survivors. I miss by a meter. You only get one chance, don't you? Can I try again? No, like in real life, always just one go.)

The outcome of the snowball experiment is as valid or deceptive as any other prediction. Other examples of such creative, sometimes literary, play are Herrndorf's willful insertions of false information into *Wikipedia* for it to match the worlds he is building in his fiction (*AS*, 151), as well as his incorporating into a diary entry the life expectancy of three to four years that a doctor predicts to him in a dream (*AS*, 153). The latter is reported in the text in the same matter-of-fact manner as the prognoses Herrndorf wrests from doctors in his waking life. Indeed, from the outset of the illness diary, fact and fiction seem to reach into each other: the author reveals that what helps him settle into life in the psychiatric ward is the fact that a fellow patient strikes him as resembling the fictional character Isa he had created for *Tschick* (*AS*, 9–14). To begin and to keep writing the diary fosters a creative perspective on the world that gives the fantastical the same ontological status as the reality that encroaches upon him, a perspective that could be labeled romantic.[79] It is the maximum degree of spirituality that Herrndorf allows himself. It is not a privileging of fiction over fact (that is, not a form of detachment from the world), but rather, it suggests an approximation of the two. *Arbeit und Struktur*'s aesthetic is one that suspends "normal" judgment and gives the realm of a playful, literary speculation as much validity as the empirical world surrounding and finally closing in on its author. In this sense, Herrndorf's illness diary demonstrates the kinship of the fictional and the nonfictional in a way that only life writing, and maybe particularly end-of-life writing, can do.

The diary documents Herrndorf's ongoing engagement with the effect of genre ascriptions—reflecting on the potential of autobiographical writing in particular. In this context, he compares Karl Philipp Moritz's *Anton Reiser* (1785–90) and Rousseau's *Confessions* (1782 and 1788) and by doing so goes back to texts that are today canonized as two of the first major secular autobiographies. Herrndorf appreciates Rousseau's "uneinlösbaren Anspruch" (*AS*, 292; unachievable aspiration) of wanting to show "a man in every way true to nature,"[80] as the famous opening lines have it, but he finds that Moritz's *Reiser* comes much closer to realizing this aim. With *Reiser*, Herrndorf notably favors a book that entered literary history for revolutionizing both the novel genre and that of autobiography,[81] as well as the relative underdog in the equation.

Thus relating his writing *Arbeit und Struktur* to Rousseau (critically) and Moritz (favorably), as well as the literary history of autobiographical writing that they stand for, Herrndorf comments explicitly on his own approach to the practice of diary writing from the contemporary margins of that tradition, culminating in the following ellipsis: "Das Gefasel von der Unzuverlässigkeit des Gedächtnisses und der Unzulänglichkeit der Sprache spare ich mir, allein der berufsbedingt ununterdrückbare Impuls, *dem Leben wie einem Roman zu Leibe zu rücken,* die sich im Akt des Schreibens immer wieder einstellende, das Weiterleben enorm erleichternde, falsche und nur im Text richtige Vorstellung, die Fäden in der Hand zu halten und das seit langem bekannte und im Kopf ständig schon vor- und ausformulierte Ende selbst bestimmen und den tragischen Helden mit wohlgesetzten, naturnotwendigen, fröhlichen Worten in den Abgrund stürzen zu dürfen wie gewohnt—" (*AS*, 292; emphasis mine; I spare myself ramblings about the unreliability of memory or the shortcomings of language, solely the impulse—irrepressible and down to my occupation—*to approach life like a novel*, the notion that again and again sets in during the act of writing of holding the reins, which is wrong, only right in text, yet makes going on living so much easier; and to decide over the long-known and in the mind's eye perpetually pre- and fully formulated ending; and with words that are well placed, cheerful, and by their nature, essential to bring ruin on the tragic hero as per usual—); this, one surmises, is what he permits himself to do.

For one, the autothanatographer claims his right to speak here. By pointing out that his work as life writer is not so different from his work as novelist, moreover, he moves the diary in the proximity of the novel with this statement. In doing so, he builds on Moritz's remodeling of his own autobiographical story into *Anton Reiser*, a publication that sparked a new genre, that of the "psychological novel," as is established in the text's subheading. This resonated with Herrndorf, who found it apt "to approach life like a novel" and who, by keeping *Arbeit und Struktur*, takes up the "Prinzip der Selbstbeobachtung" (principle of self-observation) advocated by Moritz,[82] identifying threads and themes that run through his life and feeding them into the diary. It is what gives *Arbeit und Struktur*, when read as a whole, a certain narrative coherence and invites readers to treat the text as "life fiction,"[83] subject to one condition: that they do not repudiate the actuality of the diarist's existence, which Herrndorf strips down to this: "Im einen Moment belebte Materie, im nächsten dasselbe, nur ohne Adjektiv" (*AS*, 255; One moment [you are] live matter, the next, [you're] the same, just lacking the adjective).

Creative life writing as Herrndorf practices it deconstructs any traditionalist binary thinking about fictional genres on the one hand and nonfictional (e.g., autobiographical) genres on the other—or the novel and the diary more specifically. It rehabilitates the diary as literature and demonstrates, once more for literary history, that the diary can be and is being put to poetic and to narrative uses. Lastly, it shows that out of the snapshots that are individual entries, over time and as the diarist writes on, unrestrained by aspirations to conform to ideals of any one genre, an image of a self emerges.

Posthumous Reading Practices and Herrndorf's Selfies

When studying autothanatographical diaries published online, one must bear in mind that one's reading from a posthumous stance is a different reading from that of the contemporary blog follower. The latter reads entries in what comes close to real time, most likely beginning with the latest rather than the oldest post, and of necessity does so discontinuously, in a pattern primarily determined by the rhythm in which entries are published. The posthumous reader of the diary as an archived site or book can be assumed to read a larger number of passages at a time and in chronological order, and—as an effect—may not become aware of days of silence quite the same. In a sense, the posthumous reader (and maybe especially the book reader) fast-forwards the illness narrative, somewhat overriding a defining characteristic of the diary form, namely the interval between "Unterbrechung und Wiederaufnahme" (disruption and resumption) of the act of writing.[84] In this respect, posthumous reading habits of Herrndorf's diary also move it closer to the novel form. This almost inevitable change in reading practice in part stems from the knowledge later readers have of *Arbeit und Struktur*'s ending, marked by the deterioration of Herrndorf's health as well as his suicide, which takes place outside the text yet is incorporated in the blog in the form of a concluding death note.[85] And to those later readers who approach *Arbeit und Struktur* in book format, the form of the printed book itself suggests completion and closure. Readers coming to the text after Herrndorf's death on August 26, 2013, be it on- or offline, necessarily and unavoidably wear a different interpretative hat. Herrndorf's role since is confined to that of protagonist in the diary text, as he himself had anticipated.

Herrndorf, in fact, tested out his becoming a character when writing himself into *Bilder deiner großen Liebe*, the last piece of fiction he was working on in parallel to *Arbeit und Struktur*. Narrator-protagonist Isa renders Herrndorf's cameo appearance as follows: "'Was machst du da?,' fragt ein Mann, der wie aus dem Boden neben mir aufgetaucht ist. Er trägt eine grüne Trainingsjacke."[86] ("What are you doing there?" asks a man who has popped up next to me out of nowhere. He is wearing a green tracksuit top.) It is his trademark Adidas jacket that Herrndorf can be seen wearing in a widely used author's portrait that makes him so recognizable here. Poignantly, the dying author's fictional self appears to Isa in a graveyard and strikes up a conversation about commemoration rituals with her. Just as the lines of fiction and reality can come to blur within the diary, the author here crosses over into the narrative world of Isa to become a character in his own fiction—if only for a moment, as after a short exchange he disappears again.

On the one hand, Herrndorf points out the permeability of the boundaries between fact and fiction, diary and novel in his late work. On the other, he corroborates the extratextual referentiality of *Arbeit und Struktur* as a piece of life writing by incorporating photographs into the diary/blog. The majority of the inserted photos are so-called selfies; the angle and quality of the images suggest that they have been taken with the built-in camera of Herrndorf's laptop computer. Most of these snapshots depict the diarist looking straight at the camera lens—thereby complying with a classic feature of self-portraiture.[87] Thus making reference to self-representations in painting is yet another way of dismissing the charges that autobiographical writing incurred within literary studies. After all, in visual art, self-portraiture has been an established, reputable genre for centuries. (Yet, of course, the diary is to autobiographical writing what the selfie is to self-portraiture: its most popular, in the sense of most widely practiced, "low" form.)

In the no-frills shots he takes of himself, Herrndorf displays hardly any facial expression, keeps posing to a minimum, and rarely comments on a picture. This marks them as matter-of-fact, documentary material that not exactly invites but nonetheless allows for readers to have an emotional reaction to these images. The diarist takes the photographs in his apartment (*AS*, 70, 269, 345), outdoors (*AS*, 82, 159), and in hospital rooms (*AS*, 174, 265, 297), as can be gathered from the background of the pictures. Most of them have been carried over from the blog into the book publication, too, although reproduced in black and white.

On a documentary level, and as they accumulate over time, the images capture physical changes in the author. These changes are often subtle but can sometimes be drastic, as when Herrndorf—back home from hospital—holds the back of his head squarely into the webcam, taking a picture that shows off a fresh scar, complete with staples; a result of the latest operation (*AS*, 269). The diarist himself can, with some justification, be seen as the primary beholder of these visual records of illness and its treatment that he produces; without taking the picture of the scar, for example, Herrndorf himself would not have been able to view it in the first place. What is more, this and other photos allow Herrndorf momentarily to externalize his viewpoint and relate to the images as if he were a reader. Adopting Roland Barthes's terminology from *Camera Lucida*, the diarist is tempted by the possibility of taking up the position of operator, spectrum and spectator all at once; in other words, he who takes the selfie is subject in it and views it too.[88] With Herrndorf's diary otherwise consisting largely of text, each of these photographic self-portraits—especially in the way they appear to blog readers as they scroll down, and in full color—is a calculated disruption of the flow of reading. Conscious of the media at his disposal, the diarist employs photography in this way to remind his readership that this diary is—now was—lived reality for him.

Through insertion of these images, readers are prompted to consider the ways in which they themselves are implicated in the illness diary. Herrndorf offers a face to his diaristic voice and thus honors expectations of intimacy that readers bring to life writing, and above all diary texts. Yet it depends on whether individual readers can pause, linger, and endure the gaze that the dying author directs at them from the self-portraits, or whether they find themselves quickly scrolling past them. Herrndorf, who made his diary available for anyone to read, and himself to be looked at, is looking back; perhaps more defiantly so than Schlingensief from *So schön*'s cover. Herrndorf's insertion of these images can be seen as a way of ensuring a balance between inviting readers who come to his blog from the vastness of the Internet to read his illness story as they would fiction, and visually confronting them with the fact that he is—at least at the time of writing—one of them, one of the living. Part of accepting that likeness with the author means that readers must accept the more difficult truth of their own mortality. Herrndorf's use of amateur photography in this way echoes Schlingensief's more direct verbal and, when on stage, also physical provocations of readerships/audiences. Both end-of-life writers knowingly confronted the public with their thanatophobia. They knew of its shock value. In the words of Walter Benjamin, which Schlingensief chose as epigraph to his diary publication: "Es gibt für die Menschen, wie sie heute sind, nur eine radikale Neuigkeit—und das ist immer die gleiche: der Tod" (There is only one radical piece of news for people, the way they are today—and that is always the same: death).

The use of photography in the autothanatographical diary addresses directly the dying author's anticipated transformation from subject to object. As Susan Sontag has rightly highlighted, "All photographs are *memento mori*. To take a photograph is to participate in another person's (or thing's) mortality, vulnerability, mutability. Precisely by slicing out this moment and freezing it, all photographs testify to time's relentless melt."[89] Like the diary genre, then, the medium of photography takes issue with time, without being able to halt it. What it can do, however, is attempt to give reassurance that "something [or somebody] exists, or did exist."[90] If, in life, the diarist's self-portraits emphasized the author's presence, they now, in his death, reinforce his absence. Through the visual aesthetic of pop culture rather than that of high art, Herrndorf's selfies indicate, too, how the diarist would like to be read, namely, with a minimum of "elegies, praise, and idealization" that typically launch a dead celebrity's "posthumous career" as public negotiations of that person's after-image begin.[91] The decision to tap into and combine the everyday practices of taking selfies and keeping a diary reinforces an important message to later readers: *Arbeit und Struktur* asks us not to endow its author posthumously with sanctity but instead to engage with the works he left behind.

Sounding Out the Limits of Human Experience at the Margins of Literature

With some justification, *Arbeit und Struktur* could be called the most experimental text of Herrndorf's oeuvre. Questioning genre boundaries, crisscrossing the line from high art to popular culture and back, the diarist discomforts readers in their urge to classify the text and asks them instead to deal with ambiguity and uncertainty, both in content and in form. In effect, *Arbeit und Struktur* is a text that suggests to readers that they abandon their diagnostic impulse, their need to categorize that puts them in a position of power over the writer not unlike that of a medical professional—and instead dares them to see themselves as on an equal footing with the author.

In *Arbeit und Struktur*, Herrndorf exhibits his poetological convictions with renewed vigor. Much of what the diary form has to offer intuitively appealed to him at the time of terminal illness: accessibility, precision, and clarity come to matter more than ever, as is expressed, for instance, in the stated ambition for the diary to recall, in style, the *Code civil*, that is the sober style of legal texts (*AS*, 444). Herrndorf's dislike for stilted writing as for traditional philosophy was amplified from the perspective of terminal illness (*AS*, 313–14, 64). As an author inspired by Popliteratur and Romanticism in equal measure, he violates any distinctions between high and low literature in writing *Arbeit und Struktur*—as did Schlingensief regarding low and high art on and beyond the theatrical stage. Just as Schlingensief in his *Tagebuch*, Herrndorf through *Arbeit und Struktur* expresses a wariness of cultural elitism. In writing autothanatographically, both authors turned to the diary as a tangible, quotidian genre that derives its concerns from concrete reality and everyday life; in each case, this must be understood as a conscious decision informed by what ultimately proved to be terminal illness.

It is commonplace to stress the therapeutic value of illness narratives—for literary scholarship, however, this assumption can only be a starting point for investigations into cultural productions arising from personal illness experiences. It certainly should not be the end point. The diaries analyzed in the chapter at hand focus on selves in crisis, yet they do so in the context of their culture and their time. Acknowledging this is to recognize the diary—and maybe especially the end-of-life diary—as a socially relevant and politically potent genre beyond the personal meaning it can take on for the individual writer and reader. It is no coincidence that Herrndorf's diary/blog fueled the ongoing debate around liberalizing assisted dying in Germany. As it wove the mesh of an individual life and set forth the challenges of cancer as they affected Herrndorf's everyday life and his literary convictions, it also became the means through which the writer entered into the politics of the personal.

In contrast to Schlingensief, Herrndorf withdrew from the media, critics, and public in all but this one way. Through the means of his diary/blog, he too claimed his right to participate in literary debates and in societal matters generally, and indeed to provoke, such as in the case of the German assisted dying debate. Relatively suddenly finding himself in the limelight of the German literary scene, through the medium of the blog, Herrndorf also exercised his right to influence narratives that had begun to emerge about him as a person and as an author. Along the way, he asserted the literary value of the diary—and the resulting text *Arbeit und Struktur* is now seen by many as his magnum opus.

As early as June 2011, a little over a year after the blog's inception, Wolfgang Höbel, writing for *Der Spiegel*, hailed Herrndorf's diary/blog as a "Literaturereignis" (literary sensation), and the accolades continued from then on.[92] Herrndorf, interestingly, was subjected to much less of the doubt and clear rejection that Schlingensief, so shortly before him, had to experience when publishing his cancer diary.[93] Despite the difference in reception, both illness diaries notably triggered extreme reactions. These seemingly arbitrary and contradictory judgments of outright rejection, even hostility, on the one hand, and overwhelming praise, on the other, can, however, be related to each other.

In the context of Holocaust testimony, Dori Laub has delineated "hazards to the listening to trauma."[94] Among the reactions he describes being displayed by overchallenged readers or listeners to difficult stories of personal experiences, we recognize both of the opposing reactions that came to bear on the cancer diaries discussed in this chapter: Laub finds that in some cases, a "sense of outrage and of anger" is directed at the victim/narrator—which is very much the reaction Schlingensief's text (and his subsequent strong media presence) elicited in a large, or at least particularly vocal, part of his readership.[95] Astonishingly, Laub even uses the example of disablist reactions to disclosures of serious illness as a point of reference in this context. He explains the psychological cause of such feelings of anger toward an ill person thus: "We are torn apart by the inadequacy of our ability to properly respond, and inadvertently wish for the illness to be the patient's responsibility and wrongdoing."[96] This latter tendency that Laub detects (without explicitly criticizing it) is certainly one that has been at work in popular negotiations of illness—one needs only to recall myths about a supposed *Krebspersönlichkeit*, or cancer personality, widespread in the 1970s and 1980s and beyond.[97] It has certainly done much harm to people living with, and dying from, serious illness.

In other cases, Laub points out that the victim/narrator is met with a "flood of awe and fear."[98] His explanation for this reaction, which I find exemplified in reactions to *Arbeit und Struktur* and which only intensified after Herrndorf's death, goes as follows: "We endow the survivor [or the cancer diarist] with a kind of sanctity, both to pay our tribute to him and to keep him at a distance, to avoid the intimacy entailed in knowing."[99] It is a way of avoiding confrontation with one's own fears surrounding mortality and the limits of one's agency. Although expressed in a different manner, this distancing strategy is ultimately also a refusal to engage or empathize with another's pain. This psychological dynamic at work on the side of the readership obscures the complex and multilayered text Herrndorf's autothanatographical diary has become and may explain the way in which the media reported on the writer's late achievements.[100]

I introduced this chapter by stressing the important role time plays in diaries. Time may be the only element that separates a readership from the experiences captured by these autothanatographical writers. Because as readers we are implicated in their stories more than we would like to admit, in ways both illness diarists have indeed anticipated, our own emotions can get in the way of reading or listening adequately, and may at worst prevent us from reading their texts at all. Reactions that negate the social or the literary relevance of these autothanatographical diaries must be understood in this light. With Felman and Laub in mind, we might take this as a refusal to act as another's witness.

As Schlingensief made clear in the context of the feuilleton debate of 2009,[101] he believed there was a pressing need to explore personal narratives of illness and dying in a public space in a way that goes beyond the emotive media coverage of daytime TV but retains the individual aspect lacking in philosophical treatise. By taking up the diary genre and making it suit their needs and aspirations as illness enters and alters their lives, both Schlingensief and Herrndorf count on the power of the personal and begin to fill the gap in reading matter identified by Schlingensief for a contemporary audience. The provocative nature of the cancer diary lies in its mundanity, both in its liminal literary form and in its autothanatographical content. Negotiating their illnesses between the poles of cliché and exceptionality, working with and across different media, as well as through their prompt publishing of at least parts of their diary recordings, the two autothanatographers have demonstrated this genre's potential for the twenty-first century.

Conclusion: "Und was dann"; Recent Developments and Research Desiderata

THIS BOOK HAS HIGHLIGHTED autobiographically motivated writing centering on illness/disability and dying as a neglected field of study in German literary and cultural scholarship. In response to this finding, it has demonstrated productive ways of reading this kind of literature, exemplifying in each chapter a number of approaches that could be taken further in the future.

Going against the tendency in the German-speaking world of regarding life writing as artless per se, and works centering on illness/disability as all the more so, this study brings the tools of literary studies to bear upon a selection of contemporary, personal narratives dealing with these themes from an inside perspective. In particular, it interrogates the ways authors capture their experiences in texts and how they negotiate positions of being in illness and of authorship in a cultural context that, until recently, has not seen a large number of publications telling personally of the lived experience of illness/disability including, sometimes, that of dying. By grounding the research in the field of disability studies, I have given the literary analysis of each individual text an innovative perspective, and, crucially, this has enabled me to identify gaps and contortions in the dominant readings of these texts, readings that often effectively disregard the illness experience at their center or contest the narrative's literary quality.

The research presented here found much of the political weight of a text to be carried by its formal features—which have typically been overlooked. For Charlotte Roche (chapter 1), for example, the choice of an autofictional representational mode must be read as governed by the need to reclaim agency over the story of her traumatic bereavement from the media without making herself vulnerable to fresh media intrusions and hurtful publicity. In Kathrin Schmidt's text (chapter 2), the narrative device of staring helps to fulfill the didactic aim of *Du stirbst nicht* to destabilize a readership's ableist and potentially disablist beliefs about illness/disability and conditions of speechlessness. For Verena Stefan, intertextuality becomes the crucial means in *Fremdschläfer* to align herself with the positions and values of feminist forerunners who negotiated illness publicly (chapter 3), while the text's Certeaudian poetics stresses the democratic relationship she as life writer strives for in regard to her readership. Lastly, the preference of Christoph Schlingensief and Wolfgang Herrndorf for the diary form (chapter 4) can be explained by the genre's ordinariness and mundanity. By choosing to write illness in this everyday form, both authors implicitly make a point about their strange growth in cultural status as they confront terminal illness publicly and as it occurs. Together, these revealing findings demonstrate the need to establish a literary disability studies field within Germanistik. One compelling reason for this is that contemporary writing about illness/disability and dying is more reflective and complex in its construction—that is, more literary, if one will—than is generally assumed both in the public discourse as well as within academia. That is to say, such autobiographical writing can be an artistic practice as much as, and at the same time as, being an important social practice.

Through the lens of disability studies, arguments against attending to this kind of writing from an academic stance have been recognized as strategies of avoidance. This avoidance has its origins partly in the low/high culture divide along which traditional German studies scholarship still operates, especially within Germany, but it is markedly aggravated by a widespread unease with confronting the reality of illness/disability and dying that pervades hegemonic culture. The texts this book focuses on may be at times difficult reads, yet their intensified rate of publication alone (from circa 2007 onward) should qualify them as being of interest to German literary studies. Together with their widespread reception, the texts' presence points to the fact that we are living through a moment of cultural change in the German-speaking world—a moment in which it becomes possible, for the first time, to write of illness/disability personally and reach a large, mainstream audience. This, at least, was the fundamental observation with which I set out on this study, intrigued by the power that autobiographical writing on matters of illness/disability and death evidently holds over a contemporary reading public.

Despite the fact that this study has dealt with a different contemporary author and text in each chapter, thematizing diverse illness experiences in a range of life-writing genres and across different media, the unifying methodological approach of disability studies has revealed a number of overarching themes. In this conclusion, I review how German illness narratives address and affect their readership, the way in which these texts go beyond binary thinking about factual and fictional writing (frequently drawing on features from both), and their questioning of prevalent notions of what is public and what is private, before returning to the authors' potential motivations for voicing illness autobiographically, despite the risks involved.

In the search for literature that can "shift prejudices about disability,"[1] Pauline Eyre in the conclusion to her 2009 PhD thesis came to favor fiction over autobiographical writing as more likely to accomplish this aim. Allowing for more subversive storytelling, she finds fiction more likely to change people's mind-sets. Eyre states boldly that "mere autobiographical representation of disability is ineffective as a means of engaging with the nondisabled reader, since it enshrines the very difference it sets out to problematize, institutionalizing, in effect, the disabled autobiographer and her narrative."[2] She comes to this conclusion on the basis of analyzing German-language texts from across the spectrum of autobiographical and fictional writing from the 1970s.[3] Recalling, for example, my observations regarding the development of the public discourse on Kathrin Schmidt's text *Du stirbst nicht*, especially once its author had been honored with the Deutscher Buchpreis (chapter 2), Eyre's concern here can certainly not be dismissed as unfounded. It is, in fact, a worry shared by the large majority of the life writers whose work I examined; accordingly, the question of whether they will be known only for their illness writing from the point of publication onward, or not be taken seriously anymore as professional writers, looms large in their texts.

Notwithstanding this, some strengths of the autobiographical mode may shed light on its rediscovery in recent years for the writing of illness/disability in the German context. As a rhetorical stance, writers of illness/disability employ the autobiographical to signal authenticity or commitment to a cause, or as a tactic to draw in the largest possible readership—and sometimes to achieve all this at once. Displaying a high awareness of the pitfalls of autobiographical representation, the contemporary authors considered in this book problematize the author-reader relationship of illness narrative in the texts themselves, both on the level of content and on the level of form. From Roche to Herrndorf, these authors find their own narrative strategies and aesthetic forms to relate illness/disability to what they know to be a potentially hostile reception. They tend to do so in a markedly contemporary manner, in the context of reflecting on their lives as a whole (thus avoiding isolating the experience of illness/disability), and in ways that, in many cases, can be called novelistic. This indicates the authors' aspirations to produce a piece of writing that will continue to be read, in other words, a work with the impact of "literature." The authors can be seen to strive to reach diverse audiences: refusing to be pigeonholed, they do not write exclusively for fellow ill or disabled people, nor do they exclusively address those as yet untouched by the issues and questions central to their texts.

Maybe most significantly, each text—though in some ways relating an "extraordinary" experience—at the same time stresses the mundanity of illness/disability, death, and dying. Crucially, the writers discussed here are at pains to demonstrate that they are not other, and thus approximate their subject position to that of the reader. There is a daring element to this, and it is one that is exclusive to autobiographical modes. Such writing cannot be dismissed by readers as being "merely" fiction, an intellectual game at best. Instead, readers of a personal illness narrative are challenged to confront their own feelings in relation to the "real" person speaking from between the book's covers and must acknowledge that their own life is as vulnerable to illness/disability as that of the author/narrator, and equally unstable. Especially in the case of narratives of serious and potentially terminal illness, rather than narratives of "stable" disability,[4] doing so means confronting the reality of one's own eventual death.

Recognizing both the realness of illness/disability as well as its unimaginability for at least a section of their readership, many of the examined texts blur the lines between autobiographical and fictional writing, drawing on techniques from both (consider, for instance, Herrndorf's diary writing, chapter 4). They can be observed to make use of the protective mask that the fictional offers them as vulnerable writers when they need it. What is more, it appears that, for a significant number of authors, only by writing closely along the boundaries of fact and fiction does it become possible to find an authorial position from which to write personally and yet openly about illness/disability and, in the case of autothanatography, the liminal experience of one's own dying.

Strategies used by the authors of the texts analyzed here are becoming more common in newer texts. Reminiscent of the legal statement we find placed in front the beginning of Roche's autofictional narrative *Schoßgebete* (chapter 1), David Wagner's 2013 novel *Leben* (Life/Living) is prefaced with the words, "Alles war genau so / und auch ganz anders"[5] (Everything was exactly like this / as well as totally different). This ambivalent narrative positioning is crucially what gives him the authorial freedom and creative space to begin to tell this story of life, love, loss, and identity based on his own struggles with autoimmune disease and the events surrounding his liver transplant. Richard Wagner, taking a similar line, opens *Herr Parkinson* (Mister Parkinson, 2015) by stating, "Ich wäre natürlich das 'Ich,' aber nicht ganz"[6] (I am this "I," as it were, but not quite). At the end of the paragraph this quotation is taken from, in a playful manner, he notes about the other characters that appear in his text, "Auch für sie gilt, dass jede Ähnlichkeit mit lebenden Personen zufällig ist, was im Übrigen durch unseren Herrn Parkinson jederzeit bestätigt werden kann" (For them it equally pertains that any resemblance to living persons is coincidental, which by the way our Mister Parkinson can confirm at any time). The way these authors navigate the autobiographical for our contemporary times thus invites the reader's gaze at the same time as resisting it, making us reflect, with Rosemarie Garland-Thomson,[7] on the way we stare at difference.

Just as through their texts, many contemporary illness writers question any all-too-rigid demarcation of autobiographical and fictional modes of representation; so do these authors challenge notions of what is deemed public and what is to be kept private through the mere act of publication. "So, Schluss ... das darf nicht an die Öffentlichkeit!" (Right, stop here ... this must not fall into the hands of the public!) Schlingensief's voice can be heard to laugh dryly as the audio book version of *Ich weiß, ich war's* fades out.[8] By going public with illness, he knowingly upset widespread cultural sensibilities about the privacy of illness, as did the other authors whose work I examined. To share what are still perceived to be "private" stories with a wider audience is to seek to renegotiate boundaries between the private and public, as it questions who is served by adhering to them. In the age of the Internet and social media, for illness writers, and maybe especially for autothanatographers like Schlingensief and Herrndorf whose texts are analyzed in the chapter preceding this conclusion, it applies that "Menschsein heißt, medial sein wollen"[9] (Being human [today] is to want to be part of the media landscape).

Through both traditional (i.e., book) and more modern (online/multimedia) channels, the ill claim the same right as everyone else to participate in both off- and online discourses on matters of concern to them. Their self-image as well as their life and work more generally may be altered by the experience of illness/disability (sometimes dramatically so), but despite, or rather exactly because of this, they refuse to be written off prematurely. In many cases, their experience gives authors new political impetus as they come to reassess their place in the world. As I see it, the prevalent interpretative models of the therapeutic and the confessional, which are so often put forward as offering explanations for writing illness in the public realm, today need to be supplemented by an author's desire to participate in a social media landscape which reflects on illness/disability. Although this explanation may arouse the readerly imagination less than the confessional mode, for instance, does, it may offer a better explanation for the rising number of illness narratives not just in book (or even textual) form, but across all media and including visual narrative.

Despite the relatively small number of texts I looked at for this study, Büchner's *Woyzeck* and *Lenz*, Woolf's *On Being Ill*, and Sontag's *Illness as Metaphor* consistently featured as canonical reference points. Barring Roche, all of the authors whose work is discussed in the main chapters refer to one or more of these. The impact they themselves are now having on writers following suit proves the cultural significance of the work they have begun anew, for our contemporary times, in their negotiations of illness/disability, self, and society. While it may be too soon to talk about the formation of a "community" of ill/disabled writers, at least with regard to the Germanic context at the outset of the twenty-first century focused on here, many of the recent illness narratives display a newly politicized consciousness about what it means to be ill/disabled today. Of the ones analyzed here, Stefan's and Schlingensief's texts in particular begin to invoke illness as a communal experience (chapter 3 and 4).

As more texts come out, these illness narratives weave a net of diverse experiences and positions, and—taken together—they are developing a language to speak about illness today.

Intertextual ties—even when they remain unacknowledged—are increasing in number and visibility. Christoph Schlingensief's handling of his cancer served as example for his friend Henning Mankell once he fell ill, and it strengthened his resolve to write and publish *Kvicksand*.[10] Richard Wagner, giving a somber outlook on the progression of his Parkinson's at the end of his meditative account takes up the image of the "black square" first used in the context of illness writing by Herrndorf, in *Arbeit und Struktur* (384).[11] Herrndorf coined the phrase "schwarzes Quadrat auf schwarzem Grund" (black square on black background) in a twist on Kasimir Malevich's famous abstract painting *Black Square* (NB: on a white background) to grasp the nothingness of his anticipated death. Beyond the emotivity the black square contains for both authors, for Wagner, it furthermore is an apt description of the location of Parkinson's disease in his brain: "im schwarzen Quadrat der Nigra."[12] My prediction for the future is that texts will begin to relate to and reference each other more, and more explicitly so, as more personal illness narratives come out responding to the social, medial, political, and economic conditions of their, that is, our time. What I described as a "wave" or trend at the outset of this book can be expected to develop into a lasting tradition of writing the ill/disabled or dying self publicly, as, when confronted with illness, we are likely to continue to wonder, as Richard Wagner does in the final lines of *Herr Parkinson*: "Und was dann. / Und was noch. / Und was immer. / Und was auch. / Und was nicht."[13] (And what then. / And what ever. / And what else. / And what not.)

Accordingly, it will only become more important that, as literary scholars, we develop ways to read these texts well and do them justice. The research presented in this book lays bare a curious disconnect between what cultural studies has observed to be a new "Sichtbarkeit des Todes" (visibility of death), with the dead returning to mainstream media, high art, and public discourse,[14] and academic foci of interest as displayed in German literary studies. In the wake of this new visibility, the potential for a wider conversation about illness and dying beyond perceived boundaries of the private and public realms has opened up. Yet, hitherto, German literary and cultural studies remains more focused on—more comfortable with?—death rather than dying, taking impulses from philosophy and art history in dealing with it in a discourse that will always be theoretical, often relatively abstract, and indeed necessarily fictional. As a discipline, to date, German studies seem less keen to turn toward analyzing representations of the more troubling threat of death as we encounter it in this new life writing, and the process of actual dying as autothanatographies relay it, with all its physical and metaphysical pain.[15]

At the outset of my research I observed that disability studies is not yet an established field within Germanistik. This remains true as I am closing this book. Equally, Eyre's call for cultural disability studies to widen its scope beyond the English-language context has not yet been met satisfactorily.[15] Meanwhile, a special issue of *Life Writing*, titled "Body Language: Illness, Disability, and Life Writing" has appeared, confirming the experience of illness/disability as a central impulse leading writers to engage in the auto/biographical.[16] While this publication is extremely timely and welcome, its focus, being an English-language journal, is also on English-language cultures. Pointing to future directions for the study of personal representations of life with illness/disability, German studies scholars could take inspiration from such research and test, explore, and advance it by putting it into dialogue with narratives from the Germanic cultural realm.

As my final, comparative chapter 4 indicated, illness narratives do not always necessarily take on a traditional, written form. The autothanatographical diary keeping of Schlingensief and Herrndorf crossed and switched between media in ways that can be expected to become more common. And, while I had not been able to find much relevant recent research in preparing that chapter, with a recent issue of *Zeitschrift für Germanistik*, an important contribution has been made taking a fresh look at the diary genre from a firm literary studies angle, including also a new article on Herrndorf's *Arbeit und Struktur*.[17] Remaining with questions of genre, one area that has only lately attracted scholarly interest is that of the graphic novel. Although graphic novels currently seem more prevalent in English-language contexts,[18] examples from the Germanic field come to mind that point toward the (autobiographical) graphic novel as a nascent genre of storying illness/disability here too as well as confirming comics more generally as a suitable medium. Remembering comics that came out in the context of the AIDS crisis, such as *Die verlorene Zukunft* (The lost future, 1992),[19] we might grasp this as a returning rather than an entirely new trend. One example for a contemporary graphic novel dealing, semi-autobiographically, with illness and death is *Toen David zijn stem verloor* (*When David Lost His Voice*, 2012), by the Flemish artist Judith Vanistendael; many other, both autobiographical and fictional, comics increasingly subsumed under the label "graphic medicine" could be named.[20]

As a final specific research desideratum brought out by the work on this book, I suggest revisiting German-language illness narratives from previous decades, in particular those from the 1970s and 1980s. Based on my findings about recent literature and considering the critical reactions at the time of their publication and later, one inevitably wonders whether a subterranean tradition of writing the self in illness has been missed by literary scholarship, because the texts themselves were all too quickly dismissed from the sphere of literature. Subjecting these older texts to "unpatterned" reading from the stance of disability studies today, as I argued in the introduction,[21] maybe even reading them in tandem with more contemporary narratives, might reveal surprising lines of tradition and highlight early emancipatory achievements of such illness writing, or throw into sharp relief the differences between illness writing in German then and now.

In summary, the aim of this book was twofold yet intertwined: to open up a new theoretical field for Germanistik and apply its principles to specific texts, all recent and underexplored, to show what can be gained by marrying a disability studies approach with German literary/cultural studies. Beyond the borders of its discipline, this study has contributed to our contemporary societal conversation about health and illness, death and dying. Literary studies can contribute practices of close reading and critical thinking to this wider conversation that is all too often conducted simplistically and at the expense of those whose voices and insights should be at its center.

Notes

Introduction

[1] Virginia Woolf, *On Being Ill* (Ashfield, MA: Paris Press, 2002; orig.: London: Hogarth, 1930), 3–4.

[2] Ibid., 12.

[3] Judith Shulevitz, "The Close Reader: The Poetry of Illness," *New York Times*, December 29, 2002, http://www.nytimes.com/2002/12/29/books/the-close-reader-the-poetry-of-illness.html. Looking at the broader development in Western literature during the period, indeed it could be said that it was exactly during modernism that illness and disability were inscribed into the cultural production, being a time when many writers and artists rediscovered their appreciation for the grotesque and developed a liking for what Tobin Siebers, for visual culture, calls "disability aesthetics." Tobin Siebers, *Disability Aesthetics* (Ann Arbor: University of Michigan Press, 2010).

[4] Shulevitz, "Close Reader."

[5] I will come back to this debate. The kind of illness narrative I have in mind and that is discussed in contemporary Germany is written, although illness experiences can and are being shared orally, through dance, painting, and many other ways; and, of course, not all illness writing is strictly speaking narrative in structure.

[6] Quotation from the online comment section beneath the article: Richard Kämmerlings, "Krebsliteratur: Der Schleier über den letzten Dingen," *Frankfurter Allgemeine*, August 14, 2009, http://www.faz.net/aktuell/feuilleton/buecher/krebsliteratur-der-schleier-ueber-den-letzten-dingen-1841182.html.

[7] Unless otherwise noted, all translations in this book are mine.

[8] G. Thomas Couser, *Vulnerable Subjects: Ethics and Life Writing* (Ithaca, NY: Cornell University Press, 2004), ix.

[9] An example of an auto/biographical text that focuses particularly on the demands of caring for one's ill and dying parents is the provocatively titled *Mother, When Will You Finally Die? When Caring for Your Ill Parents Becomes an Ordeal*. Martina Rosenberg, *Mutter, wann stirbst du endlich? Wenn die Pflege der kranken Eltern zur Zerreißprobe wird* (Munich: Blanvalet, 2012).

[10] Previous to that, the book was published in Dutch in 2011, Czech, Danish, Polish, Slovakian, and Slovenian in 2012, as well as in French and Spanish in 2013.

[11] *Fremdschläfer* was published in French as *D'ailleurs* (Montréal: Héliotrope, 2008). Schmidt's Buchpreis-winning novel has so far been translated into Czech,

Estonian, Finnish, Greek, Italian, Norwegian, and Romanian. Schlingensief's *Tagebuch* in translation was published 2011 by Kirja Kerrallaan in Finland and 2012 by Maarten Muntinga in the Netherlands. Wolfgang Herrndorf's diary has been translated into Dutch and published in 2014 as *Leven met het pistool op tafel: Een Berlijns dagboek* (Amsterdam: Uitgeverij Cossee). It came out in French in 2015 as *Suivons en dansant l'ombre de la nuit* (Paris: Éditions Thierry Magnier). The fact that these texts are picked for translation demonstrates their impact in the German cultural sphere and their potential impact beyond it. (Information compiled from worldcat.org queries, personal communication with publishing houses, and publishers' websites.)

[12] Rosamund Dalziell, "Shame and Life Writing," in Jolly, *Encyclopedia of Life Writing*, 2:808.

[13] Arthur W. Frank, "Illness and Autobiographical Work: Dialogue as Narrative Destabilization," *Qualitative Sociology* 23, no. 1 (2000): 135.

[14] Helga Schwalm, "Autobiography," in *The Living Handbook of Narratology*, ed. Peter Hühn et al. (Hamburg: Hamburg University), last modified April 11, 2014, http://www.lhn.uni-hamburg.de/article/autobiography, para. 9 of 28.

[15] Dennis Schep, "I Problems: Blindness and Autobiography," *European Journal of Life Writing* 4 (2015): 18. This extends to administrative, legal, and medical contexts too, within which aspects of people's lives became more commonly recorded—in the form of statistical data or as criminal/medical case studies.

[16] For a more extensive summary of the literary history of autobiography, see, from a Germanist's perspective, Martina Wagner-Egelhaaf, *Autobiographie*, Sammlung Metzler 323 (Stuttgart: Metzler, 2000), 100–201; for an English-language publication on the development of autobiography from Saint Augustine until today, Linda R. Anderson, *Autobiography*, 2nd ed. (London: Routledge, 2011).

[17] Schwalm, "Autobiography," para. 2 of 28.

[18] To suggest further reading on this, Sidonie Smith writes of the genre's transformation in her article "Self, Subject, and Resistance: Marginalities and Twentieth-Century Autobiographical Practice," *Tulsa Studies in Women's Literature* 9, no. 1 (1990): 11–24.

[19] Ibid., 21.

[20] Paul John Eakin, *How Our Lives Become Stories: Making Selves* (Ithaca, NY: Cornell University Press, 1999), see esp. chapter 2: "Relational Selves, Relational Lives."

[21] So does the term "life writing," which extends to letters, diaries, blogs, and more.

[22] Often, these worlds can and do intersect.

[23] See, for example, the breadth of topics covered by a recent edited volume on autobiographical forms: Carsten Heinze and Alfred Hornung, *Medialisierungsformen des (Auto-)Biografischen* (Konstanz: UVK, 2013).

[24] Max Saunders, *Self Impression: Life-Writing, Autobiografiction, and the Forms of Modern Literature* (Oxford: Oxford University Press, 2010), 5.

[25] A debate that is ongoing ever since the publication of Paul de Man's provocative essay "Autobiography as De-facement," *MLN* 94, no. 5 (1979): 919–30.

[26] Saunders, *Self Impression*, 524.

[27] Ibid.

[28] Ibid.

[29] Ibid., 526.

[30] Gerrit Bartels, "Überlebensgroß," *Der Tagesspiegel*, October 15, 2009.

[31] Frank, "Illness and Autobiographical Work," 135.

[32] Informed by an engagement with phenomenology and influenced by the work of S. Kay Toombs.

[33] Havi Carel and Rachel Cooper, introduction to *Health, Illness and Disease: Philosophical Essays*, ed. Havi Carel and Rachel Cooper (Durham: Acumen, 2012), 8.

[34] Woolf, *On Being Ill*, 3.

[35] Frank, "Illness and Autobiographical Work," 135.

[36] Kay Cook, "Illness and Life Writing," in Jolly, *Encyclopedia of Life Writing*, 1:456–57.

[37] G. Thomas Couser, *Recovering Bodies: Illness, Disability, and Life Writing* (Madison: University of Wisconsin Press, 1997), 8.

[38] The fourth chapter of *Recovering Bodies* attends to English-language HIV/AIDS stories. From a comparative cultural studies perspective, Beate Schappach analyzes the varying degrees to which French and German personal narratives from the time politicized individual and collective suffering from HIV/AIDS: Schappach, *Aids in Literatur, Theater und Film: Zur kulturellen Dramaturgie eines Störfalls*, Materialien des ITW Bern 12 (Zurich: Chronos, 2012), 111–28.

[39] Couser, *Recovering Bodies*, 12.

[40] Frank, "Illness and Autobiographical Work," 135.

[41] The notion that illness narrative is therapeutic reaches back to the nineteenth century and Freud's "talking cure," at least for psychological illness. For physical illness, the idea gained momentum from 1988, when Arthur Kleinman published *The Illness Narratives*, a book that emphasizes the importance for medical practitioners to listen to patients' accounts and that highlights the storying of the illness in dialogue with the patient as therapeutic. From there, it runs like a golden thread through research on illness narratives, especially when undertaken from the perspective of medical sociology (e.g., also Frank), psychology (Lucius-Hoene), or the medical humanities (Hawkins). Aside from this, a whole field of scholarly work, bibliotherapy, rests firmly on the belief in the therapeutic functions of writing the ill self and reading about others' experiences. Arthur Kleinman, *The Illness Narratives: Suffering, Healing and the Human Condition* (New York: Basic Books, 1988); Gabriele Lucius-Hoene, "Erzählen von Krankheit und Behinderung," *Psychotherapie, Psychosomatik, Medizinische Psychologie* 48 (1998): 108–13; Anne Hunsaker Hawkins, "Writing about Illness: Therapy? Or Testimony?," in *Unfitting Stories: Narrative Approaches to Disease, Disability, and*

Trauma, ed. Valerie Raoul et al. (Waterloo, ON: Wilfrid Laurier University Press, 2007), 113–27.

[42] According to Dominic Manganiello, Augustine's *Confessions* from around the year 400 "established the prototype confessional autobiography" (228). With the story of his conversion to Christianity being the highlight and indeed the trigger of the self-narrative, it is because of Augustine that the confessional as a genre or model in life writing studies, up until today, evokes connotations of religion, sin, and redemption; the focus of the narrative, however, being on God (and praising God) rather than the individual. Rousseau shifted this emphasis dramatically in his *Confessions* (completed in 1765), with the text marking "the secular transformation of the genre" (Manganiello, 228). Rousseau's confessions are made to the reader instead of God (229). Dominic Manganiello, "Confessions," in Jolly, *Encyclopedia of Life Writing*, 1:228–29. Anne Hunsaker Hawkins, in *Reconstructing Illness*, contends that contemporary "pathographies" (i.e., illness narratives) have replaced stories of religious conversion popular in earlier eras. She highlights the extent to which mythical thinking pervades the English-language illness narratives in her corpus and identifies the main metaphors used in storying and coping with illness: battle, journey, and death and rebirth. Her thesis has had a strong influence on subsequent research into narratives of illness/disability. Anne Hunsaker Hawkins, *Reconstructing Illness: Studies in Pathography*, 2nd ed. (West Lafayette, IN: Purdue University Press, 1999). Kay Cook points out that "historically, . . . illness narratives were closely linked with spiritual and mystical autobiographies and [illness] constituted the central event—the vision or the conversion—in the narrator's life." Cook, "Illness and Life Writing," 457.

[43] Woolf, *On Being Ill*, 11.

[44] Einat Avrahami, *The Invading Body: Reading Illness Autobiographies* (Charlottesville: University of Virginia Press, 2007), 76.

[45] Ibid.

[46] Reinhold Schwarz, "Die 'Krebspersönlichkeit'—Mythen und Forschungsresultate," *psychoneuro* 30, no. 4 (2004): 209.

[47] Picking up, like me, on the pervasiveness within scholarship of the confessional as an interpretive model for personal illness narratives, Avrahami makes it central to her analysis of Harold Brodkey's *This Wild Darkness: The Story of My Death* (1996). She details how in his account, the US-American author navigates the confessional mode "both in earnest and as a literary ploy" (Avrahami, *Invading Body*, 76). He is drawn to it in two ways: first as an AIDS sufferer who "internalized abjection" and second as an author seeking an audience (77). For more, see 73–96.

[48] Avrahami, *Invading Body*, 96.

[49] Ibid.

[50] Shlomith Rimmon-Kenan, "The Story of 'I': Illness and Narrative Identity," *Narrative* 10, no. 1 (2002): 24; Arthur W. Frank, *The Wounded Storyteller: Body, Illness, and Ethics*, 2nd ed. (Chicago: University of Chicago Press, 2013), 122–26.

[51] Rimmon-Kenan, "Story of 'I,'" 24.

[52] Couser, *Recovering Bodies*, 290.

[53] Ibid.

[54] Paul John Eakin, foreword to Lejeune, *On Autobiography*, xvi.

[55] See, for instance, Roy Pascal's *Design and Truth in Autobiography* (London: Routledge & Kegan Paul, 1960)—a publication that started to change this.

[56] Shirley Jordan, "Autofiction in the Feminine," *French Studies* 67, no. 1 (2013): 80; Franz K. Stanzel, "Autobiographie: Wo ein Ich erzählt, ist immer Fiktion," *Sprachkunst* 37, no. 2 (2006): 326; Wagner-Egelhaaf, *Autobiographie*, 65.

[57] In a German and Austrian context in particular, discussions of truth and truthfulness understandably continue to surface: the relation of fact and fiction continues to be problematized in the case of autobiographies by notable authors and public intellectuals, such as Günter Grass, Walter Jens, and others who for a long time kept secret memberships in the SS (Grass) or NSDAP (Jens). One symptomatic example of the ongoing discussion and remaining dissent among scholars in this respect is narratologist Franz K. Stanzel's essay in the yearbook *Sprachkunst* (2006), together with the criticism it received from the yearbook's editor, Hans Höller. Stanzel, "Autobiographie"; Hans Höller, "Brief zu Franz K. Stanzels Akademie-Vortrag vom 19. Januar 2007: 'Autobiographie. Wo ein Ich erzählt, ist immer Fiktion,'" *Sprachkunst* 37, no. 2 (2006).

[58] Philippe Lejeune, "The Autobiographical Pact (bis)," in Lejeune, *On Autobiography*, 120.

[59] Eakin, foreword, ix.

[60] See especially the first three texts discussed for examples that veer from traditional usage of a first-person voice, as well as for their use of pseudonyms or alter ego characters. Engaging in more complex disguising of the factual and fictional in and beyond her text, Charlotte Roche's *Schoßgebete* is identified in chapter 1 as an autofiction.

[61] Lejeune, "Autobiographical Pact (bis)," 134.

[62] G. Thomas Couser, "Genre Matters: Form, Force, and Filiation," *Life Writing* 2, no. 2 (2005): 145.

[63] Ibid., 144.

[64] Lejeune sees this too: Lejeune, "Autobiographical Pact (bis)," 124.

[65] Philippe Lejeune, "The Autobiographical Pact," in Lejeune, *On Autobiography*, 14.

[66] Eakin, foreword, ix. Importantly, Lejeune himself later opened up his definition to accommodate more experimental forms of autobiographical writing that were emerging. In "The Autobiographical Pact (bis)," he qualified the previously fairly rigid criterion concerning the identity of the names: "The name of the character can be at the same time similar to the name of the author and different: same initials, different names . . .; same first name, different last names" (134). Both Charlotte Roche and Kathrin Schmidt give the protagonists of their illness narratives names that are "the same but different" in this sense (chapters 1 and 2).

[67] Eakin, foreword, xi.

[68] Ibid., xxiii.

[69] Lennard J. Davis, *Enforcing Normalcy: Disability, Deafness, and the Body* (London: Verso, 1995), 2.

[70] When thinking of a subject such as Sonderpädagogik (special needs education), a degree course offered at many German universities, it does become clear which academic subjects have an affinity with the critical thinking that underlies disability studies as a field, and which less so. Markus Dederich, himself professor of rehabilitation sciences, sees contradictory intentions ultimately keeping apart the fields of disability studies and Sonderpädagogik, for example. For more, see Markus Dederich, *Körper, Kultur und Behinderung: Eine Einführung in die Disability Studies*, Disability Studies: Körper—Macht—Differenz 2 (Bielefeld: Transcript, 2007), 51–54.

[71] David T. Mitchell and Sharon L. Snyder, "Representation and Its Discontents: The Uneasy Home of Disability in Literature and Film," in Albrecht, Seelman, and Bury, *Handbook of Disability Studies*, 203.

[72] This is not to say that this norm is fixed; disability historians have shown that what is understood to be health or ablebodiedness continues to change, just like the meaning that is ascribed to various disabilities does.

[73] For more, see, for instance, Bill Hughes and Kevin Paterson, "The Social Model of Disability and the Disappearing Body: Towards a Sociology of Impairment," *Disability & Society* 12, no. 3 (1997): 325–40; Tom Shakespeare, "The Social Model of Disability," in Davis, *Disability Studies Reader*, 214–21; Tom Shakespeare, *Disability Rights and Wrongs Revisited* (London: Routledge, 2014).

[74] Including an analysis of a trauma narrative as a matter of course, this book plays its part in this development. Although I cannot claim to have fully interlinked the vocabularies of disability studies and trauma theory in chapter 1, both schools of thought significantly shaped my understanding of Roche's *Schoßgebete* and the story of emotional/psychological suffering caused by bereavement that it tells. I agree with James Berger that there is considerable overlap in interest between the fields (he writes, "Both . . . are concerned with devastating injury and its lasting effects; both place individual disability and trauma in broad social and historical contexts; both focus intensively on problematics of representation"), and, from the stance of disability studies, it is important to stress, like he does, that "trauma is not sacred. Trauma is utterly secular. It is . . . something that happens." James Berger, "Trauma without Disability, Disability without Trauma: A Disciplinary Divide," *JAC* 24, no. 3 (2004): 563, 567. For more than I can offer here on the distance trauma studies and disability studies have kept from each other, possible reasons for this, and potential benefits of a rapprochement, see Berger's article.

[75] G. Thomas Couser, *Signifying Bodies: Disability in Contemporary Life Writing* (Ann Arbor: University of Michigan Press, 2009), 9.

[76] Davis's sentence continues: "But also by working in factories, driving insufficiently safe cars, living in toxic environments or high-crime areas." Davis, *Enforcing Normalcy*, 8; Shakespeare, "Social Model of Disability," 221.

[77] Carol Poore explains, "This new direction in research and teaching about disability has been developed mostly by disabled scholars in the United States and in Great Britain rather than in a country such as Germany where disabled people have been excluded much more strictly from the regular educational system."

Carol Poore, *Disability in Twentieth-Century German Culture* (Ann Arbor: University of Michigan Press, 2007), 300.

[78] Mitchell and Snyder, "Representation and Its Discontents," 200.

[79] Gary L. Albrecht, Katherine D. Seelman, and Michael Bury, eds., *Handbook of Disability Studies* (London: Sage, 2001); Lennard J. Davis, ed., *The Disability Studies Reader*, 4th ed. (New York: Routledge, 2013); Carol Thomas, Nick Watson, and Alan Roulstone, eds., *Routledge Handbook of Disability Studies* (London: Routledge, 2012).

[80] Running initially under the name *Journal of Literary Disability*.

[81] The critical perspective offered by disability studies has entered some American studies departments in Germany. Apart from that, it has been taken up primarily by social scientists, with Anne Waldschmidt and Theresia Degener having founded the Arbeitsgemeinschaft Disability Studies in Deutschland—Wir forschen selbst (Working Group Disability Studies in Germany—We Do Research Ourselves) in 2002. For a more extensive assessment of the state of disability studies in German academia than can be offered here, see Poore, *Disability in Twentieth-Century German Culture*, 299–306, from the perspective of an arts and humanities scholar; see also the special topic section of *Disability Studies Quarterly* headed "Disability Studies in German Speaking Countries," guest edited by Swantje Köbsell and Anne Waldschmidt: Beth Haller and Corinne Kirchner, eds., "Education," special issue, *Disability Studies Quarterly* 26, no. 2 (2006).

[82] Elizabeth C. Hamilton, "From Social Welfare to Civil Rights: The Representation of Disability in Twentieth-Century German Literature," in *The Body and Physical Difference: Discourses of Disability*, ed. David T. Mitchell and Sharon L. Snyder (Ann Arbor: University of Michigan Press, 1997), 223–39; Poore, *Disability in Twentieth-Century German Culture*; Eleoma Joshua and Michael Schillmeier, eds., *Disability in German Literature, Film, and Theatre*, Edinburgh German Yearbook 4 (Rochester, NY: Camden House, 2010); Pauline Eyre, "Permission to Speak: Representations of Disability in German Women's Literature of the 1970s and 1980s" (PhD diss., University of Manchester, 2009); Petra-Andelka Anders, *Behinderung und psychische Krankheit im zeitgenössischen deutschen Spielfilm*, KONNEX Studien im Schnittbereich von Literatur, Kultur und Natur 9 (Würzburg: Königshausen & Neumann, 2014); Allison G. Cattell, "Disability Drama: Semiotic Bodies and Diegetic Subjectivities in Post-WWI German Expressionist Drama" (PhD diss., University of Waterloo, 2014), https://uwspace.uwaterloo.ca/bitstream/handle/10012/8417/Cattell_Allison.pdf?sequence=1.

[83] David Bolt, "Literary Disability Studies: The Long Awaited Response" (presented at the Inaugural Conference of the Cultural Disability Studies Research Network, Liverpool John Moores University, May 26, 2007), http://disability-studies.leeds.ac.uk/files/library/bolt-Long-Awaited-Response.pdf, 2.

[84] I am borrowing the term "nervousness" from Ato Quayson yet identifying less a crisis of representation than a crisis of academic/critical reading practices for the contemporary Germanic realm. Ato Quayson, *Aesthetic Nervousness: Disability and the Crisis of Representation* (New York: Columbia University Press, 2007).

[85] This is in keeping with other scholars' use. Carel and Cooper, "Introduction," 8.

[86] Shakespeare, "Social Model of Disability," 215.

[87] Carel and Cooper, "Introduction," 8.

[88] Davis, *Enforcing Normalcy*, 10.

[89] Quayson, *Aesthetic Nervousness*, 4.

[90] Alice Hall, *Literature and Disability* (London: Routledge, 2016), 8.

[91] David Bolt, "Epilogue: Attitudes and Action," in Bolt, *Changing Social Attitudes toward Disability*, 172.

[92] David Bolt, introduction to Bolt, *Changing Social Attitudes toward Disability*, 3.

[93] Susan Wendell, "Unhealthy Disabled: Treating Chronic Illnesses as Disabilities," in Davis, *Disability Studies Reader*, 161–73. Wendell previously published a book-length study on the topic: Susan Wendell, *The Rejected Body: Feminist Philosophical Reflections on Disability* (New York: Routledge, 1996).

[94] Wendell, "Unhealthy Disabled," 165.

[95] Anders, *Behinderung*, 443.

[96] Ibid., 64.

[97] Pauline Eyre, "From Impairment to Empowerment: A Re-assessment of Libuše Moníková's Representation of Disability in *Pavane für eine verstorbene Infantin*," in Joshua and Schillmeier, *Disability in German Literature, Film, and Theatre*, 212.

[98] David T. Mitchell and Sharon L. Snyder, *Narrative Prosthesis: Disability and the Dependencies of Discourse* (Ann Arbor: University of Michigan Press, 2000), 47.

[99] Ibid., 47.

[100] Günter Grass, *Die Blechtrommel* (Darmstadt: Luchterhand, 1959). For more, see Hamilton, "From Social Welfare to Civil Rights."

[101] Mitchell and Snyder, *Narrative Prosthesis*, 61.

[102] Ibid., 48.

[103] Christoph Schlingensief, *So schön wie hier kanns im Himmel gar nicht sein! Tagebuch einer Krebserkrankung* (Munich: btb, 2010; orig.: Cologne: Kiepenheuer & Witsch, 2009), 9.

[104] Ibid., 9.

[105] Articles that contributed to the debate (in order of publication): Kämmerlings, "Krebsliteratur"; Michael Angele, "Wer hat geil Krebs?," *Der Freitag*, September 3, 2009, http://www.freitag.de/autoren/michael-angele/wer-hat-geil-krebs; Iris Radisch, "Metaphysik des Tumors," *Zeit Online*, September 19, 2009, http://www.zeit.de/2009/39/Krebsbuecher; Dirk Peitz, "Die Ich-Erzähler," *Berliner Zeitung*, October 10, 2009, http://www.berliner-zeitung.de/archiv/immer-mehr-autoren-berichten-in-ihren-buechern-von-sich-selbst--und-von-ihren-krankheiten-die-ich-erzaehler,10810590,10671790.html; Christoph Schröder, "Die Kunst der Krankheit: Wir kommen nicht von uns los," *Der Tagesspiegel*, October 24, 2009, http://www.tagesspiegel.de/kultur/die-kunst-der-krankheit-wir-kommen-nicht-von-uns-los/1621152.html; Thomas Macho, "Wer redet, ist nicht tot," *Neue Zürcher Zeitung*, November 19, 2009, http://www.nzz.ch/wer-redet-ist-nicht-tot-1.4036808.

[106] It is one that lasts beyond this particular feuilleton debate, as much newer articles demonstrate when they repeat arguments similar to those used in 2009. One example (triggered, this time, by Henning Mankell's cancer writing) is Ulrich Greiner's "Man sollte diskret sterben," *Zeit Online*, January 31, 2014, http://www.zeit.de/kultur/literatur/2014-01/mankell-krebsdiagnose-literatur-krankheit.

[107] Kämmerlings, "Krebsliteratur."

[108] In the article, Kämmerlings asks the rhetorical question, "Was aber berührt nun an diesen Beispielen . . . so unangenehm?" (What is it in these examples that we find so unpleasant?)

[109] Ibid.

[110] Angele, "Wer hat geil Krebs?"

[111] Note that Schlingensief's idiosyncratic spelling has been retained in the German quotation.

[112] Bill Hughes, "Fear, Pity and Disgust. Emotions and the Non-disabled Imaginary," in Thomas, Watson, and Roulstone, *Routledge Handbook of Disability Studies*, 69.

[113] Ibid.

[114] Tina Klopp, "Todgeweihte leben länger: Über die Interpretation von Künstlerbiografien," *Deutschlandfunk*, May 31, 2015, http://www.deutschlandfunk.de/kunst-todgeweihte-leben-laenger.1184.de.html?dram:article_id=317368.

[115] Angele, "Wer hat geil Krebs?"

[116] Peitz, "Die Ich-Erzähler."

[117] This indicates that if "creative" books of fiction and "factual" nonfiction are the two most established understandings of what writing can be in the German public/cultural sphere, lyric poetry and dramatic art lose out to (commonly booklength) prose in public attention, as does anything like life writing that would have to be characterized both as creative/artistic writing yet nonfictional in essence.

[118] Thomas Anz, *Gesund oder krank? Medizin, Moral und Ästhetik in der deutschen Gegenwartsliteratur* (Stuttgart: Metzler, 1989).

[119] Although, as Sander L. Gilman has objected, the study omits analysis of the Nazi escalation of such rhetoric, as well as ignoring relevant English-language research on the topic. Sander L. Gilman, review of *Gesund oder krank? Medizin, Moral und Ästhetik in der deutschen Gegenwartsliteratur*, by Thomas Anz, *German Quarterly* 64, no. 4 (1991): 603–5.

[120] Anz, *Gesund oder krank?*, xi.

[121] Ibid.

[122] Ibid., 4.

[123] Georg Büchner later based his novella *Lenz* (written in 1836) on Oberlin's descriptions. Of the contemporary authors whose texts this study deals with in detail, both Kathrin Schmidt and Wolfgang Herrndorf refer to Büchner's *Lenz* as an exemplary literary portrait that sensitively animates Oberlin's case study. The original moralistic interpretation of illness by Oberlin, taking Lenz's "Wahnsinn als selbstverschuldete Folge normwidrigen Verhaltens" (madness as a self-inflicted

consequence of behavior that is outside the norm), mitigates considerably in Büchner's retelling. Foreshadowing modernism, Büchner's narrative instead questions this logic. Anz, *Gesund oder krank?*, 7.

[124] Anz, *Gesund oder krank?*, 52. Judith Ricker-Abderhalden's research into illness writing of the late 1970s / early 1980s further confirms this; she finds that many authors at the time rhetorically position society as ill and themselves (or the protagonists of their narratives, in the case of fiction) as sane. For more, see Judith Ricker-Abderhalden, "Schreiben über Krankheit: Bemerkungen zur Zerstörung eines literarischen Tabus," *Neophilologus* 71, no. 3 (1987): 474–79.

[125] Anz, *Gesund oder krank?*, 57.

[126] Ibid., 60.

[127] Ibid., 64. The term *Verständigungstexte*, which is difficult to translate adequately, was a popular label used for life-writing texts by, for instance, women, authors from the LGBT community, or disabled people published in the wake of 1968, and it tends today to be employed interchangeably with other, similar terms such as *Betroffenheitsliteratur* (roughly, literature of concernment, or literature by/for those affected) and minority literature, in a comparably pejorative sense. Speaking of *Verständigungstexte* puts the emphasis on the aspect of communication; the texts thus described are seen primarily as an outlet for their author's experiences of hardship or social oppression. As querying Google Books' Ngram Viewer confirms, *Verständigungstext* entered literary critics' vocabulary in the late 1970s and was used widely throughout the 1980s. Malcolm Pender in 1998 translates it simply as "non-literary personal account[ ]," which shows that, by then, the status of the texts understood to belong to this group as extraliterary was consensus. Malcolm Pender, *Contemporary Images of Death and Sickness: A Theme in Swiss-German Literature* (Sheffield: Sheffield Academic Press, 1998), 158. Anita Konrad criticizes all of the aforementioned labels in an article analyzing the effects of talking about literature by authors with a migration background in such terms: Anita Konrad, "Minderheiten—Literatur?," *Stimme von und für Minderheiten* 55 (2005), http://minderheiten.at/stat/stimme/stimme55c.htm.

[128] Anz, *Gesund oder krank?*, 64.

[129] Ibid., 70.

[130] Ibid., 63.

[131] Ibid.

[132] He remains vague here and does not pursue this point further.

[133] Anz, *Gesund oder krank?*, 66. (Anz lists many more examples of texts that would fall into this category; see 65.) Expressing a comparable stance yet, to her credit, doing so in much less polemical language, Ricker-Abderhalden writes of a comparable set of texts as "nur in einem beschränktem Masse Literatur" (only in a limited sense literature), and as "in einem Grenzbezirk zwischen Fiktion und Fachliteratur, zwischen Roman und Reportage angesiedelt" (situated in a borderland between fiction and specialist literature, between novel and report). Ricker-Abderhalden, "Schreiben über Krankheit," 474.

[134] Anz, *Gesund oder krank?*, 199.

[135] Corina Caduff, *Szenen des Todes* (Basel: Lenos, 2013); Thomas Macho and Kristin Marek, eds., *Die neue Sichtbarkeit des Todes* (Munich: Wilhelm Fink, 2007).

[136] Caduff, *Szenen des Todes*, 151–72.

[137] Ibid., 166.

[138] Frank Degler and Christian Kohlroß, eds., *Epochen/Krankheiten: Konstellationen von Literatur und Pathologie*, Das Wissen der Literatur 1 (St. Ingbert: Röhrig, 2006); Katrin Max, *Liegekur und Bakterienrausch: Literarische Deutungen der Tuberkulose im "Zauberberg" und anderswo* (Würzburg: Königshausen & Neumann, 2012).

[139] Kafka is the paradigmatic example here: Sander L. Gilman, *Franz Kafka: The Jewish Patient* (New York: Routledge, 1995); Johannes Groß, *Kafkas Krankheiten* (Marburg: LiteraturWissenschaft.de, 2012).

[140] Cattell, "Disability Drama," 175. Prototypical examples of this tendency are works such as Andreas Dawidowicz, *Die metaphorische Krankheit als Gesellschaftskritik in den Werken von Franz Kafka, Friedrich Dürrenmatt und Thomas Bernhard*, Germanistik 42 (Berlin: LIT, 2013); Steffi Ehlebracht, *Gelingendes Scheitern: Epilepsie als Metapher in der deutschsprachigen Literatur des 20. Jahrhunderts* (Würzburg: Königshausen & Neumann, 2008).

[141] Mitchell and Snyder, *Narrative Prosthesis*.

[142] Yvonne Wübben and Carsten Zelle, eds., *Krankheit schreiben: Aufzeichnungsverfahren in Medizin und Literatur* (Göttingen: Wallstein, 2013).

[143] Fitting in with what in Anglo-American academia is subsumed under the medical humanities. For more on the disciplinary or ideological divide between the medical humanities and disability studies approaches, see Diane Price Herndl, "Disease versus Disability: The Medical Humanities and Disability Studies," *PMLA* 120, no. 2 (2005): 593–98.

[144] Bettina von Jagow and Florian Steger are joint authors of *Was treibt die Literatur zur Medizin? Ein kulturwissenschaftlicher Dialog* (Göttingen: Vandenhoeck & Ruprecht, 2009) and editors of *Repräsentationen: Medizin und Ethik in Literatur und Kunst der Moderne* (Heidelberg: Winter, 2004); *Literatur und Medizin: Ein Lexikon* (Göttingen: Vandenhoeck & Ruprecht, 2005).

[145] See, for instance, Dietrich von Engelhardt and Felix Unger, eds., *Ästhetik und Ethik in der Medizin*, Edition Weimar 4 (Weimar: VDG, 2006).

[146] Pauline Eyre, "Impaired or Empowered? Mapping Disability onto European Literature," in Bolt, *Changing Social Attitudes toward Disability*, 99.

[147] Davis, *Enforcing Normalcy*, 13.

[148] Ibid.

[149] Verena Stefan, *Fremdschläfer* (Zurich: Ammann, 2007), 92.

[150] My application of the term "autofiction" goes back to Serge Doubrovsky, who developed the concept in direct reaction to Lejeune's theoretical work on autobiography. Setting out to trouble Lejeune's suggestion of the autobiographical pact, Doubrovsky presented him with his novel *Fils* (Son/Threads) in 1977, therein

testing out how far it was possible stretch the boundaries of autobiography's need for referential truth. Lejeune, "Autobiographical Pact (bis)," 135.

[151] Hughes, "Fear, Pity and Disgust," 72–75.

[152] A facial expression that Daniel Kelly and others term the "gape face." Daniel Kelly, *Yuck! The Nature and Moral Significance of Disgust* (Cambridge, MA: MIT, 2011), 64–66.

[153] Carolyn Korsmeyer, *Savoring Disgust: The Foul and the Fair in Aesthetics* (New York: Oxford University Press, 2011), 7.

[154] This is because I see their work as decisive starting points for disgust theory in the arts and humanities. Bakhtin must be credited for drawing our attention to other facets of the grotesque in art that accompany and, to him, outweigh, the outright disgusting (such as the carnivalesque, i.e., its humorous and subversive elements). As a linguist, psychoanalyst, and literary scholar, Kristeva examines the causes and workings of disgust in both literature and beyond, reading the experience of disgust as a threat of psychic regression. Mikhail Bakhtin, *Rabelais and His World*, trans. Hélène Iswolsky (Bloomington: Indiana University Press, 1984); Julia Kristeva, *Powers of Horror: An Essay on Abjection*, trans. Leon S. Roudiez (New York: Columbia University Press, 1982).

[155] From the *Oxford English Dictionary* definition of "aesthetics," which distinguishes among three meanings of the term: "The philosophy of the beautiful or of art; a system of principles for the appreciation of the beautiful, etc.; the distinctive underlying principles of a work of art or a genre, the works of an artist, the arts of a culture, etc." Traditionally, disgust has been dismissed as an emotion not worth contemplating or representing through art, with Kant going so far as to claim that it refuses representation. Florence Vatan, "The Lure of Disgust: Musil and Kolnai," *Germanic Review* 88 (2013): 29–31.

[156] Felicitas von Lovenberg, "Ein Gespräch mit Charlotte Roche: Ich bin keine Frau, die andere Frauen verrät," *Frankfurter Allgemeine*, August 10, 2011, http://www.faz.net/aktuell/feuilleton/buecher/autoren/ein-gespraech-mit-charlotte-roche-ich-bin-keine-frau-die-andere-frauen-verraet-11104662.html?printPagedArticle=true#pageIndex_2.

[157] Martina Wagner-Egelhaaf, for example, identifies the autofictional mode across a range of texts: she finds it in Emine Sevgi Özdamar's oeuvre, Walter Benjamin's *Berliner Kindheit um neunzehnhundert*, and Günter Grass's divisive memoir *Beim Häuten der Zwiebel*. The edited volume *". . . all diese fingierten, notierten, in meinem Kopf ungefähr wieder zusammengesetzten Ichs": Autobiographie und Autofiktion* (2012) discusses Swiss writers Robert Walser, Annemarie Schwarzenbach, Friedrich Dürrenmatt, and Paul Nizon from a perspective informed by autofiction theory. Innokentij Kreknin focuses on stagings of the authorial self across literary texts and new media in the work of Rainald Goetz, Joachim Lottmann, and Alban Nikolai Herbst, identifying them as autofictional. Martina Wagner-Egelhaaf, "Autofiktion oder: Autobiographie nach der Autobiographie; Goethe—Barthes—Özdamar," in *Grenzen der Identität und der Fiktionalität*, ed. Ulrich Breuer and Beatrice Sandberg (Munich: iudicium, 2006), 353–68; Martina Wagner-Egelhaaf, "Autofiktion—Theorie und Praxis des autobiographischen Schreibens," in *Schreiben im Kontext von Schule, Universität,*

Beruf und Lebensalltag, ed. Johannes Berning et al., Schreiben interdisziplinär 1 (Berlin: LIT, 2006), 80–101; Martina Wagner-Egelhaaf, "Zum Stand und zu den Perspektiven der Autobiographieforschung in der Literaturwissenschaft," *Bios— Zeitschrift für Biographieforschung, Oral History und Lebensverlaufsanalysen* 23, no. 2 (2010): 188–200; Peter Gasser, "Autobiographie und Autofiktion: Einige begriffskritische Bemerkungen," in *". . . all diese fingierten, notierten, in meinem Kopf ungefähr wieder zusammengesetzten Ichs": Autobiographie und Autofiktion*, ed. Elio Pellin and Ulrich Weber (Göttingen: Wallstein, 2012), 13–28; Innokentij Kreknin, *Poetiken des Selbst: Identität, Autorschaft und Autofiktion am Beispiel von Rainald Goetz, Joachim Lottmann und Alban Nikolai Herbst*, Studien zur deutschen Literatur 206 (Berlin: De Gruyter, 2014).

[158] Davis, *Enforcing Normalcy*, 12. Davis harks back to Erving Goffman's notion of stigma here. Goffman too contended it is most often on the visual plane that stigma unfolds.

[159] Ibid.

[160] He writes, "These responses can include horror, fear, pity, compassion, and avoidance" (ibid.).

[161] Ibid.

[162] Rosemarie Garland-Thomson, *Staring: How We Look* (Oxford: Oxford University Press, 2009).

[163] Ibid., 6.

[164] G. Thomas Couser, "Disability, Life Narrative, and Representation," in Davis, *Disability Studies Reader*, 458.

[165] Jürgen Link, *Versuch über den Normalismus: Wie Normalität produziert wird*, 3rd ed. (Göttingen: Vandenhoeck & Ruprecht, 2006), 355–57, for more on "das Paradox der Normalitätsgrenze" (the paradox of the normality limit). For an article that considers Link's "These von der flexiblen Normalisierung" (5; hypothesis of flexible normalization) from a sociological vantage point, testing it against the reality of disabled people's negotiations of their place in society today, see Anne Waldschmidt, "Flexible Normalisierung oder stabile Ausgrenzung: Veränderungen im Verhältnis Behinderung und Normalität," *Soziale Probleme* 9, no. 1 (1998): 3–25.

[166] Chantelle Warner points out that the descriptor *Betroffenheitsliteratur* "ambiguously refers both to the affected nature of the experiences and the emotional response elicited from the book's readers." Chantelle Warner, *The Pragmatics of Literary Testimony: Authenticity Effects in German Social Autobiographies* (New York: Routledge, 2013), 27.

[167] Monique Wittig, "The Point of View: Universal or Particular?," *Feminist Issues* 3, no. 2 (1983): 61–69.

[168] As quoted in Andrea Spiegl, "Gross, schlank, blond, attraktiv: Schweizer Schriftstellerinnen der 1970er," *literaturkritik.at*, September 23, 2013, http://www.uibk.ac.at/literaturkritik/zeitschrift/1111216.html#Dreizehn.

[169] Anne Betten, "Entwicklungen und Formen der deutschen Literatursprache nach 1945," in *Sprachgeschichte: Ein Handbuch zur Geschichte der deutschen Sprache und ihrer Erforschung*, ed. Werner Besch et al., 2nd ed. (Berlin: De Gruyter, 2004), 4:3141.

[170] See, for instance, ibid., 3138, 3140.

[171] See "working notes" to Verena Stefan, "Doe a Deer," *TRIVIA: Voices of Feminism* 4 (2006), www. triviavoices.com/doe-a-deer.html.

[172] Wittig, "Point of View," 68.

[173] Philippe Lejeune, *On Diary*, ed. Jeremy D. Popkin and Julie Rak, trans. Katherine Durnin (Honolulu: Biographical Research Center, 2009); Kylie Cardell, *De@r World: Contemporary Uses of the Diary* (Madison: University of Wisconsin Press, 2014). Building on Lejeune, my final comparative analysis takes into account the sociology and history of the diary genre as well as the individual contexts of the two texts specifically, hoping to break through preconceptions about the form, replacing these with findings from close literary analysis. Cardell's study must be highlighted as key for having formulated contemporary, public uses of the diary form, having begun to examine its place as a published genre in popular culture today and with that the meaning it takes on as a mode of self-expression in times of the Internet and in various (often oppressive) contexts and conflicts.

[174] To list the existing secondary literature on *Arbeit und Struktur* published in the meantime: Lilla Balint, "Sickness unto Death in the Age of 24/7: Wolfgang Herrndorf's *Arbeit und Struktur*," *Studies in 20th & 21st Century Literature* 40, no. 2 (2016): 1–19; Maximilian Burk, "'dem Leben wie einem Roman zu Leibe rücken': Wolfgang Herrndorf's Blog *Arbeit und Struktur*," in *Wolfgang Herrndorf*, ed. Annina Klappert (Weimar: VDG, 2015); Elisabeth Michelbach, "Dem Leben wie einem Roman zu Leibe rücken: Wolfgang Herrndorfs Blog und Buch *Arbeit und Struktur* zwischen digitalem Gebrauchstext und literarischem Werk," *Textpraxis: Digitales Journal für Philologie* 2 (2016); Elke Siegel, "'die mühsame Verschriftlichung meiner peinlichen Existenz': Wolfgang Herrndorfs *Arbeit und Struktur* zwischen Tagebuch, Blog und Buch," *Zeitschrift für Germanistik* 26, no. 2 (2016): 348–72.

[175] Phrase from Marcy Westerling's cancer blog that describes "the process of *livingly dying*" as "staring at imminent mortality and yet residing in the world of the living." Marcy Westerling, "Welcome to Livingly Dying," *Livingly Dying* (blog), May 27, 2013, https://livinglydying.wordpress.com/.

[176] Frank Fischer, "Der Autor als Medienjongleur: Die Inszenierung literarischer Modernität im Internet," in *Autorinszenierungen: Autorschaft und literarisches Werk im Kontext der Medien*, ed. Christine Künzel and Jörg Schönert (Würzburg: Königshausen & Neumann, 2007). Reading Fischer, what becomes clear is that, until relatively recently, both the choice of the diary genre and that of the Internet as place of publication disqualified texts from consideration as literature in most German-language critics' eyes.

[177] Some authors of the period have been named above; others that come to mind are Hildegard Knef, Peter Noll, Brigitte Reimann, and Maxie Wander. For more names of authors and texts and more in-depth commentary on the writing of the 1970s and 1980s than can be provided here, see, for instance, Christa Karpenstein-Eßbach, "Krebs—Literatur—Wissen: Von der Krebspersönlichkeit zur totalen Kommunikation," in Degler and Kohlroß, *Epochen/Krankheiten*, 233–64; Marion Moamai, *Krebs schreiben: Deutschsprachige Literatur der siebziger und achtziger Jahre*, Mannheimer Studien zur Literatur- und Kulturwissenschaft

13 (St. Ingbert: Röhrig, 1997); Pender, *Contemporary Images of Death and Sickness*; Ricker-Abderhalden, "Schreiben über Krankheit."

Chapter One

[1] Charlotte Roche, *Schoßgebete* (Munich: Piper, 2011). Hereafter referenced parenthetically as *SG*.

[2] Charlotte Roche, *Feuchtgebiete* (Cologne: DuMont, 2008); Charlotte Roche, *Wetlands*, trans. Tim Mohr (London: Fourth Estate, 2009).

[3] Serge Doubrovsky, *Fils: Roman* (Paris: Galilée, 1977).

[4] Johnnie Gratton, "Autofiction," in Jolly, *Encyclopedia of Life Writing*, 1:86.

[5] *Dictionnaire des termes littéraires*, ed. Hendrik van Gorp et al. (Paris: Champion, 2001), s.v. "Autofiction." Claudia Gronemann imported the French concept of autofiction into German-language autobiography studies around the year 2000. Claudia Gronemann, *Postmoderne/postkoloniale Konzepte der Autobiographie in der französischen und maghrebinischen Literatur: Autofiction—Nouvelle Autobiographie—Double Autobiographie—Aventure du texte* (Hildesheim: Georg Olms, 2002).

[6] Isabelle Grell, "Pourquoi Serge Doubrovsky n'a pu eviter le terme d'autofiction," in *Genèse et autofiction*, ed. Jean-Louis Jeannelle and Catherine Viollet (Louvain-la-Neuve: Academia-Bruylant, 2007), 51.

[7] Korsmeyer, *Savoring Disgust*, 7.

[8] Both confession and apology are classic functions of autobiographical writing since antiquity. Wagner-Egelhaaf, *Autobiographie*, 4.

[9] The existing scholarly work on Roche's texts mostly concentrates on *Feuchtgebiete* and tends to center on discussions of gender, the female body, the author's pop feminism, her use of pornographic imagery, and performative aspects of her public appearances. Particularly notable are Maria Stehle's application of Judith Butler's concept of rebellious speech to Roche's debut novel and further Claudia Liebrand's article "Pornografische Pathografie," because it recognizes the role of illness in *Feuchtgebiete*. Maria Stehle, "Pop, Porn, and Rebellious Speech: Feminist Politics and the Multi-media Performances of Elfriede Jelinek, Charlotte Roche, and Lady Bitch Ray," *Feminist Media Studies* 12, no. 2 (2012): 229–47; Claudia Liebrand, "Pornografische Pathologie: Charlotte Roches *Feuchtgebiete*," *Literatur für Leser* 34, no. 1 (2011): 13–22. For further reading, see Margaret McCarthy, "Feminism and Generational Conflicts in Alexa Hennig von Lange's *Relax*, Elke Naters's *Lügen*, and Charlotte Roche's *Feuchtgebiete*," *Studies in 20th & 21st Century Literature* 35, no. 1 (2011): 56–73; Carrie Smith-Prei, "'Knaller-Sex Für Alle': Popfeminist Body Politics in Lady Bitch Ray, Charlotte Roche, and Sarah Kuttner," *Studies in 20th & 21st Century Literature* 35, no. 1 (2011): 3–39.

[10] Interestingly, this was done only with Roche's German-language audience in mind. The official English-language title of the text—*Wrecked*—shifts the emphasis away from the protagonist's sex life and onto the central car accident. Charlotte Roche, *Wrecked*, trans. Tim Mohr (London: Fourth Estate, 2013).

¹¹ "Kulturzeitinterview über das Buch *Schoßgebete* von Charlotte Roche mit Denis Scheck," YouTube video, 6:17, from the program *Kulturzeit* televised by 3sat, posted by "missmodprofi," December 11, 2011, http://www.youtube.com/watch?v=YBm2wLvEeqA; "Langatmige Beichte in Schrumpfdeutsch," mp3, 6:14, from the program *SWR2 am Morgen* broadcast on August 10, 2011, accessed December 11, 2012, http://www.swr.de/swr2/literatur/charlotte-roche-schossgebete/-/id=6891032/nid=6891032/did=8445458/1tlszgk/ (site discontinued); Christian Buß, "Sexautorin Charlotte Roche: 'Meine Therapeutin hat mir das Leben gerettet,'" *Spiegel Online*, August 7, 2011, http://www.spiegel.de/kultur/literatur/sexautorin-charlotte-roche-meine-therapeutin-hat-mir-das-leben-gerettet-a-778812.html.

¹² Hester Baer, "Sex, Death, and Motherhood in the Eurozone: Contemporary Women's Writing in German," *World Literature Today* 86, no. 3 (2012): 59–65.

¹³ Emily Spiers, "The Long March through the Institutions: From Alice Schwarzer to Pop Feminism and the New German Girls," *Oxford German Studies* 43, no. 1 (2014): 69.

¹⁴ Ibid., 82.

¹⁵ For more on "unpatterned reading," see the section on "Illness and the Attraction of the Personal" in this book's introduction.

¹⁶ German *Schoß* translates into English as "lap" or, more poetically, as "womb/bosom."

¹⁷ A now rarely used equivalent in English for such a prayer is the word "ejaculation," which for a contemporary audience connects back to the sexual connotations of Roche's title. The *Oxford English Dictionary* defines its older, religious meaning as "the putting up of short earnest prayers in moments of emergency; the hasty utterance of words expressing emotion." The term was commonly understood in this latter sense from the seventeenth century through the nineteenth.

¹⁸ Tony Paterson, "Charlotte Roche: Troubled Mind of a Taboo-Buster," *Independent*, August 26, 2011, http://www.independent.co.uk/news/people/profiles/charlotte-roche-troubled-mind-of-a-taboo-buster-2344746.html.

¹⁹ Cathy Caruth, "Unclaimed Experience: Trauma, and the Possibility of History," *Yale French Studies* 79 (1991): 181.

²⁰ American Psychiatric Association, *Diagnostic and Statistical Manual of Mental Disorders*, 3rd ed. (Washington, DC: APA, 1980), 236–39.

²¹ Caruth, "Unclaimed Experience," 186–87.

²² Cathy Caruth, "Introduction: The Wound and the Voice," in *Unclaimed Experience: Trauma, Narrative, and History*, by Cathy Caruth (Baltimore: Johns Hopkins University Press, 1996), 4. The trope of the wound is no coincidence: etymologically, the Greek noun *trauma* describes a physical wound. Only much later did it come to signify, as it does here, a (metaphorical) wounding of the mind.

²³ Ibid., 9.

²⁴ Ibid., 55.

²⁵ Ibid., 6. Caruth's choice of words here is reminiscent of Grell's characterization of autofiction as bearing a "transparence énigmatique" (referred to at the outset

of this chapter), which already indicates the autofictional mode as potentially fitting for the representation of stories of trauma.

[26] Ibid.

[27] Judith Lewis Herman, *Trauma and Recovery: From Domestic Abuse to Political Terror*, 2nd ed. (London: Pandora, 2001), 1.

[28] My translation of her spoken words. "Charlotte Roche bei Markus Lanz (18. August 2011)," YouTube video, 14:34, televised by ZDF, posted by "Aphexxx83," September 1, 2011, https://www.youtube.com/watch?v=26I7h2u5ntY.

[29] Gasser, "Autobiographie und Autofiktion. Einige begriffskritische Bemerkungen," 23.

[30] Cathy Caruth, "Introduction: Trauma and Experience," in Caruth, *Trauma*, 7; Caruth, "Introduction: The Wound and the Voice," 6–7.

[31] APA, *DSM-III*, 236.

[32] Laura S. Brown, "Not Outside the Range: One Feminist Perspective on Psychic Trauma," in Caruth, *Trauma*, 100–112.

[33] Jeffrey Kauffman, "On the Primacy of Pain," in *The Shame of Death, Grief, and Trauma*, ed. Jeffrey Kauffman (London: Routledge, 2010), 12–13.

[34] Bessel A. van der Kolk and Onno van der Hart, "The Intrusive Past: The Flexibility of Memory and the Engraving of Trauma," in Caruth, *Trauma*, 160.

[35] Cathy Caruth, "Introduction: Recapturing the Past," in Caruth, *Trauma*, 151.

[36] Ibid., 152.

[37] Caruth, "Introduction: Trauma and Experience," 4–5.

[38] Ibid., 8–9.

[39] To recommend further reading, Hawkins very concisely summarizes trauma studies' history: Hunsaker Hawkins, "Writing about Illness," 115–19. Herman does so at more length in her milestone publication *Trauma and Recovery*. For an overview on the emergence of trauma theory in cultural studies and a contextualization of Caruth's understanding of trauma, and especially for more in-depth remarks on Caruth in relation to Paul de Man's and Shoshana Felman's work, see Roger Luckhurst, "Mixing Memory and Desire: Psychoanalysis, Psychology, and Trauma Theory," in *Literary Theory and Criticism: An Oxford Guide*, ed. Patricia Waugh (Oxford: Oxford University Press, 2006); and Petar Ramadanovic, "Introduction: Trauma and Crisis," *Postmodern Culture: An Electronic Journal of Interdisciplinary Criticism* 11, no. 2 (2001), http://pmc.iath.virginia.edu/text-only/issue.101/11.2introduction.txt. Among the Yale school scholars, de Man has especially influenced Caruthian theory, most notably in his identification of a paradoxical "gap between reference and representation" (Luckhurst, 501) with view to language. This idea that language undermines its own meaning in the act of stating it is one that Caruth transferred to trauma theory.

[40] The narrator states this in the context of feeling hungry and the family's decision to have pizza and beers in the hospital on the day after the accident.

[41] Kristeva, *Powers of Horror*, 3.

[42] Elizabeth Grosz explicates with recourse to Lacan: "Although the ego is formed through a recognition of its body in the mirror phase, it recoils from the idea of being tied to or limited by the body's form." Elizabeth Grosz, *Sexual Subversions: Three French Feminists* (Crows Nest: Allen & Unwin, 1989), 77.

[43] Korsmeyer, *Savoring Disgust*, 129. Examples of passages in which Elizabeth is actively wishing for death: *SG*, 65, 168.

[44] Grosz, *Sexual Subversions*, 73.

[45] Jordan gives an overview of the studies already carried out on women's autofiction as well as examples of French writers whom she considers deserve attention in this respect. She then goes on to point out the—fewer—studies that are concerned with autofictional trauma writing, all by French literary scholars, focusing on French-speaking authors. Jordan, "Autofiction in the Feminine."

[46] Asked about it in an interview, Doubrovsky himself speculated as to why so many of the contemporary writers who take up the autofictional mode are female: "Il y a effectivement plus de femmes 'autofictionneuses.' Pour la première fois, elles peuvent s'assumer dans leur désir. Ainsi, Catherine Millet n'y va pas par quatre chemins en racontant qu'elle aime les partouzes. Les femmes ont besoin de se déshabiller et que ce ne soit pas toujours un homme qui le fasse, comme Zola avec *Nana* ou Flaubert avec *Madame Bovary*. Je crois que c'est une libération historique, quitte à choquer certains. Il y a un besoin de vérité." (There are indeed more female "autofictionists." For the first time, they can be at ease with their desire. This is why Catherine Millet doesn't beat around the bush when talking about her penchant for orgies. Women need to strip off and it should not always be a man who does it for them, such as Zola with *Nana* or Flaubert with *Madame Bovary*. I think that this is a historically significant liberation [on the part of the female writers], which risks shocking certain people. There is a need for truth.) "Serge Doubrovsky: 'Écrire sur soi, c'est écrire sur les autres,'" *Le Point*, February 22, 2011, http://www.lepoint.fr/grands-entretiens/serge-doubrovsky-ecrire-sur-soi-c-est-ecrire-sur-les-autres-22-02-2011-1298292_326.php.

[47] In German-language autobiography studies, autofiction has emerged in the past decade as one of the areas incurring intensified research interest, alongside that of memory and its relation to autobiography, and spatial theory and autobiography. Wagner-Egelhaaf, "Zum Stand und zu den Perspektiven der Autobiographieforschung in der Literaturwissenschaft."

[48] Arnaud Schmitt, "Making the Case for Self-Narration against Autofiction," *a/b: Auto/Biography Studies* 25, no. 1 (2010): 122–23; Frank Zipfel, "Autofiktion: Zwischen den Grenzen von Faktualität, Fiktionalität und Literarität?," in *Grenzen der Literatur: Zu Begriff und Phänomen des Literarischen*, ed. Simone Winko et al. (Berlin: De Gruyter, 2009), 286.

[49] Wagner-Egelhaaf, "Autofiktion—Theorie und Praxis," 100.

[50] Schmitt, "Making the Case for Self-Narration against Autofiction," 123.

[51] Zipfel, with recourse to Marie Darrieussecq's work: Zipfel, "Autofiktion," 304–5.

[52] In reaction to this, Schwarzer published a furious open letter to Roche on her website *aliceschwarzer.de*. This letter, captioned "Hallo Charlotte," is not retrievable anymore.

[53] Note that this has tradition: Doubrovsky's *Fils* and many subsequent autofictional publications in French have similarly been labeled "roman."

[54] *The Literary Encyclopedia*, s.v. "Charlotte Elisabeth Grace Roche," first published February 10, 2010, http://www.litencyc.com/php/speople.php?rec=true&UID=12646.

[55] Lejeune, "Autobiographical Pact (bis)," 134.

[56] Wagner-Egelhaaf, "Autofiktion—Theorie und Praxis," 97.

[57] Susanna Egan, *Burdens of Proof: Faith, Doubt and Identity in Autobiography* (Waterloo, ON: Wilfrid Laurier University Press, 2011), 17.

[58] The lasting dispute that involved several court proceedings is well summarized on *Bildblog*, a watchblog that specializes in publicly addressing erroneous media reports and unethical methods of journalists, especially focusing on the tabloid paper it is named after.

[59] The strange power that disgusting art can exert on its onlooker or reader, respectively, is described by Korsmeyer as its "magnetism" (see *Savoring Disgust*, esp. chapter 5), a term that tries to catch exactly how one can simultaneously be drawn to and repelled by the abject. Kristeva too discusses this in *Powers of Horror* (esp. chapter 1). Within intellectual thought, disgust's alluring, fascinating side is perhaps most evident in Bakhtin's positively biased rewriting of the sensation and its function in art and culture in his essays on the grotesque: Bakhtin, *Rabelais and His World*.

[60] Wagner-Egelhaaf, "Autofiktion—Theorie und Praxis," 97.

[61] Kristeva, *Powers of Horror*, 210.

[62] Wagner-Egelhaaf, "Autofiktion—Theorie und Praxis," 98.

[63] Note, too, that the passage, despite being set in the past, is narrated in the present tense.

[64] Luckhurst, "Mixing Memory and Desire," 499.

[65] Armine Kotin Mortimer, "Autofiction as Allofiction: Doubrovsky's *L'Après-vivre*," *L'Esprit Créateur* 49, no. 3 (2009): 33.

[66] Suzette A. Henke, *Shattered Subjects: Trauma and Testimony in Women's Life Writing* (London: Macmillan, 1998), 53.

[67] "5 Fragen an Charlotte Roche zu *Schoßgebete*," YouTube video, 4:19, promotional video, posted by "Piper Verlag," August 25, 2011, http://www.youtube.com/watch?v=Ag4amSRETSY.

[68] She uses the adjectives *lustig*, *krass*, *ehrlich*, and *wahrhaftig* in the German-language video.

[69] The author's exact wording in the video is "Ich sitze dann zuhause und warte auf den Tod."

[70] "Charlotte Roche bei Markus Lanz (18. August 2011)," YouTube video.

[71] Thomas Steinfeld, "Verlogenheit zwischen den Beinen," *Süddeutsche Zeitung*, July 27, 2012, http://www.sueddeutsche.de/kultur/charlotte-roches-neuer-roman-schossgebete-verlogenheit-zwischen-den-beinen-1.1129744.

[72] Carsten Heidböhmer, "Trauerspiel statt Sexskandal," *stern.de*, August 10, 2011, http://www.stern.de/kultur/buecher/-schossgebete----zweiter-roman-von-charlotte-roche-trauerspiel-statt-sexskandal-3779768.html.

[73] In her article "Pop, Porn, and Rebellious Speech" focusing on female writers and performers employing sexually explicit language, Stehle has written about this mechanism much more extensively than can be done here.

[74] Kotin Mortimer, "Autofiction as Allofiction," 33.

[75] According to the *Oxford English Dictionary*, a fable is a "short story devised to convey some useful lesson; *esp.* one in which animals or inanimate things are the speakers or actors."

[76] Caruth, "Introduction: Trauma and Experience," 10.

[77] Philip Oltermann, "Interview: Charlotte Roche," *GRANTA*, May 10, 2008, http://www.granta.com/New-Writing/Interview-Charlotte-Roche.

[78] Which are those readers who bear with Elizabeth through this opening scene and the repeated bold encounters with the unsexy, ill, and oozing bodies one encounters throughout the narrative.

[79] "NDR Talkshow 26.08.2011—Charlotte Roche (1/2)," YouTube video, 9:29, from the program *NDR Talkshow* televised by NDR, posted by "s2thepoweroftwo," August 29, 2011, https://www.youtube.com/watch?v=V71mDxERvIw.

[80] Zipfel, "Autofiktion," 301.

[81] Herman, *Trauma and Recovery*, 1.

[82] Buß, "Sexautorin Charlotte Roche."

[83] Hawkins, "Writing about Illness," 117. She draws on Robert J. Lifton's research on Hiroshima survivors in making this point.

[84] "NDR Talkshow 26.08.2011," YouTube video.

[85] Gasser, "Autobiographie und Autofiktion," 25; similarly: Wagner-Egelhaaf, "Zum Stand und zu den Perspektiven der Autobiographieforschung in der Literaturwissenschaft," 197.

[86] Bakhtin, *Rabelais and His World*, 319.

[87] Kathrin Schmidt, *Du stirbst nicht* (Munich: btb, 2011; orig.: Cologne: Kiepenheuer & Witsch, 2009).

[88] Kathleen Fietz, Kristina Pezzei, and Detlev Schilke, "Montagsinterview Kathrin Schmidt: Ich wusste schnell wieder, wer ich bin," *taz*, January 4, 2010, http://www.taz.de/!46202/.

Chapter Two

[1] Aphasia is an impairment of language owing to brain damage, often the result of a stroke, an infection, a brain tumor, or a traumatic brain injury, such as the aneurysm that burst in Schmidt's head. Aphasia can affect all language abilities, both one's production of language as well as one's processing of others' speech (be it written or spoken). Fluent and nonfluent aphasia are the two most frequent

forms of aphasia—the latter is associated with damage in the Broca's area of the brain and manifests itself in vocabulary and pronunciation problems, which are particularly severe when trying to find verbs. People with aphasia further experience problems producing grammatical sentences.

² The character and its creator share year of birth, have worked in the same professions (as psychologist and writer), both lived in the GDR, and are mothers of five children. For more, see, for example, Kathrin Krause, "Schmidt, Kathrin," in *Munzinger Online / KLG—Kritisches Lexikon zur deutschsprachigen Gegenwartsliteratur*, last modified March 1, 2017, http://www.munzinger.de/document/16000000689; Nina Schmidt, "Kathrin Schmidt," author page for the *Centre for the Study of Contemporary Women's Writing*, n.d. [2014], accessed August 24, 2017, https://modernlanguages.sas.ac.uk/research-centres/centre-study-contemporary-womens-writing/languages/german/kathrin-schmidt.

³ Bartels, "Überlebensgroß."

⁴ Ibid.

⁵ Walter Fabian Schmid, "Kathrin Schmidt im Gespräch: Das ist ein anderes Schreiben, als es vorher war," *Poet* 7 (2009): 182. She repeatedly expresses such concerns about being pigeonholed as *Betroffenheitsliteratur* or self-help literature across various interviews. See also, for example, Frank Quilitzsch, "'Literaturpreis für Kathrin Schmidt: 'Schreiben war immer meine Fluchtburg,'" *Thüringische Landeszeitung*, September 25, 2013, http://www.tlz.de/web/zgt/kultur/detail/-/specific/Heimkehr-durch-die-Raeume-meiner-Kindheit-und-Jugend-922015597.

⁶ Marina Neubert, "Lebendig begraben," *Berliner Morgenpost*, March 27, 2009, http://www.morgenpost.de/printarchiv/kultur/article1062623/Lebendig-begraben.html.

⁷ Kathleen Fietz, Kristina Pezzei, and Detlev Schilke, "Montagsinterview Kathrin Schmidt: Ich wusste schnell wieder, wer ich bin," *taz*, January 4, 2010, http://www.taz.de/!46202/.

⁸ Eyre, "From Impairment to Empowerment," 212.

⁹ Jörg Magenau, "Auf der Suche nach dem verlorenen Leben," *Literaturen* 10, no. 4 (2009): 56.

¹⁰ Anne-Ev Ustorf, "Es ist ein großes Glück, dass ich diesen Beruf hatte, als ich erkrankte: Kathrin Schmidt im Gespräch," *Psychologie Heute*, January 2011, http://www.ustorf.de/dateien/Interview_Kathrin_Schmidt.pdf.

¹¹ Ibid.

¹² Elmar Krekeler, "Wie ich die Sprache wiederfand," *Die Welt*, October 14, 2009, http://www.welt.de/welt_print/kultur/article4840308/Wie-ich-die-Sprache-wiederfand.html.

¹³ Von Lovenberg, "Ein Gespräch mit Charlotte Roche."

¹⁴ Katrin Hillgruber, "Erinnerungsroman: Aufschlussreiche Sprachbefreiung," *Spiegel Online*, April 20, 2009, http://www.spiegel.de/kultur/literatur/erinnerungsroman-aufschlussreiche-sprachbefreiung-a-619620.html; Anja Hirsch, "Steh auf und erinnere dich," *Frankfurter Allgemeine*, April 11, 2009, http://www.

faz.net/aktuell/feuilleton/buecher/rezensionen/belletristik/kathrin-schmidts-roman-du-stirbst-nicht-steh-auf-und-erinnere-dich-1792428.html; Sonja E. Klocke, "Kathrin Schmidt, *Du stirbst nicht*: A Woman's Quest for Agency," in *Emerging German-Language Novelists of the Twenty-First Century*, ed. Lyn Marven and Stuart Taberner (Rochester, NY: Camden House, 2011), 228.

[15] Christa Wolf's *Der geteilte Himmel* (*Divided Heaven / They Divided the Sky*, 1963) needs to be acknowledged as a model here, at least for Schmidt's choice of narrative structure and perspective: in Wolf's piece of fiction, Rita Seidel wakes up from coma, having suffered a mysterious accident at her factory workplace that can be interpreted as a suicide attempt. From this moment of crisis, little by little she begins to review her relationship with Manfred, his decision to leave for West Berlin, and her ultimate decision to stay in the East just as the Wall is built. Just like *Du stirbst nicht*, it is narrated in the third person, with two levels of storytelling interlacing: that of the narrative present in the hospital and that of the remembered past, retrospectively assessed. Christa Wolf, *Der geteilte Himmel* (Halle: Mitteldeutscher Verlag, 1963).

[16] Schmidt, *Du stirbst nicht*, 39, 74. Hereafter referenced parenthetically as *DSN*.

[17] Viktor/Viola is strongly reminiscent of another "Vatermutter" of Schmidt's, namely the character Lutz/Lucia in the author's debut novel *Die Gunnar-Lennefsen-Expedition* (The Gunnar-Lennefsen-expedition, 1998). For more on Lutz/Lucia's function within the novel, see Sonja E. Klocke, "Die frohe Botschaft der Kathrin Schmidt? Transsexuality, Racism, and Feminist Historiography in *Die Gunnar-Lennefsen-Expedition*," in *Sexual-Textual Border-Crossings: Lesbian Identity in German-Language Literature, Film, and Culture*, ed. Cordula Böcking-Politis and Carrie Smith-Prei, Germanistik in Ireland 5 (Konstanz: Hartung-Gorre, 2010).

[18] Krekeler, "Wie ich die Sprache wiederfand." She makes a similar assertion in conversation with Walter Fabian Schmid for *Poet*. Schmid, "Kathrin Schmidt im Gespräch," 181.

[19] Wagner-Egelhaaf, *Autobiographie*, 40–42.

[20] The narratologist Monika Fludernik stresses the creation of "experientiality" in narrative as central to the definition of narrative, hoping to move scholarly attention away from the plot or depiction of events and onto the mediation of the cognitive processing of events or experiences by a human or anthropomorphic character. According to Fludernik, it is experientiality, above all else, that makes a story imaginable for the reader. For more, see Monika Fludernik, *Towards a "Natural" Narratology* (New York: Routledge, 1996).

[21] Garland-Thomson, *Staring*.

[22] Ibid., 17, 49. To be seen is, of course, of equal importance (75).

[23] And there are, of course, a significant number of disabled people who voluntarily search the limelight too. *Staring* accounts for many such disabled starees by choice who purposely expose themselves to the public eye (such as, for instance, the New York-based artist and photographer Matuschka).

[24] Susan Sontag, *Regarding the Pain of Others* (London: Hamish Hamilton, 2003).

[25] Garland-Thomson, *Staring*, 6, 3.

[26] Ibid., 22–23.

[27] Ibid., 33.

[28] Ibid., 13.

[29] Garland-Thomson agrees, for example, that there is pleasure in looking as well as pleasure in being looked at (Mulvey, 423)—however, this is not its central concern, nor can pleasure be staring's only effect. She does not deny the extent to which the gaze permeates Western patriarchal society. Similar to others, her book takes as its basis the paradox displayed by the starer (or cinemagoer, in Mulvey's work) of oscillating between othering and identifying with the staree (the object of one's gaze) and the difficulty of finding a balance in both impulses. Laura Mulvey, "Visual Pleasure and Narrative Cinema," in *Contemporary Literary Criticism: Literary and Cultural Studies*, ed. Robert Con Davis and Ronald Schleifer, 3rd ed. (New York: Longman, 1994), 422–31.

[30] Mulvey, "Visual Pleasure and Narrative Cinema." For more on "staring as dominance," as Garland-Thomson titles her subchapter on the gaze, see *Staring*, 40–44. Here, Garland-Thomson herself discusses the relevant literature on the male as well as the postcolonial gaze, including Berger's, Fanon's, Saïd's, Foucault's, and Sartre's work.

[31] Garland-Thomson, *Staring*, 20. The exhibition "Der [im-]perfekte Mensch" (brackets in the original), curated by the Deutsches Hygiene-Museum Dresden in 2000/2001, too displayed a great interest in the stare. This seems to confirm Garland-Thomson's claim. A significant part of the exhibition, which was a landmark for an emerging disability studies in Germany, was devoted to the "Blick" (look/gaze) and its various dimensions. For more, see, for example, Poore, *Disability in Twentieth-Century German Culture*, 300.

[32] Garland-Thomson, *Staring*, 39.

[33] Ibid., 194. For more detail, see her concluding chapter in *Staring* or its reprint: Rosemarie Garland-Thomson, "Beholding," in Davis, *Disability Studies Reader*, 199–208.

[34] Klocke, "Kathrin Schmidt, *Du stirbst nicht*," 228.

[35] Deirdre Byrnes, "Writing on the Threshold: Memory, Language and Identity in Kathrin Schmidt's *Du stirbst nicht*," in *Transitions: Emerging Women Writers in German-Language Literature*, ed. Valerie Heffernan and Gillian Pye, German Monitor 76 (Amsterdam: Rodopi, 2013), 172, 169. In a chapter of her book on constructions of gender in the contemporary European novel, Yuan Xue focuses on the importance of the act of remembering Viola for Helene's recuperation. Unfortunately, Xue's work appears flawed both in some of its basic interpretation of the plot, as well as in the problematic language with which it discusses Helene's disability. Yuan Xue, *Über den Körper hinaus: Geschlechterkonstruktionen im europäischen Roman seit Ende der 1990er Jahre* (Bielefeld: Transcript, 2014), 94–115.

[36] Klocke, "Kathrin Schmidt, *Du stirbst nicht*," 228.

[37] Byrnes, "Writing on the Threshold," 173.

38 Garland-Thomson, *Staring*, 51.

39 Darian Leader and Judy Groves, *Introducing Lacan* (Cambridge: Icon Books UK, 1995), 22.

40 Jacques Lacan, "The Mirror Stage as Formative of the Function of the I," in *Écrits: A Selection*, trans. Alan Sheridan (London: Tavistock, 1977; orig.: Paris: Seuil, 1966), 4. The German terms have been retained in the translation; one might be able to translate them as "inner world" or "the world within," and "environment" or "the surrounding world."

41 Dino Felluga, "Modules on Lacan: On Psychosexual Development," *Introductory Guide to Critical Theory*, last modified January 31, 2011, http://www.purdue.edu/guidetotheory/psychoanalysis/lacandevelop.html.

42 Grosz, *Sexual Subversions*, 22.

43 For more on phenomenology's philosophical distinction between Körper and Leib, see, for instance, Emmanuel Alloa et al., eds., *Leiblichkeit: Geschichte und Aktualität eines Konzepts*, UTB 3633 (Tübingen: Mohr Siebeck, 2012).

44 Garland-Thomson, *Staring*, 52.

45 Schmidt's protagonist is generally quick to come up with nicknames for other patients around her, and these are telling. Apart from "the defective," for instance, there is also "hängende[s] Augenlid" (*DSN*, 176; droopy eyelid). As *partes pro toto*, these nicknames—although most certainly to be taken with a pinch of salt—negate their bearers any individuality. Instead, they turn impairment into all-consuming stigma and reveal some of the societally prevalent ableist mind-set Helene's thinking is also steeped in, at least at the beginning of the novel, which denotes the beginning of the protagonist's learning process.

46 Garland-Thomson, *Staring*, 6.

47 She notes, "Ob man ihm tatsächlich den Fuß verkehrt herum ans Knie genäht hat, kann sie jetzt nicht überprüfen" (*DSN*, 170; She has no chance to check in this moment if they indeed sewed his foot onto his knee the wrong way around).

48 This is alluding to a children's game where one floats on the water (in a swimming pool or the sea) on one's back for as long as possible, as if "dead." An alternative, less literal translation could therefore be "let him do star floats for a while."

49 Garland-Thomson, *Staring*, 19.

50 Besides Wojziech, Viktor/Viola is another intertextual character in *Du stirbst nicht*, one whose name amalgamates several cultural and historical references. It is evocative of Viola/Cesario in Shakespeare's comedy of errors *Twelfth Night, or What You Will* as well as the 1933 Reinhold Schünzel film *Viktor und Viktoria*, one of the last German cross-dressing comedies typical of the Weimar Republic, about a female cabaret star who pretends that she is in drag to get more work during the Great Depression. However, in *Du stirbst nicht*, Viola's fate is tragic rather than comical. The name Viola is further reminiscent of the Damenklub Violetta, an organization that represented the interests of queer women in 1920s Germany (especially Berlin).

51 "Von dem sich ja doch niemand lösen kann, so frei er sich auch wähnt," as Viola says in an email to Helene (*DSN*, 152; From which nobody can ultimately break away, no matter how free one thinks oneself).

52 Judith Butler, *Gender Trouble: Feminism and the Subversion of Identity* (New York: Taylor & Francis e-Library, 2002; orig.: New York: Routledge, 1990), 9.

53 Rosemarie Garland-Thomson, "Integrating Disability, Transforming Feminist Theory," *NWSA* 14, no. 3 (2002): 1–32. The fields intersect in their interest in the sociohistorical embeddedness of representations of bodies, the effects of culture on real/material bodies, and the formation of identities. They share critical attitudes toward understandings of normality and difference, and are equally keen to analyze power structures at work between people and in society. A further shared feature of disability and gender studies is their historic emergence from and continuing proximity to political activism.

54 NB: Helene has a pacemaker.

55 This is on account of the priority we assign it, being "celebrated and scorned, pronounced to be manipulative, liberating, rapacious, pornographic, gendered, or dominating." Garland-Thomson, *Staring*, 25.

56 Susan Sontag, *Illness as Metaphor and AIDS and Its Metaphors* (London: Penguin Books, 2002; orig.: New York: Anchor Books Doubleday, 1989), 3.

57 Davis, *Enforcing Normalcy*.

58 Dalziell, "Shame and Life Writing," 2:808.

59 Matthias Weichelt, "Kathrin Schmidt: You Are Not Going to Die," trans. Isabel Cole, *Litrix.de—German Literature online*, August 2010, http://www.litrix.de/buecher/belletristik/jahr/2010/stirbstnicht/buchbesprechung/enindex.htm.

60 Elmar Krekeler, "Bester Roman des Jahres: *Du stirbst nicht*," *Die Welt*, October 14, 2009, www.welt.de/welt_print/kultur/article4840309/Bester-Roman-des-Jahres-Du-stirbst-nicht.html.

61 See, for example, Fietz, Pezzei, and Schilke, "Montagsinterview."

62 Stefan, *Fremdschläfer*.

63 See, for instance, Betten, "Entwicklungen und Formen," 4:3138, 3140.

64 Verena Stefan, *Häutungen* (Munich: Frauenoffensive, 1975). First published in English as *Shedding* in 1978 by an American publishing house (New York: Daughters), and a year later in the UK (London: Women's Press).

65 Compare my assessment of literary scholars' reactions to personal illness narratives from the 1970s and 1980s in the introduction to this study, see especially the section "German Studies Scholarship and Its Attitude toward Illness in Literature."

66 Verena Stefan, *Es ist reich gewesen: Bericht vom Sterben meiner Mutter* (Frankfurt am Main: Fischer Taschenbuch, 1993). Allyson Fiddler translates the German title as "There Were Riches: On the Death of My Mother." Allyson Fiddler, "Subjectivity and Women's Writing of the 1970s and Early 1980s," in *The Cambridge Companion to the Modern German Novel*, ed. Graham Bartram (Cambridge: Cambridge University Press, 2004), 256.

Chapter Three

[1] Ingo Arend, "Eine undurchsichtige Größe," *Der Freitag*, May 9, 2008, www.freitag.de/autoren/der-freitag/eine-undurchsichtige-grosse. Stefan has continued to publish since. In 2014, *Die Befragung der Zeit* (Inquiry into time) came out—a text based on the story of Stefan's grandfather, who, as a doctor in the Bernese region of Switzerland, was arrested repeatedly for illegally performing abortions in the 1940s and 1950s. Verena Stefan, *Die Befragung der Zeit* (Munich: Nagel & Kimche, 2014).

[2] Stefan, *Fremdschläfer*, 218. Hereafter referenced parenthetically as *F*.

[3] Stefan, *Häutungen*, 3. Hereafter referenced parenthetically as *H*.

[4] Christa Binswanger and Kathy Davis indeed draw this parallel and highlight aspects in which the books are comparable: both *Feuchtgebiete* and *Häutungen* tell the coming-of-age story of a girl or young woman, respectively. They do so using a vocabulary and style specifically developed by each author in an attempt to find an independent language to describe the female body as well as to express female protagonists' sexual desires and pleasures in a new way. Media discussions in both cases revolved around notions of taboo, their limits, and transgression, and resulted in assessments of the books as either advancing or setting back feminist concerns. Christa Binswanger and Kathy Davis, "Sexy Stories and Postfeminist Empowerment: From *Häutungen* to *Wetlands*," *Feminist Theory* 13, no. 3 (2012): 245–63.

[5] A chapter centering on this is titled "Entzugserscheinungen" (*H*, 59; Withdrawal symptoms).

[6] Binswanger and Davies, "Sexy Stories," 246.

[7] Allyson Fiddler describes *Häutungen* as a "phenomenally successful" book, adding that "its first print run sold out in a matter of months." Fiddler, "Subjectivity and Women's Writing of the 1970s and early 1980s," 250. As Binswanger and Davies note, "By the end of 1977, 150,000 copies had been sold and in 1985, the book was still a German bestseller. . . . By 1994, 300,000 German copies had been sold and *Häutungen* had already been translated into seven European languages as well as Japanese." Binswanger and Davies, "Sexy Stories," 259.

[8] As quoted in Spiegl, "Gross, schlank, blond, attraktiv."

[9] Over the years, more reasonable criticism of the book has emerged, too. See, for instance, Joanne Leal, "The Politics of 'Innerlichkeit': Karin Struck's *Klassenliebe* and Verena Stefan's *Häutungen*," *German Life and Letters* 50, no. 4 (1997): 508–28. Leal criticizes *Häutungen*'s ending for offering only a private solution (with the main character retreating from society) and reads it as one of political resignation. Others have grappled with Stefan's radical feminism as unwittingly reinscribing a biological determinism into gender relations and thus, as they see it, ultimately reaffirming gender stereotypes: Cordula Böcking-Politis and Carrie Smith-Prei, introduction to *Sexual-Textual Border-Crossings: Lesbian Identity in German-Language Literature, Film, and Culture*, ed. Böcking-Politis and Smith-Prei, Germanistik in Ireland 5 (Konstanz: Hartung-Gorre, 2010), 7.

[10] For a discussion of the genre designation "novel" and its possible functions in the context of contemporary life writing, see the introduction to this book, section "Illness and the Attraction of the Personal."

[11] Ruth Klüger, "Einwandern, auswandern, wandern," *Die Welt*, October 6, 2007, http://www.welt.de/welt_print/article1239740/Einwandern-auswandern-wandern.html.

[12] See "working notes" to Stefan, "Doe a Deer."

[13] See ibid.

[14] Wittig, "Point of View." Wittig has had a strong influence on Stefan throughout her writing career. Stefan regularly uses Wittig's theorizations to explain her choice of words in the last lines of *Häutungen*—having put "der mensch [instead of 'the woman'] meines lebens bin ich" (*H*, 124; the person of my life is me)— and in the 1980s, Stefan cotranslated *Lesbian Peoples: Material for a Dictionary* by Monique Wittig and Sande Zeig into German. Monique Wittig and Sande Zeig, *Lesbische Völker: Ein Wörterbuch*, trans. Gabriele Meixner and Verena Stefan (Munich: Frauenoffensive, 1983).

[15] Wittig, "Point of View," 65. Wittig deliberately uses the description "minority writer" rather than homosexual or gay author to keep the category, and with it her argument, open for appropriation. After all, authors can find themselves pigeonholed as "minority writers" for a variety of reasons. Stefan, in the case at hand, fits this description as a creative person dealing publicly with serious illness but also as a foreigner in Canada, as a lesbian writer among heterosexuals, and, not least, as a female author under patriarchy.

[16] For more on the term *Betroffenheitsliteratur* and similar labels, as well as the ways in which they can prove problematic for authors, see the introduction to this book, especially the section "German Studies Scholarship and Its Attitude toward Illness in Literature."

[17] Konrad, "Minderheiten—Literatur?" All other quotations in this paragraph from Wittig, "Point of View," 65.

[18] Wittig, "Point of View," 68.

[19] Ibid., 65.

[20] In this focus, my analysis of Stefan's *Fremdschläfer* varies significantly from Sonja Klocke's. Klocke's chief interest lies in the "significance of the female body for the ways in which immigration, cancer, and kinship are linked," as she makes explicit. Sonja Klocke, "'Committed from Head to Toe?' Cancer, Immigration, and Kinship in Verena Stefan's *Fremdschläfer*," *Women in German Yearbook: Feminist Studies in German Literature & Culture* 26 (2010): 118.

[21] For more on the stigma of breast cancer, see, for example, Sontag, *Illness as Metaphor*; Couser, *Recovering Bodies*, esp. chapter 3: "Self-Reconstruction: Personal Narratives of Breast Cancer."

[22] Thatcher Carter, "Body Count: Autobiographies by Women Living with Breast Cancer," *Journal of Popular Culture* 36, no. 4 (2003): 653.

[23] All medical/statistical information in this paragraph is from M. Malvezzi et al., "European Cancer Mortality Predictions for the Year 2013," *Annals of Oncology* 24, no. 3 (2013): 792–800.

[24] Brenda L. Blondeau and Eva C. Karpinski, editorial, *Canadian Woman Studies / Les Cahiers de la Femme* 28, nos. 2/3 (2010): 3.

25 Ibid.

26 Sontag, *Illness as Metaphor*, 19.

27 Marion Moamai, for example, maintains personal cancer literature's function "als Lebenshilfe" (as providing emotional or moral support / counseling) to be primary. Moamai, *Krebs schreiben*, 37.

28 Diane Price Herndl, "Our Breasts, Our Selves: Identity, Community, and Ethics in Cancer Autobiographies," *Signs* 32, no. 1 (2006): 229. Herndl explains the psychological dynamic she sees at work in what are, to a large extent, narratives of recovery: when recasting their role as writer-helper, authors who were affected by breast cancer and have been reliant on help as they underwent treatment distance themselves from their patient role as they provide to others the support they once received.

29 Ulrich Teucher, "The Incomprehensible Density of Being: Aestheticizing Cancer," in *Unfitting Stories: Narrative Approaches to Disease, Disability, and Trauma*, ed. Valérie Raoul (Waterloo, ON: Wilfrid Laurier University Press, 2007), 73.

30 Couser, *Recovering Bodies*, 40; Mary K. DeShazer, *Fractured Borders: Reading Women's Cancer Literature* (Ann Arbor: University of Michigan Press, 2005), 4. For Herndl, writing about more recent breast cancer narratives (also from the US context), the canon appears less homogenous: "Typically, these narratives do end on an upbeat note, but often that tone is shown to be provisional, subject to unpredictable change." Herndl, "Our Breasts," 232.

31 Herndl, "Our Breasts," 222.

32 Teucher, "Incomprehensible Density of Being," 74.

33 DeShazer, *Fractured Borders*, 1–10.

34 See the diversity in autobiographical writings by, for example, Musa Mayer, Christina Middlebrook, Susan Wendell, Barbara Rosenblum, and Treya Killam Wilber, as discussed by Einat Avrahami in *The Invading Body*, chapter 2.

35 Maxie Wander, *Tagebücher und Briefe*, ed. Fred Wander (Berlin: Buchverlag Der Morgen, 1980), later republished as *Leben wär' eine prima Alternative: Tagebücher und Briefe*. Ruth Picardie's *Before I Say Goodbye* (London: Penguin, 1998) is a posthumously published collection of the journalist's end-of-life *Observer* columns.

36 Miriam Engelberg, *Cancer Made Me a Shallower Person: A Memoir in Comics* (New York: Harper, 2006); Marisa Acocella Marchetto, *Cancer Vixen: A True Story* (New York: Alfred A. Knopf, 2006). For more, see, for instance, Dina Georgis's review of six postmillennial graphic memoirs by women about their personal cancer experience: Dina Georgis, "Bearing Cancer in Graphic Memoir," *Canadian Woman Studies / Les Cahiers de la Femme* 28, nos. 2/3 (2010): 105–9.

37 Teucher, "Incomprehensible Density of Being," 73.

38 For a recent study of postmillennial breast cancer narratives (albeit, like the large majority of scholarly work, discussing exclusively English-language examples) and the ways in which these twenty-first-century narratives differ from older ones, see Mary K. DeShazer, *Mammographies: The Cultural Discourses of Breast Cancer Narratives* (Ann Arbor: University of Michigan Press, 2013).

[39] Such questions are repeated, especially throughout the first part of the book. On page 41, for instance, one reads: "Was ist es, das in dir gewachsen ist, warum hast du nicht gemerkt, daß sich ein Knoten bildet, zu dem du augenblicklich Fremdkörper sagst?" (What is it that has grown inside you, why haven't you noticed that a lump was forming, one that immediately you call a foreign body?)

[40] Woolf, *On Being Ill*.

[41] Sontag, *Illness as Metaphor*.

[42] Audre Lorde, *The Cancer Journals* (London: Sheba Feminist, 1985; orig.: San Francisco: Spinsters Ink, 1980).

[43] Lucy Grealy, *Autobiography of a Face* (Boston: Houghton Mifflin, 1994).

[44] Wittig, "Point of View," 65.

[45] Sontag, *Illness as Metaphor*, 3. Despite the fact that Sontag later called the one-page preamble "a brief, hectic flourish of metaphor, [composed] in mock exorcism of the seductiveness of metaphorical thinking" (91), today the preface is the most widely cited part of the book—proof, at the very least, of the persistent intuitive appeal of metaphorical thinking. Sontag nonetheless held on to her opinion, as voiced in the main part of the essay, that it is "sometimes correct to be 'against' interpretation" (91). The determination with which she avoided a personal tone in writing the essay can be interpreted as her own distancing strategy, as indeed Christoph Schlingensief did (see introduction to this book). Scholars have stressed that with *Illness as Metaphor*, Sontag was buying into a myth herself, namely that of metaphorlessness: Barbara Clow, "Who's Afraid of Susan Sontag? or, The Myths and Metaphors of Cancer Reconsidered," *Social History of Medicine* 14, no. 2 (2001): 293–312. Anne Hunsaker Hawkins provides the needed corrective to Sontag's polemic when she insists that "myths about illness may be enabling as well as disabling." Hunsaker Hawkins, *Reconstructing Illness*, 24. In Audre Lorde's text *The Cancer Journals*, which Lorde wrote at virtually the same time as Sontag hers, we can observe the benefits of metaphorical thinking at work: the image of herself as "warrior poet" fighting cancer helps Lorde to conceive of herself as more than just passive victim. It is a more potent and livable subject position for her. Lorde, *Cancer Journals*, 26.

[46] Woolf, *On Being Ill*, 3.

[47] Note Stefan's stylistic decision against putting full stops at the end of many paragraphs in *Fremdschläfer*. This gives the writing in the book a distinctly open-ended, reverberating quality.

[48] Sontag's exact words: "Cancer is a rare and still scandalous subject for poetry; and it seems unimaginable to aestheticize the disease." Sontag, *Illness as Metaphor*, 20. In the German literary realm, Judith Ricker-Abderhalden proved her wrong as early as 1987, when she was able to look back on a variety of German-language illness writings (in challenging, literary/poetic form) from the late 1970s and early 1980s. Ricker-Abderhalden, "Schreiben über Krankheit."

[49] Sontag, *Illness as Metaphor*, 15.

[50] In the epigraph, Stefan quotes (in her own translation) Woolf's words: "Here we go alone, and like it better so. Always to have sympathy, always to be accompanied, always to be understood would be intolerable." Woolf, *On Being Ill*, 12.

51 Woolf, *On Being Ill*, 4.

52 Hermione Lee, introduction to *On Being Ill*, by Virginia Woolf (Ashfield, MA: Paris Press, 2002), xxviii.

53 Woolf, *On Being Ill*, p. 12.

54 As observed about Woolf, by Lee, introduction, xxxii.

55 My interpretation here runs counter that of Sonja Klocke, who reads *Fremdschläfer*'s shifts in pronoun usage as introducing gradations of distance (increasing from first to second to third person). Klocke takes the supposed need to establish emotional distance between the narrating and the experiencing persona as decisive of this idiosyncratic use of personal pronouns. Klocke, "Committed from Head to Toe?," 125.

56 Lorde, *Cancer Journals*, 4.

57 Ibid., 32.

58 Heide Oestreich, "Schriftstellerin Verena Stefan: 'Ich bin keine Frau. Punkt,'" *taz*, May 10, 2008, http://www.taz.de/Schriftstellerin-Verena-Stefan/!17049/. On the subject of the lesbian woman as other, note also the following autobiographical short story: Verena Stefan, "We Live as Two Lesbians," *TRIVIA: Voices of Feminism* 11, no. 2 (2010), http://www.triviavoices.com/we-live-as-two-lesbians.html.

59 One example of a text from the German-language context that one might expect to be referenced in Stefan's writing about cancer is *Fuss fassen* by fellow Swiss-German author Maja Beutler, a personal cancer narrative from 1980. Beutler in fact shares her hometown of Bern with Verena Stefan. As this demonstrates, however, Stefan seems to have consciously avoided establishing such all-too-obvious lines of reference. Maja Beutler, *Fuss fassen* (Bern: Zytglogge, 1980).

60 Published in English as *The Practice of Everyday Life*. Michel de Certeau, *The Practice of Everyday Life*, trans. Steven Rendall (Berkeley: University of California Press, 1984; orig.: *L'invention du quotidien: 1. arts de faire*, Paris: Union générale d'éditions, 1980).

61 De Certeau, *The Practice of Everyday Life*, qtd. from the book's dedication.

62 Ian Buchanan, "Introduction to Part III: Other People: Ethnography and Social Practice," in *The Certeau Reader*, ed. Graham Ward (Oxford: Blackwell, 2000), 100.

63 Ibid., 100.

64 Rendall's translation of the French original. De Certeau, *Practice of Everyday Life*, 97.

65 Very similarly, in the phrase "Dein Text könnte abreißen" (*F*, 159; your text might break off), text equals life.

66 Hardy Ruoss, "Verena Stefan: *Fremdschläfer*—die Autorin im Gespräch mit Hardy Ruoss," mp3, 28:43, from the program *Schweizer Radio DRS—Reflexe*, broadcast on November 8, 2007, http://www.srf.ch/sendungen/reflexe/verena-stefan-fremdschlaefer-die-autorin-im-gespraech-mit-hardy-ruoss.

67 Oestreich, "Schriftstellerin Verena Stefan."

⁶⁸ As is made clear in its preface, *Häutungen* arose from Stefan's desire at the time to ignite a sociopolitical debate in Germany (i.e., precisely to intervene in the German context), declaring "dessen inhalt *hierzulande* überfällig" (*H*, 3; emphasis mine; its content [i.e., the content of the book] overdue *in this country*).

⁶⁹ Although born in Switzerland, because of her Swiss mother's marriage to her German father, Stefan was officially regarded a foreigner herself (*F*, 195).

⁷⁰ Stefan's work today certainly needs to be read in the context of not just German- but English- and French-language literatures too, as she inserts her voice into these discourses in translation, having been published, for instance, in *TRIVIA: Voices of Feminism* (in English) and with excerpts of *Fremdschläfer/ D'ailleurs* (in French) reprinted in "Women and Cancer," a special issue of *Canadian Woman Studies / Les Cahiers de la Femme* 28, nos. 2/3 (2010). Her latest novel *Die Befragung der Zeit* was published in French in 2017 as *Qui maîtrise les vents connaît son chemin*.

⁷¹ Virginia Woolf, *A Room of One's Own & Three Guineas* (London: Vintage, 1996; orig.: London: Chatto & Windus / Hogarth, 1984), 229.

⁷² Verena Stefan in an interview with Jeremy M. Davies from *Dalkey Archive Press*, July/August 2010, currently retrievable in slightly altered form to the original only from a personal blog, accessed February 3, 2014, ginster-plantagenet.blogspot.co.uk/2011/07/verena-stefan-poet-author-from-another.html.

⁷³ Carter, "Body Count," 657.

⁷⁴ Ibid., 657–58.

⁷⁵ Verena Stefan, *D'ailleurs*, trans. Louis Bouchard and Marie-Elisabeth Morf (Montréal: Héliotrope, 2008).

⁷⁶ Oestreich, "Schriftstellerin Verena Stefan."

⁷⁷ Herndl, "Our Breasts," 241. On the basis of her analyses of breast cancer narratives published between 1997 and 2002, Herndl stresses that cancer narratives are aimed at an audience that shares the cancer experience, the implied reader being "almost always assumed to be another woman with breast cancer or someone close to a woman with breast cancer" (231).

⁷⁸ Couser, *Recovering Bodies*, 37.

⁷⁹ Stefan, "We Live as Two Lesbians." I am thinking in particular of geographical, cultural, and linguistic boundaries.

⁸⁰ "Writing" and "text" are to be understood in the widest possible sense, as there are many forms in which lives find shape in a digitized society. In their incorporation of various media (audio, video, photography) and use of the Internet, Schlingensief and Herrndorf are very contemporary examples of diaristic self-expression.

⁸¹ Schlingensief, *So schön wie hier kanns im Himmel gar nicht sein!*; Wolfgang Herrndorf, *Arbeit und Struktur* (Berlin: Rowohlt, 2013).

⁸² Considering the immediacy of blogging is one way of troubling this perspective, because authors signal with every post that they are still alive. The act of writing, in blogging, conveys life.

Chapter Four

[1] Schlingensief, *So schön wie hier kanns im Himmel gar nicht sein!*; Herrndorf, *Arbeit und Struktur*. Hereafter referenced parenthetically as *So schön* and *AS*, respectively. Schlingensief's *Tagebuch* (hardcover) was the fourth-best-selling book on May 4, 2009; in week thirty-nine of 2010 it still ranked twenty-fourth in the *Spiegel*-Bestsellerliste. Its paperback version took fifth place overall in week forty of 2010. Following its hardcover publication in early December 2013, Herrndorf's *Arbeit und Struktur* ranked twelfth in the *Spiegel*-Bestsellerliste by December 23, 2013. It remained one of the most sold books on the German-language market throughout 2014—remaining in the top twenty for the first half of the year and in the top fifty for the second half. Interestingly, while Herrndorf's diary was included in the *Belletristik* list (belles lettres/fiction), Schlingensief's was considered a *Sachbuch* (nonfiction), indicating neither book to be a neat fit in its assigned category. (All data from *buchreport.de*.)

[2] Philippe Lejeune, "How Do Diaries End?," in Lejeune, *On Diary*, 193; Burkhard Meyer-Sickendiek, "Der Schmerz im Tagebuch," in *Affektpoetik: Eine Kulturgeschichte literarischer Emotionen*, by Burkhard Meyer-Sickendiek (Würzburg: Königshausen & Neumann, 2005).

[3] Kathryn Carter, "Death and the Diary, or Tragedies in the Archive," *Journal of Canadian Studies / Revue d'études canadiennes* 40, no. 2 (2006): 56.

[4] Literary scholarship came to the diary as an object of study in its own right comparatively late. Within psychology, especially since the psychoanalytic movement, interest in the diary arose out of the hope of tracing the inner workings of the human mind and revealing the unconscious; historians appreciate diaries as original sources. Sociologists use diaries both to gain insight into the lived social reality of sections of society and, though this is a more recent trend, as research tools in themselves. Christiane Holm, "Montag Ich. Dienstag Ich. Mittwoch Ich. Versuch einer Phänomenologie des Diaristischen," in Gold, *@bsolut? Privat! Vom Tagebuch zum Weblog*, 10; Kenneth Plummer, *Documents of Life: An Introduction to the Problems and Literature of a Humanistic Method*, Contemporary Social Research Series 7 (London: Allen & Unwin, 1983).

[5] Trailblazers include Peter Boerner, who produced one of the first systematizations of the diary (its phenomenology, history, and modern form) for German studies, and Philippe Lejeune, for his more philosophical and experimental analyses of diaries' emergence, aesthetic, and functions, and for having introduced the diary as a valid subject for scholars of life writing internationally. Researching Holocaust diaries, Alexandra Zapruder has discussed the dangers that come with imposing preconceived ideas of such diaries onto individual texts, obfuscating their design and content. In the context of World War II and the Holocaust, she has exposed the tendency to glorify victims' diaries as reflecting readers' needs. Another recent publication in English to be highlighted is Cardell's *De@r World*. Peter Boerner, *Tagebuch* (Stuttgart: Metzler, 1969); Lejeune, *On Diary*; Alexandra Zapruder, *Salvaged Pages: Young Writers' Diaries of the Holocaust* (New Haven, CT: Yale University Press, 2002), 1–12.

[6] Helmut Gold, "@bsolut privat!? Vom Tagebuch zum Weblog," in Gold, *@bsolut? Privat!*, 6–7.

⁷ This is an understanding many contemporary researchers of the diary now share; see by way of example Günter Butzer, "Sich selbst schreiben: Das Tagebuch als Weblog avant la lettre," in Gold, *@bsolut? Privat!*, 94–96.

⁸ Philippe Lejeune, "The Diary as 'Antifiction,'" in Lejeune, *On Diary*, 204. Although Lejeune's exploratory research into the diary does not have a particular focus on autothanatography as such, it provided a valuable springboard for the ideas underlying this chapter and does include considerations of diaries' endings and the diarist's death.

⁹ Rachel Cottam, "Diaries and Journals: General Survey," in Jolly, *Encyclopedia of Life Writing*, 1:269.

¹⁰ Philippe Lejeune, "The Continuous and Discontinuous," in Lejeune, *On Diary*, 179. In his use of the term "trace," Lejeune also brings in the idea that diarists invest much of themselves into the diaristic text (without offering further comment at this point), and that their "having been present" has a lasting impact in a near-physical sense, like a footprint (my example).

¹¹ Martin Lindner, "Ich Schreiben im Falschen Leben: Tagebuch-Literatur seit 1950; Eine kurze Geschichte der deutschsprachigen Literatur am Leitfaden der Diaristik" (unpublished habilitation diss., Universität Passau, 1998; last revised 2005), n.p. (section headed "Vorschlag einer formalen Definition der Textsorte 'Tagebuch'").

¹² Lejeune, "Diary as 'Antifiction,'" 204.

¹³ Philippe Lejeune, *On Autobiography*, ed. Paul John Eakin, trans. Katherine Leary, Theory and History of Literature 52 (Minneapolis: University of Minnesota Press, 1989).

¹⁴ Philippe Lejeune, "The Diary on Trial," in Lejeune, *On Diary*, 153.

¹⁵ Catherina Gilles shares this view in *Kunst und Nichtkunst: Das Theater von Christoph Schlingensief* (Würzburg: Königshausen & Neumann, 2009), 153.

¹⁶ Klaus Biesenbach et al., eds., *Christoph Schlingensief* (Cologne: Walther König, 2014), 21.

¹⁷ It is not known to what extent the diary entries were edited. What is clear is that the published diary presents the reader with a selection of available material, as the whole of the transcripts are said to take up between one (Diez) and three (Schors) bulging ring binders, amounting to 450 pages of text (Diez). Horst Willi Schors, "Der Tod als Bühnenstück," *Kölner Stadt-Anzeiger*, September 22, 2009, n.p.; Georg Diez, "Ich habe den Tod gespürt, er saß in mir: Ich habe gekämpft," *Süddeutsche Zeitung Magazin* 38 (2008), http://sz-magazin.sueddeutsche.de/texte/anzeigen/26434/1/1.

¹⁸ Schlingensief used the art action and later documentary film *Die Piloten—eine Talkshow in sechs Folgen, die nie ausgestrahlt wird* (2009) as a forum to discuss his fears of losing his father, who lay in hospital dying at the time. Exhibitions that dealt with his father's death were to follow: "18 Bilder pro Sekunde" in Munich (Haus der Kunst, May 25–Sept. 16, 2007) and "Querverstümmelung" in Zurich (Migros Museum für Gegenwartskunst, Nov. 3, 2007–Feb. 3, 2008).

¹⁹ Conceptually, the diary stands at the very beginning of that period. Other—theatrical and operatic—works honing in on the artist's illness experience include

Der Zwischenstand der Dinge (which had a private showing to invited guests only at the Maxim Gorki Theater Berlin in July 2008 and three public showings in Nov. 2008), *Eine Kirche der Angst vor dem Fremden in mir: Fluxus-Oratorium von Christoph Schlingensief* (premiered as part of the Ruhrtriennale in Sept. 2008), *Mea Culpa—Eine ReadyMadeOper* (opened at the Burgtheater Wien in March 2009), and *Sterben lernen! Herr Andersen stirbt in 60 Minuten* (which premiered at the Theater Neumarkt in Zurich in Dec. 2009). While producing these stage works, Schlingensief also set up his *Schlingenblog* and the online forum *Geschockte Patienten*. Additionally, his long-term vision, Operndorf Afrika, was initiated then. It runs to this day.

[20] The diary passes unheeded in the following examples of academic studies on Schlingensief's late work: Kaspar Mühlemann, *Christoph Schlingensief und seine Auseinandersetzung mit Joseph Beuys*, Europäische Hochschulschriften: Kunstgeschichte 439 (Frankfurt am Main: Lang, 2011); Sarah Ralfs, "'Wir sind eins'— total total: Selbst-Inszenierungen in Christoph Schlingensiefs späten Arbeiten," in Janke and Kovacs, *Der Gesamtkünstler Christoph Schlingensief*, 307–26; Sandra Umathum, "Die Kunst des Abschiednehmens: Überlegungen zu Christoph Schlingensiefs Inszenierung von eigenem Sterben und Tod," in *Theater und Subjektkonstitution: Theatrale Praktiken zwischen Affirmation und Subversion*, ed. Michael Bachmann et al., Theater 33 (Bielefeld: Transcript, 2012).

[21] This is evidenced in the feuilletons of the newspapers, and it also matches the attitude toward personal illness writings of German-language literary scholarship. Terms quoted here as used in Angele, "Wer hat geil Krebs?"; Kämmerlings, "Krebsliteratur"; Peitz, "Die Ich-Erzähler."

[22] Christoph Schlingensief, *Ich weiß, ich war's*, ed. Aino Laberenz (Cologne: Kiepenheuer & Witsch, 2012), 30.

[23] This appears to be a reference to Nietzsche's *Ecce homo: Wie man wird, was man ist* (written 1888, published 1908).

[24] For a thorough study of Beuys's place in Schlingensief's thinking, see Mühlemann, *Christoph Schlingensief*.

[25] Beuys's piece too was generally understood as being highly autobiographical in meaning, with the artist having suffered a heart attack in 1975. Ibid., 95.

[26] Schappach, *Aids in Literatur, Theater und Film*, 154.

[27] They base this observation on research done in the field of trauma studies, and in particular on Shoshana Felman and Dori Laub's seminal *Testimony: Crises of Witnessing in Literature, Psychoanalysis, and History* (New York: Routledge, 1992).

[28] Nancy K. Miller and Jason Tougaw, "Introduction: Extremities," in *Extremities: Trauma, Testimony, and Community*, ed. Nancy K. Miller and Jason Tougaw (Urbana: University of Illinois Press, 2002), 11.

[29] The Opera Village is a nonprofit project located near Ouagadougou. Its construction began in 2009. It will eventually be a self-sufficient village with a festival hall at its center, complete with a hospital and a school that puts a special emphasis on the practice of the arts.

[30] When this book went into print, the site hosting the forum was still accessible via two links: http://www.krank-und-autonom.de/ and http://www.geschockte-patienten.org/.

[31] Lindner, "Ich Schreiben im Falschen Leben," n.p. (section headed "Vorschlag einer formalen Definition der Textsorte 'Tagebuch'").

[32] Eakin, foreword, ix.

[33] This, however, remains Egan's only remark on the suitability of the diary form for autothanatographical expression. Susanna Egan, "The Life and Times of Autothanatography" (workshop discussion paper for the Pain and Suffering Interdisciplinary Research Network, 2001), accessed October 9, 2014, http://www.english.ubc.ca/PROJECTS/PAIN/DEGAN.HTM (site discontinued).

[34] Ibid.

[35] Philippe Lejeune, "Rereading your Diary," in Lejeune, *On Diary*, 324.

[36] Schlingensief, *Ich weiß, ich war's*, 51.

[37] Jeremy D. Popkin, "Philippe Lejeune, Explorer of the Diary," preface to Lejeune, *On Diary*, 2.

[38] Arno Dusini argues that such reductions go along with any editing of original diary material. Arno Dusini, *Tagebuch. Möglichkeiten einer Gattung* (Munich: Wilhelm Fink, 2005), 55.

[39] Susanna Egan, *Mirror Talk: Genres of Crisis in Contemporary Autobiography* (Chapel Hill: University of North Carolina Press, 1999), 197.

[40] See especially the section "The (Non)place of Narratives of Illness/Disability in Contemporary German Literature."

[41] Egan, *Mirror Talk*, 197.

[42] See http://www.peter-deutschmark.de/blog or http://www.peter-deutschmark.de/schlingenblog/category/schlingenblog/. Both links appear to lead to the same page. The oldest available entry on the site dates back to November 25, 2008. Parts of the blog can also be found at http://schlingenblog.wordpress.com, yet the Wordpress site reaches back only to November 2009. According to Lore Knapp, the original URL was http://www.schlingenblog-posterous.com/ (site discontinued). Whereas I see no contradiction in regarding the blog as artful and simultaneously recognizing its diary form, Lore Knapp reads the *Schlingenblog* as an "artblog" and perceives it to resemble more "dem Lit-, dem Fach- oder dem Reiseblog" (the literary, specialist, or travel blog) than a personal blog or diary. It must suffice to point out that the blog does, however, carry all the defining features of the text type as outlined, with the help of Lejeune and Lindner, in this chapter's introduction. Lore Knapp, "Christoph Schlingensiefs Blog: Multimediale Autofiktion im Künstlerblog," in *Narrative Genres im Internet: Theoretische Bezugsrahmen, Mediengattungstypologie und Funktionen*, ed. Ansgar Nünning and Jan Rupp (Trier: Wissenschaftlicher Verlag, 2012), 117.

[43] Lejeune, "How Do Diaries End?," 191.

[44] Ibid.

[45] Ibid.

46 I am using the term author/producer to emphasize that it is not just the uploaded content that bears Schlingensief's hallmarks, but that the conception of the blog as a whole (including a number of layout decisions even when using blogging software such as that provided by Posterous and Wordpress) and the maintenance of the site were in his hands.

47 Schlingensief, *Ich weiß, ich war's*, 19.

48 In all quotations from the *Schlingenblog*, Schlingensief's idiosyncratic spelling and spacing has been retained exactly as in the original.

49 For background reading on Muschg's and Frisch's respective interest in the themes carried forward by *Mars* and *Diktate*, see Pender, *Contemporary Images of Death and Sickness*.

50 This is not a direct quotation from the article by Johannes Seibel published in the newspaper on September 11, 2008, but Schlingensief's own paraphrase of its content. An excerpt from Seibel's original article is included in Pia Janke and Teresa Kovacs, eds., *Der Gesamtkünstler Christoph Schlingensief*, Diskurse—Kontexte—Impulse 8 (Vienna: Praesens, 2011), 330.

51 The diary was begun in March 2010 and is still accessible online under http://www.wolfgang-herrndorf.de/. Unless stated otherwise, quotations used in this chapter follow the book version of Wolfgang, *Arbeit und Struktur*.

52 Cardell, *De@r World*, 97.

53 Herrndorf holds off from narrating the moment of diagnosis in any detail until the decision to make the blog freely available online in September 2010; he then incorporates it into the beginning of a series of "Rückblenden" (flashbacks; *AS*, 97–149). He writes these in order to provide a more narrative back story to his diary that by its nature began in situ. The passages serve as orientation for a general reader outside of the author's closer circle of friends and family. They prepare the diary for a wider readership that, one can infer, the author expects from this point.

54 The late blogger Marcy Westerling used the phrase to describe her life since diagnosis with stage IV ovarian cancer. She credited Christopher Hitchens as having inspired her to use it. Marcy Westerling, "About Marcy Westerling," *Livingly Dying* (blog), n.d., https://livinglydying.wordpress.com/about/. The editors of a special issue on death and dying in contemporary (largely German-language) literature speak of the "Ausdehnung des Sterbeprozesses" (extension of the process of dying) in this context. Anna Katharina Neufeld and Ulrike Vedder, "An der Grenze: Sterben und Tod in der Gegenwartsliteratur; Einleitung," *Zeitschrift für Germanistik* 25, no. 3 (2015): 495.

55 The majority of whom first took notice of Herrndorf as the author of *Tschick* and distinguished winner of the Deutscher Jugendliteraturpreis 2011 (German Children's Literature Award, category YA Fiction).

56 Wolfgang Herrndorf, *Tschick* (Berlin: Rowohlt, 2010); *Sand* (Berlin: Rowohlt, 2011); *Bilder deiner großen Liebe: Ein unvollendeter Roman* (Berlin: Rowohlt, 2014). *Tschick* has since been translated into English and published as *Why We Took the Car*, trans. Tim Mohr (London: Andersen, 2014; New York: Arthur A. Levine, 2014). An English translation of *Sand* came out with Pushkin Press (London: Pushkin Press, 2017).

[57] Couser, *Signifying Bodies*, 2.

[58] See, for example, Philippe Lejeune, "Counting and Managing," in Lejeune, *On Diary*, 51–60.

[59] Compare Sascha Lobo and Holm Friebe's tongue-in-cheek self-ascription as digital bohemians in their popular nonfiction book *Wir nennen es Arbeit: Die digitale Bohème oder Intelligentes Leben jenseits der Festanstellung* (Munich: Heyne, 2006).

[60] *Wir höflichen Paparazzi* was a literary Internet forum where those invited to join portrayed coincidental encounters with celebrities. The site had been moderated by fellow Rowohlt author Tex Rubinowitz. Some texts are still online and retrievable under http://www.hoeflichepaparazzi.de/index.html (accessed November 6, 2017). *Riesenmaschine* (http://riesenmaschine.de/, accessed November 6, 2017) exposes the absurdities of modern life, often through a focus on inventions and trends, analyzing contemporary culture and its products in a humorous, satirical fashion.

[61] Quotation from the blurb. Rainald Goetz, *Abfall für alle: Roman eines Jahres* (Frankfurt am Main: Suhrkamp, 1999). The "novel," as the diary was called when published in book form, forms part of a five-part cycle titled *Heute Morgen: Geschichte der Gegenwart*. For more on German language writers' first big literary online projects from the mid-1990s (driven especially by those authors associated with the Popliteratur movement, such as Goetz), and critics' reactions to them, see Frank Fischer, "Der Autor als Medienjongleur: Die Inszenierung literarischer Modernität im Internet," in *Autorinszenierungen: Autorschaft und literarisches Werk im Kontext der Medien*, ed. Christine Künzel and Jörg Schönert (Würzburg: Königshausen & Neumann, 2007), 271–80.

[62] Klaus Schönberger speaks of online blogs as reaching "Mikroöffentlichkeiten" or "Teilöffentlichkeiten" (micro or partial public spheres) in this context, Jan Schmidt writes of "persönlichen Öffentlichkeiten" (personal public spheres). Klaus Schönberger, "Von der Lesewut zur Schreibwut?," in Gold, *@bsolut? Privat!*, 113; Jan Schmidt, "Die A-List und der Long Tail: Persönliche Öffentlichkeiten in der Blogosphäre," in Gold, *@bsolut? Privat!*, 115–17.

[63] For more on how bloggers tap into the diary's aesthetic, see Cardell, *De@r World*, 95–101.

[64] For more on the appeal of blogging about one's experience of illness, see Anthony McCosker, "Blogging Illness: Recovering in Public," *M/C Journal* 11, no. 6 (2008), http://journal.media-culture.org.au/index.php/mcjournal/article/view/104.

[65] BBC journalist Ivan Noble, who was diagnosed with a brain tumor in 2002, began to write a personal column on *BBC News* online postdiagnosis. After his death, his illness writing was published in book form together with e-mails he had received from readers in response as *Like a Hole in the Head: Living with a Brain Tumour* (London: Hodder & Stoughton, 2005). Noble calls this book his "diary" (18). Tom Lubbock too was a journalist; he wrote in the *Observer* about his life with a glioblastoma. Herrndorf came across Lubbock's writing online; he references it twice in *Arbeit und Struktur* (158–59, 179). Lubbock's words and finally his death affected Herrndorf deeply, as he felt he had much in common with the

professional writer and art critic, not least the type of tumor they both suffered from. Also posthumously, Granta published Lubbock's "memoir," entitled *Until Further Notice, I Am Alive* (London: Granta, 2012), consisting of excerpts from the journal Lubbock had kept since diagnosis, plus a reprint of a substantial article on the illness experience he wrote for the *Observer* in 2010.

66 In reaction to Herrndorf's death, the site notice has been changed several times; the statement quoted here, which was relevant only as long as the blog's author was alive, has since been removed.

67 See, for example, Martin Schulte, "Schreiben für die Unsterblichkeit," *sh:z Schleswig-Holsteinischer Zeitungsverlag*, December 9, 2011, http://www.shz.de/incoming/schreiben-fuer-die-unsterblichkeit-id1878506.html. After Herrndorf's suicide, the media responses took on yet another quality, interpreting his literary production through the lens of his death, falling back on conventional cultural reactions to authors' suicides. For more on these culture patterns, see Marie-Isabel Matthews-Schlinzig, "Der Suizid des Autors: Texte und Reaktionen (am Beispiel von Édouard Levé, André Gorz und Heinrich von Kleist)," *Zeitschrift für Germanistik* 25, no. 3 (2015): 589–602.

68 "Isa" is Herrndorf's working title of the manuscript that, in accordance with Herrndorf's wishes at the end of his life, would later be published (in unfinished form) as *Bilder deiner großen Liebe*.

69 Thomas Mann, *Tagebücher, 1953–1955*, ed. Inge Jens (Frankfurt am Main: Fischer, 1995), 242.

70 For more on Mann's diaries, see T. J. Reed, "Mann as Diarist," in *The Cambridge Companion to Thomas Mann*, ed. Ritchie Robertson (Cambridge: Cambridge University Press, 2001), 227.

71 Lejeune, "Diary as 'Antifiction,'" 208.

72 The term first crops up in the preface as the author describes his younger self as "durch einen sonderbaren Zufall zu Bewusstsein gekommen" (having become conscious through a peculiar circumstance); see discussion of *Dämmerung* above.

73 The film is not mentioned by title, but it can be assumed to be Hanspeter Bäni's 2011 documentary *Tod nach Plan* (A planned death).

74 Lejeune, "Diary as 'Antifiction,'" 204.

75 Sales figures for Anne Frank's diary exceed thirty million copies; the text has been published in at least sixty-five languages. Tine Nowak, "Das meistgelesene Tagebuch der Welt," in Gold, *@bsolut? Privat!*, 144. In 2009, UNESCO added Anne Frank's manuscripts to the World Heritage List for documents, the so-called Memory of the World Register.

76 Lejeune, "Diary as 'Antifiction,'" 209.

77 Ibid. Lejeune isolates this characteristic of the diary as one that is essential to its reception; it accounts for the reader's fascination with it and ontologically distinguishes the diary from fiction.

78 Felicitas von Lovenberg, "Zum Tod Wolfgang Herrndorfs: Dieses Zuviel ist niemals genug," *Frankfurter Allgemeine*, August 27, 2013, http://www.faz.net/

aktuell/feuilleton/buecher/zum-tod-wolfgang-herrndorfs-dieses-zuviel-ist-niemals-genug-12549002.html.

[79] At the risk of simplification, I would draw out two aspects of Herrndorf's diary aesthetic as influenced by romanticism: first, the attempt to conciliate an emphasis on reason with a distinct focus on emotion and individuality, and, second, Herrndorf's aspirations, as highlighted in this section, of cutting across traditional ideas of genre and their boundaries; for the romantics, part of their striving toward an "Universalpoesie" (universal poetry).

[80] The second sentence of Rousseau's *Confessions*, as translated by J. M. Cohen, reads in full: "My purpose is to display to my kind a portrait in every way true to nature, and the man I shall portray will be myself." Jean-Jacques Rousseau, *The Confessions*, trans. J. M. Cohen (London: Penguin, 1953), 17.

[81] Martina Wagner-Egelhaaf, *Autobiographie*, Sammlung Metzler 323 (Stuttgart: Metzler, 2000), 152.

[82] Wagner-Egelhaaf, *Autobiographie*, 153.

[83] Laurie McNeill, "Teaching an Old Genre New Tricks: The Diary on the Internet," *Biography* 26, no. 1 (2003), 45.

[84] Günter Oesterle, "Die Intervalle des Tagebuchs—das Tagebuch als Intervall," in Gold, *@bsolut? Privat!*, 100.

[85] The death note appears on the blog but not in the book as, by the time the book came out, the facts of when, where, and how the author had died were widely known: http://www.wolfgang-herrndorf.de/page/2/ (accessed November 16, 2017).

[86] Herrndorf, *Bilder deiner großen Liebe*, 20.

[87] Corina Caduff, "Selbstporträt, Autobiografie, Autorschaft," in *Autorschaft in den Künsten: Konzepte—Praktiken—Medien*, ed. Corina Caduff and Tan Wälchli, Zürcher Jahrbuch der Künste 4 (Zurich: Zürcher Hochschule der Künste, 2008), 58.

[88] Roland Barthes, *Camera Lucida: Reflections on Photography*, trans. Richard Howard (London: Vintage, 1993; orig.: *La Chambre Claire*, Paris: Gallimard/Seuil, 1980).

[89] Susan Sontag, *On Photography* (New York: Anchor Books, 1990), 15.

[90] Ibid., 5.

[91] Joli Jensen, "Introduction—on Fandom, Celebrity, and Mediation: Posthumous Possibilities," in *Afterlife as Afterimage: Understanding Posthumous Fame*, ed. Steve Jones and Joli Jensen (New York: Peter Lang, 2005), xx.

[92] Wolfgang Höbel, "Warum denn nicht ich?," *Der Spiegel* 6 (2011): 122.

[93] Although there is a point at which suspicions arise that the illness diary may be a "Marketingcoup" (*AS*, 321) of Herrndorf's. The allegations were made by Joachim Lottmann in "Joachim Lottmann vs. Wolfgang Koeppen," *taz.blogs*, April 25, 2012, http://blogs.taz.de/lottmann/2012/04/25/joachim-lottmann-vs-wolfgang-koeppen/.

[94] Felman and Laub, *Testimony*, 72–73.

[95] Ibid., 72.

[96] Ibid.

[97] Schwarz, "Die 'Krebspersönlichkeit.'"

[98] Felman and Laub, *Testimony*, 72.

[99] Ibid.

[100] Herrndorf's dissatisfaction with any kind of mythologizing of his figure during his lifetime comes through in statements such as the one recorded in the diary on September 12, 2012, in which (presumably upon reading another such article about his achievements in the light of cancer) he retorts, provocatively, "Ich nenn euch [Journalisten] doch auch nicht dauernd behindert, nur weil ihr es seid" (*AS*, 355; I for my part don't constantly call you [journalists] retarded just because you are).

[101] See quotation at the beginning of this book's introduction.

Conclusion

[1] Eyre, "Permission to Speak," 214.

[2] Ibid., 215.

[3] She regards the two autobiographical accounts she examines—Luise Habel's *Herrgott, schaff die Treppen ab!* (Good Lord, do abolish stairways!, 1978) and Christa Reinig's *Die himmlische und die irdische Geometrie* (The heavenly and the earthly geometry, 1975)—as "flawed" (122), the former for foregrounding the disabled experience to the extent that it takes on undesirable qualities of the medical case study (113), the latter for distracting from its author's disabled identity to the extent that this identity has been largely overlooked (110–22).

[4] Wendell, "Unhealthy Disabled," 162.

[5] David Wagner, *Leben* (Reinbek: Rowohlt, 2013).

[6] Richard Wagner, *Herr Parkinson* (Munich: Albrecht Knaus, 2015).

[7] For more, see Garland-Thomson, *Staring*, or my chapter 2.

[8] Christoph Schlingensief, *Ich weiß, ich war's*, with text inserts read by Martin Wuttke (Tacheles / Roof Music, 2012), CD 4 of 4, track 13, minutes 11.50–12.00.

[9] Harro Segeberg, "Menschsein heißt, medial sein wollen: Autorinszenierungen im Medienzeitalter," in *Autorinszenierungen: Autorschaft und literarisches Werk im Kontext der Medien*, ed. Christine Künzel and Jörg Schönert (Würzburg: Königshausen & Neumann, 2007), 245.

[10] Thus reports journalist Martin Scholz in his obituary for Mankell, recalling a conversation with the best-selling author from 2014: Martin Scholz, "Ich hatte ein fantastisches Leben," *Welt.de*, October 5, 2015, https://www.welt.de/kultur/literarischewelt/article147239728/Ich-hatte-ein-fantastisches-Leben.html; Henning Mankell, *Kvicksand* (Stockholm: Leopard, 2014).

[11] Wagner entitles the fourth and final part to his book "Im schwarzen Quadrat." Richard Wagner, *Herr Parkinson*, 131.

[12] Ibid., 36.

[13] Ibid., 144.

[14] Thus argues the influential edited volume by Macho and Marek, *Die neue Sichtbarkeit des Todes* (Munich: Wilhelm Fink, 2007).

[15] A notable exception (also for its contemporary rather than historic frame of reference) is the recent issue of the *Zeitschrift für Germanistik* entitled "An der Grenze: Sterben und Tod in der Gegenwartsliteratur." Anna Katharina Neufeld and Ulrike Vedder, eds., "An der Grenze: Sterben und Tod in der Gegenwartsliteratur," special issue, *Zeitschrift für Germanistik* 25, no. 3 (2015).

[16] Quoted in the introduction, section "Academic Nervousness in the Face of the Real?"

[17] G. Thomas Couser, ed., "Body Language: Illness, Disability, and Life Writing," special issue, *Life Writing* 13, no. 1 (2016).

[18] Sabine Kalff and Ulrike Vedder, eds., "Tagebuch und Diaristik seit 1900," special issue, *Zeitschrift für Germanistik* 26, no. 2 (2016). As pointed out in the introduction ("Overview of the Chapters"), more and more research is being published on *Arbeit und Struktur* in particular.

[19] I pointed out Miriam Engelberg's *Cancer Made Me a Shallower Person* and Marisa Acocella Marchetto's *Cancer Vixen* in chapter 3, section "Traditions in Breast Cancer Writing and Their Diversification."

[20] Jón S. Jónsson, Andreas C. Knigge, and Annie Goetzinger, *Die verlorene Zukunft* (Hamburg: Carlsen Comics, 1992).

[21] M. K. Czerwiec et al., *Graphic Medicine Manifesto* (University Park: Penn State University Press, 2015). Comics artists Borretsch, Reto Gloor, and Daniela Schreiter, to name but a few, have all published what could be described as German-language graphic medicine.

[22] Einat Avrahami's term; for more, see section "Illness and the Attraction of the Personal" in the introduction.

Bibliography

Albrecht, Gary L., Katherine D. Seelman, and Michael Bury, eds. *Handbook of Disability Studies*. London: Sage, 2001.
Alloa, Emmanuel, et al., eds. *Leiblichkeit: Geschichte und Aktualität eines Konzepts*. UTB 3633. Tübingen: Mohr Siebeck, 2012.
American Psychiatric Association. *Diagnostic and Statistical Manual of Mental Disorders*. 3rd ed. Washington, DC: APA, 1980.
Anders, Petra-Andelka. *Behinderung und psychische Krankheit im zeitgenössischen deutschen Spielfilm*. KONNEX Studien im Schnittbereich von Literatur, Kultur und Natur 9. Würzburg: Königshausen & Neumann, 2014.
Anderson, Linda R. *Autobiography*. 2nd ed. London: Routledge, 2011.
Angele, Michael. "Wer hat geil Krebs?" *Der Freitag*, September 3, 2009. http://www.freitag.de/autoren/michael-angele/wer-hat-geil-krebs.
Anz, Thomas. *Gesund oder krank? Medizin, Moral und Ästhetik in der deutschen Gegenwartsliteratur*. Stuttgart: Metzler, 1989.
Arend, Ingo. "Eine undurchsichtige Größe." *Der Freitag*, May 9, 2008. www.freitag.de/autoren/der-freitag/eine-undurchsichtige-grosse.
Avrahami, Einat. *The Invading Body: Reading Illness Autobiographies*. Charlottesville: University of Virginia Press, 2007.
Baer, Hester. "Sex, Death, and Motherhood in the Eurozone: Contemporary Women's Writing in German." *World Literature Today* 86, no. 3 (2012): 59–65.
Bakhtin, Mikhail. *Rabelais and His World*. Translated by Hélène Iswolsky. Bloomington: Indiana University Press, 1984.
Balint, Lilla. "Sickness unto Death in the Age of 24/7: Wolfgang Herrndorf's *Arbeit und Struktur*." *Studies in 20th & 21st Century Literature* 40, no. 2 (2016): 1–19.
Bartels, Gerrit. "Überlebensgroß." *Der Tagesspiegel*, October 15, 2009.
Barthes, Roland. *Camera Lucida: Reflections on Photography*. Translated by Richard Howard. London: Vintage Books, 1993. Originally published as *La Chambre Claire* in Paris by Gallimard/Seuil, 1980.
Berger, James. "Trauma without Disability, Disability without Trauma: A Disciplinary Divide." *JAC* 24, no. 3 (2004): 563–82.
Berger, John. *Ways of Seeing*. London: BBC / Penguin Books, n.d. [c. 1990].
Berkéwicz, Ulla. *Überlebnis*. Frankfurt am Main: Suhrkamp, 2008.
Betten, Anne. "Entwicklungen und Formen der deutschen Literatursprache nach 1945." In *Sprachgeschichte: Ein Handbuch zur Geschichte der deutschen Sprache und ihrer Erforschung*, edited by Werner Besch et al., 2nd ed., 4:3117–59. Berlin: De Gruyter, 2004.

Beutler, Maja. *Fuss fassen*. Bern: Zytglogge, 1980.
Biesenbach, Klaus, et al., eds. *Christoph Schlingensief*. Cologne: Walther König, 2014.
Binswanger, Christa, and Kathy Davis. "Sexy Stories and Postfeminist Empowerment: From *Häutungen* to *Wetlands*." *Feminist Theory* 13, no. 3 (2012): 245–63.
Blondeau, Brenda L., and Eva C. Karpinski. Editorial. *Canadian Woman Studies / Les Cahiers de la Femme* 28, nos. 2/3 (2010): 3, 5.
Böcking-Politis, Cordula, and Carrie Smith-Prei. Introduction to *Sexual-Textual Border-Crossings: Lesbian Identity in German-Language Literature, Film, and Culture*, edited by Böcking-Politis and Smith-Prei, 7–10. Germanistik in Ireland 5. Konstanz: Hartung-Gorre, 2010.
Boerner, Peter. *Tagebuch*. Stuttgart: Metzler, 1969.
Bolt, David, ed. *Changing Social Attitudes toward Disability: Perspectives from Historical, Cultural, and Educational Studies*. London: Routledge, 2014.
———. "Epilogue: Attitudes and Action." In Bolt, *Changing Social Attitudes toward Disability*, 172–75.
———. Introduction to Bolt, *Changing Social Attitudes toward Disability*, 1–11.
———. "Literary Disability Studies: The Long Awaited Response." Presented at the Inaugural Conference of the Cultural Disability Studies Research Network. Liverpool John Moores University, May 26, 2007. http://disability-studies.leeds.ac.uk/files/library/bolt-Long-Awaited-Response.pdf.
Brown, Laura S. "Not Outside the Range: One Feminist Perspective on Psychic Trauma." In Caruth, *Trauma*, 100–112.
Buchanan, Ian. "Introduction to Part III: Other People; Ethnography and Social Practice." In *The Certeau Reader*, edited by Graham Ward, 97–100. Oxford: Blackwell, 2000.
Büchner, Georg. *Lenz* and *Der Hessische Landbote*. Stuttgart: Philipp Reclam Jun., 1988.
———. *Woyzeck* and *Leonce und Lena*. Stuttgart: Philipp Reclam Jun., 2001.
Burk, Maximilian. "'dem Leben wie einem Roman zu Leibe rücken': Wolfgang Herrndorf's Blog *Arbeit und Struktur*." In *Wolfgang Herrndorf*, edited by Annina Klappert, 85–99. Weimar: VDG, 2015.
Buß, Christian. "Sexautorin Charlotte Roche: 'Meine Therapeutin hat mir das Leben gerettet.'" *Spiegel Online*, August 7, 2011. http://www.spiegel.de/kultur/literatur/sexautorin-charlotte-roche-meine-therapeutinhat-mir-das-leben-gerettet-a-778812.html.
Butler, Judith, *Gender Trouble: Feminism and the Subversion of Identity*. New York: Taylor & Francis e-Library, 2002. Originally published in New York by Routledge, 1990.
———. "Wittig's Material Practice: Universalizing a Minority Point of View." *GLQ: A Journal of Lesbian and Gay Studies* 13, no. 4 (2007): 519–33.

Butzer, Günter. "Sich selbst schreiben: Das Tagebuch als Weblog avant la lettre." In Gold, *@bsolut? Privat!*, 94–96.

Byrnes, Deirdre. "Writing on the Threshold: Memory, Language and Identity in Kathrin Schmidt's *Du stirbst nicht*." In *Transitions: Emerging Women Writers in German-Language Literature*, edited by Valerie Heffernan and Gillian Pye, 169–85. German Monitor 76. Amsterdam: Rodopi, 2013.

Caduff, Corina. "Selbstporträt, Autobiografie, Autorschaft." In *Autorschaft in den Künsten: Konzepte—Praktiken—Medien*, edited by Corina Caduff and Tan Wälchli, 54–67. Zürcher Jahrbuch der Künste 4. Zurich: Zürcher Hochschule der Künste, 2008.

———. *Szenen des Todes*. Basel: Lenos, 2013.

Cardell, Kylie. *De@r World: Contemporary Uses of the Diary*. Madison: University of Wisconsin Press, 2014.

Carel, Havi, and Rachel Cooper. Introduction to *Health, Illness and Disease: Philosophical Essays*, edited by Havi Carel and Rachel Cooper, 1–20. Durham: Acumen, 2012.

Carter, Kathryn. "Death and the Diary, or Tragedies in the Archive." *Journal of Canadian Studies / Revue d'études canadiennes* 40, no. 2 (2006): 42–59.

Carter, Thatcher. "Body Count: Autobiographies by Women Living with Breast Cancer." *Journal of Popular Culture* 36, no. 4 (2003): 653–68.

Caruth, Cathy. "Introduction: Recapturing the Past." In Caruth, *Trauma*, 151–57.

———. "Introduction: Trauma and Experience." In Caruth, *Trauma*, 3–12.

———. "Introduction: The Wound and the Voice." In *Unclaimed Experience: Trauma, Narrative, and History*, edited by Cathy Caruth, 1–9. Baltimore: Johns Hopkins University Press, 1996.

———, ed. *Trauma: Explorations in Memory*. Baltimore: Johns Hopkins University Press, 1995.

———. "Unclaimed Experience: Trauma, and the Possibility of History." *Yale French Studies* 79 (1991): 181–92.

Cattell, Allison G. "Disability Drama: Semiotic Bodies and Diegetic Subjectivities in Post-WWI German Expressionist Drama." PhD Diss., University of Waterloo, 2014. https://uwspace.uwaterloo.ca/bitstream/handle/10012/8417/Cattell_Allison.pdf?sequence=1.

Clow, Barbara. "Who's Afraid of Susan Sontag? or, The Myths and Metaphors of Cancer Reconsidered." *Social History of Medicine* 14, no. 2 (2001): 293–312.

Cook, Kay. "Illness and Life Writing." In Jolly, *Encyclopedia of Life Writing*, 1:456–58.

Cottam, Rachel. "Diaries and Journals: General Survey." In Jolly, *Encyclopedia of Life Writing*, 1:267–69.

Couser, G. Thomas, ed. "Body Language: Illness, Disability, and Life Writing." Special issue, *Life Writing* 13, no. 1 (2016).

———. "Disability, Life Narrative, and Representation." In Davis, *Disability Studies Reader*, 456–59.

———. "Genre Matters: Form, Force, and Filiation." *Life Writing* 2, no. 2 (2005): 139–56.

———. *Recovering Bodies: Illness, Disability, and Life Writing*. Madison: University of Wisconsin Press, 1997.

———. *Signifying Bodies: Disability in Contemporary Life Writing*. Ann Arbor: University of Michigan Press, 2009.

———. *Vulnerable Subjects: Ethics and Life Writing*. Ithaca, NY: Cornell University Press, 2004.

Czerwiec, M. K., et al. *Graphic Medicine Manifesto*. University Park: Penn State University Press, 2015.

Dalziell, Rosamund. "Shame and Life Writing." In Jolly, *Encyclopedia of Life Writing*, 2:807–9.

Darrieussecq, Marie. "L'autofiction, un genre pas sérieux." *Poétique* 27 (1996): 367–80.

Davis, Lennard J., ed. *The Disability Studies Reader*. 4th ed. New York: Routledge, 2013.

———. *Enforcing Normalcy: Disability, Deafness, and the Body*. London: Verso, 1995.

Dawidowicz, Andreas. *Die metaphorische Krankheit als Gesellschaftskritik in den Werken von Franz Kafka, Friedrich Dürrenmatt und Thomas Bernhard*. Germanistik 42. Berlin: LIT, 2013.

De Certeau, Michel. *The Practice of Everyday Life*. Translated by Steven Rendall. Berkeley: University of California Press, 1984. Originally published as *L'invention du quotidien: 1. arts de faire* in Paris by Union générale d'éditions, 1980.

De Man, Paul. "Autobiography as De-facement." *MLN* 94, no. 5 (1979): 919–30.

Dederich, Markus. *Körper, Kultur und Behinderung: Eine Einführung in die Disability Studies*. Disability Studies: Körper—Macht—Differenz 2. Bielefeld: Transcript, 2007.

Degler, Frank, and Christian Kohlroß, eds. *Epochen/Krankheiten: Konstellationen von Literatur und Pathologie*. Das Wissen der Literatur 1. St. Ingbert: Röhrig, 2006.

DeShazer, Mary K. *Fractured Borders: Reading Women's Cancer Literature*. Ann Arbor: University of Michigan Press, 2005.

———. *Mammographies: The Cultural Discourses of Breast Cancer Narratives*. Ann Arbor: University of Michigan Press, 2013.

Diez, Georg. *Der Tod meiner Mutter*. Cologne: Kiepenheuer & Witsch, 2009.

———. "Ich habe den Tod gespürt, er saß in mir: Ich habe gekämpft." *Süddeutsche Zeitung Magazin* 38 (2008). http://sz-magazin.sueddeutsche.de/texte/anzeigen/26434/1/1.

Doubrovsky, Serge. *Fils: Roman*. Paris: Galilée, 1977.

———. "Textes en main." In *Autofictions & Cie*, edited by Serge Doubrovsky, Jacques Lecarme and Philippe Lejeune, 207–17. RITM 6. Nanterre: Université Paris X-Nanterre, 1993.

Dubiel, Helmut. *Tief im Hirn*. Munich: Kunstmann, 2006.

Dusini, Arno. *Tagebuch: Möglichkeiten einer Gattung.* Munich: Wilhelm Fink, 2005.
Eakin, Paul John. Foreword to Lejeune, *On Autobiography*, vii–xxviii.
——. *How Our Lives Become Stories: Making Selves.* Ithaca, NY: Cornell University Press, 1999.
Egan, Susanna. *Burdens of Proof: Faith, Doubt and Identity in Autobiography.* Waterloo, ON: Wilfrid Laurier, 2011.
——. "The Life and Times of Autothanatography." Workshop discussion paper for the Pain and Suffering Interdisciplinary Research Network, 2001. Accessed October 9, 2014. http://www.english.ubc.ca/PROJECTS/PAIN/DEGAN.HTM (site discontinued).
——. *Mirror Talk: Genres of Crisis in Contemporary Autobiography.* Chapel Hill: University of North Carolina Press, 1999.
Ehlebracht, Steffi. *Gelingendes Scheitern: Epilepsie als Metapher in der deutschsprachigen Literatur des 20. Jahrhunderts.* Würzburg: Königshausen & Neumann, 2008.
Engelberg, Miriam. *Cancer Made Me a Shallower Person: A Memoir in Comics.* New York: Harper, 2006.
Eyre, Pauline. "From Impairment to Empowerment: A Re-assessment of Libuše Moníková's Representation of Disability in *Pavane für eine verstorbene Infantin*." In Joshua and Schillmeier, *Disability in German Literature, Film, and Theatre*, 197–212.
——. "Impaired or Empowered? Mapping Disability onto European Literature." In Bolt, *Changing Social Attitudes toward Disability*, 99–108.
——. "Permission to Speak: Representations of Disability in German Women's Literature of the 1970s and 1980s." PhD diss., University of Manchester, 2009.
Fanon, Frantz. *Black Skin, White Masks.* Translated by Charles Lam Markmann. New York: Grove Press, 1967.
Felluga, Dino. "Modules on Lacan: On Psychosexual Development." In *Introductory Guide to Critical Theory.* Last modified January 31, 2011. http://www.purdue.edu/guidetotheory/psychoanalysis/lacandevelop.html.
Felman, Shoshana, and Dori Laub. *Testimony: Crises of Witnessing in Literature, Psychoanalysis, and History.* New York: Routledge, 1992.
Fiddler, Allyson. "Subjectivity and Women's Writing of the 1970s and Early 1980s." In *The Cambridge Companion to the Modern German Novel*, edited by Graham Bartram, 249–65. Cambridge: Cambridge University Press, 2004.
Fietz, Kathleen, Kristina Pezzei, and Detlev Schilke. "Montagsinterview Kathrin Schmidt: Ich wusste schnell wieder, wer ich bin." *taz*, January 4, 2010. http://www.taz.de/!46202/.
Fischer, Frank. "Der Autor als Medienjongleur: Die Inszenierung literarischer Modernität im Internet." In *Autorinszenierungen: Autorschaft und literarisches Werk im Kontext der Medien*, edited by Christine Künzel and Jörg Schönert, 271–80. Würzburg: Königshausen & Neumann, 2007.

Fludernik, Monika. *Towards a "Natural" Narratology*. London: Routledge, 1996.
Foucault, Michel. *Discipline and Punish: The Birth of the Prison*. Translated by Alan Sheridan. 2nd ed. New York: Vintage Books, 1995.
Frank, Anne. *Das Tagebuch der Anne Frank, 12. Juni 1942–1. August 1944*. Translated by Anneliese Schütz. 33rd ed. Frankfurt am Main: Fischer Bücherei, 1971.
Frank, Arthur W. "Illness and Autobiographical Work: Dialogue as Narrative Destabilization." *Qualitative Sociology* 23, no. 1 (2000): 135–56.
———. *The Wounded Storyteller: Body, Illness, and Ethics*. 2nd ed. Chicago: University of Chicago Press, 2013.
Garland-Thomson, Rosemarie. "Beholding." In Davis, *Disability Studies Reader*, 3rd ed., 199–208. New York: Routledge, 2010.
———. *Extraordinary Bodies: Figuring Physical Disability in American Culture and Literature*. New York: Columbia University Press, 1997.
———. "Integrating Disability, Transforming Feminist Theory." *NWSA* 14, no. 3 (2002): 1–32.
———. *Staring: How We Look*. Oxford: Oxford University Press, 2009.
Gasser, Peter. "Autobiographie und Autofiktion: Einige begriffskritische Bemerkungen." In *"... all diese fingierten, notierten, in meinem Kopf ungefähr wieder zusammengesetzten Ichs": Autobiographie und Autofiktion*, edited by Elio Pellin and Ulrich Weber, 13–28. Göttingen: Wallstein, 2012.
Geiger, Arno. *Der alte König in seinem Exil*. Munich: Carl Hanser, 2011.
Georgis, Dina. "Bearing Cancer in Graphic Memoir." *Canadian Woman Studies / Les Cahiers de la Femme* 28, nos. 2/3 (2010): 105–9.
Gernhardt, Robert. *Die K-Gedichte*. Frankfurt am Main: Fischer, 2004.
———. *Später Spagat*. Frankfurt am Main: Fischer, 2006.
Gilles, Catherina. *Kunst und Nichtkunst: Das Theater von Christoph Schlingensief*. Würzburg: Königshausen & Neumann, 2009.
Gilman, Sander L. *Franz Kafka: The Jewish Patient*. New York: Routledge, 1995.
———. Review of *Gesund oder krank? Medizin, Moral und Ästhetik in der deutschen Gegenwartsliteratur*, by Thomas Anz. *German Quarterly* 64, no. 4 (1991): 603–5.
Goetz, Rainald. *Abfall für alle: Roman eines Jahres*. Frankfurt am Main: Suhrkamp, 1999.
Gold, Helmut, ed. *@bsolut? Privat! Vom Tagebuch zum Weblog*. Kataloge der Museumsstiftung Post und Telekommunikation 26. Heidelberg: Edition Braus, 2008.
———. "@bsolut privat!? Vom Tagebuch zum Weblog." In Gold, *@bsolut? Privat!*, 6–7.
Görsdorf, Alexander. *Taube Nuss: Nichtgehörtes aus dem Leben eines Schwerhörigen*. Reinbek: Rowohlt, 2013.
Grass, Günter. *Die Blechtrommel*. Darmstadt: Luchterhand, 1959.
Gratton, Johnnie. "Autofiction." In Jolly, *Encyclopedia of Life Writing*, 1:86–87.

Graves, Peter J. "Karen Duve, Kathrin Schmidt, Judith Hermann: 'Ein literarisches Fräuleinwunder'?" *German Life and Letters* 55, no. 2 (2002): 197–207.
Grealy, Lucy. *Autobiography of a Face*. Boston: Houghton Mifflin, 1994.
Greiner, Ulrich. "Man sollte diskret sterben." *Zeit Online*. January 31, 2014. http://www.zeit.de/kultur/literatur/2014-01/mankell-krebsdiagnose-literatur-krankheit.
Grell, Isabelle. "Pourquoi Serge Doubrovsky n'a pu eviter le terme d'autofiction." In *Genèse et autofiction*, edited by Jean-Louis Jeannelle and Catherine Viollet, 39–51. Louvain-la-Neuve: Academia-Bruylant, 2007.
Gronemann, Claudia. *Postmoderne/postkoloniale Konzepte der Autobiographie in der französischen und maghrebinischen Literatur: Autofiction—Nouvelle Autobiographie—Double Autobiographie—Aventure du texte*. Hildesheim: Georg Olms, 2002.
Grosz, Elizabeth. *Sexual Subversions: Three French Feminists*. Crows Nest: Allen & Unwin, 1989.
Groß, Johannes. *Kafkas Krankheiten*. Marburg: LiteraturWissenschaft.de, 2012.
Großklaus, Götz. "Versuch einer Dekolonisierung des Körpers. Notiz zu *Häutungen* von Verena Stefan—1986—." In *Vierzig Jahre Literaturwissenschaft, 1969–2009: Zur Geschichte der kultur- und medienwissenschaftlichen Öffnung*, edited by Götz Großklaus, 95–103. Frankfurt am Main: Peter Lang, 2011.
Habel, Luise. *Herrgott, schaff die Treppen ab! Erfahrungen einer Behinderten*. Stuttgart: Kreuz, 1978.
Hall, Alice. *Literature and Disability*. London: Routledge, 2016.
Haller, Beth, and Corinne Kirchner, eds. "Education." Special issue, *Disability Studies Quarterly* 26, no. 2 (2006).
Hamilton, Elizabeth C. "From Social Welfare to Civil Rights: The Representation of Disability in Twentieth-Century German Literature." In *The Body and Physical Difference: Discourses of Disability*, edited by David T. Mitchell and Sharon L. Snyder, 223–39. Ann Arbor: University of Michigan Press, 1997.
Heidböhmer, Carsten. "Trauerspiel statt Sexskandal." *Stern.de*, August 10, 2011. http://www.stern.de/kultur/buecher/-schossgebete----zweiter-roman-von-charlotte-roche-trauerspiel-statt-sexskandal-3779768.html.
Heinze, Carsten. "Zum Stand und den Perspektiven der Autobiographie in der Soziologie: Sozialkommunikative Konzepte zur Beschreibung einer literarischen Gattung." *Bios—Zeitschrift für Biographieforschung, Oral History und Lebensverlaufsanalysen* 23, no. 2 (2010): 201–31.
Heinze, Carsten, and Alfred Hornung. *Medialisierungsformen des (Auto-) Biografischen*. Konstanz: UVK, 2013.
Henke, Suzette A. *Shattered Subjects: Trauma and Testimony in Women's Life Writing*. London: Macmillan, 1998.

Herman, Judith Lewis. *Trauma and Recovery: From Domestic Abuse to Political Terror*. 2nd ed. London: Pandora, 2001.
Herrndorf, Wolfgang. *Arbeit und Struktur*. Berlin: Rowohlt, 2013.
———. *Bilder deiner großen Liebe: Ein unvollendeter Roman*. Berlin: Rowohlt, 2014.
———. *Sand*. Berlin: Rowohlt, 2011. English translation published in London by Pushkin Press, 2017.
———. *Tschick*. Berlin: Rowohlt, 2010.
———. *Why We Took the Car*. Translated by Tim Mohr. London: Andersen, 2014; New York: Arthur A. Levine, 2014.
Hillgruber, Katrin. "Erinnerungsroman: Aufschlussreiche Sprachbefreiung." *Spiegel Online*, April 20, 2009. http://www.spiegel.de/kultur/literatur/erinnerungsroman-aufschlussreiche-sprachbefreiung-a-619620.html.
Hirsch, Anja. "Steh auf und erinnere dich." *Frankfurter Allgemeine*, April 11, 2009. http://www.faz.net/aktuell/feuilleton/buecher/rezensionen/belletristik/kathrin-schmidts-roman-du-stirbst-nicht-steh-auf-und-erinnere-dich-1792428.html.
Höbel, Wolfgang. "Warum denn nicht ich?" *Der Spiegel* 6 (2011): 122–25.
Höller, Hans. "Brief zu Franz K. Stanzels Akademie-Vortrag vom 19. Januar 2007: 'Autobiographie. Wo ein Ich erzählt, ist immer Fiktion.'" *Sprachkunst* 37, no. 2 (2006): 341–42.
Holm, Christiane. "Montag Ich. Dienstag Ich. Mittwoch Ich. Versuch einer Phänomenologie des Diaristischen." In Gold, *@bsolut? Privat!*, 10–50.
Hughes, Bill. "Fear, Pity and Disgust: Emotions and the Non-disabled Imaginary." In Thomas, Watson, and Roulstone, *Routledge Handbook of Disability Studies*, 67–77.
Hughes, Bill, and Kevin Paterson. "The Social Model of Disability and the Disappearing Body: Towards a Sociology of Impairment." *Disability & Society* 12, no. 3 (1997): 325–40.
Hunsaker Hawkins, Anne. *Reconstructing Illness: Studies in Pathography*. 2nd ed. West Lafayette, IN: Purdue University Press, 1999.
———. "Writing about Illness: Therapy? Or Testimony?" In *Unfitting Stories: Narrative Approaches to Disease, Disability, and Trauma*, edited by Valerie Raoul et al., 113–27. Waterloo, ON: Wilfrid Laurier University Press, 2007.
Janke, Pia, and Teresa Kovacs, eds. *Der Gesamtkünstler Christoph Schlingensief*. Diskurse—Kontexte—Impulse 8. Vienna: Praesens, 2011.
Jens, Tilman. *Demenz: Abschied von meinem Vater*. Gütersloh: Gütersloher Verlagshaus, 2009.
———. *Vatermord: Wider einen Generalverdacht*. Gütersloh: Gütersloher Verlagshaus, 2010.
Jensen, Joli. "Introduction—on Fandom, Celebrity, and Mediation: Posthumous Possibilities." In *Afterlife as Afterimage: Understanding Posthumous Fame*, edited by Steve Jones and Joli Jensen, xv–xxiii. New York: Peter Lang, 2005.

Jolly, Margaretta, ed. *Encyclopedia of Life Writing: Autobiographical and Biographical Forms.* Vol. 1, A–K. London: Fitzroy Dearborn, 2001.

———. *Encyclopedia of Life Writing: Autobiographical and Biographical Forms.* Vol. 2, L–Z. London: Fitzroy Dearborn, 2001.

Jónsson, Jón S., Andreas C. Knigge, and Annie Goetzinger. *Die verlorene Zukunft.* Hamburg: Carlsen Comics, 1992.

Jordan, Shirley. "Autofiction in the Feminine." *French Studies* 67, no. 1 (2013): 76–84.

Joshua, Eleoma, and Michael Schillmeier, eds. *Disability in German Literature, Film, and Theatre.* Edinburgh German Yearbook 4. Rochester, NY: Camden House, 2010.

Kalff, Sabine, and Ulrike Vedder, eds. "Tagebuch und Diaristik seit 1900." Special issue, *Zeitschrift für Germanistik* 26, no. 2 (2016).

Kämmerlings, Richard. "Krebsliteratur: Der Schleier über den letzten Dingen." *Frankfurter Allgemeine,* August 14, 2009. http://www.faz.net/aktuell/feuilleton/buecher/krebsliteratur-der-schleier-ueber-den-letzten-dingen-1841182.html.

Karpenstein-Eßbach, Christa. "Krebs—Literatur—Wissen: Von der Krebspersönlichkeit zur totalen Kommunikation." In Degler and Kohlroß, *Epochen/Krankheiten,* 233–64.

Kauffman, Jeffrey. "On the Primacy of Pain." In *The Shame of Death, Grief, and Trauma,* edited by Jeffrey Kauffman, 3–24. London: Routledge, 2010.

Kaysen, Susanna. *Girl, Interrupted.* New York: Vintage Books, 1993.

Kekes, John. "Disgust and Moral Taboos." *Philosophy* 67, no. 262 (1992): 431–46.

Kelly, Daniel. *Yuck! The Nature and Moral Significance of Disgust.* Cambridge, MA: MIT Press, 2011.

Kleinman, Arthur. *The Illness Narratives: Suffering, Healing and the Human Condition.* New York: Basic Books, 1988.

Klocke, Sonja E. "'Committed from Head to Toe?' Cancer, Immigration, and Kinship in Verena Stefan's *Fremdschläfer.*" *Women in German Yearbook: Feminist Studies in German Literature & Culture* 26 (2010): 117–35.

———. "Die frohe Botschaft der Kathrin Schmidt? Transsexuality, Racism, and Feminist Historiography in *Die Gunnar-Lennefsen-Expedition.*" In *Sexual-Textual Border-Crossings: Lesbian Identity in German-Language Literature, Film, and Culture,* edited by Cordula Böcking-Politis and Carrie Smith-Prei, 143–58. Germanistik in Ireland 5. Konstanz: Hartung-Gorre, 2010.

———. "Kathrin Schmidt, *Du stirbst nicht*: A Woman's Quest for Agency." In *Emerging German-Language Novelists of the Twenty-First Century,* edited by Lyn Marven and Stuart Taberner, 228–42. Rochester, NY: Camden House, 2011.

Klopp, Tina. "Todgeweihte leben länger: Über die Interpretation von Künstlerbiografien." *Deutschlandfunk,* May 31, 2015. http://

www.deutschlandfunk.de/kunst-todgeweihte-leben-laenger.1184. de.html?dram:article_id=317368.

Klüger, Ruth. "Einwandern, auswandern, wandern." *Die Welt*, October 6, 2007. http://www.welt.de/welt_print/article1239740/Einwandern-auswandern-wandern.html.

Knapp, Lore. "Christoph Schlingensiefs Blog: Multimediale Autofiktion im Künstlerblog." In *Narrative Genres im Internet: Theoretische Bezugsrahmen, Mediengattungstypologie und Funktionen*, edited by Ansgar Nünning and Jan Rupp, 117–32. Trier: Wissenschaftlicher Verlag, 2012.

Knef, Hildegard. *Das Urteil oder der Gegenmensch*. Vienna: Fritz Molden, 1975.

Kohler Riessman, Catherine. "Women and Medicalization: A New Perspective." In *The Politics of Women's Bodies: Sexuality, Appearance, and Behavior*, edited by Rose Weitz, 46–63. New York: Oxford University Press, 2003.

Konrad, Anita. "Minderheiten—Literatur?" *Stimme von und für Minderheiten* 55 (2005). http://minderheiten.at/stat/stimme/stimme55c.htm.

Korsmeyer, Carolyn. *Savoring Disgust: The Foul and the Fair in Aesthetics*. New York: Oxford University Press, 2011.

Köster, Gaby, and Till Hoheneder. *Ein Schnupfen hätte auch gereicht: Meine zweite Chance*. Frankfurt am Main: Scherz, 2011.

Köster, Gaby, and Thomas Köller. *Die Chefin*. Munich: Pendo, 2015.

Kotin Mortimer, Armine. "Autofiction as Allofiction: Doubrovsky's *L'Après-vivre*." *L'Esprit Créateur* 49, no. 3 (2009): 2–35.

Kotte, Andreas. "Der Performer als Objekt seiner selbst. Das Prinzip Schlingensief." In *Theater und Subjektkonstitution: Theatrale Praktiken zwischen Affirmation und Subversion*, edited by Michael Bachmann et al., 241–52. Theater 33. Bielefeld: Transcript, 2012.

Krause, Kathrin. "Schmidt, Kathrin." In *Munzinger Online / KLG—Kritisches Lexikon zur deutschsprachigen Gegenwartsliteratur*, last modified March 1, 2017. http://www.munzinger.de/document/16000000689.

Krekeler, Elmar. "Bester Roman des Jahres: *Du stirbst nicht*." *Die Welt*, October 14, 2009. www.welt.de/welt_print/kultur/article4840309/Bester-Roman-des-Jahres-Du-stirbst-nicht.html.

———. "Wie ich die Sprache wiederfand." *Die Welt*, October 14, 2009. http://www.welt.de/welt_print/kultur/article4840308/Wie-ich-die-Sprache-wiederfand.html.

Kreknin, Innokentij. *Poetiken des Selbst: Identität, Autorschaft und Autofiktion am Beispiel von Rainald Goetz, Joachim Lottmann und Alban Nikolai Herbst*. Studien zur deutschen Literatur 206. Berlin: De Gruyter, 2014.

Kristeva, Julia. *Powers of Horror: An Essay on Abjection*. Translated by Leon S. Roudiez. New York: Columbia University Press, 1982.

Lacan, Jacques. "The Mirror Stage as Formative of the Function of the I." In *Écrits: A Selection*, translated by Alan Sheridan, 1–7. London: Tavistock, 1977. Originally published in Paris by Seuil, 1966.

Leader, Darian, and Judy Groves. *Introducing Lacan*. Cambridge: Icon Books UK, 1995.
Leal, Joanne. "The Politics of 'Innerlichkeit': Karin Struck's *Klassenliebe* and Verena Stefan's *Häutungen*." *German Life and Letters* 50, no. 4 (1997): 508–28.
Lee, Hermione. Introduction to *On Being Ill*, by Virginia Woolf, xi–xxxii. Ashfield, MA: Paris Press, 2002.
Leinemann, Jürgen. *Das Leben ist der Ernstfall*. Hamburg: Hoffmann und Campe, 2009.
Lejeune, Philippe. "The Autobiographical Pact." In Lejeune, *On Autobiography*, 3–30.
———. "The Autobiographical Pact (bis)." In Lejeune, *On Autobiography*, 119–37.
———. "Autofictions & Cie: Pièce en cinq actes." In *Autofictions & Cie*, edited by Serge Doubrovsky, Jacques Lecarme, and Philippe Lejeune, 5–15. RITM 6. Nanterre: Université Paris X-Nanterre, 1993.
———. "The Continuous and Discontinuous." In Lejeune, *On Diary*, 175–86.
———. "Counting and Managing." In Lejeune, *On Diary*, 51–60.
———. "Diaries on the Internet: A Year of Reading." In Lejeune, *On Diary*, 299–316.
———. "The Diary as 'Antifiction.'" In Lejeune, *On Diary*, 201–10.
———. "The Diary on Trial." In Lejeune, *On Diary*, 147–67.
———. "How Do Diaries End?" In Lejeune, *On Diary*, 187–200.
———. *On Autobiography*. Edited by Paul John Eakin. Translated by Katherine Leary. Theory and History of Literature 52. Minneapolis: University of Minnesota Press, 1989.
———. *On Diary*. Edited by Jeremy D. Popkin and Julie Rak. Translated by Katherine Durnin. Honolulu: Biographical Research Center, 2009.
———. "Rereading your Diary." In Lejeune, *On Diary*, 324–26.
Liebrand, Claudia. "Pornografische Pathologie: Charlotte Roches *Feuchtgebiete*." *Literatur für Leser* 34, no. 1 (2011): 13–22.
Lindner, Martin. "Ich Schreiben im Falschen Leben: Tagebuch-Literatur seit 1950; Eine kurze Geschichte der deutschsprachigen Literatur am Leitfaden der Diaristik." Unpublished habilitation diss., Universität Passau, 1998. Last revised 2005. Microsoft Word file.
Link, Jürgen. *Versuch über den Normalismus: Wie Normalität produziert wird*. 3rd ed. Göttingen: Vandenhoeck & Ruprecht, 2006.
Lobo, Sascha, and Holm Friebe. *Wir nennen es Arbeit: Die digitale Bohème oder Intelligentes Leben jenseits der Festanstellung*. Munich: Heyne, 2006.
Lorde, Audre. *The Cancer Journals*. London: Sheba Feminist, 1985. Originally published in San Francisco by Spinsters Ink, 1980.
Lubbock, Tom. *Until Further Notice, I Am Alive*. London: Granta, 2012.
Lucius-Hoene, Gabriele. "Erzählen von Krankheit und Behinderung." *Psychotherapie, Psychosomatik, Medizinische Psychologie* 48 (1998): 108–13.

Luckhurst, Roger. "Mixing Memory and Desire: Psychoanalysis, Psychology, and Trauma Theory." In *Literary Theory and Criticism: An Oxford Guide*, edited by Patricia Waugh, 497–507. Oxford: Oxford University Press, 2006.
Macho, Thomas. "Wer redet, ist nicht tot." *Neue Zürcher Zeitung*, November 19, 2009. http://www.nzz.ch/wer-redet-ist-nicht-tot-1.4036808.
Macho, Thomas, and Kristin Marek, eds. *Die neue Sichtbarkeit des Todes*. Munich: Wilhelm Fink, 2007.
Magenau, Jörg. "Auf der Suche nach dem verlorenen Leben." *Literaturen* 10, no. 4 (2009): 54–59.
Malvezzi, M., et al. "European Cancer Mortality Predictions for the Year 2013." *Annals of Oncology* 24, no. 3 (2013): 792–800.
Manganiello, Dominic. "Confessions." In Jolly, *Encyclopedia of Life Writing*, 1:228–29.
Mankell, Henning. *Kvicksand*. Stockholm: Leopard, 2014.
Mann, Thomas. *Tagebücher, 1953–1955*. Edited by Inge Jens. Frankfurt am Main: Fischer, 1995.
Marchetto, Marisa Acocella. *Cancer Vixen: A True Story*. New York: Alfred A. Knopf, 2006.
Matthews-Schlinzig, Marie-Isabel. "Der Suizid des Autors: Texte und Reaktionen (am Beispiel von Édouard Levé, André Gorz und Heinrich von Kleist)." *Zeitschrift für Germanistik* 25, no. 3 (2015): 589–602.
Max, Katrin. *Liegekur und Bakterienrausch: Literarische Deutungen der Tuberkulose im "Zauberberg" und anderswo*. Würzburg: Königshausen & Neumann, 2012.
McCarthy, Margaret. "Feminism and Generational Conflicts in Alexa Hennig von Lange's *Relax*, Elke Naters's *Lügen*, and Charlotte Roche's *Feuchtgebiete*." *Studies in 20th & 21st Century Literature* 35, no. 1 (2011): 56–73.
McCosker, Anthony. "Blogging Illness: Recovering in Public." *M/C Journal* 11, no. 6 (2008). http://journal.media-culture.org.au/index.php/mcjournal/article/view/104.
McNeill, Laurie. "Teaching an Old Genre New Tricks: The Diary on the Internet." *Biography* 26, no. 1 (2003): 24–47.
Meckel, Miriam. *Brief an mein Leben: Erfahrungen mit einem Burnout*. Reinbek: Rowohlt Taschenbuch Verlag, 2011.
Meyer-Sickendiek, Burkhard. "Der Schmerz im Tagebuch." In *Affektpoetik: Eine Kulturgeschichte literarischer Emotionen*, by Meyer-Sickendiek, 424–53. Würzburg: Königshausen & Neumann, 2005.
Michelbach, Elisabeth. "Dem Leben wie einem Roman zu Leibe rücken: Wolfgang Herrndorfs Blog und Buch *Arbeit und Struktur* zwischen digitalem Gebrauchstext und literarischem Werk." *Textpraxis: Digitales Journal für Philologie* 2 (2016): 107–29.
Miller, Nancy K., and Jason Tougaw. "Introduction: Extremities." In *Extremities: Trauma, Testimony, and Community*, edited by Nancy K. Miller and Jason Tougaw, 1–22. Urbana: University of Illinois Press, 2002.

Mitchell, David T., and Sharon L. Snyder. *Narrative Prosthesis: Disability and the Dependencies of Discourse*. Ann Arbor: University of Michigan Press, 2000.

———. "Representation and Its Discontents: The Uneasy Home of Disability in Literature and Film." In Albrecht, Seelman, and Bury, *Handbook of Disability Studies*, 195–218.

Moamai, Marion. *Krebs schreiben: Deutschsprachige Literatur der siebziger und achtziger Jahre*. Mannheimer Studien zur Literatur- und Kulturwissenschaft 13. St. Ingbert: Röhrig, 1997.

Moritz, Karl Philipp. *Anton Reiser: Ein psychologischer Roman*. Stuttgart: Philipp Reclam Jun., 1972.

Mühlemann, Kaspar. *Christoph Schlingensief und seine Auseinandersetzung mit Joseph Beuys*. Europäische Hochschulschriften: Kunstgeschichte 439. Frankfurt am Main: Peter Lang, 2011.

Mulvey, Laura. "Visual Pleasure and Narrative Cinema." In *Contemporary Literary Criticism: Literary and Cultural Studies*, edited by Robert Con Davis and Ronald Schleifer, 3rd ed., 422–31. New York: Longman, 1994.

Neubert, Marina. "Lebendig begraben." *Berliner Morgenpost*, March 27, 2009. http://www.morgenpost.de/printarchiv/kultur/article1062623/Lebendig-begraben.html.

Neufeld, Anna Katharina, and Ulrike Vedder, eds. "An der Grenze: Sterben und Tod in der Gegenwartsliteratur." Special issue, *Zeitschrift für Germanistik* 25, no. 3 (2015).

———. "An der Grenze: Sterben und Tod in der Gegenwartsliteratur; Einleitung." *Zeitschrift für Germanistik* 25, no. 3 (2015): 495–98.

Noble, Ivan. *Like a Hole in the Head: Living with a Brain Tumour*. London: Hodder & Stoughton, 2005.

Noll, Peter. *Diktate über Sterben & Tod*. Zurich: Pendo, n.d. [1984].

Nowak, Tine. "Das meistgelesene Tagebuch der Welt." In Gold, *@bsolut? Privat!*, 142–45.

Oesterle, Günter. "Die Intervalle des Tagebuchs—das Tagebuch als Intervall." In Gold, *@bsolut? Privat!*, 100–103.

Oestreich, Heide. "Schriftstellerin Verena Stefan: 'Ich bin keine Frau. Punkt.'" *taz*, May 10, 2008. http://www.taz.de/Schriftstellerin-Verena-Stefan/!17049/.

Oltermann, Philip. "Interview: Charlotte Roche." *GRANTA*, May 10, 2008. http://www.granta.com/New-Writing/Interview-Charlotte-Roche.

Pascal, Roy. *Design and Truth in Autobiography*. London: Routledge & Kegan Paul, 1960.

Paterson, Tony. "Charlotte Roche: Troubled Mind of a Taboo-Buster." *Independent*, August 26, 2011. http://www.independent.co.uk/news/people/profiles/charlotte-roche-troubled-mind-of-a-taboo-buster-2344746.html.

Peitz, Dirk. "Die Ich-Erzähler." *Berliner Zeitung*, October 10, 2009. http://www.berliner-zeitung.de/archiv/immer-mehr-autoren-berichten-in-

ihren-buechern-von-sich-selbst--und-von-ihren-krankheiten-die-ich-erzaehler,10810590,10671790.html.
Pender, Malcolm. *Contemporary Images of Death and Sickness: A Theme in German-Swiss Literature*. Sheffield: Sheffield Academic Press, 1998.
Picardie, Ruth. *Before I Say Goodbye*. London: Penguin, 1998.
Pielhau, Miriam. *Fremdkörper*. Munich: MVG, 2009.
Plummer, Kenneth. *Documents of Life: An Introduction to the Problems and Literature of a Humanistic Method*. Contemporary Social Research Series 7. London: Allen & Unwin, 1983.
Poore, Carol. *Disability in Twentieth-Century German Culture*. Ann Arbor: University of Michigan Press, 2007.
Popkin, Jeremy D. "Philippe Lejeune, Explorer of the Diary." Preface to Lejeune, *On Diary*, 1–15.
Preußer, Heinz-Peter, and Helmut Schmitz. "Autobiografik zwischen Literaturwissenschaft und Geschichtsschreibung: Eine Einleitung." In *Autobiografie und historische Krisenerfahrung*, edited by Heinz-Peter Preußer and Helmut Schmitz, 7–20. Jahrbuch Literatur und Politik 5. Heidelberg: Winter, 2010.
Price Herndl, Diane. "Disease versus Disability: The Medical Humanities and Disability Studies." *PMLA* 120, no. 2 (2005): 593–98.
———. "Our Breasts, Our Selves: Identity, Community, and Ethics in Cancer Autobiographies." *Signs* 32, no. 1 (2006): 221–45.
Quayson, Ato. *Aesthetic Nervousness: Disability and the Crisis of Representation*. New York: Columbia University Press, 2007.
Quilitzsch, Frank. "Literaturpreis für Kathrin Schmidt: 'Schreiben war immer meine Fluchtburg.'" *Thüringische Landeszeitung*, September 25, 2013. http://www.tlz.de/web/zgt/kultur/detail/-/specific/Heimkehr-durch-die-Raeume-meiner-Kindheit-und-Jugend-922015597.
Radisch, Iris. "Metaphysik des Tumors." *Zeit Online*, September 19, 2009. http://www.zeit.de/2009/39/Krebsbuecher.
Ralfs, Sarah. "'Wir sind eins'—total total: Selbst-Inszenierungen in Christoph Schlingensiefs späten Arbeiten." In Janke and Kovacs, *Der Gesamtkünstler Christoph Schlingensief*, 307–26.
Ramadanovic, Petar. "Introduction: Trauma and Crisis." *Postmodern Culture: An Electronic Journal of Interdisciplinary Criticism* 11, no. 2 (2001). http://pmc.iath.virginia.edu/text-only/issue.101/11.2introduction.txt.
Reed, T. J. "Mann as Diarist." In *The Cambridge Companion to Thomas Mann*, edited by Ritchie Robertson, 226–34. Cambridge: Cambridge University Press, 2001.
Reimann, Brigitte, and Christa Wolf. *Sei gegrüßt und lebe: Eine Freundschaft in Briefen, 1964–1973*. Edited by Angela Drescher. Berlin: Aufbau, 1993.
Reinig, Christa. *Die himmlische und die irdische Geometrie*. Düsseldorf: Eremiten-Presse, 1975.

Ricker-Abderhalden, Judith. "Schreiben über Krankheit: Bemerkungen zur Zerstörung eines literarischen Tabus." *Neophilologus* 71, no. 3 (1987): 474–79.
Rimmon-Kenan, Shlomith. "The Story of 'I': Illness and Narrative Identity." *Narrative* 10, no. 1 (2002): 9–27.
Roche, Charlotte. *Feuchtgebiete*. Cologne: DuMont, 2008.
———. *Schoßgebete*. Munich: Piper, 2011.
———. *Wetlands*. Translated by Tim Mohr. London: Fourth Estate, 2009.
———. *Wrecked*. Translated by Tim Mohr. London: Fourth Estate, 2013.
Rosenberg, Martina. *Mutter, wann stirbst du endlich? Wenn die Pflege der kranken Eltern zur Zerreißprobe wird*. Munich: Blanvalet, 2012.
Rousseau, Jean-Jacques. *The Confessions*. Translated by J. M. Cohen. London: Penguin, 1953.
Russo, Mary. *The Female Grotesque: Risk, Excess and Modernity*. New York: Routledge, 1995.
Sartre, Jean-Paul. *Being and Nothingness: An Essay on Phenomenological Ontology*. Translated by Hazel E. Barnes. London: Routledge, 2003.
Saunders, Max. *Self Impression: Life-Writing, Autobiografiction, and the Forms of Modern Literature*. Oxford: Oxford University Press, 2010.
Schadek, Sandra. *Ich bin eine Insel: Gefangen im eigenen Körper*. Reinbek: Rowohlt, 2009.
Schappach, Beate. *Aids in Literatur, Theater und Film: Zur kulturellen Dramaturgie eines Störfalls*. Materialien des ITW Bern 12. Zurich: Chronos, 2012.
Schep, Dennis. "I Problems: Blindness and Autobiography." *European Journal of Life Writing* 4 (2015): 17–35.
Schlingensief, Christoph. *Ich weiß, ich war's*. Edited by Aino Laberenz. Cologne: Kiepenheuer & Witsch, 2012.
———. *Ich weiß, ich war's*. With text inserts read by Martin Wuttke. Tacheles / Roof Music, 2012. 4 audio CDs.
———. *So schön wie hier kanns im Himmel gar nicht sein! Tagebuch einer Krebserkrankung*. Munich: btb, 2010. Originally published in Cologne by Kiepenheuer & Witsch, 2009.
Schmid, Walter Fabian. "Kathrin Schmidt im Gespräch: Das ist ein anderes Schreiben, als es vorher war." *Poet* 7 (2009): 183–91.
Schmidt, Jan. "Die A-List und der Long Tail: Persönliche Öffentlichkeiten in der Blogosphäre." In Gold, *@bsolut? Privat!*, 115–17.
Schmidt, Kathrin. *Blinde Bienen*. Cologne: Kiepenheuer & Witsch, 2010.
———. *Die Gunnar-Lennefsen-Expedition*. Cologne: Kiepenheuer & Witsch, 1998.
———. *Du stirbst nicht*. Munich: btb, 2011. Originally published in Cologne by Kiepenheuer & Witsch, 2009.
Schmidt, Nina. "Kathrin Schmidt." Author page for the *Centre for the Study of Contemporary Women's Writing*, n.d. [2014]. Accessed August 24, 2017. https://modernlanguages.sas.ac.uk/research-centres/centre-study-contemporary-womens-writing/languages/german/kathrin-schmidt.

Schmitt, Arnaud. "Making the Case for Self-Narration against Autofiction." *a/b: Auto/Biography Studies* 25, no. 1 (2010): 122–37.
Scholz, Martin. "Ich hatte ein fantastisches Leben." *Welt.de*, October 5, 2015. https://www.welt.de/kultur/literarischewelt/article147239728/Ich-hatte-ein-fantastisches-Leben.html.
Schönberger, Klaus. "Von der Lesewut zur Schreibwut?" In Gold, *@bsolut? Privat!*, 112–14.
Schors, Horst Willi. "Der Tod als Bühnenstück." *Kölner Stadt-Anzeiger*, September 22, 2009.
Schröder, Christoph. "Die Kunst der Krankheit: Wir kommen nicht von uns los." *Der Tagesspiegel*, October 24, 2009. http://www.tagesspiegel.de/kultur/die-kunst-der-krankheit-wir-kommen-nicht-von-uns-los/1621152.html.
Schulte, Martin. "Schreiben für die Unsterblichkeit." *sh:z Schleswig-Holsteinischer Zeitungsverlag*, December 9, 2011. http://www.shz.de/incoming/schreiben-fuer-die-unsterblichkeit-id1878506.html.
Schwalm, Helga. "Autobiography." In *The Living Handbook of Narratology*, edited by Peter Hühn et al. Hamburg: Hamburg University, last modified April 11, 2014. http://www.lhn.uni-hamburg.de/article/autobiography.
Schwarz, Reinhold. "Die 'Krebspersönlichkeit'—Mythen und Forschungsresultate." *psychoneuro* 30, no. 4 (2004): 201–9.
Segeberg, Harro. "Menschsein heißt, medial sein wollen: Autorinszenierungen im Medienzeitalter." In *Autorinszenierungen: Autorschaft und literarisches Werk im Kontext der Medien*, edited by Christine Künzel and Jörg Schönert, 245–56. Würzburg: Königshausen & Neumann, 2007.
Shakespeare, Tom. *Disability Rights and Wrongs Revisited*. London: Routledge, 2014.
———. "The Social Model of Disability." In Davis, *Disability Studies Reader*, 4th ed., 214–21.
Shulevitz, Judith. "The Close Reader: The Poetry of Illness." *New York Times*, December 29, 2002. http://www.nytimes.com/2002/12/29/books/the-close-reader-the-poetry-of-illness.html.
Siebers, Tobin. *Disability Aesthetics*. Ann Arbor: University of Michigan Press, 2010.
———. *Disability Theory*. Ann Arbor: University of Michigan Press, 2008.
Siegel, Elke. "'die mühsame Verschriftlichung meiner peinlichen Existenz': Wolfgang Herrndorfs *Arbeit und Struktur* zwischen Tagebuch, Blog und Buch." *Zeitschrift für Germanistik* 26, no. 2 (2016): 348–72.
Sighişorean, Christian. *Rose und Gebrochen Deutsch*. Rottenburg: Mauer, 2009.
———. *VerLetztes*. Vallendar: Patris, 2011.
Smith, Sidonie. "Self, Subject, and Resistance: Marginalities and Twentieth-Century Autobiographical Practice." *Tulsa Studies in Women's Literature* 9, no. 1 (1990): 11–24.

Smith, Sidonie, and Julia Watson. *Reading Autobiography: A Guide for Interpreting Life Narratives.* 2nd ed. Minneapolis: University of Minnesota Press, 2010.

———. "The Rumpled Bed of Autobiography: Extravagant Lives, Extravagant Questions." *Biography* 24, no. 1 (2001): 1–14.

Smith-Prei, Carrie. "'Knaller-Sex Für Alle': Popfeminist Body Politics in Lady Bitch Ray, Charlotte Roche, and Sarah Kuttner." *Studies in 20th & 21st Century Literature* 35, no. 1 (2011): 3–39.

Sontag, Susan. *Illness as Metaphor and AIDS and Its Metaphors.* London: Penguin Books, 2002. Originally published in New York by Anchor Books Doubleday, 1989.

———. *On Photography.* New York: Anchor Books, 1990.

———. *Regarding the Pain of Others.* London: Hamish Hamilton, 2003.

Spiegl, Andrea. "Gross, schlank, blond, attraktiv: Schweizer Schriftstellerinnen der 1970er." *literaturkritik.at*, September 23, 2013. http://www.uibk.ac.at/literaturkritik/zeitschrift/1111216.html#Dreizehn.

Spiers, Emily. "The Long March through the Institutions: From Alice Schwarzer to Pop Feminism and the New German Girls." *Oxford German Studies* 43, no. 1 (2014): 69–88.

Stallybrass, Peter, and Allon White. *The Politics and Poetics of Transgression.* London: Methuen, 1986.

Stanzel, Franz K. "Autobiographie: Wo ein Ich erzählt, ist immer Fiktion." *Sprachkunst* 37, no. 2 (2006): 325–40.

Stefan, Verena. *D'ailleurs.* Translated by Louis Bouchard and Marie-Elisabeth Morf. Montréal: Héliotrope, 2008.

———. *Die Befragung der Zeit.* Munich: Nagel & Kimche, 2014.

———. "Doe a Deer." *TRIVIA: Voices of Feminism* 4 (2006). www.triviavoices.com/doe-a-deer.html.

———. *Es ist reich gewesen: Bericht vom Sterben meiner Mutter.* Frankfurt am Main: Fischer, 1993.

———. *Fremdschläfer.* Zurich: Ammann, 2007.

———. "Fremdschläfer/D'ailleurs." *Canadian Woman Studies / Les Cahiers de la Femme* 28, nos. 2/3 (2010): 139–41.

———. *Häutungen.* Munich: Frauenoffensive, 1975. English translation published as *Shedding* in New York by Daughters, 1978; in London by the Women's Press, 1979.

———. *Qui maîtrise les vents connaît son chemin.* Translated by Céline Hostion. Montréal: Héliotrope, 2017.

———. "We Live as Two Lesbians." *TRIVIA: Voices of Feminism* 11, no. 2 (2010). http://www.triviavoices.com/we-live-as-two-lesbians.html.

Stehle, Maria. "Pop, Porn, and Rebellious Speech: Feminist Politics and the Multi-media Performances of Elfriede Jelinek, Charlotte Roche, and Lady Bitch Ray." *Feminist Media Studies* 12, no. 2 (2012): 229–47.

Steinfeld, Thomas. "Verlogenheit zwischen den Beinen." *Süddeutsche Zeitung*, July 27, 2012. http://www.sueddeutsche.de/kultur/charlotte-roches-neuer-roman-schossgebete-verlogenheit-zwischen-den-beinen-1.1129744.

Teucher, Ulrich. "The Incomprehensible Density of Being: Aestheticizing Cancer." In *Unfitting Stories: Narrative Approaches to Disease, Disability, and Trauma*, edited by Valérie Raoul, 71–78. Waterloo, ON: Wilfrid Laurier University Press, 2007.

Thomas, Carol, Nick Watson, and Alan Roulstone, eds. *Routledge Handbook of Disability Studies*. London: Routledge, 2012.

Umathum, Sandra. "Die Kunst des Abschiednehmens: Überlegungen zu Christoph Schlingensiefs Inszenierung von eigenem Sterben und Tod." In *Theater und Subjektkonstitution: Theatrale Praktiken zwischen Affirmation und Subversion*, edited by Michael Bachmann et al., 253–62. Theater 33. Bielefeld: Transcript, 2012.

Ustorf, Anne-Ev. "Es ist ein großes Glück, dass ich diesen Beruf hatte, als ich erkrankte: Kathrin Schmidt im Gespräch." *Psychologie Heute*, January 2011. http://www.ustorf.de/dateien/Interview_Kathrin_Schmidt.pdf.

Van der Kolk, Bessel A., and Onno van der Hart. "The Intrusive Past: The Flexibility of Memory and the Engraving of Trauma." In Caruth, *Trauma*, 158–82.

Vanistendael, Judith. *Toen David zijn stem verloor*. Amsterdam: Oog & Blik, 2012. English translation published as *When David Lost His Voice* in London by SelfMadeHero, 2012.

Vatan, Florence. "The Lure of Disgust: Musil and Kolnai." *Germanic Review* 88 (2013): 29–46.

Vice, Sue. "Bakhtin and Kristeva: Grotesque Body, Abject Self." In *Face to Face: Bakhtin in Russia and the West*, edited by Carol Adlam et al., 160–74. Sheffield: Sheffield Academic Press, 1997.

Von Engelhardt, Dietrich, and Felix Unger, eds. *Ästhetik und Ethik in der Medizin*. Edition Weimar 4. Weimar: VDG, 2006.

Von Jagow, Bettina, and Florian Steger, eds. *Literatur und Medizin: Ein Lexikon*. Göttingen: Vandenhoeck & Ruprecht, 2005.

———, eds. *Repräsentationen: Medizin und Ethik in Literatur und Kunst der Moderne*. Heidelberg: Winter, 2004.

———. *Was treibt die Literatur zur Medizin? Ein kulturwissenschaftlicher Dialog*. Göttingen: Vandenhoeck & Ruprecht, 2009.

Von Lovenberg, Felicitas. "Ein Gespräch mit Charlotte Roche: Ich bin keine Frau, die andere Frauen verrät." *Frankfurter Allgemeine*, August 10, 2011. http://www.faz.net/aktuell/feuilleton/buecher/autoren/ein-gespraech-mit-charlotte-roche-ich-bin-keine-frau-die-andere-frauen-verraet-11104662.html?printPagedArticle=true#pageIndex_2.

———. "Zum Tod Wolfgang Herrndorfs: Dieses Zuviel ist niemals genug." *Frankfurter Allgemeine*, August 27, 2013. http://www.faz.net/aktuell/feuilleton/buecher/zum-tod-wolfgang-herrndorfs-dieses-zuviel-ist-niemals-genug-12549002.html.

Wagner, David. "Für neue Leben." *Merkur* 62, no. 715 (2008): 1113–22.

———. *Leben*. Reinbek: Rowohlt, 2013.

Wagner, Richard. *Herr Parkinson*. Munich: Albrecht Knaus, 2015.
Wagner-Egelhaaf, Martina. *Autobiographie*. Sammlung Metzler 323. Stuttgart: Metzler, 2000.
———. "Autofiktion oder: Autobiographie nach der Autobiographie; Goethe—Barthes—Özdamar." In *Grenzen der Identität und der Fiktionalität*, edited by Ulrich Breuer and Beatrice Sandberg, 353–68. Munich: iudicium, 2006.
———. "Autofiktion—Theorie und Praxis des autobiographischen Schreibens." In *Schreiben im Kontext von Schule, Universität, Beruf und Lebensalltag*, edited by Johannes Berning et al., 80–101. Schreiben interdisziplinär 1. Berlin: LIT, 2006.
———. "Zum Stand und zu den Perspektiven der Autobiographieforschung in der Literaturwissenschaft." *Bios—Zeitschrift für Biographieforschung, Oral History und Lebensverlaufsanalysen* 23, no. 2 (2010): 188–200.
Waldschmidt, Anne. "Flexible Normalisierung oder stabile Ausgrenzung: Veränderungen im Verhältnis Behinderung und Normalität." *Soziale Probleme* 9, no. 1 (1998): 3–25.
Wander, Maxie. *Tagebücher und Briefe*. Edited by Fred Wander. Berlin: Buchverlag Der Morgen, 1980.
Warner, Chantelle. *The Pragmatics of Literary Testimony: Authenticity Effects in German Social Autobiographies*. New York: Routledge, 2013.
———. "Speaking from Experience: Narrative Schemas, Deixis, and Authenticity Effects in Verena Stefan's Feminist Confession *Shedding*." *Language and Literature* 18, no. 1 (2009): 7–23.
Weichelt, Matthias. "Kathrin Schmidt: You Are Not Going to Die." Translated by Isabel Cole. *Litrix.de—German Literature online*, August 2010. http://www.litrix.de/buecher/belletristik/jahr/2010/stirbstnicht/buchbesprechung/enindex.htm.
Wendell, Susan. *The Rejected Body: Feminist Philosophical Reflections on Disability*. New York: Routledge, 1996.
———. "Unhealthy Disabled: Treating Chronic Illnesses as Disabilities." In Davis, *Disability Studies Reader*, 161–73.
Westerwelle, Guido, and Dominik Wichmann. *Zwischen zwei Leben: Von Liebe, Tod und Zuversicht*. Hamburg: Hoffmann und Campe, 2015.
Wittig, Monique. "The Point of View: Universal or Particular?" *Feminist Issues* 3, no. 2 (1983): 61–69.
Wittig, Monique, and Sande Zeig. *Lesbische Völker: Ein Wörterbuch*. Translated by Gabriele Meixner and Verena Stefan. Munich: Frauenoffensive, 1983.
Wolf, Christa. *Der geteilte Himmel*. Halle: Mitteldeutscher Verlag, 1963.
Woolf, Virginia. *On Being Ill*. Ashfield, MA: Paris Press, 2002. Originally published in London by Hogarth, 1930.
———. *A Room of One's Own & Three Guineas*. London: Vintage Books, 1996. Originally published in London by Chatto & Windus / Hogarth, 1984.

Wübben, Yvonne, and Carsten Zelle, eds. *Krankheit schreiben: Aufzeichnungsverfahren in Medizin und Literatur*. Göttingen: Wallstein, 2013.
Xue, Yuan. *Über den Körper hinaus: Geschlechterkonstruktionen im europäischen Roman seit Ende der 1990er Jahre*. Bielefeld: Transcript, 2014.
Zapruder, Alexandra. *Salvaged Pages: Young Writers' Diaries of the Holocaust*. New Haven, CT: Yale University Press, 2002.
Zipfel, Frank. "Autofiktion: Zwischen den Grenzen von Faktualität, Fiktionalität und Literarität?" In *Grenzen der Literatur: Zu Begriff und Phänomen des Literarischen*, edited by Simone Winko et al., 285–314. Berlin: De Gruyter, 2009.
Zorn, Fritz. *Mars*. Munich: Kindler, 1977.

Index

abjection, 34, 49–50, 55
ablebodiedness, 16, 19, 21
ableism, 19, 21, 143. *See also* disablism
activism: academic, 16–17, 21; disability rights, 17, 21; disability studies and, 16–17, 20; political, 104
agency: authorial, 34, 58, 59, 108, 110, 143, 159; of ill people, 10, 36, 73; lack of, 79, 92, 150, 157
AIDS, 2, 3, 10, 121, 165. *See also* HIV/AIDS
alter ego, 15, 36, 60, 66, 67, 89
anger: at self, 77–78; toward ill person, 157; toward others, 52
Antipsychiatrie, 28
assisted dying, 26, 134, 156
Augustine, Saint, 11
authenticity: of author, 35, 71, 90, 123; of text, 14, 26, 50, 51, 71, 85, 90, 115, 161
author: feminist, 100, 104, 108, 110, 159; lesbian, 94, 100, 102, 110; minority, 31, 37, 94, 95, 100
authorial motivations, 1, 5, 12, 25, 39, 65, 107, 131, 134, 138, 147, 160
autobiografiction, 9
autobiographic effect, 9
autobiographical pact, 14–15, 51, 135
autobiography, 5, 7–16, 46, 54, 116, 127; auto/biography, 4; as confession, 11–12, 31, 53, 111, 115, 119, 163; the occasion for, 6, 10; as therapy, 29, 57, 68. *See also* memoir
autofiction, 4, 9, 15, 33, 34, 35, 36, 41–66, 159. *See also* factual fiction

autonomy: of the author, 8, 139, 141; of the ill, 23, 141, 143
autothanatography, 10, 113, 116, 121–29, 131–36, 142, 150–52, 158

Bakhtin, Mikhail, 34, 49, 55, 65
Barthes, Roland, 51, 154
beholding, 72, 73, 79
Bekenntnisliteratur, 26, 118
belonging, 94
Benjamin, Walter, 155
bereavement, 4, 34, 48, 50, 159
Berkéwicz, Ulla, 3, 4
Betroffenheitsliteratur, 37, 70, 90, 91, 95, 112
Beutler, Maja, 98
Beuys, Joseph, 121, 122
Bewusstsein, 146
Bildungsgeschichte, 8
binary thought, 27, 86–89, 152, 160
blog, 39–40, 98, 114–58
blogosphere, 133
body: alienation from the, 70, 92, 99; as battleground, 77; the extraordinary, 72, 79, 85; and femininity, 96–97; physicality of the, 1, 10, 16, 44, 49, 54, 62, 64, 77, 83, 97; regulation of, 16, 65, 72, 96; and the self, 10, 78; and sexuality, 44, 96; and shame, 96
border: beyond the, 38, 111; disciplinary, 30, 41, 104, 166; geographical, 111; linguistic, 32
Breuer, Joseph, 56
Brontë, Charlotte, 145–46

cancer: and identity, 97; living with, 22, 37, 40 93–95, 102, 121, 127–28, 131, 135, 156; and "personality," 12, 157; and politics, 23, 120; as unknowable, 105–6; women and, 95–97, 111–12
cancer writing: and feuilleton debates, 2–4, 24–26; as shared experience, 132, 140–41, 143, 164; and topography, 38, 100–101, 107–8; traditions of, 97–99, 104
canonization, of illness writing, 8, 27, 30, 40, 82, 91, 110, 151, 163. *See also* cultural elitism
Cartesian dualism, 6
censorship, 65
clinic, 25, 79, 97, 107, 126
comic, 165. *See also* graphic novel
commonality, of illness experience, 112
community: of ill/disabled writers, 103, 163; online, 128; of suffering, 29, 121
confessional literature, 26, 118. See also *Bekenntnisliteratur*
control: over illness experience, 10, 34, 64; over one's body, 55, 72, 78, 80, 124, 143, 144
corporeality, 49. *See also* body: physicality of the
corpse, 49, 61, 62, 148; as metaphor, 49
Couser, G. Thomas, 5, 10–11, 13, 15, 17, 36, 97, 111, 133
cross-media performance, 41–42
cultural elitism, 40, 156. *See also* canonization, of illness writing

de Certeau, Michel, 108, 159
death: confronting, 54, 162, 164; fear of, 48–49, 99–100, 137, 157; focus on author's, 112–13, 153, 155; and legacy, 112, 119, 146–47; managing, 119, 132; nearness to, 39, 105, 113, 115, 119, 126, 127, 129, 130, 131, 134, 135, 138–39, 141–42, 144, 148; possibility of, 17, 104; premature, 17, 57, 62, 133; storying, 42; and trauma, 34, 43, 46–49, 55–56, 65

destigmatization, 10
Deutscher Buchpreis, 36, 67, 70, 161
diagnosis, 10, 113, 118, 119, 121; cancer, 93, 96, 97, 99, 100, 131, 132, 134
diaristic: pact, 116, 135; persona, 124, 154
diary: as aesthetic form, 115, 151, 161; and the confessional, 118–19, 163; and creativity, 118, 122, 125, 129, 150–52, 162; as dialogic space, 40, 102, 115, 121, 130–31; literary value of the, 111, 133–34, 145, 147, 156; as widespread cultural practice, 113–14, 135, 160
Diez, Georg, 3, 4, 68
disability: diversity in, 4, 21, 110–11; as identity, 5, 8, 17, 20, 84, 89, 94; as metaphor, 22–24, 39, 69, 97, 98, 101, 104, 107; as minority status, 17, 37; pride, 22, 96; and social exclusion, 20, 91, 119, 147; "stable," 16, 19, 162; as undiscussable, 13, 17, 19
Disability Studies, 6, 16–24; and Anglo-American literary studies, 18, 20, 32, 38, 111–12; and gender studies, 17, 86; and German literary studies, 6–7, 18–20, 24–32, 160, 165–66
disablism, 18, 19, 21. *See also* ableism
discrimination, 20, 33, 59
disease, 19, 20, 27–28, 45, 96, 97, 101, 124, 162, 164
disgust, 26, 34–36, 42, 49, 53–55, 58, 63–65, 73, 75, 80
Doubrovsky, Serge, 9, 41, 50, 54, 57
Drescher, Angela, 130
dual citizenship, as metaphor, 100
Dubiel, Helmut, 3, 4
Dürer, Albrecht, 149
dying: public negotiations of, 26; speechlessness of, 24

emotion: authorial, 3, 106; protagonist's struggle with, 84, 104, 139, 141, 144; and reader response, 34–36, 49, 119, 158

emotional porn, 52, 53
empathy, 53, 84, 88, 145
enfant terrible, 116–17, 126
Entwicklungsroman, 36, 87
epidemiology, 24
Erinnerungsroman, 35, 68
Erlenberger, Maria, 29
exhibitionism, 56, 115

factual fiction, 50. *See also* autofiction
fear: of alienation, 26, 126; of dying, 42, 48, 49, 99, 109, 137; of illness, 23, 25, 88, 100, 125, 157; of losing selfhood, 74, 157; of rejection, 64
feminism, 43; second-wave, 38, 51
feminist writer, 100, 104, 108, 110, 159
feuilleton debate, 2, 6, 24, 43, 158
Frank, Anne, 116, 148–49
Frank, Arthur W., 10–13
free indirect discourse, 71, 75
Fremdbild, 71, 75, 77, 85. See also *Selbstbild*
Freud, Sigmund, 28, 45–46, 56
Frisch, Max, 130
Foucauldian analysis, 17; theorizations, 108

Garland-Thomson, Rosemarie, 36, 71–74, 79, 82, 86, 162
gaze, the, 35–36, 53, 64, 72–73, 115, 148; diagnostic, 6; medical, 55; reader, 66, 90, 162. *See also* staring
Geiger, Arno, 4
gender norms, 84–85, 96, 102
genre: autobiography as, 7–8, 15, 27, 38, 59, 89, 132; boundaries of, 9, 14, 29, 33, 35, 92, 112, 146, 151–52, 155; diary as, 38–40, 51, 113–16, 123, 128, 156, 158, 165
German Reunification, 69, 117
Goethe, Johann Wolfgang von, 8, 28
Goetz, Rainald, 136
Görsdorf, Alexander, 4
graphic medicine, 165
graphic novel, 98, 165
Grass, Günter, 23, 70
Grealy, Lucy, 18, 99, 104

grief, 46, 55, 86
grotesqueness, 34, 64, 78, 80
guilt, 28, 64, 80, 83

happy ending, 25
healing, process of, 49, 70, 74, 88, 90, 97, 110, 121, 122
healthy disabled, 21
heaven, 1, 39, 112, 133
Heimat, 106, 109. *See also* home
Herrndorf, Wolfgang, 4–5, 33, 38–40, 112, 114–58, 160–65; and the canon, 40, 132–33, 143, 145–46, 148–49, 151–52; and celebrity status, 140–41; self-portraits of, 153–55; suicide, 134, 143, 153; unfinished work, 135, 144, 153
Herrndorf, Wolfgang, works by: *Arbeit und Struktur*, 4, 5, 39, 40, 112–58, 164, 165; *Bilder deiner großen Liebe*, 114, 132, 153; *Sand*, 132; *Tschick*, 132, 140, 151
heteronormativity, 93–94
high literature/low literature debate, 4, 14, 35, 40, 82, 155–56, 160, 166
HIV/AIDS, 3, 10. *See also* AIDS
Hoheneder, Till, 4
Holocaust, the, 26, 121, 157
home, 57, 67, 106, 107–9, 110, 149, 154. See also *Heimat*
homeopathic treatment, 140
hope, 24, 124, 125, 146, 147
hospital experience, 44, 79, 84, 103, 107, 119, 131, 133, 138, 144
hygiene, 44, 49, 64–65

identity: authorial, 15, 67, 89, 110, 135, 162; changes in, 36, 78, 79, 84, 94; gender, 84, 85, 96, 97; minority, 95
illness (meanings and interpretation): appreciating, 1; as communal experience, 20, 163; glorification of, 2, 28, 133, 155; as identity, 5, 8, 10, 17, 20, 22, 89, 94, 97; knowledge gained through, 6, 132, 142; normalizing, 10, 80, 102, 110; symbolic uses of, 23, 31, 94

illness (symptoms and diseases): ALS (amyotrophic lateral sclerosis), 4; Alzheimer's disease, 4; amnesia, 46–47; amputation, 101, 105; aneurysm, 66, 71, 75, 84; anxiety, 49, 126; autoimmune diseases, 4; brain hemorrhage, 67; Broca's aphasia, 67, 70, 76–77, 85; burnout, 4; chemotherapy, 104–5; dementia, 4; depression, 48, 126, 147; glioblastoma, 131–32, 137, 141; hemiplegia, 67; hypomania, 13; influenza, 1; leukemia, 4; mastectomy, 99, 102; metastases, 25, 127; Parkinson's disease, 4, 162, 164; phobia, 48; posttraumatic stress disorder, 45; prosthesis, 35, 99, 104; spasticity, 79; stroke, 4, 22, 25, 36, 66–67, 86; transplants, 4, 162

illness literature: as art, 1, 6, 13, 25–26, 32, 39, 118–20, 145; as confession, 11–12, 26, 31, 42, 111, 115, 118–19, 163; literary value of, 24, 27, 30, 68, 94, 146, 156; as political, 5, 9, 11, 33, 38, 44, 74, 97, 104, 120, 134, 156, 159, 163–64; as popular literature, 4, 25, 35, 40, 133, 155

immigration, 93, 106, 111. *See also* migration

impairment, 6, 10, 16, 19–22, 36, 70

individuality, 7, 143; and autonomy, 8, 139, 141, 143; and selfhood, 49, 141

institutionalization, 18, 33, 161

Internet: as public space, 136, 154, 163; as publication space, 40, 136–37, 154

intersubjectivity, 8

intertextuality, 38, 60, 82, 91, 95, 99–104, 142, 159, 164

Janet, Pierre, 45, 46
Jens, Tilman, 3, 4
journey, metaphorical, 105

Kafka, Franz, 70

Kaysen, Susanna, 18
Kindler, Helmut, 130
Köster, Gaby, 4
Kristeva, Julia, 34, 49, 55

Lacan, Jacques, 74–75, 77
language: female, 93, 111; feminine, 93; as homeland, 109; hybridity, 9, 64; for illness, 164; loss of, 63, 89; medical, 10, 107; memory and, 41, 70, 73, 77; person-centered, 20; performativity of, 51; sign, 35; as symbolic system, 75; and the unspeakable, 48, 99, 146, 151

legacy, textual, 40, 146; author, 112, 116, 119

Leinemann, Jürgen, 3, 25, 68

Lejeune, Philippe, 13, 14–15, 39, 50, 51, 114, 115, 116, 125, 127, 135, 144, 149

letters, diaries and, 116, 130; reader, 140–42

literary case study, 28, 82

"livingly dying," 40, 132

loneliness, 23

Lorde, Audre, 18, 38, 99, 102, 103, 104, 110

loss: death and, 43, 121; of future, 143; reality of, 26; of speech ability, 73; traumatic, 34

Lubbock, Tom, 136

madness, 28, 82
magic realism, 62, 110
Malevich, Kasimir, 164
Mankell, Henning, 164
Mann, Thomas, 2, 142
marginalization, 96, 103
Meckel, Miriam, 4
media, debates, 26, 43; policing, 59
medical: advances, 96, 131, 132; diagnosis, 6, 97, 132; establishment, 10, 18, 65, 85; jargon, 10, 19, 77, 107; metaphor, 24; models, 17; paraphernalia, 103; research, 150; subjects, 16; treatment, 21, 24, 99; truths, 28

medicalization: of experience, 19, 104; of society, 28
medicine: history and ethics of, 31; and literature, 31, 32, 165; modern, 10, 72
memoir, 4, 15, 98, 133; fake, 14. *See also* autobiography
memory archive, 142, 152
mental health, 22, 82, 93, 132
mental illness, 18, 21, 22, 28, 44
migration, 37, 38, 94, 95, 99, 100, 101. *See also* immigration
minority literature, 31, 100
minority writer, 37, 94, 95
mirror stage, 74–75
morality, 23, 34, 58, 59, 118, 122; boundaries of, 54
Moritz, Karl Philipp, 151–52
Muschg, Adolf, 130

narcissism, 55–56, 58, 115
narrative "prosthesis," 22–23
narrative strategy: collaborative, 4–5; distancing, 71, 127, 157; immersive, 71
narrative structure: and chronology, 59, 97, 99, 116, 124, 153; phoenix, 13; quest, 13, 73
National Socialism, 28
neologism, 44, 50, 62. *See also* language: hybridity
Neue Frauenbewegung (new women's movement), 38, 91
Neue Subjektivität (New Subjectivity), 3, 28, 38, 91
Nietzsche, Friedrich, 28, 120, 143
nihilism, 147
Noble, Ivan, 136
Noll, Peter, 130
normality, myth of, 17, 89
norms and expectations: bodily, 80, 83, 85–86, 88; gender, 21, 84, 86, 102; social construction of, 12, 16, 21, 30, 35, 44, 65, 72, 79, 88, 90, 102, 137

objectification, 36, 73

online community, 128; illness narratives, 98, 112, 131, 135–39, 141, 148, 152; reading public, 134, 147
Ostentatio Vulnerum, 121
other, the, 26, 53, 75, 102, 106, 108; colonization of, 73

pain, emotional, 61, 86, 94, 106, 120, 142, 164; physical, 1, 17, 21, 26, 63, 64, 77, 81–82, 114, 126, 157, 164
paratext, 15, 42
Passig, Kathrin, 132
patienthood, 10, 65, 84, 96, 98, 103–5, 108, 119; celebrity, 140, 148
patriarchy, 21, 92, 93, 102
Picardie, Ruth, 98
Pielhau, Miriam, 3
Pietist movement, 7
politics: of patienthood, 32; of the personal, 129, 156; of representation, 8
pop culture, 9, 155
Popliteratur, 156
postmodernism, 17, 119
prayer, 5, 44
privilege, 38, 106, 111
privacy, 27, 44, 136, 140, 163
psyche, 18, 42, 48, 54, 64
public eye, 84, 89, 120, 136

rape, 46; as metaphor, 52, 53
readership: author's relationship with, 12, 16, 29, 34, 35, 66, 95, 106, 157; diverse, 38, 111; imagined, 45, 105, 115, 119, 125, 130, 150; mainstream, 36, 133, 161, 162
reading: lifelong, 101; normative, 36, 37, 90; posthumous, 40, 112, 146, 152–55
recordings: audio, 117, 119–21, 124, 127, 128, 130, 133; diary, 2, 125, 130, 158
recovery: mental, 57, 70; physical, 74, 88, 90, 97, 110
Reimann, Brigitte, 130
religion, 7, 44, 133, 140

remedy, 141
Rieder, André, 147, 148
Roche, Charlotte, 4, 5, 11–12, 25, 33–36, 41–67, 70, 140, 159, 161–63; *Bild-Zeitung*, 34, 52–53; celebrity status, 34, 51, 55, 64; family tragedy, 47, 52–53, 58–60; media appearances, 57–58, 66; Sexautorin, 43, 64
Roche, Charlotte, works by: *Feuchtgebiete*, 41, 43, 44, 57, 92; *Schoßgebete*, 4, 5, 12, 15, 33, 34, 35, 36, 41–66, 70, 162
Romanticism, 156
Rousseau, Jean-Jacques, 8, 11, 151
Rowohlt (publishing house), 137, 139

Schadek, Sandra, 3, 4
Schlingensief, Christoph, 2–3, 5–6, 11–12, 23, 25, 30, 33, 38–40, 67, 112–58, 160, 163–65; as artist, 116–17; navigating personal and public life, 117–18, 121–23; recordings, 120–25; *Schlingenblog*, 127–28, 135, 136, 142
Schlingensief, Christoph, works by: *18 Bilder pro Sekunde*, 129; *100 Jahre CDU—Spiel ohne Grenzen*, 117; *Bitte liebt Österreich*, 117; *Chance 2000*, 117; *Das deutsche Kettensägenmassaker*, 117; *Freakstars*, 117; *Hamlet*, 117; *Jeanne D'Arc*, 123; *Kunst und Gemüse*, 117; *Mea Culpa*, 119, 128, 141; *Mein Filz, mein Fett, mein Hase—48 Stunden Überleben für Deutschland*, 117; *Parsifal*, 117, 129; *Querverstümmelung*, 129; *So schön wie hier kanns im Himmel gar nicht sein! Tagebuch einer Krebserkrankung*, 39, 112–58; *Terror 2000*, 117; *United Trash*, 117
Schmidt, Kathrin, 4–5, 10, 25, 33, 35–37, 65–91, 94, 159, 161; brain hemorrhage, 67; Deutscher Buchpreis, 36, 67; and gender, 83–86; and literary canon, 67–70, 82–83, 89–90

Schmidt, Kathrin, works by: *Blinde Bienen*, 67; *Die Gunnar-Lennefsen-Expedition*, 188; *Du stirbst nicht*, 3, 5, 15, 25, 33, 35, 36, 65–91, 159, 161
Schneider, Peter, 29
Schwarzer, Alice, 43, 51
scriptotherapy, 57
secularization, 7
Selbstbild, 71, 75, 85. See also *Fremdbild*
self: -admiration, 87; alienation from, 26, 70, 99, 199; altered, 6, 85, 163; -attention, 6, 89; body's relationship to, 6, 10, 43, 48–49, 72–73, 75, 77–78, 85, 97, 99, 101; -healing, 11, 97; -image, 71, 86, 88; mortal, the, 49; -mutilation, 44; -portraits, 155; -realization, 92; -scrutiny, 7, 77; sense of, 22, 74–77, 140; -transcendence, 97
self-help books, 29, 31, 97
selfie, 152–55
separatism, lesbian, 92, 103
sex: as coping strategy, 44, 48–49, 57; and desire, 42; and disgust, 53–54
sex change, 84
sexuality, 17, 44, 49, 86, 94
shame, 6, 64, 73, 77–78, 80, 83, 96, 142
Sighişorean, Christian, 4
social exclusion, 20, 91, 95, 119
Sontag, Susan, 2, 3, 28, 38, 72, 87, 97, 99, 100, 155, 163
soul, 1, 57, 121
speech act, 121
spiritual change, 1, 10
starer/staree, 72, 73, 84, 87, 90
"staring": conceptualizations of, 71–74; as narrative device, 68, 90, 159; as natural impulse, 36, 72, 83; as self-reflection, 79, 82; as storytelling, 36; as two-way encounter, 72, 79, 81; as violence, 35, 37, 84. See also gaze, the
Stefan, Verena, 3, 5, 12, 33, 37–38, 90–113, 159, 163; and breast cancer, 94, 97–98, 105, 112; and feminism, 91, 93, 99–104, 110;

and migration, 92, 93, 94, 100, 101, 107–10
Stefan, Verena, works by: *Es ist reich gewesen: Bericht vom Sterben meiner Mutter*, 91; *Fremdschläfer*, 3, 5, 15, 33, 37, 38, 90–113, 159, 167; *Häutungen*, 37, 38, 91, 92, 93, 95, 110, 111; "We Live as Two Lesbians," 92
stigma, 17, 73, 96, 111, 119; and mental illness, 22, 28. *See also* destigmatization; taboo
Storz, Claudia, 29
Struck, Karin, 29
subjectivity, 112; radical, 144
suicide, 84, 134, 143, 153; thoughts of, 42, 47, 49, 57, 149
surfiction, 50
survivor, 4, 104, 157

taboo, 25, 44, 54, 65, 148. *See also* stigma
temporary ablebodiedness, 21
thanatophobia, 155
therapy, 29, 55, 68, 81. *See also* treatment; writing: as therapy
time, touching, 148–50
transgender, 84
transnational stance, 38, 95, 109, 110, 111, 112
trauma: and autofiction, 50; childhood, 44; and the everyday, 42, 47–48, 54; and the extraordinary, 46, 49; and grieving, 46, 48, 159; and loss, 34; and memory, 47, 56, 63; paradoxes of, 47; psychological, 4, 22, 34, 41, 44; sources of, 59, 65; storying, 42, 45, 70; studies, 35; symptoms of, 45, 49; as "unspeakable," 45; women and, 46, 50, 55, 57
treatment, 18, 21, 84, 93, 96–97, 99, 103–4, 107, 119, 130, 133, 140, 154. *See also* therapy

truth: and autobiography, 14, 15, 29, 50, 116; and illness, 132; of mortality, 83, 155; one's own, 107; and trauma, 45, 46, 56, 60

unhealthy disabled, 22
unpatterned reading, 12, 43, 166
Urszene, 138

Vergangenheitsbewältigung, 117
victim, 29, 45, 81, 157
vision, primacy of, 86
visibility: of death, 30; as human, 92; of illness, 35, 72, 78, 99; as survivor, 104
Volkskrankheit, 24
voyeurism, 53, 72, 115, 147

Wagner, David, 4, 162
Wagner, Richard, 4, 162, 164
Wander, Fred, 130
Wander, Maxie, 98, 130
Westerwelle, Guido, 4, 5
Wichmann, Dominik, 4, 5
Wikipedia, 150
Wittig, Monique, 37, 94, 95, 100
Wolf, Christa, 29, 130
Woolf, Virginia, 1–3, 10, 11, 12, 27, 38, 99, 100, 101, 102, 104, 110, 163
wound, 61, 65, 81; metaphorical, 121, 122; societal, 118; trauma as, 45, 55, 64, 122
writing: the dying self, 39, 118; end-of-life, 39, 40, 112, 115, 127, 128, 146, 148, 151, 156; in extremis, 122, 124, 131–34; "from below," 108; as lifeline, 109, 142; subject, 46, 116, 123, 124, 125; as therapy, 11–12, 29, 37, 40, 57, 65, 68, 112, 119, 156 163

Zentrale Intelligenz Agentur (Central Intelligence Agency), 135
Zorn, Fritz, 29, 130

www.ingramcontent.com/pod-product-compliance
Lightning Source LLC
Chambersburg PA
CBHW070800230426
43665CB00017B/2437